Biology Education for Social and Sustainable Development

Biology Education for Social and Sustainable Development

Edited by

Mijung Kim
University of Victoria, Canada

and

C. H. Diong
Nanyang Technological University, National Institute of Education, Singapore

SENSE PUBLISHERS
ROTTERDAM/BOSTON/TAIPEI

A C.I.P. record for this book is available from the Library of Congress.

ISBN: 978-94-6091-925-1 (paperback)
ISBN: 978-94-6091-926-8 (hardback)
ISBN: 978-94-6091-927-5 (e-book)

Published by: Sense Publishers,
P.O. Box 21858,
3001 AW Rotterdam,
The Netherlands
https://www.sensepublishers.com/

Printed on acid-free paper

TABLE OF CONTENTS

III. Theme 3: Teaching Practice & Student Learning of Biology and the Environment

FOREWORD

The Asian Association for Biology Education (AABE) has held its meetings in many Asian countries. Its 2010 meeting in Singapore is the second time AABE meets in this garden city. I am pleased the university's National Institute of Education (NIE) was able to partner the AABE to co-organise the conference with AABE, and to host the conference on this beautiful campus. I believe the conference has opened further opportunities for future collaboration.

Biological sciences have advanced rapidly during the last decades. This new biocentury has made us more conscious than ever before of the social, economic, and environmental challenges that man faces in an increasingly urbanised, but ecologically interconnected global environment. Biological knowledge, as we all know, is intrinsically related to building a sustainable relationship between nature and human society. Hence the role of biology education needs to be rethought to respond to life in this century. The theme of the conference- Rethinking Biology Education for Social and Sustainable Development- was indeed timely and relevant for biologists and biology educators to discuss responsible and responsive roles for practitioners and researchers in biology education.

This publication of selected papers presented at the conference will further help disseminate the key ideas on sustainable development and biology education that were discussed at the conference to an even wider audience. I congratulate the contributors and editors for making this publication possible.

With best wishes,

Prof Lee Sing Kong, PhD, BSc (Hons), FSIBiol.
Director
National Institute of Education
Nanyang Technological University
1 Nanyang Walk
Singapore 637616

MESSAGE FROM THE EDITORS

In an era of globalization and urbanization, the world faces many social, economic, and environmental challenges as well as ethical problems around advances in biotechnology and biomedicine. Considering how biological knowledge is intrinsically related to building a sustainable relationship between nature and human society, the roles of biology education need to be thoroughly rethought to respond to issues and changes in life and the world in the twenty-first century.

A key measure of the value of an academic discipline is its capacity to offer perspectives and solutions that positively impact societies, communities and people beyond the confines of the classroom. How can biology be relevant across societies all over the world that face uniquely local conditions, but are also very much interdependent in today's globalized world? Biology is undoubtedly a key discipline in understanding and responding to some of the most pressing issues of the day, from the many challenges arising from population growth, human impacts on ecosystems and services to climate change and sustainability.

The papers in this book were first presented at the 23rd Biennial Conference of the Asian Association for Biology Education (AABE) held at the National Institute of Education, Nanyang Technological University, 18–20 Oct 2010. To promote responsible and responsive roles for researchers and practitioners in biology education in the Asian region and beyond, the AABE 2010 Conference was intended to build a platform for Asian biologists and biology educators to: (i) *identify* current and future challenges in society and the environment, (ii) *rethink* the roles and goals of biology education to meet these challenges, and (iii) *discuss* possible frameworks and strategies for knowledge building and implementation. The theme of the conference, *Biology Education for Social and Sustainable Development*, further reflects the need for biologists and biology educators from diverse cultures and societies to come together to discuss several current issues under the subthemes of biology education curriculum and policy, teacher learning and education, student learning in K-12 levels, biology education at tertiary levels, environmental and social issues in biology, and assessment and evaluation.

The 42 papers in this book, *Biology Education for Social and Sustainable Development*, explore how biology education can contribute to social and sustainable development. They are organized around four main themes: (i) *Visions and Challenges of Biology Education for Sustainability*, (ii) *Biology, Community and Higher Education*, (iii) *Teaching Practice and Student Learning of Biology and the Environment*, and (iv) *Developing Teacher Education and Biology Science Curriculum*. The book is informative, stimulating, and thought-provoking to read, and is a useful resource for graduate seminar courses in science education and anyone interested in biology education in the region.

Because the concept of sustainable development is rooted in specific and unique local contexts, the case studies presented in this book offer valuable insights into the varied ways in which biology education can foster sustainability. A broad spectrum of issues is discussed, from the exploration of alternative fuel supplies in the Philippines, adult education programs that empower small farmers in Asia and bioentrepreneurship projects.

Several studies in this book also present recommendations on how to improve learning outcomes for students. They range from teaching students writing strategies to the use of advance organizers, the provision of timely and targeted feedback and the use of cues to facilitate inference, to cite a few. Studies were also done to assess the effectiveness of educational field trips to increase student interest in science and knowledge integration.

The development of teacher training programs and science curriculum is also discussed through case studies taken from countries such as China, South Korea, Thailand, Indonesia, Japan and Ukraine. The power a science teacher has to spark a thirst for learning and the core beliefs that guide a good science teacher are explored in those studies as well as the need for strategic professional development programs. Several researchers sound the call for reform of science curriculum and teaching methodologies to provide more relevant contexts for learning, and to foster meaningful collaboration amongst students and local communities.

The papers and studies presented here paint an exciting picture for the future of biology education in promoting sustainability. Critical reviews of the challenges highlight the possibilities for growth and positive case studies of effective collaboration point the way towards greater interdisciplinary integration and networking. Whether one is a science student, educator or field worker, the issues raised in this book will provoke thought and action towards fostering sustainability.

We thank the keynote speakers for their invited papers and authors for the contributed papers. It has been our pleasure to acknowledge and appreciate all your contributions to this publication. Your enthusiastic participation in the conference contributed richly to the discussions and at the same time extended and enlarged the existing network of biology educators, as well as helped propel biology education for social and sustainable development.

Rethinking and reconstruction of biology education in the Asia-Pacific region is increasingly grounded in deep understandings of what counts as valuable local knowledge, practices, culture, and ideologies for the global issues. Collaborative approach among us plays an undeniably significant role in those challenges and contributes to the richness and diversity of problem solving in Asia and around the world. It is our sincere hope that this publication will act as a catalyst to further promote education for sustainable development and enliven on-going discussions and collaborations among the community of science educators in the Asia-Pacific region and beyond. We look forward to opportunities for further collaboration in the near future.

Mijung Kim and C. H. Diong
Editors

LIST OF CONTRIBUTORS

Ashikin ABU BAKAR
Ngee Ann Secondary School,
Singapore
ashikin_abu_bakar@ngeeannsec
.edu.sg

Agustin B. ANCOG
Bohol Island State University
Tagbilaran City,Bohol, Philippines
agustinancog@yahoo.com

Jan BARKMANN
Department of Agricultural
Economics and Rural Development,
Environmental and Resource
Economics, Georg-August-
Universität Göttingen, Germany
jbarkma@gwdg.d

Maria Cristina A. BORDALLO
De La Salle-College of Saint Benilde
2544 Taft Avenue, Manila,
Philippines tinbordallo@yahoo.com

Rumila P. BULLECER
Bohol Island State University
6300 Tagbilaran City,Bohol,
Philippines
mslling@yahoo.com

Susan BYRNE
Environmental Sustainability
Research Centre, School of Life and
Environmental Science, Deakin
University, Warrnambool, Australia
susan.byrne@deakin.edu.au

Alma Linda ABUBAKAR
FAO Regional Office for Asia and
Pacific in Bangkok
Thailand
Almalinda.Abubakar@fao.org

Manuel B. BARQUILLA
Department of Science and Mathematics
Education, College of Education,
MSU-Iligan Institute of Technology,
Iligan City, Philippines
stitch_mbb@yahoo.com

Susanne BÖGEHOLZ
Faculty of Biology, Albrecht-von-
Haller-Institute for Plant Sciences,
Didactics of Biology,
Georg-August-Universität Göttingen,
Germany
zeusbio@gwdg.de

Ricardo P. BULLECER
University of Bohol, Philippines
ricbullecer@yahoo.com

Nida G. BUTRON
Bohol Island State University
6300 Tagbilaran City, Bohol, Philippines
nida_butron@yahoo.com

Josefino R. CASTILLO
Department of Biological Sciences,
College of Science University of Santo
Tomas, Manila, Philippines
jrcast327@yahoo.com

Rosalinda Mercedes E. CASTILLO
La Consolacion College Manila,
8 Mendiola Street, 1005 Manila,
Philippines
lyndy_312@yahoo.com

Chun-Yen CHANG
Graduate Institute of Science Education
Science Education Center, Department
of Earth Sciences
National Taiwan Normal University,
Taiwan
changcy@ntnu.edu.tw
http://w1.ceels.org/chunyen/index_
eng.html

Esther DANIEL
Department of Mathematics &
Science Education, Faculty of
Education, University of Malaya,
Kuala Lumpur 50603, Malaysia
esther@um.edu.my

Nenita M. DAYRIT
University of the Philippines Diliman
Clarkfield, Pampanga, Philippines
dayritnitz@yahoo.com

Narendra D. DESHMUKH
Homi Bhabha Centre for Science
Education, TIFR, Mumbai, India
nddeshmukh1965@gmail.com

Emmanuel ESPINEDA
Department of Biology, Ateneo de
Manila University,
Loyola Schools, Katipunan Road,
Loyola Heights 1108, Quezon City,
Philippines
vtolentino2001@yahoo.com

Emilia FÄGERSTAM
Department of Behavioural Sciences
and Learning, Linkoping University,
581 83 Linkoping,
Sweden
emilia.fagerstam@liu.se

Woon Keat FOO-LAM
Hwa Chong Institution, 661 Bukit
Timah Road, Singapore 269734
foowk@hci.edu.sg

Kseniya FOMICHOVA
Department of Eco-social System
Engineering
University of Yamanashi, 4-3-11,
Takeda, Kofu Yamanashi, 400-8511,
Japan
white_kirin@ymail.com

Melinda M. GARABATO
Odiongan National High School,
Odiongan
Gingoog City, Philippines
mgsky_815@yahoo.com

Michelle GRAYMORE.
Horsham Campus Research Precinct,
University of Ballarat, Horsham,
Australia
Michelle.graymore@ballaratuni
.edu.au

Yuhong HUANG
Sanming College, Fujian, China

Reizl P. JOSE
Bohol Island State University,
Tagbilaran City, Bohol, Philippines
gzl_4@yahoo.com

Jashanan KASINATHAN
Si Ling Primary School, No 61,
Woodlands Avenue 1, Singapore
739067
jashanan_kasinathan@moe.edu.sg

Futaba KAZAMA
Department of Eco-social System
Engineering, University of
Yamanashi, 4-3-11, Takeda, Kofu
Yamanashi, 400-8511, Japan
kfutaba@yamanashi.ac.jp

Heui-Baik KIM
Seoul National University, Shillim-
dong, Gwanak-gu, Seoul, Korea,
151–748
hbkim56@snu.ac.kr

Sebastian KOCH
Faculty of Biology, Albrecht-von-
Haller-Institute for Plant Sciences,
Didactics of Biology, Georg-August-
Universität Göttingen, Germany
skoch@gwdg.de

Ching-San LAI
National Taipei University of
Education,
Taipei, Taiwan
clai@tea.ntue.edu.tw

Minjoo LEE
Seoul National University
Gwanak-gu, Seoul, Korea
mjtree@snu.ac.kr

Eunhee KANG
Seoul National University, 599 Gwanak-
ro,Gwanak-gu Seoul, Korea, 151-748
chukbai@hanmail.net

Shogo KAWAKAMI
Gamagori Museum of Earth, Life and
the Sea
Gamagori City, Aichi, Japan
kawakami@nrc.gamagori.aichi.jp

Jan Willem KETELAAR
FAO Regional Office for Asia and
Pacific in Bangkok
Thailand
Johannes.Ketelaar@fao.org

Mijung KIM
National Institute of Education,
Nanyang Technological University,
Singapore 637616
Current address: University of Victoria,
BC, Canada
mjkim@uvic.ca

Marina A. LABONITE
Bohol Island State University
6300 Tagbilaran City, Bohol, Philippines
mtalabonite@yahoo.com.ph

Jane Jiyoung LEE
Seoul National University, Shillim-
dong, Gwanak-gu, Seoul, Korea, 151-
748
jlee@cph.osu.edu

Sun-Kyung LEE
Cheongju National University of
Education
Cheongju, Chungbuk 361-712, Korea
sklee@cje.ac.kr

Milarosa L. LIBREA
Ateneo High School, Ateneo de
Manila University, Katipunan Road,
Loyola Heights, 1108, Quezon City,
Philippines
milarosalibrea@yahoo.com

Sheau-Wen LIN
Graduate Institute of Mathematics and
Science Education, Pingtung University
of Education, Taiwan
linshewen@mail.npue.edu.tw

Enshan LIU
The College of Life Sciences
Beijing Normal University, 100875,
China
liues@bnu.edu.cn

Vivianne LOW
Si Ling Primary School, No 61,
Woodlands Avenue 1, Singapore 739067
goh_lee_teng@moe.edu.sg

Lalevie Casas LUBOS
Bukidnon State University,
Malaybalay City, Bukidnon
Province, Philippines
lal2004love@yahoo.com

Lesley Casas LUBOS
Research and Publication Office, Liceo
De Cagayan University, Liceo Arcade,
Rodolfo N. Pelaez Boulevard, Carmen,
9000 Cagayan De Oro City, Philippines
dawsonia@yahoo.com

Wendel T. MARCELO
Department of Biology, Ateneo de
Manila University, Loyola Schools,
Katipunan Road, Loyola Heights
1108, Quezon City, Philippines

Aya MATSUMOTO
Meiho Lower Secondary School
Nagoya, Japan

Ty G MATTHEWS
Environmental Sustainability
Research Centre, School of Life and
Environmental Science, Deakin
University, Warrnambool, Australia
ty.matthews@deakin.edu.au

Koichi MORIMOTO
Nara University of Education
Takabatakecho Nara, Japan
morimoto@nara-edu.ac.jp

Irving Brian MOSBERGEN
Si Ling Primary School,
No 61, Woodlands Avenue 1,
Singapore 739067
mosbergen_irving_brian@moe.edu.sg

Chi-Yao Ni
Chung-Hu Elementary School
Taipei County, Taiwan
twnicy@gmail.com

Glorina P. OROZCO
Far Eastern University, Manila,
Philippines
Nicanor Reyes St., Sampaloc
Manila, Philippines 1008
orozcogp@yahoo.com

Myrna PAEZ-QUINTO
Department of Biological Sciences,
Far Eastern University, Manila
Philippines
myrnazaldy2003@yahoo.com

Jocelyn D. PARTOSA
College of Science and Information
Technology
Ateneo de Zamboanga University
Zamboanga City,
Philippines
Ojdpartosa@yahoo.com

Sherry P. RAMAYLA
Philippine Science High School-
Central Visayas Campus and
University of the Philippines of the
Visayas Cebu Campus, Philippines
platenae@yahoo.com

Ashri B. SHUKRI
Si Ling Primary School,
No 61, Woodlands Avenue 1,
Singapore 739067
ashri_b_shukri@moe.edu.sg

Yen Ping SOH
Hwa Chong Institution,
661 Bukit Timah Road, Singapore
269734
sohyp@hci.edu.sg

Hassan H. TAIRAB
Department of Curriculum &
Instruction,
Faculty of Education,
United Arab Emirates University,
UAE
tairab@uaeu.ac.ae

Hong Kim TAN
Natural Sciences and Science
Education, National Institute of
Education, Nanyang Technological
University, Singapore
hongkim.tan@moe.edu.sg

Meng Leng POH
Hwa Chong Institution,
661 Bukit Timah Road, Singapore
269734
Pohml@hci.edu.sg

Thasaneeya R.
NOPPARATJAMJOMRAS
Institute for Innovative Learning,
999 Phuttamonthon 4 Road, Nakhon
Pathom 73170
Mahidol University, Thailand
iltrt@mahidol.ac.th

Mark Joseph SIBAL
Department of Biology, Ateneo de
Manila University, Loyola Schools,
Katipunan Road, Loyola Heights 1108,
Quezon City, Philippines

Leti SUNDAWATI
Faculty of Forestry, Department of
Forest Management, Social Forestry
Unit, Institut Pertanian Bogor (IPB),
Indonesia

Hoe Teck TAN
Singapore School of Science and
Technology
Singapore
tanhoeteck@hotmail.com

Merle C. TAN
National Institute for Science and
Mathematics Education Development
University of the Philippines
merle.tan@up.edu.ph

Yan-Ting TANG
College of Life Sciences, Shaanxi
Normal University, South Chang'an
Road,Xi'an, 710062, P.R.China,
mabean@126.com

Paul P.S. TENG
Dean, Graduate Studies and
Professional Learning
National Institute of Education,
Nanyang Technological University
Singapore 637616
paul.teng@nie.edu.sg

Anne WALLIS
Environmental Sustainability
Research Centre
School of Life and Environmental
Science
Deakin University, Warrnambool,
Australia.
PO Box 423, Warrnambool, Victoria,
3280, Australia,
anne.wallis@deakin.edu.au

Koichiro WATANABE
Kanare Elementary School, Nagoya,
Japan

Marcelo WENDEL
Department of Biology, Ateneo de
Manila University, Loyola Schools,
Katipunan Road, Loyola Heights
1108, Quezon City, Philippines

Ting-Kuang YEH
Graduate Institute of Science
Education
Department of Earth Sciences
National Taiwan Normal University,
Taiwan
895440089@ntnu.edu.tw

Hang Chuan TENG
Si Ling Primary School,
Woodlands Avenue 1 Singapore 739067
teng_heng_chuan@moe.edu.sg

Vivian S. TOLENTINO
Department of Biology, Ateneo de
Manila University, Loyola Schools,
Katipunan Road, Loyola Heights 1108,
Quezon City, Philippines
vtolentino2001@yahoo.com

Robert L. WALLIS
School of Science & Engineering,
University of Ballarat, Australia
r.wallis@ballarat.edu.au

Margaret WATERMAN
Biology Department,
Southeast Missouri State University
Cape Girardeau, Missouri 63701 USA
mwaterman@semo.edu

Baojun YAO
School of Life Science, Jiangxi Normal
University, Jiangxi, China
755782564@qq.com

Macrina T. ZAFARALLA
University of the Philippines at Los
Baños
Institute of Biological Sciences,
College of Arts and Sciences,
Philippines
ctzafaralla@yahoo.com

YING-Chun ZHANG
College of Life Sciences, Shaanxi
Normal University South Chang'an
Road, Xi'an, 710062, China
yingchunzcn@yahoo.com.cn

VISIONS AND CHALLENGES OF BIOLOGY EDUCATION FOR SUSTAINABILITY: KEYNOTE PAPERS

There are many challenges of social and environmental problems in our local and global society. Overpopulation and the depletion of natural resources, food security, overexploitation of ecosystems for direct use and non-use utility are among the human-environmental issues that have created social and ecological injustice by polarizing human life between the developed and developing countries. To survive in the global economy and capitalistic society, science and technology has been the means of advancing human life. This approach has however been criticized as mechanical and aggressive, without taking into account the biocapacity and sustainability of the earth. It is timely that we shift our paradigm of "doing" science and "teaching" science away from the mechanistic exploitative approach to a sustainable harmonistic approach to Nature and the society.

More practically, it is questioned how school biology education could respond to those timely issues. How can biology education in schools be more related to the needs of different target groups, ranging from school children to illiterate farmers? While bioscience enterprises have certainly helped improve livelihoods of farmers and fueled national development, how can what is taught in the classroom further contribute to the wellbeing of the people through bioentrepreneurship projects? How can real-life issues be integrated into biology education? These questions are discussed in Paul Teng's paper, *"Linking Education to Bioentreprenuership for Sustainable Development "*. By emphasizing food security as one of the essential elements of sustainable development in Asian countries, Teng is leading his readers to think about the challenges and strategies of sustainable development such as through bioentrepreneurship and education. An added challenge is that adult educational programs, with an emphasis on andragogy, must be responsive to the rapid pace of scientific and technological advances to improve scientific literacy and the livelihoods of poor communities in developing countries.

Since the meaning of sustainable development (SD) is heavily context-dependent in social, cultural, and environmental situations, the visions and strategies of SD can differ from one country to another. Merle Tan raises fundamental questions on the concept of SD and the role of science education to develop scientifically, technologically and environmentally literate citizens for sustainability in society in her paper, *"Promoting Public Understanding of Sustainable Development: Opportunities for Science Education"*. For example, to what extent can concepts of sustainable development be contextualized in schools, so that students can be equipped with knowledge and skills to analyze and address community problems? Could teachers and students become model citizens who become leaders of advocacy programs, through inquiry-based science teaching? Introducing the examples of current educational efforts in the Philippines, Tan emphasizes students' understandings of SD based on their community contexts and integrated approach to science curriculum planning, and teaching and learning in schools to enhance students' scientific literacy for sustainable development. A case study based in the Philippines also presents interesting findings on a proposed STE-based science curriculum. A study of the scientific literacy of Grade 6 to high school students in the Philippines found decreasing performance levels for Grade 6 and Year 4 students. These findings suggest that students have been trained to give the right answers rather than exploring questions, seen from their difficulty in evaluating information drawn from tables or real-life contexts. Tan highlights the implications for instruction and teacher education, for example, focusing on experiential activities rather than training students to follow steps and instructions.

These same issues on how biology education can promote sustainable development are explored by Margaret Waterman from a North American perspective in her paper "*Action and Opportunities: A North American perspective on Undergraduate Biology Education for Social and Sustainable Development*". For now, progress appears to be uneven, with non-governmental organizations (NGO) taking the lead in promoting sustainable development through education, rather than national governments. Waterman singles out UNESCO as leading the way, specifically in international networking. What are the factors that account for the slow progress in the introduction of education for sustainable development in North American teacher training programs? Waterman cites several reasons for this, for example, decentralized control over education, lack of official standards for ESD and optional national accreditation of teacher education programs. Emphasizing the changes of pedagogy in science teaching, she shares possible strategies of Education for Sustainable Development (ESD) in teacher education, such as offering academic programs with sustainability emphases, using ESD as a co-curricular theme, greening of campus and curriculum, creating new courses on sustainability itself, and injecting ESD units or modules into individual courses. Her paper presents an overview of these issues, and discusses two common approaches – the SENCER approach and Problem based learning (PBL)– that can engage students in analyzing complex problems and encourage active civic engagement.

The experience of China also offers an intriguing case study. With the major shift from a centralized planned economy to a market economy, the educational needs of the country have also undergone a sea change. Reforms started in the year 2000 to prepare the new generation of Chinese school students for the new century. They have centered on maximizing human capital and building a creative thinking economy. What are some key areas that reform has focused on? Enshan Liu examines the five-fold mission of China's education reform in "*Biology Education in China 2000–2010: A Review of Curricular Trends and Teacher Preparation Models for a Changing Society*". His paper also explores the change in principles undergirding biology education, for example, a shift away from elitist thinking that limited biology education to a few excellent students while neglecting the bulk of the student population.

Another exciting area for educational science is genetic and neuroscience research. To contemplate on education, science, and the future in our modern society, questions on cognition and students' learning are one of the key factors to delve into. The integration of multiple disciplines like education, cognitive psychology, and neuroscience can provide many meaningful frameworks for research, learning and instruction. Chun-Yen Chang and Ting-Kuang Yeh propose an interdisciplinary research framework and preliminary work in exploring associations between genotypes and student abilities and achievements. They introduce their innovative and creative research framework with regard to students' cognitive development. In their paper " *From Gene to Education – The ECNG Research Framework: Education, Cognition, Neuroscience, and Gene*", they provide instructional approaches (施教) and learning strategies to fit with students' aptitudes or characteristics (因材) based on the interactional effects of Education, Cognition, Neuroscience, and the Gene (the ECNG model). The ultimate goal of Chang and Yeh's ECNG model is to provide instructional approaches and learning strategies that are best suited to students' aptitudes, thus, for learning development.

How can the discipline of Biology continue to be relevant and powerful in shaping the way the global community understands the scientific basis of life? This question is all the more important in light of unprecedented challenges that biology educators face, as highlighted in Robert Wallis' paper, *"Biology Education in the Future"*. These include the explosion of knowledge that may leave educators overwhelmed, challenges to the scientific method from fundamentalist and other pressure groups, the challenge to integrate and generalize knowledge, urgency of challenges that confront society, and the lure of short-term solutions over long-term ones that may lack scientific rigor. Wallis also addresses some guiding principles that can ensure the continued importance and success of biology education, including ensuring relevance and stressing scientific applications as much as discoveries. Wallis is hopeful that our awareness and wisdom on economic, social, cultural and environmental sustainability will lead us to make meaningful decisions on educational approaches for the future.

A recurring concept in all the papers is the issue of relevance – how can biology education promote sustainable development in modern societies? Because the concept of sustainable development is so rooted in local contexts, it is difficult to come up with a universal definition. While this presents challenges, the papers point to exciting opportunities for biology education to contemplate on its roles in local and global societies.

PAUL P.S. TENG

1. LINKING EDUCATION TO SOCIALLY-RELEVANT BIOENTREPRENEURSHIP FOR SUSTAINABLE DEVELOPMENT

ABSTRACT

Sustainable development requires, inter alia, that efforts be made to eliminate poverty and reduce the number of hungry people. Many of the poor do not have access to the means to improve their livelihoods. Those involved in agriculture generally find difficulty in increasing the value of outcomes from their efforts. The 20th Century saw humankind dramatically expand in the diversity and magnitude of bioscience enterprises, i.e. enterprises which create value using biology. These bioscience enterprises include raw bio-commodities like rubber and palm oil produced using modern plantation technology, high quality seed material using hybrids, high quality seed material using tissue culture, biofermentation, biofertilizers, biopesticides, biofuels, bioremediation and biotech seeds. Each of these enterprises is based on sound science and contributes to key needs of modern societies. Such enterprises have contributed to improving livelihoods and aggregatively, to national development. However, technology and entrepreneurship together are not enough, and require andragogy and pedagogy through education programs developed for specific target groups, ranging from school children to uneducated farmers. Science education generally, and biology focused education specifically, at the school level need to be linked to "real-world" situations to have relevance to societal issues. In this respect, Science Centres are pivotal to the broader education of the citizenry to ensure continued support of the rural base that feeds cities. Similarly, the rapid pace of scientific and technological advances requires that adult education programs – mainly implemented by extension systems – be designed with simplicity to facilitate the adoption of new seeds and modern agronomy.

KEYWORDS

Andragogy, Pedagogy, Asia, Biology Education

INTRODUCTION

Education is central to sustainable development (SD) as it empowers people and strengthens nations. It is a powerful "equalizer" to reduce the distinctions made by class, race and culture, and opens doors to all to lift themselves out of poverty. As noted by the International Council for Science (ICSU), one of the biggest

Mijung Kim and C. H. Diong (Eds.), Biology Education for Social and Sustainable Development, 5–18.

challenges facing governments today is how to build capacity in science and technology to achieve the goal of sustainable development (Malcolm et al., 2002). In today's context of increasing food prices and increasing numbers of poor and hungry, education becomes even more important to reinforce efforts aimed at providing livelihood and reducing poverty, so that the poor can have economic access to food (Escaler, Teng & Caballero-Anthony, 2010).

Education on its own, however, is no guarantor of success in achieving the goal of SD and an intermediary is needed in the form of gainful employment which provides livelihoods and therefore accesses to the material goods which are so essential for modern living. Education enables entrepreneurship, which in poor, rural communities, is often seen in the form of bio-enterprises such as the growing and selling of crops and animals. This link between education, entrepreneurship and SD is illustrated in Figure 1.

That education promotes economic growth, national productivity and innovation is generally accepted by the development community. So too is education's role to promote the values of democracy and social cohesion. An educated and science-skilled workforce is one of the pillars of the knowledge-based economy. Increasingly, comparative advantages among nations come less from natural resources or cheap labor and more from technical innovations and the competitive use of knowledge. Studies also link education to economic growth: education contributes to improved productivity which in theory should lead to higher income and improved economic performance. Countries with higher primary schooling and a smaller gap between rates of boys' and girls' schooling tend to enjoy greater democracy. Democratic political institutions (such as power-sharing and clean elections) are more likely to exist in countries with higher literacy rates and education levels. Education, especially adult education, can further enhance natural resource management and national capacity for disaster prevention and adoption of new, environmentally friendly technologies.

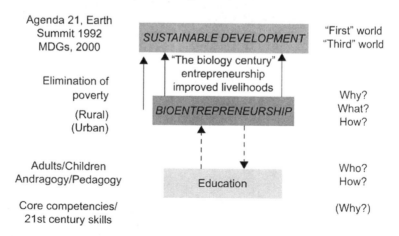

Figure 1. Schematic showing the relationship between education to facilitate bioentrepreneurship in support of sustainable development.

THE CHALLENGES OF SUSTAINABLE DEVELOPMENT

Sustainable development is the goal of most developing nations. International consensus such as the "Agenda 21" arising from the Earth Summit (Sitarz, 1994) has stressed the important role played by education. The Millennium Development goals (MDGs), which may be likened to development targets set by governments through the platform of the United Nations, have seen much progress towards their attainment in many parts of Asia. Two of the eight MDGs pertain to education— namely, universal primary completion and gender parity in primary and secondary schooling. Moreover, education—especially girls' education—has a direct and proven impact on the goals related to child and reproductive health and environmental sustainability.

Many definitions and interpretations of "sustainable development" have been proposed. Sustainable development is development that "meets the needs of the present without compromising the ability of future generations to meet their own needs" (WCED, 1987), while the International Institute of Sustainable Development prefers to view sustainable development (SD) as "improving the quality of life for all of the Earth's citizens without increasing the use of natural resources beyond the capacity of the environment to supply them indefinitely". This author has used SD to mean development which is economically rewarding, environmentally friendly and socially just.

What does this mean in an Asian context? Social equity, Economic viability and Environmental friendliness are descriptors which have been used in various situations. A set of rubrics is possible to characterize SD, for example,

- People
    - Economically empowered (livelihoods, incomes)
    - Food Secured
    - Access to education, shelter and healthcare
- Environment
    - Conservation of natural ecosystems
    - Minimizing anthropogenic effects on nature
- Governance
    - Transparency, Meritocracy
    - Gender neutrality
    - Social justice

Regardless of the definition, SD needs to benefit the 4 Billion people at the "bottom of the pyramid" (Prahalad, 2010) who are generally considered to be the "poor" of the world and earn less than US $1–2 per day. This part of humankind is most susceptible to the vagaries of the marketplace in an increasingly globalized world. For example, most of the estimated 1.02 Billion hungry people in the world are part of this "bottom of the pyramid" and are greatly affected by the increases in food pricing evidenced in 2007–08 and more recently (Escaler, Teng & Caballero-Anthony, 2010). For Asia, this is one of our biggest paradoxes, as 642 Million of these 1.02 Billion are estimated to live in the Asia, a continent which has seen some of the fastest wealth creation for individuals and spectacular double-digit economic growth. It is not possible or logical to have sustainable development if there is food insecurity arising from poverty and environmental degradation.

The Food and Agriculture Organization, U.N. considers *"Food Security"* to exist when all people, at all times, have physical, social and economic access to sufficient, safe and nutritious food that meets their dietary needs and food preferences for an active and healthy life. Food security is therefore an important measure of sustainable development as well, as implicitly, the capacity to purchase food due to livelihood means which depend on education in schools and for adults. In rural communities, bioenterprises have contributed and have high potential to provide the livelihood means to life people out of their poverty trap; some of these will be described in the following sections.

ROLE OF ENTREPRENEURSHIP IN MEETING THE CHALLENGES OF SUSTAINABLE DEVELOPMENT

The 21st Century has been called a "Biology" century because of the many advances in humankind's understanding of the basic processes and components of life. At the same time that exciting discoveries and applications based on biology have been made, the lingering problems of hunger and poverty among almost a quarter of humankind still remain. Profound challenges face the world even as we advance technologically. Biology offers great scope to meet these challenges, especially in the assurance of food security, and in the use of biology to meet the needs for more fuel, fiber and animal feed – the 4 F's (Teng, 2007a).

In the 1990's, Asia saw much interest in "biobusinesses", premised mainly in the potential of the new life science industry to spill over into pharmaceuticals and biomedical applications with the rapid developments in biotechnology. In reality, there has been limited success to enter into this highly competitive area in which large multinational companies and industrialized countries have secured their strong "first entry" advantage. A few countries, exemplified by Singapore, have been able to capitalize, *albeit* after large multi-billion dollar investments, and grow their own biomedical sectors. By and large, most Asian countries have not been able to tap into the "biobusiness" potential so ably desribed by the pioneering book, *BioBusiness in Asia* by Gurinder S. Shahi (2004, Pearson Education South Asia.). In retrospect, the Asian financial crisis of 1996–97 played a role in dampening investment interest but also raising consciousness on the need to address basics before embarking on new ventures. Thailand, through the urging of its Royal Family, embarked on a program of self sufficiency to address its own food needs; Malaysia refocussed its national development plan to move agriculture away from a "sunset industry" status. China's continued economic growth and the corresponding overall uplift in its people's standard of living also contributed to renewed interest to ensure secured supplies of the fundamentals – food, fiber, fuel. The recent spiking of petroleum prices, the general optimism in the Asian region about continued prosperity, the availability of capital through high national average savings rates, are additional factors which have spurred a renaissance in bioscience enterprises for value creation and to meet Asia's growing needs (Teng, 2007a).

The year 2008 saw the re-emergence of food security as a global issue that has precipitated social upheaval across all world regions (Escaler, Teng & Caballero-Anthony, 2010). Scientific and popular media have seen a plethora of literature and articles on food riots, the spectacular increase in commodity prices of corn, rice and wheat, and the alarming effects of high food costs on the poor (The Economist Magazine, April 19–25 2008). Thai rice breached the US1000 per milled ton barrier in April 2008, a 300 percent increase compared to January 2008! Key rice countries like Vietnam and India stopped their exports. World stocks of cereal grains reached their lowest in a decade, and the Food and Agriculture Organization, United Nations, warned that most Asian countries would become net grain importers in twenty years if no significant changes are achieved in productivity (FAO, U.N. -- http://www.fao.org/Ag/magazine/9809/spot1.htm). Because of the large number of small farmers in Asia, and the relatively small size of land holdings, Asian food security will depend on the ability to mobilize and empower this large number with the means to produce more food through education and access to modern technology. For Asia to feed itself, there must therefore be a renaissance in thinking and action, in which a "New Agriculture", based on modern bioscientific knowledge, and harnessing the best of biology, *is translated into products through entrepreneurship by the millions of small farmers.* Tremendous opportunities are provided by bioscience entrepreneurship to contribute to sustainable development in Asia, including in the islamic states of the middle-east.

The use of biological knowledge to serve human needs is not new and neither are the enterprises associated with exploiting that knowledge. Human society has tapped biological knowledge for millennia to produce food, feed, beverages and fiber, but the advent of modern technologies and new biological knowledge has vastly expanded the applications of biology. Our early ancestors domesticated plants and animals and with the selective breeding of preferred species, they formed the biological foundation for today's plant and animal varieties, many of which are vastly different from their original parents. Indeed, few of today's crop plants are unimproved or harvested from the wild. The bulk of fish is now farmed, not captured from the wild. A Bioscience Enterprise is any commercial activity which involves the application of biology and the understanding of life processes and creates economic value for its owner (Teng, 2008a, Chapter 1). What bioenterprises enable sustainable communities? This generally would include enterprises involving raw bio-commodities, high quality seed material using hybrids, high quality seed material using tissue culture, biofermentation, biofertilizers, biopesticides, biofuels, bioremediation, and biotech seeds.

Raw Bio-Commodities

Asia has been an important producer of some of the world's major bio-commodities, such as rice, corn (maize), cashew nuts, rubber, palm oil and cacao. Asia also is the world's largest producer of natural timber and aquacultured fish. With the exception of the cash crops such as rubber and oil palm, most other crops are grown by small farmers. While the commodities themselves remain important as food sources, increasing pressure is being put on their traditional role to supply calories for humans and feed for animals, especially on those commodities with potential for secondary exploitation such as conversion into higher valued biofuel or pharmaceuticals. This development is not surprising as plants have always been viewed as "primary producers" in the food chain because of their ability to capture energy from sunlight to make useful products. It is logical to expect that plants as "bio factories" will evolve in their role as human society evolves in its relative needs to use plants. "Biofarming" is traditional, while "biopharming" is a new application based on progress in science and technology in the molecular sciences and a host of new technologies. As a value proposition in bioscience entrepreneurship however, experience has shown that more value is created during the secondary and tertiary processing of raw commodities.

High Quality Seed Material Using Hybrids

The seed market includes both hybrid and non-hybrid, improved seed. The global seed market is valued at over US$ 30 Billion per year, dominated by multinational companies. There is no major seed company of Asian origin even though Asia potentially is the world's biggest market for certified, high quality seed. The value capture in the seed industry is through Intellectual Property ownership of plant varieties protected by law, but also offering value to growers who purchase the seed material. Hybridization as a bioscience technical process is well studied but its use as a enterprise only started in the 1920s with corn in the U.S.A. and led to the founding of one of today's largest seed companies (PIONEER HI-BRED). Hybrids offer a scientific means to preserve value as such seeds commonly loose their hybrid vigor (which confers 10–15% yield advantage over non-hybrids) if the seeds from hybrids are re-used for subsequent planting. Small farmers can participate in producing hybrid seeds but would require new skills and knowledge to do so, through innovative andragogy programs.

Tissue Culture

Tissue culture refers to a set of techniques and scientific knowledge, which enables the growth of cells into tissues and whole organisms under artificial conditions. Tissue culture was among the earliest applications of modern bioscience to develop into a multi-million dollar business for producing genetically identical seed material with the desired characteristics such as high yield, good eating quality or resistance to pests and diseases. The technique was also one of the earliest commonly included in biotechnology to create value for investors. However, even on its own, it has led to important applications, for example, the selection and subsequent mass-propagation of plant varieties showing resistance to specific diseases. Indeed, most of the large plantations of rubber and palm oil in South East Asia have their origins in tissue cultured clones.

The varieties of plants propagated by tissue culture in Asia and around the world are numerous and include herbaceous ornamentals, ferns, orchids, roots, tubers, tree species, tropical and subtropical crops. The benefits of propagating plants using tissue culture are manifold, apart from the uniformity in all the plants and the rapid multiplication. Plants grown in tissue culture are often disease and virus free. The economic value also is that tissue cultured plants are easily exported in small light-weight containers. As plants are free of soil, disease quarantine problems are minimized. With these advantages, export and import of tissue culture products are greatly facilitated. Tissue culture is a multi-million dollar business in several Asian countries such as Singapore, Thailand, Australia, China and Taiwan. Tissue culture plants me be found even in remote areas.

Biofermentation

Biofermentation is a process whereby food and organic products are produced through fermentation in a bioreactor by organisms like yeast, fungi and algae. Some of the more familiar products produced through the process of biofermentation include natto and tempe. The process of biofermentation involves selection of a suitable microbial culture that has the metabolic potential to produce the desired end product. The medium in which the culture is fermented is carefully chosen. The development of a suitable, economical medium is a balance between the nutritional requirements of the microorganism and the cost and availability of the medium components. Bioreactors range from small, relatively unsophisticated ones to large units with highly controlled internal growing conditions. Production by biofermentation has been deemed advantageous as fermentation utilizes renewable feedstocks instead of petrochemicals, some of the renewable feedstocks are agricultural waste. Also, the by-products of fermentation are usually environmentally benign compared to the organic chemicals and reaction by-products of chemical manufacturing. Often the cell mass and other major by-products are highly nutritious and can be used in animal feeds.

Biofertilizers

Fertilizers are needed to provide plants with the macro-nutrients for growth and development. In the modern era, high crop yields have been achieved because proper levels of fertilizer application have allowed the genetic potential of seeds to be expressed. Most of the fertilizer use today is made from petroleum-based products (i.e. synthetic fertilizers); some are organic. The high cost of synthetic fertilizers, coupled with concerns on sustainability, has led to the search for alternatives. Biofertilizers are organisms that enrich the quality of the soil through their natural processes and are commonly bacteria, fungi and cynobacteria (blue-green algae). Some of the more common types of biofertilizers include mycorrhiza, rhizobium, and cyanophyceae. Natural soil already serves as a reservoir of millions of micro-organisms, of which more than 85% are beneficial to plant life. Fertile soil usually consists of 93% mineral and 7% bio-organic substances. In Asia, fungi-based concoctions are commonly sold to augment synthetic fertilizers and have proven effective in maintaining high crop yields while reducing the overall cost of fertilizer per unit area. Several countries, have for environmental health reasons, launched campaigns to promote increased use of biofertilizers for food and plantation, commercial crops (e.g. Palm Oil in Malaysia), so too to reduce dependency on synthetic, often imported fertilizers.

Biopesticides

Pests cause an estimated 20–30% loss in production per crop harvest and the global pesticide market is a multi-billion one. Almost every modern crop is produced using one or more pesticides and much has been invested in R & D to produce new plant varieties which can naturally resist pests and diseases. Most of the pesticides in current use are synthetic petro-chemicals, hence their costs to growers has risen in response to the increase in oil. Pesticides are regulated by governments but often their misuse has had negative effects on human health and also on ecosystems. Biopesticides are considered a safe alternative and have sparked renewed attention in the 21st century due to current social issues surrounding pesticide usage, notably, market globalization and sustainable development. The term "biopesticide" refers to any living microbial agent which selectively infests and kills its insect or weed host or which is a microbial antagonist of a plant pathogen. The agent is mass produced and its infective stage is applied to control the target pest. Microorganisms used for weed control are often termed "bioherbicides" while those used for insect control are often termed "bioinsecticide". The use of certain types of biopesticides is based mainly on the ability of selected bacterial, fungal or viral strains to produce specific microbial, insecticidal or herbicidal compounds which are detrimental to their host – insects, weeds or other bacteria and viruses which are harmful to the target crop plant. Biopesticides act against insect pests which feed on plant tissues and act as an antagonist for the suppression of plant diseases. The main types of biopesticides were considered by Teng (2008a) to be Living microbes, Insecticidal toxins, Bacteria for biocontrol of plant diseases, Fungi for biocontrol of weeds, and Viruses for biocontrol of insect pests. Perhaps the most well known of the biopesticides is the group of insecticidal toxins referred to commonly as *Bacillus* toxins produced naturally by various *Bacilli*, especially *Bacillus thuringiensis* (Bt), found to be toxic to the Colorado Potato Beetle, the Diamond Back Moth, black flies and mosquitoes.

Biofuels

Biofuels are fuel sources that utilize biomass to produce bioenergy in order to provide a wide variety of energy services and to produce biomaterials as substitutes for those presently manufactured from petro-chemicals. Biofuels could be an integrating response to a number of global problems including equity, development, energy supply severity, rural employment and climate change mitigation. Biomass provides fuel flexibility to match a wide range of energy demands and is a renewable energy source that can be stored, which is an advantage over several other forms of renewable energy. Two principal biofuels are currently in use – bioethanol produced from sugarcane, corn and other starchy grains, and biodiesel produced from oil sources such as palm oil, soybean and rapeseed. In Asia, several countries have embarked on accelerated programs to produce biofuel, notably the giant countries like China and India, and also ASEAN countries like Malaysia, Thailand, the Philippines and Singapore. Energy crops are important to long-term energy strategies because they can be expanded to significantly shift the pattern of world energy supply. Volumes of other forms of waste biomass available are limited as they are by-products of other processes. Plant species that can be grown as energy crops and used for bioenergy purposes are so diverse that they can be grown in virtually every part of the world, including marginal lands and by small farmers.

Bioremediation

Industrial and farming activities have contaminated large tracts of land with toxic chemicals such as arsenic, mercury or high levels of salts, making the land uninhabitable or unsuitable for crops. Fresh water bodies have similarly been contaminated. While mechanical and chemical cures are known for removing the toxic or unwanted chemicals, government is increasingly searching for environment friendly techniques to make suck lands and waters usable again. One such set of techniques is collectively called "bioremediation", or the use of microbes, plants or their enzymes to remedy contaminated land and water. Several types of bioremediation techniques are in use; in the case where plants are the main tool, then the technique is called "phytoremediation" – phytoextraction, phytodegradation, phytotransformation, phytostabilization, and rhizofiltration (use of plant roots to reduce contamination in wetlands and estuaries). Phytoextraction is popular and much experience has built up to use specific plants for cleaning soil contaminated with heavy metals; the plant material is subsequently removed from the locale and incinerated. About 400 plants have been reported to hyperaccumulate metals. Several common aquatic species also have the ability to remove heavy metals from water, e.g., water hyacinth (*Eichhornia crassipes* (Mart.) Solms); and duckweed (*Lemna minor* L.). Microbes that are known to degrade pesticides and hydrocarbons generally are exemplified by species like *Pseudomonas, Alcaligenes*, which use the contaminant as a source of energy and carbon. Even mushroom fungi such as *Phanaerochate chrysosporium* have been shown capable of degrading environmental pollutants. Laboratory studies in Singapore have shown that common ferns (*Pteris vittata, Pityrogramma calomelanos*) are able to bio-accumulate arsenic at levels significantly higher than those found in the environment. Bioremediation is not a new phenomenon but modern science has made it a potentially powerful ally by improving the efficiency of the organisms concerned either using conventional selection or through genetic improvement. Much "upside" has yet to be exploited and can be done only through further investments in R & D and then capacity building.

Biotech Seeds

More than a decade ago, a significant new phenomenon emerged on the agriculture scene – biotech seeds (also known as genetically modified seeds) in which new traits had been introduced using the new tools of biotechnology such as "gene-splicing". Despite controversy over the use of such "gene-splicing" techniques, the uptake of biotech seeds has been remarkable and many independent academic studies have shown their value to poor farmers and commercial growers alike, as well as attesting to their biosafety and food/feed safety. The international non-profit organization based at Cornell University in the U.S.A., called the International Service for the Acquisition of Agribiotech Applications (www.ISAAA.org) has documented this remarkable phenomenon and shown that more than 145 Million ha of biotech crops were grown in 26 countries in 2010. ISAAA has projected the area of biotech crops to grow to a global area of 200 Million ha by 2015 (James, 2007). Given the proven benefits of biotech crops to farming and the consumer, it is likely that Asia will increase its adoption of such crops and capitalize on the multi-million dollar investments already made in R & D. Small farmers of cotton and maize have benefited greatly by growing these new crops, while some are deriving livelihood by producing seeds under contract with the knowledge owners.

ROLE OF EDUCATION IN ENABLING BIOENTREPRENEURSHIP FOR SUSTAINABLE DEVELOPMENT: ANDRAGOGY AND PEDAGOGY

Appropriate education is key to ensuring that biology provides the knowledge base to support entrepreneurship. Biology has been singled out due to the primacy placed on this discipline in its potential to affect humankind in the 21st Century. Indeed, the 21st Century has been touted as the "Biology Century" (Woese, 2004). However, biology education has to be viewed in the broader context of science education, and in particular, science education for development. In this broader context, science (biology) education must be considered for creating science literacy in adult populations and not just in schools. The UNESCO's "Science for All" initiative of the 1980s was primarily aimed at science literacy at the school level and not that of the public (Fensham & Harlen, 1999). In a contemporary context, this is not sufficient as science and its concomitant technology have become such an integral part of our lives that generalized science literacy is needed to form a basis for society to make informed decisions. In Figure 2, the schematic shows the three general goals of science education along the slope. Science education in schools involves pedagogy which stimulates enquiry and yet conveys the right degree of core knowledge; this has been the focus of most curriculum reform such as those in Singapore's Science Curriculum Framework (www.moe.gov.sg) and has economic goals associated with it. In Singapore, one of the Government's thrusts has been in the life sciences and biotechnology applications. Biology curricula were revamped in the early 2000's to focus on these as a basis for developing human resources (scientists and technologists) required to sustain a life science industry. At the National Institute of Education, the Ministry of Education provided financial support to develop a "DNA Centre" as part of the effort to train a cadre of teachers capable of driving the Life Science thrust. At the same time, the Singapore Science Centre (www.science.edu.sg) was tasked with public education and it in turn mounted exhibits and "hands-on" workshops on various aspects of genomics, molecular biology and biotechnology in an attempt to educate the general public towards greater "modern biology" literacy.

Conceptually, science education at the school level requires pedagogy skills while science education for the general adult public requires a sound understanding of andragogy (Figure 2). This is particularly the case when the situation is extrapolated to poor rural communities in developing countries, where sustainable development is so much more needed than in urban, rich communities. It is argued here that the andragogy must further recognize that language and mathematics literacy is often low in rural communities, and that to derive benefits from increased science literacy, it is further necessary to link that to entrepreneurship skills so that there are tangible outcomes which improve the livelihood of the poor.

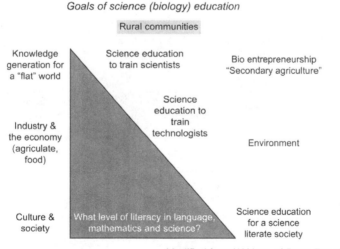

Figure 2. Schematic representation of the Goals of Science (Biology) Education.

The goals of science (biology) education are closely tied to what some workers have called the "Science for Development" model, schematically represented in Figure 3 (Drori *et al.*, 2003). The teaching of science is advocated as a necessary part of national development, implicitly, sustainable development, when issues of the environment (Figure 2) are considered together with industry and the economy. In the "Science for Development" model, school curricula are designed to meet national development goals, leading to a scientifically skilled workforce and a capacity to localize or develop local technology. While the model is fundamentally sound and is heuristic, it is still mainly focused on school science and pedagogy. As Peter Fensham and his co-workers (Fensham & Harlen, 1999) have found, there can occur disconnection between school science and the public understanding of science. Even in a relatively sophisticated urban city state like Singapore, surveys have shown that despite widespread public education initiatives on biotechnology, many surveyed thought that only genetically modified food contained genes and DNA while conventional food did not (Teng, 2008b). In Singapore, school science is now increasingly viewed from its opportunities to inculcate so called "21st Century skills", which are mainly thinking, analytical and communication in the hope that this will result in learners with greater innovation and entrepreneurship skills. As noted earlier, sustainable development depends, *inter alia*, on entrepreneurship skills and knowledge to provide livelihoods. These skills can only be gained through education programs which start with science in schools but continue into adult education programs. To be successful in one of the bioenterprises described in the previous section further requires that supportive government policies and institutions exist, and private sector financial facilities be available to marginalized communities. In rural areas in particular, linking adult science learning to the environment and to potential bioenterprises is a catalytic approach to nurturing science literacy.

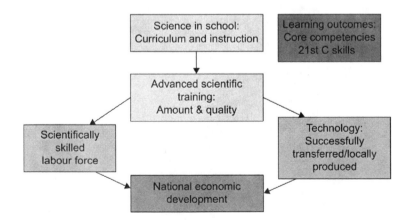

Figure 3. "Science for Development" Model – Pedagogy. (After: Drori et al., 2003).

The author's experience with rural rice farming communities has shown that adult farmer field schools made up of learning communities linked to local schools become powerful change agents for improving livelihoods based on scientific knowledge.

CONCLUDING REMARKS

Asian demographic data strongly point to the increasing number of people and an increasing demand for food, fuel, fiber, pharmaceuticals, and progressively, demand for a cleaner environment. By 2025, there will likely be more than five Billion people in Asia, characterized by an increasingly affluent but older population, most of whom will live in mega-cities with over ten million people each. Many of Asia's poor people, however, will still live in the countryside. The area of arable land for agriculture is expected to decline slightly compared to 2007, while sources of freshwater are also anticipated to decline. All these poses tremendous challenges in the coming years to produce more with less land, less water, less chemical and less labor. But it provides opportunities of high potential for bioscience entrepreneurship. The biosciences, and particularly biotechnology, offer great promise to meet these challenges in this new millennium. It is hoped that the discussion in preceding sections has shown that biology is a pivotal knowledge component to meeting humankind's requirements and thereby contributing to sustainable development. Biology's contributions can only be achieved through well planned and executed educational programs in schools and in adult populations, and focused as bioentrepreneurship.

The Asian region is uniquely placed to become the global leader in exploiting bioscience entrepreneurship to meet its needs. As physical and human capacity improves, more discoveries will fuel more innovative applications while the current deep R & D pipeline in many countries will translate into actual products and processes. By 2025, Asia will likely be a leading player in the "Biology Century".

REFERENCES

Drori, G. S., Meyer, J. W., Ramirez, F. O. & E. Schofer. (2003). Science in the Modern World Polity : Institutionalization and Globalization. Stanford: Stanford University. p. 103.

Escaler, Margarita, Paul Teng & Mely Caballero-Anthony. 2010. Ensuring Urban Food Security in ASEAN: Summary of the Findings of the Food Security Expert Group Meeting held in Singapore 4–5 August, 2010. *Food Security*, 2(4): 407–408.

Fensham, Peter J. & Harlen, Wynne (1999) School science and public understanding of science. *International Journal of Science Education*, 21(7): 755–763.

Malcolm, Shirley, Cetto, A. M., Dickson, D., Gaillard, J., Schaeffer, D. & Yves Quere. (2002). Science Education and Capacity Building for Sustainable Development. ICSU Series on Science for Sustainable Development no. 5. 31 p.

Prahalad, C. K. 2010. The fortune at the bottom of the Pyramid. Wharton School Pub. 407 p.

Sitarz, Daniel. 1994 (ed). AGENDA 21: The Earth Summit Strategy to Save Our Planet. Earth Press. 321 p.

Teng, P. S. 2007a. Accelerating the renaissance in bioscience entrepreneurship – Part 1. Asia Pacific Biotech, 11(16): 1138–1145.

Teng, P. S. 2007b. Commercialization of agricultural crop biotechnology products. In: Business Potential of Agricultural Biotechnology Products, pp 71–88. Asian Productivity Organization, Tokyo, Japan.

Teng, P. S. 2008a. BioScience Entrepreneurship in Asia: Creating Value with Biology. Singapore: World Scientific Publishing Co. 335 p.

Teng, P. S. 2008b. An Asian perspective on GMO and biotechnology issues. Asia Pacific journal of Clinical Nutrition 17 S1: 237–240.

Woese, Carl R. 2004. A New Biology for a New Century. Microbiology and Molecular Biology Reviews, Vol. 68(2): 173–186.

World Commission on Environment and Development (WCED). 1987. Our common future. Oxford: Oxford University Press, p. 43.

Paul P.S. Teng
Dean, Graduate Studies and Professional Learning
National Institute of Education, Nanyang Technological University
Singapore 637616
paul.teng@nie.edu.sg

MERLE C. TAN

2. PROMOTING PUBLIC UNDERSTANDING OF SUSTAINABLE DEVELOPMENT: OPPORTUNITIES FOR SCIENCE EDUCATION

ABSTRACT

The concept of sustainable development remains vague to many people. This is understandable because its meaning is continuously evolving as it is dependent on local contexts, needs, interests, and experiences. The concept of sustainability also means many different things to different people; those who live without access to basic necessities may not even have any association with this word! How then do we promote understanding of SD and sustainability if there is no definition that is universally accepted? One approach is to bring sustainable development and sustainability concepts in schools to contextualize their meanings. When students understand the concepts, they can use their knowledge and skills to help resolve community problems. They can make rational decisions on how to properly manage their environment and its resources. They can model sustainable practices in the community and exhibit high levels of commitment to action. These attributes are possessed by scientifically, technologically, and environmentally literate citizens. Developing STE literates is what science education aims to achieve. Are schools performing their roles to develop STE literates who can promote understanding of SD and sustainability? This paper presents the findings of a study in the Philippines on the level of STE literacy of selected students. The results of the study served as inputs to the proposed STE-based, inquiry-based science education curriculum framework for basic education that puts premium on enduring understandings needed to maintain good health and live safely, utilize energy and cope with changes, and protect and conserve the environment and its resources. The paper also describes some school-partnership programs that illustrate varied opportunities for learners and teachers to take leadership roles in organizing advocacy programs that enhance community participation and facilitate acquisition of STE literacy and promote SD. The implications of such innovations to teacher education are highlighted.

KEYWORDS

Scientific, Technological And Environmental Literacy, Inquiry-Based Science Teaching, Education For Sustainable Development, Sustainability

Mijung Kim and C. H. Diong (Eds.), Biology Education for Social and Sustainable Development, 19–28.

INTRODUCTION

In a recent gathering of educators, Dr. Lourdes Cruz, a marine scientist from the University of the Philippines talked about the relationship between poverty and education (Cruz 2010). She presented a graph that shows the estimated level of poverty in some Asian countries. Estimates refer to the population with income per capita below US$ 1.25 per day. While the poverty level of Vietnam, Indonesia and China is decreasing rapidly, that of the Philippines is almost at a steady rate. One of her inferences for the Philippine situation is that the marginalized people in varied rural communities have insufficient knowledge on how to utilize and manage their resources at a sustainable level. Her project with the Aetas, an ethnic community in the North, confirmed this.

However, many reports show that lack of knowledge about managing resources at a sustainable level is observed all over the Philippines and also in other countries (Tan & Leonardo, 2007). Environmental experts say that people from different communities have difficulty in envisioning a sustainable environment because the meaning of SD is heavily dependent on local contexts, needs, interests, and experiences. In addition, the relationship between SD and the social, economic, and environmental conditions in a community is complex. The concept of sustainability also means many different things to different people; a large part of humanity around the world still live without access to basic necessities. While it is difficult to envision a sustainable environment, many have no difficulty identifying what is unsustainable in our societies. We can quickly make a list of problems – inefficient use of energy, insufficient supply of potable water, increasing water, air, and land pollution, scarcity of fishery resources, decreasing biodiversity, low crop productivity, and many more.

SCIENCE EDUCATION AS A TOOL FOR ACHIEVING SD AND SUSTAINABILITY

The problems and concerns mentioned above are relevant context in the teaching of science in basic education. Using the STS approach, students are able to study the interaction between and among science, technology, and society. One example of such interaction was described by Rachel Carlson in 1962, when she exposed the dangers of insecticides and inspired the environmental movement. Unfortunately, 48 years after, the problem of contamination of the environment with substances of inconceivable potential for harm to living things remains. Students learn that these could accumulate in the tissues of plants and animals and alter the genetic material upon which characteristics of the future offspring depends. Sadly, many people have not realized the fact that Earth is endangered and that its interdependent species of plants and animals need to survive, endure, and thrive. Many have not understood why a world without plants and animals is not sustainable.

Another topic in science that could elucidate the relationship between SD and the social, economic, and environmental conditions in a community is climate change. Though global in context, climate change affects local people, especially the marginalized, during strong typhoons and flooding, when energy, food, and water are in limited supply, or when epidemics occur. Again, using the STS approach to teaching and learning, students gain knowledge and skills on how to maintain economic security without contaminating the water, soil, and air, and give high importance to biodiversity and human wellness, equity, and freedom. They can work with the community to design economic and social systems that meet basic human needs, at the same time enjoying the wonders of nature.

The aim of science education is to develop critical thinking and conflict resolution skills along with mathematical and scientific literacy. Science education encourages intellectual curiosity and empowers children to be life-long learners and wise consumers. Students develop a broad vision of the interconnectedness of all creatures and the concept of stewardship, cooperation, and moral responsibility. Science education teaches students to learn from their mistakes and correcting them, as well as regaining a sense of proportion and caring about the world we live in; it also opens up opportunities to develop informed civic engagement and harmonious partnerships among diverse groups in the community, simultaneously considering economic, social, and environmental needs so that all people can enjoy a decent quality of life (Tan, 2007). Thus, teaching science is also teaching towards sustainability.

The meaning of sustainable development and sustainability could be simplified by using this popular aphorism: "Give a man a fish and he'll eat for a day. Teach him how to fish and he'll eat forever." This suggests that people can make sure that the river is not polluted and can support a long-lasting population of fish. It ensures that all people in the community have access to the fish and have the skills and equipment necessary to do the fishing. It means developing strategies that allow folks to sell fish to people who don't live by the river, thereby improving the lives of the vendor and customer.

THE SCIENTIFIC, TECHNOLOGICAL, AND ENVIRONMENTAL LITERACY (STEL) STUDY

A sustainable society requires scientifically, technologically, and environmentally literate citizens. Are our schools developing such individuals? In 2005, UP NISMED studied the level of scientific literacy of Grade 6 (ages 11–12) and Fourth Year High School (ages 15–16) Filipino students in three regions. Bybee's fours levels of scientific literacy were expanded to seven to adapt it to the Philippines context, with Level 1 as the lowest and Level 7 the highest. The STEL domains cover healthy living, wise consumerism, living safely, and environmental protection/resource conservation.

The study showed a decreasing performance from Levels 1 to 7 for both Grade 6 and Y4 students. The STE literacy level of G6 and Y4 boys almost equal that of girls while urban students performed better than rural students. Interestingly, more students answered correctly items in Level 7 (can evaluate the impact of science and technology to society and environment) than Level 6 (design a scientific procedure and apply scientific methods to solve a problem).

The results suggest that Filipino Grade 6 and Year 4 students have been exposed to teaching strategies which emphasize the learning of right answers more than thinking about and exploring questions. Students have been given bits and pieces of information rather than challenged to explore issues and phenomena in real-life contexts. But students have difficulty in evaluating information drawn from tables or from given everyday situations. Both Grade 6 and Year 4 students could not explain specific observations and phenomena (UP NISMED, 2005). These findings imply that the current science curriculum is spread thinly over many topics that students acquire only fragments of assorted information. Such is contrary to the fact that concepts are learned best when encountered in various contexts and expressed in a variety ways (AAAS, 1989).

This STEL study further indicates that there is a need to focus on activities to be experienced rather than steps and instructions to be followed. Teachers should be able to set the STE contexts from the outset rather than present decontextualized concepts followed by illustrative examples. For example, it is easy to teach a child how to plant a seed if the only goal is getting the seed into the soil. The latter is in stark contrast to an activity where planting the seed is part of several carefully mediated events about plants, their role in nature, and our cultivation of them for food (Horton & Hutchinson, n.d.).

Any topic in science (or any subject for that matter), taught only in a single lesson or unit is unlikely to leave a trace by the end of schooling. In order for concepts to take hold, they must be taught in different contexts and at increasing levels of sophistication. This emphasizes the need for a thematic and spiraling curriculum based on enduring ideas and skills that students will need to use in solving problems in and outside of the school and throughout life.

THE PROPOSED STE-BASED, INQUIRY-BASED SCIENCE CURRICULUM FOR BASIC EDUCATION

Given the low level of scientific literacy of Filipino students, the high rate of dropouts in the country (Mateo, 2006) and the discipline-based science curriculum for basic education (Ogena & Tan, 2007), UP NISMED, in collaboration with various stakeholders in education, developed a science curriculum framework for basic education focused on STEL enhancement. The Framework has two features, making it different from previous curriculum documents: it focuses on the cohesiveness of the three interlocking components (scientific inquiry, attitudes, and content and connections) and looks at the total span of the basic education of students. It encourages a developmental and integrated approach to curriculum planning, teaching and learning. It enables students to progress smoothly through the grade levels and avoids the major disjunctions between stages of schooling evident in some previous approaches to curriculum. Thus, it provides the basis for continuity and consistency in the students' basic education.

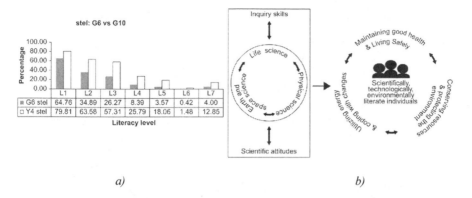

Figure 1. (a) Comparison of STE Literacy of Grade 6 and Year 4 Students, b) The Proposed Science Curriculum Framework for Basic Education.

The core content under Life Sciences, Physical Sciences, and Earth and Space Science describes the big ideas or enduring understandings (EUs) that all students are expected to learn to become STE literate and covers the competencies that indicate what students should be able to do and demonstrate at the end of G2, G4, G6, Y2, and Y4. The formulation of enduring understanding statements, essential questions, and performance indicators in the framework was inspired by the backward planning process of curriculum design espoused by Wiggins and McTighe (2005) and its emphasis on teaching with understanding. The EUs provide a conceptual focus, breadth of meaning by connecting and organizing facts, skills, and experiences, point to ideas at the heart of understanding, require "uncovering" of abstract or often misunderstood ideas and have transfer value across context and time.

The choice of topics/concepts is based on their relevance and applications to everyday life, arranged in a spiral manner from G1–6 and Y1–4 to show increasing complexity of concepts based on three science areas. The proposed curriculum shows how concepts within sciences and across subject areas are integrated. It highlights the thinking skills required to learn these concepts. The goal is scientific literacy for everyday life and gives emphasizes on acquiring and maintaining good health, using energy and coping with changes, and protecting and conserving the environment and its natural resources. An accompanying framework for science teacher education presents standards of performance of an effective science teacher, using rubrics on four levels of performance and helps teachers move from Level 1 (lowest) to the Level 4 (highest). In the professional knowledge category, teachers are required to have mastery of subject matter content; in the professional practice category, they are required to use varied strategies to develop investigations skills that promote development of 21st century skills; and in the professional attributes category, teachers are encouraged to become a member of community of learners.

SCHOOL-COMMUNITY PARTNERSHIP TO PROMOTE UNDERSTANDING OF SD

Schools alone cannot do the task of raising the quality of science education for all children. More will be accomplished if schools, families, and communities work together to promote successful students. Besides conducting research and disseminating its outputs through the curriculum and instructional materials it develops and in the professional development programs it conducts, UP NISMED links with individuals, groups, nongovernment organizations, and government agencies with the same interest and advocacy to fast-track the tasks. The following are some programs that promote the concepts of sustainable development and sustainability.

SciPol Television Program

SciPol was coined from the words "Science Serving People". UP NISMED started the program in 2006, aimed at bringing closer to the masses the work of Filipino scientists and researchers and how these work impact everyday life. Thirteen scripts in Filipino were developed by the UP College of Science and NISMED. The episodes explain in layman's language the science behind the phenomena and the nature of sustainable practices that could be adapted to protect coral reefs and groundwater, how to thwart the occurrence of red, green, and brown tides, and prevent coastal water pollution. Other titles focused on coping with natural disasters such as typhoons, landslides, earthquakes, volcanic eruptions, and tsunamis. Some health-related titles include Herbal Medicine, GMO, Dengue, and Vaccines. The National Broadcasting Network (NBN) produced the 20-min programs which were shown once a week on Channel 4. The same programs are being shown from time to time. NBN gathered data on how the viewing public receive the program; they reported that "the topics are easily understood by both children and adults." Some viewers suggested other titles.

Education for All Through Radio

In 2007, UP NISMED developed two kinds of radio program in Filipino: a 15-minuter for elementary school teachers and a 30-minuter for learners in selected communities. Later translated to *Cebuano* and *Ilokano* to suit the target listeners, both versions had 16 radio scripts (drama). These served as springboard for the radio discussion lessons. The lessons aimed to help improve the scientific, mathematical, and technological knowledge of learners on areas that affect a person's quality of life. The topics were on *Pangkalusugan (health- related)* such as poisons, balanced diet, junk food, common ailments, dengue and rabies; *Pagkaligtasan (living safely)* dealt with fire, flashfloods, typhoons, and first aid; *Pangkapaligiran* (environment-related) discussed water pollution, air pollution, solid wastes, and water as life; and *Pangkabuhayan (entrepreneurship)* introduced basic math skills in starting a small business.

An orientation workshop component for teacher trainers and community leaders were conducted in different sites. The radio lessons were then aired in 19 radio networks in Luzon, Visayas, and Mindanao. To support the implementation of the radio phase, 500 radio cassette players were distributed by the Foundation of IT Education (FIT-ED) our partner, using funds from CocaCola and Co. They studied how the radio program affected people in different communities and got encouraging feedback.

Air Care and Solid Wastes Management

Tricycles are a common mode of transportation in many communities across the Philippines. These contribute a lot to the local air pollution problem because most tricycles use two-stroke engines and recycled 2T oil. Analysis of the smoke emitted reveals high levels of carbon monoxide, nitrogen oxides, and unburned hydrocarbons. Four-stroke engines are better but more expensive. In 2004, UP NISMED partnered with the Department of Energy and Miriam College Foundation Environmental Institute in planning the Air Care Project funded by the United States Agency for International Development (USAID). UP NISMED did the production of the video lesson entitled *Beinte Beinte Lang,* a message for tricycle drivers to save Php20.00 a day for maintenance purposes. Intended to educate tricycle drivers on the preventive maintenance of tricycles, it will ultimately help in lessening air pollution caused by fumes. Copies of the video were distributed to selected tricycle drivers and operators associations of Quezon City.

Improper disposal of solid wastes is also a big problem, especially in urban areas. UP NISMED models a solid waste management system that can be adapted by teachers in schools. Posters have been prepared and distributed. The Institute developed two video lessons- one showing how to manage wastes while the other focusing on how improper disposal results to varied health problems. These materials support the Clean Air Act and Ecological Waste Management Act of the Philippines.

Sustainable and Environment-Friendly Schools Competition

Education for sustainability focuses on awareness of sustainable development issues, enhancing knowledge, influencing values and attitudes, and encouraging responsive behaviour and learning that leads to action. The school system is a vital part of our basic learning and is seen as a powerful vehicle for change. The school population, comprising of the students, teaching and non-teaching personnel, constitute a sizeable percentage of the national population. As such, any program focused on advocacy and other multi-faceted program of activities done within the school system especially relating to environmental concerns needs to be documented, encouraged, and recognized.

In 2009, the National Search for Sustainable and Eco-friendly Schools was launched as a partnership program among the Department of Environment and Natural Resources, through the Environmental Management Bureau, the Department of Education, Commission on Higher Education, with SMART

Communications Inc. UP NISMED served as one of the judges for this competition. Sustainable and Eco-Friendly schools may be described as environment-friendly schools that have initiated and integrated in their instruction, research, extension and/or administration, programs which are environment-related. The promotion of this program for the establishment and/or strengthening of sustainable and eco-friendly schools in the country had been enshrined as a priority in the ASEAN Environmental Education Plan for 2008–2012, and likewise in the Roadmap for the Implementation of Republic Act 9512 of 2008 (Environmental Awareness and Education Act) under the National Environmental Education Action Plan (2009–2014). Nine schools were declared as national champions. For 2011, another national search for Sustainable and Eco-friendly School is in place, to give recognition to the environmental initiatives of schools over the country.

Fisheries Management and Climate Change Survey

A current effort of UP NISMED in promoting SD is the development of survey questionnaires to determine the impact of a radio intervention project of WorldWideFund and FIT-ED in raising the consciousness and knowledge and skills of fisherfolks, local government units, and other stakeholders in coastal and fishing communities. The radio program includes topics on biodiversity, marine ecosystems and endangered species, sustainable livelihoods, ecotourism, ecogovernance, disaster preparedness, climate change adaptation, and ecological waste management. The result of the impact study will be the basis for future projects on SD.

CONCLUDING REMARKS

Sustainable development goes to the heart of tackling a number of interrelated global issues such as poverty, inequality, hunger, and environmental degradation. There are many ways in which the right kind of economic activity can protect or enhance the environment. The challenge of sustainable development is to promote ways of encouraging environment-friendly economic activities and discouraging environment-damaging activities. It means reconciling aspirations of communtities to achieve economic development to secure rising standards of living, both for themselves and for future generations while seeking to protect and enhance their environment, now and for their children. Prof. Wangari Maathai, Winner of the 2004 Nobel Peace Prize said that if we did a better job of managing our resources sustainably, conflicts over them would be reduced. So, protecting the environment is directly related to securing peace.

Science education has a major role to play in achieving SD and sustainability. It is a matter of shifting our view of science as exclusively an academic activity to science as a part of a larger social discourse and reflections. This way we develop STE literates who will advocate for sustainable development and sustainability.

REFERENCES

American Association for the Advancement of Science (AAAS), (1989). Science for all Americans. Washington, D.C. 2005, USA.

Bybee, R. W. (n.d.). Toward an understanding of scientific literacy. Retrieved July 13, 2004 from http://www.deacts.org/her/forum/bybee.html. In the STEL Study, UP NISMED Printing Press.

Cruz, L. (2010). *Poverty and education.* Paper presented in the General Assembly of the Foundation for Upgrading Standards of Education, May 25, 2010.

European Commission (2007). A Sustainable future in our hands. from http://ec europa.eu/sustainable /docs/sds_guide_en.pdf

Horton, R. L. & Hutchinson, S. (n.d.). *Nurturing scientific literacy among youth through experientially based curriculum materials.* Retrieved September 24, 2004, from http://www.nestafuturelab .org/research/lit_reviews.htm

Flint, Warren Flint (2010). Innovative Strategies of 5 E's, from Five E's Unlimited.

Mateo, J. (2006). *Status of Philippine Education.* Presented in the Forum for Basic Education Sector Reform Agenda, Department of Education

Ogena, E. & Tan, M. (2007). *National learning strategies in science and mathematics education.* Basic Education Sector Reform Agenda, Key Reform Thrust 3. Department of Education.

Tan, M., Gregorio L. & Leonardo L. (2005). Problems, needs and responses for promoting scientific literacy and life skills toward sustainable rural development for children, youth and adults. UNESCO International Research and Training Centre for Rural Education, Baoding, Hebie Province, China UNESCO INRULED.

Tan, M. (2007). Nurturing scientific and technological literacy through environmental education. In M. Nagao, J. Rogan, & Magno M. (Eds). *Mathematics and science education in developing countries: Issues, experiences, and cooperation prospects* (pp. 187–207). Quezon City: The University of the Philippines Press.

UP NISMED-DOST SEI-DepED (2010). Science Curriculum Framework for Basic Education (in press)

UP NISMED-DOST SEI-DepED (2010). Curriculum Framework for Science Teacher Education (in press)

UP NISMED (2005). Gender Differences in Scientific, Technological, and Environmental Literacy Among Elementary and High School Filipino Students. UP NISMED Press. Quezon City.

Wiggins G. & McTighe J. (2005) Understanding by Design. Expanded 2nd edition. ASCD, Virginia USA.

Merle C. Tan
National Institute for Science and Mathematics Education Development
University of the Philippines
merle.tan@up.edu.ph

MARGARET WATERMAN

3. ACTIONS AND OPPORTUNITIES: A NORTH AMERICAN PERSPECTIVE ON UNDERGRADUATE BIOLOGY EDUCATION FOR SOCIAL AND SUSTAINABLE DEVELOPMENT

ABSTRACT

This paper provides an overview of North American efforts to address social and sustainable development in undergraduate biology and teacher education. Progress has been uneven as non-governmental organizations (NGOs) rather than national policy are primarily responsible for infusing sustainability education into all levels of learning. Higher education addresses education for sustainable development (ESD) in several patterns: offering academic programs with sustainability emphases, using ESD as a co-curricular theme, greening of campus and curriculum, creating new courses on sustainability itself, and injecting ESD units or modules into individual courses. U.S. teacher education programs lag in the introduction of ESD topics due to decentralized control over education, existence of few official standards for ESD, and optional national accreditation of teacher education programs (they are state accredited). Changes in pedagogy are needed to facilitate integration of ESD. Common approaches are those that engage students in studying a complex problem of local to global importance from multiple perspectives, and may include active civic engagement. Two models, the SENCER approach and Problem based learning (PBL), are discussed.

KEYWORDS

PBL, Case Studies, AASHE, NGOs, SENCER, Education for Sustainable Development, ESD

INTRODUCTION

Education for Sustainable Development (ESD) is a global-level response to awareness of the interrelationships among climate change, injustice, population growth, overuse of resources, and the deterioration of the environment. The UN's Decade of Education for Sustainable Development has accelerated actions and awareness of ESD around the globe. Unlike the longstanding environmental education movement emphasizing conservation, education for sustainable development addresses the "triple bottom line" of creating a socially, economically

Mijung Kim and C. H. Diong (Eds.), Biology Education for Social and Sustainable Development, 29–40.

and environmentally sustainable world. How this plays out in colleges is expressed well in the description of the minor in sustainability at Emory University (2010).

... we acknowledge the issue of sustainability as one of the most theoretically and practically complex questions of our times. Involving far more than simply turning off lights or recycling bottles and paper, sustainability has implications for how we eat and drink; how we treat the land, sea, air, and atmosphere; how we approach health and well-being on an interspecies level; how we produce and consume goods; how we distribute the benefits and costs of that production and consumption; how we derive the energy to maintain both those economic enterprises and our everyday lifestyles; and how we assess and rethink the proper balance between profit, politics, wealth, and the common good. The challenge of sustainability is its profoundly crosscutting nature; none of these questions may be answered without consideration of the others.

This paper provides an overview of Canadian and U.S. efforts to address education for sustainable development in undergraduate biology and teacher education.

THE OVERVIEW OF ESD IN CANADA AND THE U.S.

Context of Education and What that Means for ESD

In the United States and Canada there is at present no oversight of the content of education at the national level, no national curriculum, no unified approach to schooling. Each of the 50 U.S. states develops its own standards, assessments and teacher education requirements for primary and secondary education. The 10 provinces and three territories of Canada are similarly controlled (Council of Ministers of Education, 2008).

To complicate matters in the U.S., every school district creates its own curriculum to address the state standards. Higher education is even more variable lacking national or state oversight of curriculum, as is common. Instead, each program and each individual professor creates curriculum. Because of these decentralized organizational structures, a national, top down approach to integrating ESD into education is not feasible in the U.S. and Canada.

Actions and Opportunities Supporting ESD at the Federal Level – U.S.

In 1996 President Clinton's Council on Sustainable Development (PCSD) produced the well-thought-out plan "Education for Sustainability: An agenda for action." Having only an advisory role and due to lack of funding, the PCSD was dissolved in 1999.

In 2008, President Bush signed the Higher Education Sustainability Act (a part of the Higher Education Opportunity Act) into U.S. law to provide federal funding to the Department of Education for grants "to support research and teaching initiatives that focus on multidisciplinary and integrated environmental, economic and social elements... to integrate sustainability curricula in all programs of instruction" (Higher Education Opportunity Act of 2008, p. 122). An examination of the Department's website and grants.gov did not turn up any evidence that the program is active thus far.

President Obama's Secretary for Education outlined early steps in the administration's response to ESD in his letter to the UNESCO World Conference on Education for Sustainable Development in Bonn (Duncan, 2009). His points were, first, that some of the money of the American Recovery and Reinvestment Act of 2009 is being used to create modern, green learning environments. Second was the focus on solving the U.S. energy problem and the need to educate people so as to reduce greenhouse gas emissions, to use alternative energy sources, and to prepare for jobs in this emerging field. No clear statement about ESD as such is contained in his letter. Energy sustainability seemed to be the main emphasis of this administration in 2009.

The National Science Foundation, one of the major sources of federal funding for science-related education and research in the U.S., established a new program called Science, Engineering and Education for Sustainability (SEES) that cuts across the divisions of the agency. The 2010 emphasis is on Climate Change Education Partnerships. The program "seeks to establish a coordinated national network of regionally- or thematically-based partnerships devoted to increasing the adoption of effective, high quality educational programs and resources related to the science of climate change and its impacts" (http://www.nsf.gov/geo/ sees/index.jsp). The first seven grants were awarded, with increasing numbers since 2010.

Other federal actions include the ongoing work of agencies in providing educational materials related to aspects of sustainability and climate change and focused around their missions. Leading the way are the U.S. Environmental Protection Agency (EPA) (with its longstanding environmental education – not ESD - grants programs), the Department of Energy, the National Oceanic and Atmospheric Administration (NOAA), and the Department of Agriculture. Each of these agencies has developed tools, resources and in some cases have provided grant funds for the development of ESD-related curricula. Most recently, as of this writing, NOAA requested proposals for environmental literacy education, especially as it relates to climate change (http://www.oesd.noaa.gov/funding_opps.html).

State Level Actions and Opportunities

Only two states have incorporated sustainability standards into K-12 education: Vermont in 2000 and Washington state in 2009 (Church and Skelton, 2010; Feinstein, 2009). As of 2010, only Washington state had created a sustainability endorsement as an option for teacher certification (Feinstein, 2009). While not sustainability standards exactly, many states have been guided in developing their science standards by the National Science Education Standards (NRC, 1996). These standards are advisory only, not compulsory. In particular Standard F: Science in personal and social perspectives, addresses ESD. "An important purpose of science education is to give students a means to understand and act on personal and social issues" (NRC, 1996, p. 107) including issues such as "personal and community health, natural resources; environmental quality; and natural and human-induced hazards" (ibid., p. 108).

Critical Roles of NGOs in Promoting ESD

Given the decentralized organization of education in Canada and the US, one way to initiate ESD infusion is for non-governmental organizations (NGOs) to develop resources and professional development opportunities. In addition, they establish networks of practitioners, leaders, educators, experts, and other interested persons to work with officials at every level: local, state or provincial and territorial, and national.

UNESCO of course leads the way, with its global reach and ability to bring diverse international groups of leaders together. Within UNESCO are numerous resources including networks related to reorienting teacher education for ESD as well as a curriculum toolkit to start working on ESD. It has established Regional Centers of Expertise (RCE) on ESD. The Decade of Education for Sustainable Development (DESD), announced in 2002 and begun in 2005, has led to the formation (or in some cases refocusing) of other groups to push forward the DESD goals (http://www.unesco.org/en/esd/). Canada's Learning for a Sustainable Future, (www.lsf-lst.ca) established in 1991 as a nonprofit to integrate sustainability into Canada's education system, is leading the work today. It has partnered with Education for Sustainable Development Canada (http://www.esdcanada.ca/) to create provincial or territorial committees that work with the ministries of education, schools and other agencies to incorporate ESD into the curriculum. The provincial group in British Columbia has been named a UNESCO RCE.

The U.S. Partnership for Education for Sustainable Development, formed to address the UN DESD "acts as a convener, catalyst, and communicator working across all sectors of American society. Partners join by agreeing to the vision and mission." This organization has tremendous resources and networks including sections on higher education and K-12 and teacher education (http://www. uspartnership.org).

The US Partnership's members have made a significant contribution by developing the first National Sustainability Education Standards that lay out a roadmap through the K-12 curriculum for "education for sustainability" or "EfS" (U.S. Partnership, online). Many other organizations have listed ESD learning goals, but the Partnership's set of standards brings these together. These standards are a tool that can be critical to making headway in K-12 education and teacher education, if adopted.

In the US and Canada the American College and University Presidents Climate Commitment, signed by leaders from over 650 higher education institutions, has generated significant momentum and change in higher education affecting 5.6 million U.S. university students – more than one-third of undergraduates. Signatories commit to annually assess greenhouse gas emissions, implement at least two actions to reduce those gases, create a plan to reach climate neutrality, have all students experience sustainability as part of their education, and make these reports public (ACUPCC, online).

The Association for the Advancement of Sustainability in Higher Education (AASHE) (www.aashe.org), with 840 member institutions from around the world, supports sustainability efforts in higher education by including resources for curricular and all other aspects of greening the campus: from food supplies, to energy use, to design and retrofitting of facilities, to waste management. In addition, AASHE has recently released its Sustainability Tracking, Assessment and Rating System (STARS) for assessing campus sustainability efforts – a tool that may make comparisons and evaluations easier. In October 2010, the AASHE Curriculum Convocation on Sustainability Education took place in Denver CO, where they examined existing curriculum and strategies for infusing sustainability education into the higher education curriculum.

There are many other worthy organizations whose missions relate to sustainability education that are not discussed here, such as the Sierra Club, the Natural Resources Defense Council, the Audubon Society, and the World Wildlife Fund. Most of these offer curriculum materials, policy statements and political action opportunities. At this stage it is up to individual instructors to make use of these materials in their own classrooms, thus limiting the NGOs overall reach.

Patterns of ESD in Higher Education

Higher education addresses ESD in several patterns: offering academic programs with sustainability emphases, using ESD as a co-curricular theme, greening both campus and curriculum, creating new courses on sustainability topics, and injecting ESD units or modules into individual courses. U.S. teacher education programs lag in the introduction of ESD topics due to decentralized control over education, existence of few official standards for ESD, and optional national accreditation of teacher education programs. For programs meeting National Council for the Accreditation of Teacher Education guidelines, as does the teacher education program I teach in, science education programs must meet content standards about understanding roles of science in social perspectives, issues teaching, and leading students to decision making about issues. These accreditation standards are a strong source of incentive to include ESD in teacher education.

Academic Programs: Canada and the U.S. have a long history of having academic programs in environmental sciences or environmental studies. The first U.S. program was offered by Middlebury College in 1965. Today there are 585 bachelor's level programs (www.enviroeducation.com) and 869 graduate programs or certificates (www.gradschools.com) in environmental science/studies. There are likely more than the ones listed by these companies. Many of these programs lay important conceptual groundwork for expansion into full sustainability programs as they already look at one or more of the three areas of ESD: economics, environment and society. Environmental justice programs (e.g., at Clark University Atlanta and the University of Michigan) often integrate the three pillars of sustainability education.

Programs that specifically emphasize 'sustainability' (for example, in their title) are far fewer than the environmental science/studies programs noted above.

The ACUPCC has stimulated the development of programs specifically around sustainability through their commitments. Their handbook "Education for Climate Neutrality and Sustainability" (2009) articulates this vision:

Profound change cannot be merely intellectual, it must be rooted in a place that is personally relevant and connected with an ability to take action. The educational experience of graduates would reflect an intimate connection among (1) curriculum; (2) research; (3) understanding and reducing any negative ecological and social footprint of the institution; and (4) working to improve local, regional, and global communities so that they are healthier, more socially vibrant and stable, economically secure and environmentally sustainable (pp. 5–6).

The most extensive listing of academic efforts on sustainability in the U.S. and Canada is compiled by AASHE (in collaboration with ACUPCC) in its annual Digest. This list is not comprehensive, but is drawn from newsletters and features their membership. Only a few of the many Canadian programs were reported. The number of sustainability-focused formal academic degree programs, certificates or minors reported by AASHE increased from 3 in 2005 to 27 in 2007 to 66 in 2008 to 113 in 2009, with 32 of these for undergraduate students, 36 graduate and 45 for continuing education. One graduate program in sustainability education and one add-on certificate in sustainability in teacher education are listed. Most academic offerings are interdisciplinary with degree options in social or natural sciences or in sustainability and business. Many of the continuing education programs offer certificates and are for training workers in green industries (alternative energies, engineering, design, etc.). Dalhousie University in Nova Scotia has the first Canadian College of Sustainability and in 2007 Arizona State University established the first U.S. degree-granting School of Sustainability.

An example of a sustainability minor is the one developed at Emory University in its interdisciplinary Institute for the Liberal Arts. It requires 6 courses, including a core course that examines sustainability around a theme (such as Fossil Fuels and Sustainability, a chemistry course), a required capstone course, and a developmental portfolio. Students choose from among 30 ESD related courses, distributing them across social sciences, humanities and natural sciences, including ten courses with strong biology content (e.g., plants and society, ecology and global health).

Co-Curricular Themes

AASHE listed 9 institutions that used sustainability as a theme for an academic year. Often this took the form of a series of common readings for use in courses, such as a first year seminar, as well as campus and community activities.

Green Campus, Green Curriculum

This is the model that best fits the ACUPCC vision, where efforts to make a campus sustainable create a laboratory for learning, in which students study carbon footprints, LEED (Leadership in Energy & Environmental Design) building statistics, and the food system. In addition, sustainability concepts are infused across the curriculum. According to the AASHE Digest in 2009 some 30 events (conferences, workshops, webinars) were conducted at colleges and universities to help faculty integrate sustainability into their curricula. Often partnerships with community organizations are a feature of green campus, green curriculum institutions.

The Princeton Review, a company that ranks and rates colleges and universities as a service for prospective students, provided its first list of "Green Rating of Colleges" in 2010, with Arizona State University as number one. Its criteria include how the college handles its food, waste, transportation, parking and facilities, whether or not it makes is carbon footprint publicly available and has a plan for reducing greenhouse gas emissions, as well as how it organizes its sustainability committees and offices. Most critical to us as biology educators are the criteria related to the curriculum: whether or not colleges offer "an environmental studies major or minor" and if it has "an environmental literacy" requirement (Princeton Review, 2010, online). Nearly 200 US colleges and universities are ranked based on these criteria, and in a survey conducted by the Princeton Review, 60% of prospective students say they consider green issues in their choice of college.

Emory University in Georgia is a good example of an institution organized around the model of green campus, green curriculum. (Disclosure: I taught biology there in the early 1980s.) Emory decided early on to invest in LEED certified buildings, even though they are more costly to build. They then convened the Piedmont Project in 2001 to provide year-long training to cohorts of faculty as well as making available resources for creating sustainability curriculum across and within disciplines. (Northern Arizona University's Ponderosa Project provided the prototype for this kind of faculty development on sustainability education.) The minor in sustainability was described above. On a recent visit to Emory I toured a new LEED certified building, a retrofitted building and two community gardens on campus. New furnishings were purchased from companies that use sustainable materials and production. Banners about everyday actions people can take to improve sustainability are displayed throughout the campus. Sustainability is a clearly visible part of life at Emory.

Another good example of the green campus, green curriculum approach is Chico State University in California, where students engage with sustainability using their campus and community as a total learning environment. CSU decided in 2005 to infuse sustainability concepts across the curriculum while undertaking efforts to become a sustainable campus and an involved community member. By 2010, over 100 courses were "green" which means that "Green courses encourage students to be wise stewards of scarce resources and to understand that individual and collective actions have economic, social, and environmental consequences" (Manual CPCR, online). One example of infusing sustainability into an ecology course was the use of so-called "ECOncerns" already in the textbook as the basis for weekly class discussions within a general ecology course. Extra-curricular activities are common, with active student groups around sustainability.

Creating Entirely New Courses on Sustainability Topics

This strategy is not uncommon. Perhaps sustainable development deserves examination as a thing unto itself at the level of a foundations/theory course. However, as quoted early in this paper, sustainability is a cross-cutting concept. Experts in the field advise against isolating sustainability education into a course or two "on sustainability." They argue instead for sustainability as a thread woven throughout the curriculum. Examples of such tapestries were described above in the section on green campus, green curriculum.

ESD Units or Modules in Courses

This is probably the most common approach to ESD since it is one that individuals can do without involving the entire campus. In my own course "Analysis of Biological Issues" senior biology majors critically examine case studies about social issues with a biological component (such as climate change, pandemic flu). I used a University of Michigan eco-justice case study of factory hog farming in poverty stricken North Carolina (Statter, 1996) as a way to help biology majors begin to connect the science to larger issues involving the environment, social justice and sustainable business practices. For this two week unit, my students enthusiastically researched this problem, looking not only at the biology (especially of waste disposal and spillages) but also at the legal, economic and ethical aspects of commercial hog farming and its impacts. Using similar methods for a case I co-wrote on pandemic planning, students outlined issues in planning for pandemic flu from multiple perspectives, again placing the biology into a larger social, economic, and ethical context.

At Spelman College the first semester course of biology has students examine the connections between the science they are learning and how it applies in the real world (Spelman College, 2007). The course, Biological Communities, Evolution and Biodiversity, has a syllabus that looks like a "regular" biology course. To introduce ESD, the faculty has included a series of case studies to show students how the concepts they are learning are used outside the classroom. For example, the first five week unit is ecology. While students learn about biomes, ecosystems and populations, they are working on a series of cases about mercury pollution in fisheries, in biomes (Amazon rain forest, Everglades and ocean), and as it affects human health. For the evolution unit, the case is about sickle cell disease, malaria and the evolution of malarial parasites. Weekly case activities are planned, with in class or homework assignments completed by individuals or groups. Fifteen percent of the course grade is based on the case study assignments.

Some Pedagogies Useful for ESD in Biology

Changes in pedagogy and some aspects of course and curriculum structure are needed to facilitate integration of ESD into biology education. Common approaches are those that engage students in studying a complex problem of local importance from multiple perspectives and may include active civic engagement (actions within the community or beyond). Two different approaches, SENCER and Case Study/Problem Based Learning (PBL), illustrate well the possibilities.

The Science Education for New Civic Engagements (SENCER) program (http://www.sencer.net/) established in 2001 and funded by the U.S. National Science Foundation helps scientists see how to connect social and economic development issues to science courses. "SENCER improves science education by focusing on real world problems and, by so doing, extends the impact of this learning across the curriculum to the broader community and society." Their basic educational approach is to use complex, often unsolved problems of interest to their students as the starting point. From there they explore the issues and use them to lead into the underlying science and mathematics. Civic action is frequently a component. SENCER dissemination strategies include regional and national faculty development opportunities, including a SENCER Fellows program. They also provide resources such as a collection of model courses and background papers, assessment tools, and a monthly newsletter.

SENCER model courses (approximately 25) are offered as examples of stand alone courses as well as of learning communities (several courses taken together). They are a way for faculty to get ideas for restructuring their own courses and to explore the SENCER model. Topics especially relevant to the life sciences include such model courses as Slow Food, HIV-AIDS, Pregnancy Outcomes in African women, Science of Sleep, The Urbanized Shoreline, Addiction Biology, Sustainability and Health (Stearns and Worthy, 2004) among others. Descriptions of how the courses are implemented and the course syllabi are available online.

SENCER backgrounder essays are resources that address scientific as well as teaching topics. The Biodiversity backgrounder (Sterling et al., 2003), for example, outlines how biodiversity science concepts fit with human needs. Ecological services and their disruption are an example of this kind of fit, as well as the need for diverse genetic pools for resistance to diseases, food and pharmaceutical sources. This resource contains a wealth of ideas for considering how to link social and economic development issues with the biology.

A second pedagogical approach is the family of strategies centered on case studies and Problem Based Learning (PBL). Several examples of their use have been described above, at Chico State, in my course, and at Spelman College. In the last 20 years these methods have been adapted for undergraduate science education from their early use in business and medical schools. Notable projects include BioQUEST's Investigative Case Based Learning resources (http://bioquest. org/icbl); the National Center for Case Study Teaching in Science (http://sciencecases.lib.buffalo.edu/cs/), the University of Delaware PBL project (http://www.udel.edu/pbl/), Cases Online for K-20 education http://www.cse. emory.edu/cases/; and the multimedia CaseIT! project focusing on molecular biology cases http://caseit.uwrf.edu/. In 2012, with funding from the National Science Foundation, these projects are collaborating on the ScienceCaseNetwork (http://sciencecasenet.org) as an organizer and entry point for faculty and researchers interested in using cases and PBL to teach biology.

Case study and PBL approaches begin with a story or case of some kind – real or realistic – to anchor learning in a complex context that is meaningful to the learners. Because the problems are based in real concerns, they are messy, ill structured and open to multiple solutions. They are of necessity multidisciplinary and that is what makes them ideal for the integrative nature of ESD. Once the case has been read, students work in collaborative groups to analyze the case, identifying what they know and what they need to find out more about. They then consult resources to learn more and to refine their questions. In the ICBL project that I lead with cofounder Dr. Ethel Stanley of the BioQUEST Curriculum Consortium, students then investigate their questions using laboratory, field or computational techniques (simulations, models, bioinformatics) (Waterman and Stanley, 2005, 2008). Literally hundreds of biology-related cases and PBL modules have been developed and are freely available for adaptation from the websites listed above. Topics include, for example, global health issues, water quality, ecojustice issues, food security and sustainability, genetic engineering, and invasive species. The stories in the cases are frequently taken from people going about their everyday lives.

Without the lever of nationalized education systems to create change, actions leading to the spread of ESD in the U.S. and Canada have come about by other means, resulting in an increasing number of programs, courses and modules for teaching and learning about sustainable development. Opportunities to continue and extend this work abound.

REFERENCES

American College and University Presidents Climate Commitment. Website. http://www.presidentsclimatecommitment.org/

American College and University Presidents Climate Change Commitment. Education for Climate Neutrality and Sustainability (2009). http://www2.presidentsclimatecommitment.org/html/documents/EducationforClimateNeutralitySustainability_2009.05.07_finalWEB.pdf

Anonymous. Criteria for the Princeton Review Green Rating of Colleges. 2010. http://www.princetonreview.com/uploadedFiles/Editorial_Content/Green_Material/TPR_286_Green_1.pdf

Chico State University Curriculum Manual (no date). http://www.csuchico.edu/vpaa/manual/CPCR_Instructions.shtml

Council of Ministers of Education, Canada. The education systems of Canada – Facing the Challenges of the Twenty-First Century. UNESCO. 2008 http://www.ibe.unesco.org/National_Reports/ICE_2008/canada_NR08_en.pdf

Duncan, Arne. US. Secretary of Education Letter to the Attendees of the UNESCO World Conference on Education for Sustainable Development. March 2009. https://ed.gov/about/inits/ed/internationaled/unesco-letter.pdf

Emory University. The sustainability minor. 2010 Atlanta, GA. http://www.ila.emory.edu/ila-undergraduate/sub-undergraduate-sus.shtml

Higher Education Opportunity Act of 2008, including the Higher Education Sustainability Act. Public Law 110–315. http://frwebgate.access.gpo.gov/cgi-bin/getdoc.cgi?dbname=110_cong_public_laws&docid=f:publ315.110

Presidents Council for Sustainable Development. Education for Sustainability: An Agenda for Action. 1996. http://ffof.org/pcsd/

Spelman College. Syllabus for Biology 110. Biology Department , Atlanta, GA http://www.colleges.org/enviro/alliances/cfd/syllabi/BioSyllabus2007.doc

Statter, H. Hog Farming in North Carolina: An Ecojustice Case. 1996. (http://www.umich.edu/~snre492/statter.html

Stearns, D. & K. Worthy, Sustainability and Human Health: A Learning Community. 2004 http://serc.carleton.edu/sencer/sustainability_health/index.html

Sterling, E. J., N. Bynum, M. Laverty, I. Harrison, S. Spector & E. Johnson. Why Should You Care About Biological Diversity? A SENCER Backgrounder July, 2003. http://serc.carleton.edu/files/sencer/backgrounders/why_should_you_care.pdf

U.S. Partnership for Education for Sustainable Development. National Sustainability Education Standards version 3. 2009 http://usp.umfglobal.org/resources/0000/ 0081/USP_EFS_standards_V3_10_09.pdf

Waterman, M. & E. Stanley. Investigative Case Based Learning: Teaching Scientifically While Connecting Science to Society. In Invention and Impact: Building Excellence in Undergraduate STEM Education Washington, D.C.: AAAS. 2005.

Waterman, M. & E. Stanley. Biological Inquiry: A Workbook of Investigative Cases. 2nd edition. San Francisco: Benjamin Cummings, 2008.

Margaret Waterman
Biology Department, Southeast Missouri State University
Cape Girardeau, Missouri 63701 USA
mwaterman@semo.edu

CHUN-YEN CHANG AND TING-KUANG YEH

4. FROM GENE TO EDUCATION – THE ECNG RESEARCH FRAMEWORK: EDUCATION, COGNITION, NEUROSCIENCE, AND GENE

ABSTRACT

Over the past decade, genetic and neuroscience research have provided exciting breakthroughs for cognitive and educational science. While exploring the mechanism of human behavior, the integration of multiple disciplines (Education, Cognitive psychology, Neuroscience, and Genetic or molecular biology studies) can now serve researchers in furthering their own research and at the same time derive meaningful implications and/or practices for learning and instruction. In this paper, we will first propose an interdisciplinary research framework, then briefly review related literature, and finally present our preliminary work in exploring the associations between genotypes and student cognitive abilities/science achievement. Our ultimate goal is to integrate different research fields with aims of not only exploring the mechanism of learning and behavior, but more importantly, providing instructional approaches (施教) and learning strategies to best fit with students' aptitudes or characteristics (因材) based on the interactional effects of ECNG (Education, Cognition, Neuron, and Gene).

KEYWORDS

Education, Cognition, Neuroscience, Gene

THE PROPOSED ECNG RESEARCH FRAMEWORK

The processes that underlie mental operations have perplexed pedagogues, philosophers, and scientific researchers for centuries. In addition, classical philosophers have debated issues such as the source of knowledge, the mechanisms of cognitive ability, and the nature of knowledge/ethics. Over the past few decades, breakthroughs within neuroscience and molecular biology have emerged, and the application of novel experimental methods and emerging technologies have provided some exciting new insights into the mechanisms of human behavior. Research that is relevant to behavioral mechanisms can now be performed on the following levels: the basic study of genes, analysis of the physiology of individual neurons and their interaction within the nervous system, evaluation of cognitive

Mijung Kim and C. H. Diong (Eds.), Biology Education for Social and Sustainable Development, 41–50.

abilities, and the investigation of the processes of higher-order learning in education. Contemporary behavioral science involves the integration of different research fields and the use of systematic studies to explore behavioral mechanisms (Ansari & Coch, 2006; Goswami, 2006; Kovas & Plomin, 2006; Plomin & Spinath, 2002).

In spite of these new developments, there has not been a significant increase in the frequency with which neuroscience or molecular biology is cited in important journals of education and psychology (Robins, Gosling, & Craik, 1998). This suggests that, at present, our knowledge of the components and genetics of the nervous system is insufficient to allow that knowledge to be applied in the fields of psychology and education (Bruder et al., 2005; Goswami, 2006). This might be due to the fact that most neuroscience/molecular biology research focuses on processes within single cells, whereas research into education and cognition focuses more on practical applications. In general, the study of a single neuronal cell does not provide complete information about behavioral development and, as a result, researchers in education hold a more conservative view to the application of neuroscience and molecular biology in educational practice and educational policy-making. However, we consider that a careful integration of molecular biology and neuroscience with other fields, such as cognition and education, might enable researchers from each area to work together to establish associations between brain activity and learning outcomes. In this paper, an interdisciplinary research framework, as illustrated in Figure 1, is proposed and our preliminary attempts in exploring the associations between genotypes and student science achievement and cognitive abilities are therefore presented based on this research framework.

The ECNG research framework as shown in Figure 1 consists of a four-level hierarchical structure and a complex network that covers multiple disciplines. We suggest that the integration of four different areas of research (educational, cognitive, neuroscience, and genetic studies) to form the Education, Cognition, Neuron, Gene (ECNG) research framework which will in turn provide a powerful approach for the exploration of behavioral mechanisms and its application to educational practices.

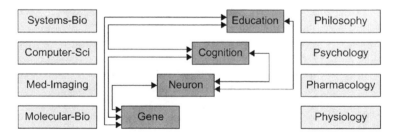

Figure 1. The ECNG Research Framework.

With respect to the integration of the ECNG research framework, two closely-related perspectives need to be considered: (1) the reductionist perspective, which focuses on explaining complex phenomena by investigating individual components in detail; and (2) the systematic thinking and synthesis perspective, which attempts to develop algorithms or machine learning tools to integrate large amounts of data (Palla, Derenyi, Farkas, & Vicsek, 2005; Saul & Filkov, 2007). From the reductionist perspective, it is vital to investigate correlations between variables in two different fields of the ECNG framework, as well as to explore the exact mechanisms that are responsible for these correlations. For example, when an association between a specific gene and neurological function is established, researchers may try to investigate how the gene controls neurological function, either directly or indirectly. The systematic thinking and synthesis approach, on the other hand, is more oriented toward processing large amounts of data that are generated by the interactions between researchers within the ECNG system.

A complex dynamic network exists between any two subsystems within the ECNG research framework. Unfortunately, these complex networks are not yet understood fully due to the current limitations of knowledge and technological development. For example, it is difficult to characterize all types of phenotype, such as protein structure, morphology, the structure of the nervous system or complex behavior. It is a priority for researchers in the different fields of the ECNG research framework to be able to characterize these phenotypes reliably, establish relationships between the variables, and investigate the mechanisms that underlie these associations and to explore the structural and functional properties of these networks.

A COMT STUDY PUBLISHED IN BRAIN AND COGNITION EXPLORING THE E AND G ASSOCIATIONS

In our previous work, we attempted to integrate the fields of education, neurophysiology, and molecular biology. We investigated the association between the academic achievement of students and polymorphism in the catechol-O-methyltransferase (COMT) gene. COMT is a methylation enzyme that catalyses the first step in the pathway by which dopamine is degraded and inactivated. It is widely accepted that COMT is involved in the modulation of dopaminergic physiology and the prefrontal cortex (PFC) function. Dopamine is postulated to be the key neurotransmitter that regulates the function of the PFC, which is involved predominantly in cognitive skills that are crucial to human language and thought, including motor planning, working memory, cognitive flexibility, abstract reasoning, temporal sequencing analysis, and generativity (Blair, Gamson, Thorne, & Baker, 2005; Egan & Weinberger, 1997; Karakuyu, Herold, Gunturkun, & Diekamp, 2007; Previc, 1999).

The COMT Val158Met polymorphism is associated with variation in COMT activity. The COMT 158Met allele may be advantageous for PFC-related cognitive abilities; however, it is associated also with increased anxiety, depression, and emotional vulnerability in response to stress or educational adversity. We found that students who were homozygous with the Met allele tended to perform relatively poorly in all components of the Taiwanese Basic Competency Test (BCT), a national standardized test that measures educational achievement, compared to students who were homozygous or heterozygous with the Val allele. In particular, the students who were homozygous with the Met allele had significantly lower performance results than the latter, notably in science and social science sub-tests (Chang *et al*, 2009). These findings provide evidence that, especially in the case of Met allele, *affective factors might overwhelm cognitive abilities* in high-stake testing environment. It is also reasonable to infer that the correlation between the COMT 158Met allele and higher academic stress/lower academic performance may be a fundamental characteristic of the adolescent population in many countries, especially within Asian countries, where national exams can make or break a student's future. We invite researchers from countries with similar high-stake testing learning environments to join us in validating the effects of the COMT 158 genetic polymorphism on learning and cognition.

Knowledge of the genotype of students could give strategic educationists an understanding of the innate cognitive abilities and emotional vulnerability of an individual student. They could then give priority to subjects that match the strongest cognitive ability of the student, and monitor the emotions of the student in relation to learning. In addition, parents of COMT 158Met allele students might need to lessen their children's emotional strain during the preparation period (approximately 3 years) before taking the high-stake test. In this way, the student's interest in learning and achievement might be increased. This study integrated the education and genetics fields. However, given that the emotional effects of the BCT and cognitive abilities at the experimental or meta-level were not measured, a connection could not be firmly established between genotype and educational performance. To extend the study, it would be interesting to test the hypothesis rigorously by recording and analyzing more complete information at the cognitive and neural levels, such as the cognitive abilities and the behaviors of the students, together with environmental information.

A RECENT BDNF PAPER UNDER REVISION TACKLING C AND G ISSUES

In a recent study, we analyzed the genotype of undergraduate students with respect to polymorphisms in the genes for COMT and brain-derived neurotrophic factor (BDNF). We have described previously the potential role of COMT in PFC (prefrontal cortex) function and human intelligence. BDNF is an important neurotrophin that is expressed throughout the brain, particularly in the PFC and hippocampus (Pezawas et al., 2004). Its impact on neurogenesis (Rossi et al., 2006), long-term memory consolidation (Alonso *et al*., 2002), neural survival (Husson et al., 2005), and neural differentiation (Lu, Pang, & Woo, 2005) has been studied extensively. BDNF has a crucial role in human memory formation: it has a pre-synaptic effect on the facilitation of vesicle docking, and postsynaptic effects on ion channels, N-methyl-D-asparte receptors, and Trk-B receptors (Kovalchuk *et al*., 2002; Tyler *et al*.,, 2002). In humans, BDNF activity is affected by a genetic polymorphism at nucleotide 196. The G to A transition results in the substitution of a methionine for a valine residue at position 66 (Val66Met); this affects the intracellular trafficking and activity-dependent secretion of

BDNF, and may influence human hippocampal function and memory (Egan et al., 2003). The analysis of these genotypes could result in findings that are relevant for researchers within the ECNG research framework in terms of enhancing students' cognitive abilities and improving understanding of the mechanisms of learning behavior.

One hundred and two Taiwanese undergraduate volunteers were recruited for this study. The memory and intelligence of the participants were evaluated using the Chinese versions of the Wechsler Memory Scale III and Wechsler Adult Intelligence Scale III. The participants were genotyped for two polymorphisms that have been implicated in memory and intelligence: the catechol-O-methyltransferase (COMT) Val158Met and brain-derived neurotrophic factor (BDNF) Val66Met polymorphisms. The results of this study revealed that 1) no significant differences in IQ and memory were detected among the different COMT158 genotypes and 2) an inverse relationship between auditory and visual memory among the three BDNF genotypes: auditory memory was superior in Val/Val individuals, whereas visual memory was superior in Met/Met individuals.

A post-hoc Scheffe analysis revealed that the BDNF 66Val/Val group outperformed the other two groups significantly in the auditory delayed memory test ($p < 0.01$). With respect to visual immediate memory, the performance of the BDNF 66Val/Val group was impaired compared with that of the Met/Met group ($p < 0.05$). Therefore, the BDNF 66Val/Val genotype seems to have an important and positive influence on auditory memory, as illustrated in Figure 2A. In contrast, this genotype appeared to have a negative influence on visual memory (Figure 2B).

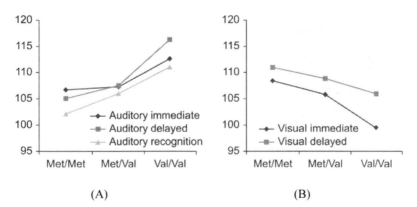

(A)   (B)

Figure 2. Trends in WMS-III scores among the BDNF genotypes. (2-A) Subjects homozygous with BDNF Val66 performed better with respect to auditory memory, including auditory immediate, delayed, and recognition memory, than the other two genotype groups, 2-B Subjects homozygous with BDNF Val66 performed worse, with respect to visual immediate and visual delayed memory, than the other two genotype groups.

DISCUSSION

Our previous study of 779 Chinese 10th grade students indicates that those who are homozygous with COMT-Met allele seemed to have impaired fluid intelligence and are less effective at processing emotionally arousing stimuli and stress than students who carry the Val allele. These factors result in impaired performance during academic testing (Chang et al., 2009). The advantageous cognitive abilities of the Met-158 genotypes may be compromised due to increased stress during the tests. However, in the present BDNF study, no significant differences in IQ were found among the three COMT genotypes. This result was expected because the subjects were streamed into the same university department on the basis of their results in the General Scholastic Ability Test (GSAT) and IQ is correlated positively with academic achievement and performance in almost all general cognitive ability tests (Strauss *et al.*, 2004).

In evaluating the association between the BDNF Val66Met polymorphism and memory, we found that the auditory delayed memory of Val/Val homozygotes was significantly superior to that of the members of the other two genotype groups. This result was consistent with the results of a previous study by Egan *et al.* (2003) of 133 healthy participants. Dempster *et al.* (2005) also have reported that the Met66 allele was associated with a lower score on the WMS (Wechsler Memory Scale) delayed measure in 114 healthy individuals; this association was not observed in their relatives who were affected with schizophrenia. Our study provides direct and strong support for a crucial role of the BDNF polymorphism in human delayed auditory memory, which is highly dependent on hippocampal function.

The role of the BDNF polymorphism in auditory function has been researched before; however, to the best of our knowledge, the association between BDNF polymorphism and visual memory has not been studied previously in a healthy population. In the BDNF study, we found that visual performance was impaired significantly in subjects who were homozygous for the Val allele, compared with that of the other two groups, however, auditory and visual memory were related inversely among the three genotypes (Figure 2B). The mechanism responsible for this inverse relationship is unclear, but it could be caused by differential effects of the BDNF polymorphism on the auditory and visual memory systems.

The aforementioned results might be considered within the ECNG research framework from two perspectives: (1) a molecular and neurophysiological approach could be employed to investigate the underlying mechanism; and (2) the results could be applied to educational practice, for example to influence instructional design. Neuroscientists and molecular biologists might be especially interested in how the BDNF polymorphism has differential effects on the auditory and visual memory systems. Educational/cognitive researchers might be interested in the implications of these effects. Impaired cognitive abilities that affect academic performance (e.g., poor visual spatial ability) can affect the willingness of students to learn. Therefore, Levine (2002) has asserted that educationists should first understand the innate cognitive abilities of individual students, and then give priority to development in subjects that match the strongest cognitive abilities of the student (e.g., auditory ability). This approach should increase the interest of the student in learning and their academic achievement. On the other hand, teachers should also consider compensating students' weaker abilities by increasing interest within them by applying different learning materials. Taken together, the results of this preliminary study within the ECNG research framework suggest that the BDNF Val66Met polymorphism has a crucial role in memory. Our findings suggest new directions for researchers in cognitive psychology and neuroscience with respect to exploring behavioral mechanisms on a cognitive/neural/molecular level. It might also be possible to apply these results within educational practice. However, such applications should be considered carefully because the neural/molecular mechanisms of learning behavior are complex and require further study.

IS IT A BRIDGE TOO FAR NOW?

It is cautioned that the aforementioned studies do have a number of limitations. First, the results, at worst, could be a statistical fluke because our sample was not big enough; this is quite common among these kinds of studies because the genetic effects on cognition are usually tiny, especially in a healthy population. Therefore, a larger sample size is required in order to substantiate the findings. As mentioned previously, researchers in cognition and education acknowledge the high degree of complexity that underlies cognitive behavior. It is reasonable to infer that the academic achievement/cognitive abilities of students might be affected by the interaction of multiple factors, such as multiple genes, various environmental factors, and epigenetic regulation. Further analysis with other possible candidate genes would greatly help researchers to discriminate the genotypic effects. In addition, we acknowledge that future studies in different groups, such as in students or patients of different ethnic origins, are especially important to validate further the interactional effects of ECNG on student learning.

FUTURE WORK AND SOME FINAL THOUGHTS

Several thousand years ago, Confucius said that we should 'teach students in accordance with their aptitude or characteristics' 「因材施教」; now a new era has emerged to really identify the learner's aptitude '材', not only by using behavior/cognitive instruments, students' self-report measures, classroom observation data (including testing and other methods), but also by leveraging on students biological markers (genes) and most importantly the interactive effects of biological markers and students' learning environment. If we can identify children's strengths and weaknesses in learning and tailor teaching to their aptitude '材', chances are we could help them overcome their weaknesses in intelligence and give rise to their full talents. It is not uncommon for children to encounter learning problems, which can be attributed to inherency, negative attitude toward learning, low motivation, passivity, uncooperativeness, or failure to adapt to the learning environment. Parents and teachers should not place too much an emphasis on academic performance or continue to force children to study hard; instead, they ought to recognize that there are individual differences that are shaped by both nature and nurturing; more importantly, they must understand the interactional effects of these differences, and that identifying learning difficulties is key to facilitate learning. Whether children enter a prominent high school or whether children are gifted, should be deemed as secondary to the act of learning itself. What truly matters is the fact that each child is granted the chance to develop his or her own aptitude. Instead of obsessing about giving children a head start, parents should also encourage students to do extensive reading, and expose them to a diverse learning environment, so that they may engage in active learning based on their interests in order to unleash their natural potential. Our research group is now taking an interdisciplinary adventure with other colleagues in Taiwan to explore the ECNG framework in more detail by using next-generation sequencing, fMRI, cognitive and educational methods.

ACKNOWLEDGEMENTS

The work in this study was supported by the National Science Council of Taiwan under contracts NSC 96-2511-S-003-022-MY2 and NSC 98-2511-S-003-050-MY3. The authors also wish to thank the Aim for the Top University (ATU) project of the National Taiwan Normal University (NTNU) for extending this study.

REFERENCES

Alonso, M., Vianna, M. R. M., Depino, A. M., Souza, T. M. E., Pereira, P., Szapiro, G., et al. (2002). BDNF-triggered events in the rat hippocampus are required for both short- and long-term memory formation. *Hippocampus, 12*(4), 551–560.

Ansari, D., & Coch, D. (2006). Bridges over troubled waters: Education and cognitive neuroscience. *Trends in Cognitive Sciences, 10*(4), 146–151.

Blair, C., Gamson, D., Thorne, S. & Baker, D. (2005). Rising mean IQ: Cognitive demand of mathematics education for young children, population exposure to formal schooling, and the neurobiology of the prefrontal cortex. *Intelligence, 33*(1), 93–106.

Bruder, G. E., Keilp, J. G., Xu, H. Y., Shikhman, M., Schori, E., Gorman, J. M., et al. (2005). Catechol-O-methyltransferase (COMT) genotypes and working memory: Associations with differing cognitive operations. *Biological Psychiatry, 58*(11), 901–907.

Yeh, T. K., Chang, C. Y.*, Hu, C. Y., Yeh, T. G. & Lin, M. Y. (2009). Association of catechol-O-methyltransferase (COMT) polymorphism and academic achievement in a Chinese cohort. *Brain and cognition, 71*(3), 300–305.

Dempster, E., Toulopoulou, T., McDonald, C., Bramon, E., Walshe, M., Filbey, F., et al. (2005). Association between BDNF Val(66)Met genotype and episodic memory. *American Journal of Medical Genetics Part B-Neuropsychiatric Genetics, 134B*(1), 73–75.

Egan, M. F., Kojima, M., Callicott, J. H., Goldberg, T. E., Kolachana, B. S., Bertolino, A. (2003). The BDNF val66met polymorphism affects activity-dependent secretion of BDNF and human memory and hippocampal function. *Cell, 112*(2), 257–269.

Egan, M. F. & Weinberger, D. R. (1997). Neurobiology of schizophrenia. *Current Opinion in Neurobiology, 7*(5), 701–707.

Goswami, U. (2006). Neuroscience and education: from research to practice? *Nature Reviews Neuroscience, 7*(5), 406–411.

Husson, I., Rangon, C. M., Lelievre, V., Bemelmans, A. P., Sachs, P., Mallet, J., et al. (2005). BDNF-induced white matter neuroprotection and stage-dependent neuronal survival following a neonatal excitotoxic challenge. *Cerebral Cortex, 15*(3), 250–261.

Karakuyu, D., Herold, C., Gunturkun, O. & Diekamp, B. (2007). Differential increase of extracellular dopamine and serotonin in the 'prefrontal cortex' and striatum of pigeons during working memory. *European Journal of Neuroscience, 26*(8), 2293–2302.

Kovalchuk, Y., Hanse, E., Kafitz, K. W. & Konnerth, A. (2002). Postsynaptic induction of BDNF-mediated long-term potentiation. *Science, 295*(5560), 1729–1734.

Kovas, Y., & Plomin, R. (2006). Generalist genes: implications for the cognitive sciences. *Trends in Cognitive Sciences, 10*(5), 198–203.

Levine, M. D. (2002). *A Mind at a Time* New York: Simon & Schuster.

Lu, B., Pang, P. T. & Woo, N. H. (2005). The yin and yang of neurotrophin action. *Nature Reviews Neuroscience, 6*(8), 603–614.

Palla, G., Derenyi, I., Farkas, I. & Vicsek, T. (2005). Uncovering the overlapping community structure of complex networks in nature and society. *Nature, 435*(7043), 814–818.

Pezawas, L., Verchinski, B. A., Mattay, V. S., Callicott, J. H., Kolachana, B. S., Straub, R. E., et al. (2004). The brain-derived neurotrophic factor val66met polymorphism and variation in human cortical morphology. *Journal of Neuroscience, 24*(45), 10099–10102.

Plomin, R. & Spinath, F. M. (2002). Genetics and general cognitive ability (g). *Trends in Cognitive Sciences, 6*(4), 169–176.

Previc, F. H. (1999). Dopamine and the origins of human intelligence. *Brain and Cognition, 41*(3), 299–350.

Robins, R. W., Gosling, S. D. & Craik, K. H. (1998). Psychological science at the crossroads. *American Scientist, 86*(4), 310–313.

Rossi, C., Angelucci, A., Costantin, L., Braschi, C., Mazzantini, M., Babbini, F., et al. (2006). Brain-derived neurotrophic factor (BDNF) is required for the enhancement of hippocampal neurogenesis following environmental enrichment. *European Journal of Neuroscience, 24*(7), 1850–1856.

Saul, Z. M. & Filkov, V. (2007). Exploring biological network structure using exponential random graph models. *Bioinformatics, 23*(19), 2604–2611.

Strauss, J., Barr, C. L., George, C. J., Ryan, C. M., King, N., Shaikh, S., et al. (2004). BDNF and COMT polymorphisms – Relation to memory phenotypes in young adults with childhood-onset mood disorder. *Neuromolecular Medicine, 5*(3), 181–192.

Tyler, W. J., Alonso, M., Bramham, C. R. & Pozzo-Miller, L. D. (2002). From acquisition to consolidation: On the role of brain-derived neurotrophic factor signaling in hippocampal-dependent learning. *Learning & Memory, 9*(5), 224–237.

*Corresponding author and project leader

*Chun-Yen Chang
Graduate Institute of Science Education, Science Education Center
Department of Earth Sciences
National Taiwan Normal University
changcy@ntnu.edu.tw, http://w1.ceels.org/chunyen/index_eng.html

Ting-Kuang Yeh
Science Education Center
National Taiwan Normal University

ENSHAN LIU

5. BIOLOGY EDUCATION IN CHINA 2000–2010: CURRICULAR TRENDS AND TEACHER PREPARATION MODELS FOR A CHANGING SOCIETY

ABSTRACT

The shift from a centralized planned economy to a market economy has brought drastic changes in mainland China at the end of the 20th century. It was apparent school education has to change to meet the challenges of the changing society. Education reforms that were started in year 2000 aim to prepare a new generation of school children for a new century. As part of the school curricula, reforms in biology teaching transitioned from a content-oriented to inquiry-based learning environment. There were three phases in the reforms in the past ten years: the identification and development of the new national school biology curricula and teaching materials (for both middle school and senior high school), trial implementation of the new curricula, and implementation to all schools. Teaching strategies and styles have been a main theme in the reform process. The reforms also include helping teachers to change their beliefs. China's education system face challenges in providing an effective teacher professional development, modeling a positive educational environment, evaluating students' learning outcomes and determining what constitutes good teaching practice for teachers.

KEY WORDS

School Biology, Teacher Professional Development, Bio-Literacy

1. BIO-EDUCATION ENVIRONMENT

Education is undergoing an unprecedented reform in mainland China. The changes aim to reform the educational strategies that have expediently managed a large population to one that maximizes human capital and build a creative thinking economy. Biology education is one of the most active areas in this national education reform, starting in 2000. This paper focuses on curricular trends and teacher preparation related to the changes in biology education.

Mijung Kim and C. H. Diong (Eds.), Biology Education for Social and Sustainable Development, 51–60.

1.1. The Rapid Changes Call for Education Reform

Rapid economic developments in China have brought great changes to people's lives. The developments of science and technology have created new job opportunities for youths. Jobs related to science and technology make up a high percentage of newly added positions and the society needs high-quality people of scientific literacy to fill these vacancies. Hence, China needs to rely heavily on educating its people to meet the needs of the society. In addition, the fast progress in economy has resulted in distinct improvements in living standards, larger wealth accumulation and changes in societal relationships, cultural perspectives, industrialization, urbanization and internationalization in the society. At the same time, problems related to a growing population, resources and environmental depletion are increasing. These factors place mainland China at a critical junction between opportunities for economic growth and challenges associated with it. Education is thus a level playing field, important in educating a new generation of well-educated citizens and labour force. Education as a priority is hence recognized as a national strategy.[1]

However, with the traditional content-centered curriculum and outdated educational beliefs where many students still follow learning by rote, China is still not ready for the new challenges. In such a school system, there is a great gap between what the students learned and what the epoch needs; schools fail to prepare the citizens to meet the needs of the society. Thus, the need for reforms in education is obvious.

1.2. The Reformed Education System

In 2000, China implemented a reformed education system to keep up with the economy and evolution of society. This reformed system required two steps: one, modify the original curricular programs and syllabuses in 2000, and two, develop and release new curricular programs and standards in 2001. The five missions of the education reform are as follows:

I.   Curriculum must be student-centered to enable students to acquire knowledge and skills as well as inculcate positive attitudes and improve students' ability to study, cooperate and behave well.
II.   Curriculum must be balanced, and integrated to involve different subjects and practical and project-based learning for a vocational education from grade 1 to 12. Elective courses should be available to cater to the different needs of students depending on school facilities.
III. Course contents, especially in science subjects, must be updated.
IV.   Active learning and problem solving are the focus of students' learning and a departure from passive learning, memory-based learning.
V.   Assessment of students' learning should be towards the alignment between student assessment and the goal of education.[2]

Since 1949, mainland China has adopted a centralized education system. This centralized education system is characterized by a national curriculum for K-12 schools. The new curriculum moves away from the over-concentrated curriculum administration and aims to implement the three-level curriculum administration – nation, local, and school, to adapt the curriculum accordingly to local areas, schools and students. The system shifts from centralization to decentralization where the establishment of the three-level administration system is helpful in being adaptive to the features of the local economy and culture and thereby, meets the demand of students' learning style and personality development.[2]

In mainland China, 12 years of general education from grades 1 to 6 are considered elementary; junior secondary (or middle) starts at grade 7 and ends at grade9 while senior high starts at grade 10 and ends at grade 12. At the elementary level, biology content is embedded in science subjects. In grades 7, 8, 10 and 11, biology is taught as a subject in a majority of schools in the mainland.[3,4] Biology education refers to both junior secondary and high school biology. Most biology teachers teach only one subject. Biology teachers are located in departments of biology at universities.

2. BIOLOGY CURRICULAR TRENDS, 2000–2010

2.1. The Steps in Biology Education Reform

Formulation of curriculum standard Biology syllabuses have been used to guide classroom teaching since the 1950's. In this curriculum reform, the Ministry of Education (MOE) organized a group of biologists and educators to formulate curriculum standards for the biology subject by finding out the status of biology curriculum in local schools and schools in other countries. In 2001, MOE issued the revised biology curriculum standards for grades 7 to 9 and grades 10 to 12 in 2003. In the newly released biology curriculum standards, some new curriculum beliefs were in place to steer Biology teaching in a new direction. The reformed curriculum standards for compulsory education were revised to accommodate the demands of citizen education. They enabled the majority of students to accomplish and reflect on the country's basic requirements for developing the literacy of citizens and aim to cultivate a desire for lifelong learning in students. Curriculum standard for high schools provides some room for levels and choices with the precondition that students meet the basic demands generally. It also establishes alternative modules to give students more subject choices and room for personal development, thus laying a foundation to cultivate lifelong learning abilities for living and responsible work and practice. All these elements are embedded in both junior secondary and high school biology curricula, making them quite different from the traditional biology syllabuses. In 2001, junior secondary biology curriculum standard was adopted by 1% of students in 38 districts/counties across the country in the initial trial phase. By 2005, all grade 7 schools started to use standard-based textbooks.

Meanwhile, reforms in high school biology curriculum have also advanced rapidly. Research work on new biology curriculum in high school was started and by 2003, MOE issued biology curriculum standards for all high schools in succession. At the end of 2004, four provinces across the country had begun trials of the new curriculum. In 2005, the coverage expanded to tens provinces. At the end of 2010, the new biology curriculum was implemented in all the high schools.

Diversity of Teaching Materials

From early 1950's to 2000, only one version of biology textbook was used in high schools in the mainland and in junior secondary schools as well. In sync with the reformed system, MOE encouraged related institutes and publishing houses to develop teaching materials according to the national curriculum standards and implemented the policy of diversity of teaching materials. It also called for more biology educators to participate in the writing of teaching materials. Many colleges, research institutes, research staff, teachers and education publishing companies jointly engage in writing biology teaching material for middle and high schools; these initiatives resulted in a wider range of teaching materials for schools.

2.2 Biology Curricular Trends

From 2000–2010, the biology curricula were again reformed to feature changes in education beliefs and subject matter.

2.2.1 New Education Beliefs Changes in belief systems and ideas in biology education shaped and defined the direction of the reformed curriculum. The following guidelines and beliefs were adopted: *biology for all, enhancement of student's biology literacy, advocacy of inquiry-based learning, teaching and learning biology with real life contexts that are relevant to students and society.* These beliefs were already quite popular in science education in the world although it was considered relatively new for biology teachers in mainland China.

Biology for All

For many years, elite education was the center stage in biology education in mainland. The elite education system was known to groom a few excellent students with a potential to enter university and study biology, but the system neglects many other aspiring students. This has resulted in a low and slow improvement of overall biological literacy for China's citizens. *Biology for All* is one of the new educational beliefs that is aimed to correct the old system. *Biology for All* ensures all students have a fair and reasonable educational opportunity regardless of age, sex, cultural or family background. It was a difficult undertaking for a developing country where citizens are placed into different societal rankings. However, the new belief system that education is for helped realize the new educational reform objectives.

All students under the reformed system need to meet the basic demands of curriculum standards. There is however no upper limit for teaching contents. Schools in provinces with fast economic growth and sound educational foundation are expected to make full use of local education resources to achieve higher academic performances for high achievers. Therefore, teachers may raise the standards of their schools and students. Student-oriented curricula did not mean that the requirements and standards of biology education were lowered.

Enhance Student's Biological Literacy

The aim of achieving biological literacy in every student should be the incentive to guide the design of secondary biology curricula. The reformed biology education in mainland China was designed for biological literacy necessary for every citizen. A graduate with biological literacy is one who has the intellectual ability to make informed judgment or decision with the science of biology and the scientific way of thinking when confronted with a phenomenon, events, and viewpoints in daily life. In this respect, biology teachers must endeavor to develop in all students the necessary biological literacy through the biology courses. In the past, biology lessons focused mainly on transfer knowledge. The revised biology curriculum emphasizes not only biological science content, but also scientific process skills, attitude, values and the understanding of science.

Advocate Inquiry-Based Learning

Traditionally, students learn biology passively from the classroom teacher. To encourage active teaching and learning in biology classrooms, the belief, *Advocate Inquiry-Based Learning*, was adopted as the biology curriculum standard. This belief system also regards the *Inquiry-Based Learning* as one of the major teaching and learning approaches. This teaching approach has thoroughly reformed the former traditional teaching and learning methods where the once passive learners are now active learners and active participants of the leaning process. Students now learn via active participation, discover and acquire knowledge through investigative exploration and research, understand thinking and problem solving approaches of scientists, master assorted skills needed for scientific research, comprehend scientific concepts and cultivate scientific spirit.

The new curriculum gives students more opportunities to experiment, discuss and to communicate their leaning experiences. The improved leaning environments are the result too of better and more varied teaching materials, learner-centred assessment and greater teacher-student rapport.

Teaching and Learning Biology with Student's Real Life Context

Students' learning in the past involves taking notes, remembering biological facts and preparing for tests. Few students have a real understanding of biology concepts in the passive way of learning. The reformed curriculum ensures students learn biology and technology in real life context. It should involve the students' personal experiences, local living thing from their environment, or issues related to the understanding of biology. Students should try to discover solutions to problems and acquire new knowledge during the process, develop a positive scientific attitude and a world view of their understanding of science, enhance their skills of science inquiry and exploration, as well as cultivate a habit of scientific thinking. In addition, emphasizing the relationship with real life contexts in school biology will help enhance their interests and initiatives in leaning and doing science.

2.2.2 Changes in Curriculum Content   Highlight inquiry and practical activities The theme "biology as inquiry" meant inquiry is embedded in both the teaching of the content as well as the pedagogy.[6] The curriculum standards further stress on experimental work and other practical activities to facilitate first hand learning of theories and contents. The new content standards provide teachers with suggestions about teaching-learning activities, which are mostly hands-on activities. In high school biology, there is a specially designed elective module called "Bio-technology Practice" to provides more opportunities for students to practice doing science. The major contents of the module are lab activities, such as the applications of microbes, enzymes, and biotechnology in food processing, and the application of biotechnology in other fields.[6,7]

Embed Bio-technology in the Content

Science and technology are two different fields that can integrate extensively. Technological literacy is of increasing concern in science education. Hence, bio-technology is embedded in both junior secondary and high school biology curriculum standards. For example, middle school biology standards require students to "practise making flour sauce and acidophilus milk", which require students to understand the knowledge about microorganisms and the fermentation process and techniques in real life. This biotechnology component facilitates students mastering of key science concepts better than just learning from books. High school biology curriculum further increases the proportion of technological contents. Technology-related contents are covered in the elective modules where there are more relevant topics on bio-technology, especially in applied and modern bio-technology. The combination of traditional technology and applied technology in junior standards will enable students to know the basics about bio-technologies. The senior biology standards have in-depth curriculum in the technologies, such as "tissue culturing", and "PCR", which help students understand the new bio-technology.

Key Concepts as Core and More Choices for Electives

Biology curriculum standards in both junior and senior high school require students to master key concepts that are necessary for living and personal decision-making. They are also the most essential requirements of their bio-literacy. The contents and topics of the two curriculum standards are mutually complementary and progressive. Biology curricula in high schools are comprise core and elective modules. The core modules are the foundations of Biology; they highlight key concepts such as cells, genetics, evolution, ecology. Elective modules lead students on to the latest developments in science and technology, its relationship with the society and to further improve their understanding of biology and ability of practice. In view of the different interests and career ambitions of students in different regions and the need for a diversified range of elective modules, the curricula are thus designed to help students select and plan their courses for future career planning.

3. TEACHER PREPARATION MODEL

Changes in the new biology curricula are distinct. With the new biology education beliefs, new curriculum aims, new contents and inquiry based teaching and learning pedagogies, the reformed curricula challenge the teachers' professional knowledge and skills. At the beginning of the implementation, many teachers had difficulty following through the curricula to teach biology. Admittedly, teacher preparation is a key issue for the success of the reform. For this purpose, both MOE and local education officers have attached much importance to teacher training. All teachers are required by the MOE to participate in at least one training program before they teach the new curriculum. Local education officers develop the teacher training schemes, as well as mobilize people to support its implementation. Each trial school has also made related training plans to ensure successful implementation of the curricula. From 2000 to 2010, different approaches have been used in teacher training and professional development. Among these approaches, one model, the on-line teacher training model was selected for in-service teacher preparation in mainland China.

On-line teacher training is an in-service teacher preparation model for pre-new-curriculum training for large number of biology/science teachers. Since 2007, the internet-based teacher preparation model has been used. This model, supported by MOE, has been used for teacher preparation at the national and provincial levels, such as in the Shandong and Hainan provinces in the last two years. This internet-based teacher training model was also piloted in other provinces. In July 2010, 5687 biology teachers from 6 provinces took part in an intensive training program that lasted 10 to 14 days. The aim of the training was to prepare teachers to teach the new school biology curriculum proficiently. The training activities were carried out using the website[8] even though most of the teachers were located in remote and rural areas such as Xinjiang and Guizhou. The on-line teacher training model comprises two stages: the preparation of on-line course materials, and the intensive on-line training. Trainer to trainee ratio was approximately one is to 20. A brief overview of the on-line teacher training model is as follows:

Design and Prepare on-Line Course Materials

The on-line course materials include approximately 20 hours of videos on different topics and further reading materials. Videos present the basic on-line course materials for the training. The following are the criteria for the selection of video course contents:

I.   Focus on topics related to teachers' concern as well as the key points of the new biology curricula

II. Main teaching-learning ideas are based on science education research or relevant educational theories

III. Contents are organized with question chains

IV. Use of classroom activities (video recording from a lesson) to explain new ideas or teaching approaches to illustrate instructional process, with suggestions

V. Content are selected based on face-to-face training experience

By understanding the anxieties and concerns of the biology teachers, the on-line video course was aimed to help them overcome their teaching difficulties and apprehension with teaching the new curriculum. The video contents contained mainly questions that were frequently asked by teachers. Before screening the videos, the textual materials were discussed and revised several times by the trainer team. Biology classroom activities, interviews with teachers and group discussions were video- recorded as basic elements for the video course. In addition, reading materials form another kind of on-line training course resources directly related to each of the topics in the video content. Reading materials consist of texts of the video captions, lesson plans, and suggestions on pedagogical content knowledge, teaching experiences, biological content knowledge, and analysis of test items which may help teachers in their teaching of the new biology curriculum.

On-line Training

During the intensive two weeks of training, biology teachers watched the videos, read on-line reading materials, held a face-to-face discussion with peers in their groups, did extension study (like a homework) on planning a lesson, up-loaded lesson plans for professional sharing with others, read daily reports issued by trainers, took part in on-line conference every three days, released comments on course contents, and made daily reports of other trainee's homework. The supervisor of each group of teachers usually lead the group discussion and work as a coordinator or facilitator as well.

Trainers and project assistants worked together during the intensive training period. Trainers had to read teachers' homework, select the best, give comments on the homework and make daily reports of them. They also need to answer questions and chair on-line conferences. Trainers were responsible for tracking the key issues that emerge on training days, respond to the issues, and report them daily. Trainers usually work more than 12 hours a day during the two weeks.

For each of the trainers, trainees and project assistants, the platform offers an on-line "office" to enable participants to do all above mentioned training activities. In the on-line office, every user can easily contact with any other user and release on-line comments or questions. Trainers and trainees are in an equal position and exchange ideas equally.

This model has been used for in-service teacher preparation and teacher professional development to solve the challenges of the new science curriculum. Although the model is not so effective in developing all aspects of teachers' PCK, it made the teachers feel more comfortable with the new curriculum. This innovative internet-based training model is not the best and perfect way for teacher preparation and professional development, but it is able to meet the professional needs of the teachers and the requirements of the new curricula in some way.

4. REVIEW AND PLANNING FOR THE NEXT STEPS

It has been 10 years since the new biology curricula was implemented. 2010 was the year for the review and assessment of the biology curricula standards. Although the data on the achievable goals thus far were not complete, it was noted that the reformed biology curricula trends with its new emphasis on inquiry based teaching and learning and advocacy for biology literacy are moving in the right direction with China's economic growth. Teachers are adopting the new belief systems of biology education and are transforming their pedagogy for active student leaning and active participation the classrooms. To ensure the future success of the reformed biology curricula standards, the teaching practices and assessment standards of teachers need to be further improved. It is important to emphasize inquiry based teaching approaches and the teaching of science concepts that are aligned with the reformed curricula standards.

REFERENCES

National Mid-long Term Scheme for Education Reform and Development Outline (2010–2020), http://www.gov.cn/jrzg/2010-07/29/content_1667143.htm

The Ministry of Education. (2001). Guideline for curriculum reform in general education

MOE, Compulsory Education Curricula Framework, http://www.ncct.gov.cn/zcwj/ShowArticle.asp?ArticleID=55

MOE, High School Curricula Framework, People Education Publishing House, Beijing, 2003

BSCS, Developing Biological Literacy, 1993.

MOE. Biology Curriculum Standard for compulsory education. Beijing Normal University Publishing Press, 2001.

MOE. Biology Curriculum Standard for high school. People Education Publishing House, Beijing, 2003.

Biology teacher training website, http://2010.cersp.com/

Enshan Liu
The College of Life Sciences
Beijing Normal University, 100875, China
liues@bnu.edu.cn

ROBERT L. WALLIS

6. BIOLOGY EDUCATION IN THE FUTURE

ABSTRACT

Biology today is a popular and influential discipline that dramatically shapes our lives and affects the development and operations of societies around the world. Biology educators thus play a crucial role in ensuring the global community is made aware of the biological bases of everything we do. However, as biology teachers and educationists, we face unprecedented challenges in making our discipline relevant, meaningful, attractive and respected. Some of the challenges include: (i) the explosion of knowledge and the feeling that we are being over-whelmed by new developments and applications, (ii) challenges to the scientific method from fundamentalist and other groups, (iii) urgency of challenges that confront society, so that long term solutions are less considered than immediate, short-term ones, (iv) shift to more applied studies that do not have the intellectual rigour that underpins disciplines like biology, and (v) specialization of the disciplinary components of biology and the challenge to integrate and generalize. On the other hand, I am optimistic about the future importance and potential success of biology education. Some guiding principles may need to be followed – these include, ensuring relevance, using the latest educational technologies wisely, stressing the applications as well as the discovery aspects of science, and ensuring biology makes meaningful contributions to economic, social, cultural and environmental sustainability.

KEY WORDS

Biology Education, Future, Conservation Biology, Natural History, Landscapes, Ecosystems

INTRODUCTION

Biology is a broad science and its teachers, lecturers and educationists face many challenges in maintaining its popularity, relevance and applicability in the Twenty First Century.

Some challenges are exciting and positive. These include the so called explosion of knowledge – the seemingly exponential growth in scientific information accompanied by an increasing number of academic publications in biology. How is it possible for faculty charged with teaching the subject BIOLOGY to keep up with all this knowledge, let alone cover so many sub-disciplines in a way that maintains the integrity of the subject and interest by our students? Another such challenge is the very

Mijung Kim and C. H. Diong (Eds.), Biology Education for Social and Sustainable Development, 61–68.

positive contribution Biology can make towards sustainable development – not only in its obvious relevance to environmental sustainability, but also in social, economic and cultural aspects. Convincing decision makers of biology's valuable contributions to advancing society's towards social sustainability is thus another important challenge!

Other challenges are threatening and negative. The rise in fundamentalist religions and zealots who pronounce biological science is anathema to their basic tenets is disturbing. Arguments raised by such groups are impossible to challenge since the very bases of their assertions are anti-science and rooted in a faith drilled into followers as unchallengeable.

There has been an emergence of new subjects that are appealing and popular with students, but which 'cherry pick' the 'entertaining' aspects of our discipline, are sometimes shallow and lack the intellectual rigour that necessarily underpins our discipline and that produce 'experts' who lack any real understanding of other related biology fields. Interestingly, many graduates of these new areas seek to acquaint themselves with 'real' biology later in life when they realize a comprehensive knowledge and understanding of the fundamentals of biology – and of the foundation sciences that underpins it – is needed.

Nonetheless, I am optimistic about the future of biology education and the role it can play in improving the world population's quality of life, health, appreciation of nature and its contributions to social, economic, environmental and cultural sustainability. I believe we can overcome the challenges and exploit the opportunities they present by ensuring biology is relevant for our students, stresses the discipline's applications and is taught using sound pedagogy and. the correct use of instructive strategies.

NEW CURRICULA

Most of the challenges I have listed above have been dealt with elsewhere and there have been recent developments that have produced novel and exciting curricula in biology that aim to address these challenges (e.g. Boulton and Panizzon, 1998; Committee on Undergraduate Biology Education to Prepare Research Scientists for the 21st Century, National Research Council, 2003; National Research Council of the National Academies, 2009).

I would instead like to concentrate on a case study for 'biology education in the future'. While this might touch on some of the aforementioned challenges, I think it addresses to me one of the most significant problems facing those of us who are concerned about developing a keen appreciation of nature in the biologists of the 21st Century; I would argue, such an appreciation is what drove so many of us in the first place to a love of our discipline.

A CASE STUDY – FIELD STUDIES, CONSERVATION BIOLOGY AND DEVELOPING AN APPRECIATION OF NATURE

Conservation biology is the scientific study of biodiversity with the aim of protecting species, their habitats and ecosystems from excessive rates of extinction.

Michael Soulé wrote an early paper describing the concept as an interdisciplinary subject applying conservation practice and policy to the theoretical bases of ecology and population biology (Soulé, 1986). Importantly, it involves ethics as with any mission- or crisis-oriented discipline. I would also argue it involves aesthetics, as people will strive to conserve a nature that they feel deeply about and appreciate for its beauty as much as its role in ecological processes.

Such a crisis-oriented discipline is warranted. The UN's Global Biodiversity Outlook 3 was released earlier this year and paints a dismal picture:

- crop production and clean water face a high risk of rapid degradation and collapse because of the record rate of animal and plant extinctions
- corals and amphibians are groups that seem to be most under stress of extinction
- 31% decline since 1970 in the size of populations of wild vertebrates
- almost 1 in 4 plant species face extinction
- genetic diversity of crops and livestock continues to decline – >60 breeds of livestock have become extinct since 2000. (http://gbo3.cbd.int/).

Conservation biology has spawned a large body of research presented in hundreds of scholarly books and many high-ranking journals. I believe one of the best such periodicals is Conservation Biology, published by the Society for Conservation Biology (SCB). In SCB's own words:

Launched in 1987, *Conservation Biology* initially was intended to provide a global voice for an emerging discipline. Since its inception, the journal has published groundbreaking papers and is instrumental in defining key issues contributing to the science and practice of conserving Earth's biological diversity. Consistent with the mission and goals of the Society for Conservation Biology, *Conservation Biology* promotes the highest standards of quality and ethics in conservation research and encourages communication of results to facilitate their application to management, policy, and education. (http://www. conbio.org/Publications/ConsBio/)

Importantly, the SCB's vision includes "a world where people understand, value, and conserve the diversity of life on Earth".

Not surprisingly, therefore, conservation biology has its roots in a much earlier study of nature called natural history. The term 'natural history' is an interesting one and seemingly quite quaint. However, it is derived from a legitimate use of the word 'history' which is derived from the Greek historia meaning a learning by inquiry. Thus my 1892 Concise Dictionary by Annandale lists some meanings of 'history':

- A verbal relation of facts or events
- A narrative
- An account of things that exist
- A description

Hence we can see that 'Natural History' is history (in any of its above meanings) applied to nature. Indeed, Annandale defines natural history as "originally the study or description of nature in its widest sense, now commonly applied collectively to the sciences of zoology and botany".

Naturalists were once a much respected group. Back in the 1880s in Australia the Field Naturalists Club of Victoria's (FNCV) annual conversaziones attracted over 800 participants – this in a city of then around 80,000! They provided detailed descriptions of wildlife, geology and landforms and indeed, of nature (including astronomy). Field naturalists played a major role in encouraging a study of nature in schools where the enquiring mind would be challenged and student learning made more interesting by field studies (as opposed to rote learning).

In the last 20 years or so of the 20th Century there was a decline in interest in natural history. The FNCV numbers dropped and university students and staff thought it contributed little to more challenging fields such as quantitative and experimental ecology.

Just how relevant is natural history in today's society? The editorial in an early issue of Conservation Biology (Noss, 1996) addressed this very question with the startling heading, **The Naturalists Are Dying Off.** It began with a quote from the Bulletin of the Ecological Society of America:

"...natural history has earned the pejorative epithet of 'alpha ecology', and it has often been considered to have little or no potential for generating ideas". The editor of Conservation Biology despaired of these views: "We are asked, albeit not often enough, by the political powers for our professional opinions on which conditions will favour the conservation of biodiversity...? What will we look for in answering these difficult questions? Our computer models? Our GIS software? The WWW? Yes in part. But if we apply these tools in the absence of a firm foundation in field experience, void of the 'naturalist's intuition' that is gained only by many years of immersion in raw Nature and through a ceaseless hunger for knowledge about living things, we are sure to go astray. Scientific abstractions and fancy technologies are no substitutes for the wisdom that springs from knowing the world and its creatures in intimate, loving detail. We owe it to ourselves for acquiring this kind of knowledge alive...."

Without a solid grounding in field experience, conservation biology is hollow. Without the years of bug-bitten trudging through hollows and bogs, how can a biologist be expected to separate biological truth from computer fabrication?" (Noss, 1996:2).

Natural history and field work provide the very bases of conservation biology as they generate the valuable data which are fed into models in the first place. Without good field data to feed into our population viability analysis models, predictions of the likelihood of extinctions or probabilities of successful reintroductions are useless, no matter how elegant the algorithms are which generate the models! And it is natural history which provides the pointers for appropriate field data collection that has to be undertaken by field ecologists. It is also natural history which inculcates a love and respect for nature which provide the basis for experience-based conservation. Naturalists may well be dying off. But with any luck and a lot of hard work, they will be replaced by a new generation of enthusiasts!"

A start might be for (schools and) universities to reinstate the field work that was common not all that long ago. Students tend to enjoy and learn the natural history experiences when they do so first hand. Unfortunately, budget cuts (field work is expensive), new technologies (easier to show a blue ray DVD) and the crowded curriculum mean students have far less exposure to the natural world. In doing so, I believe they are less likely to develop that deep empathy for nature that is really necessary if we are to succeed in reducing the alarming decline in biodiversity.

This was recently demonstrated in an article that appeared in The Daily Yomiuri in Japan entitled "Concept of 'satoumi' gaining popularity". Satoumi is the belief that an appropriate measure of human intervention in the ecology of coastal waters can produce a wider diversity of fish and shellfish. This is a very hands-on approach used with schoolchildren and involves habitat manipulation (e.g. removing sea lettuce that hampers growth of eel-grass, which is habitat for fish fingerlings).

Another trend is for active conservation management to "learn by doing" through adaptive management. Whilst adaptive management was first introduced in the 1970s it is now widely used in addressing resource and ecological problems. It addresses the difficulty in designing classical hypothesis based scientific method experiments which require controls and testing of a single variable at a time. Adaptive management thus involves:

– deliberate designing and applying management actions as experiments
– synthesizing existing knowledge, exploring alternative actions, making explicit predictions of their outcomes, monitoring these outcomes, use results for future planning (Murray and Marmorek, 2003)

The typical adaptive management cycle can be represented by CMP's (2004) diagram:

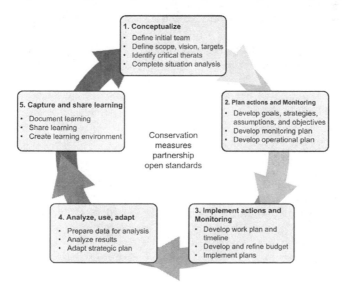

I firmly believe that adaptive management will form the bases for many future data gathering and experimental scenarios.

CONSERVATION BIOLOGY FOR THE 21ST CENTURY

Some 21 years ago the proceedings of a conference that addressed this topic was published (Western and Pearl, 1989). In it, Western and Pearl wrote an overview that speculated on 'tomorrow's world' and the possible fate of wildlife:

'Is there any point then in speculating on the fate of wildlife when our descendents may not share our concerns for wildlife, given their superior powers to create other, more fantastic worlds? I think so, for if we have one unique commodity to hand on, it is our natural world.... Should we grant to our descendents the means to advance technologically, yet deny them the chance to celebrate nature?'

And later

'But for many for us now, and I suspect many more in the future, our sense of well-being and freedom is rooted in the natural world." (Western, 1989: xiii).

Thus while many things will change in the future – our ability to create virtual worlds (Avatar?), interplanetary travel, instant communication etc. – many argue that it is the natural world and our deep understanding of it and appreciation for its value that will be important in human progress, especially in terms of ensuring a sustainable future.

Western (1989) also speculates on some interesting challenges facing conservation biologists in the 21st Century, including:

- are there common ecological and behavioural traits that distinguish threatened and tolerant life forms and processes?
- does this imply new evolutionary selection pressures, or simply a narrowing of old ones?
- how will changing selection pressures affect genomes, population structure, life histories and behavioural traits?
- is biological diversity, rather than say, ecological integrity, the right thing to be concerned about, given our future potential to enrich ecosystems?
- is it unrealistic to think we can maintain ecosystems as they are when we can tailor them to fit in better with our future world? [How natural should we aim for? Can people still derive pleasure and a deep appreciation from nature in an artificial environment like a zoo?]

Finally, on this last and very significant point, Western discusses the notion that people may well prefer artificial and manicured landscapes over wild and challenging – but natural ones. 'The most curious of naturalists, Charles Darwin, after five years circumnavigating the earth investigating its natural history, was moved to comment that "the picturesque beauty of many parts of Europe far exceeds anything we beheld". Ecosystems, no less landscapes, can be created as well as destroyed by humanity.'

I would agree and suggest it would be difficult for us to find any ecosystem untouched by human modification. To preserve everything the way it was 10, 20 or 100 years ago is a waste of energy and resources. Rather, I believe we can develop an appreciation of and respect for nature – the very essentials Noss was demanding before – in any habitat, whether it be school ground, back yard, urban creek, zoo or aquarium. The important thing is to take students into the field and enthusiastically teach them about the wonders of living things and how well they function in our world!

REFERENCES

Annandale, C. (1892). A Concise Dictionary of the English Language. (Blackie & Son, Glasgow).

Boulton, A. & Panizzou (1998). The knowledge explosion in science education: balancing practical and theoretical knowledge. Journal of Research in Science Teaching 35, 475–481.

CMP (Conservation Measures Partnership) (2004). http://www.conservationmeasures.org/

Committee on Undergraduate Biology Education to Prepare Research Scientists for the 21st Century, National Research Council (2003). BIO2010. Transforming Undergraduate Education for Future Research Biologists. http://www.nap.edu/catalog.php?record_id=10497

Murray, C & Marmorek, D. (2003). Adaptive management and ecological restoration. Ch 24, pp. 417–428 in Freiderici, P (ed). Ecological Restoration of Southwestern Ponderosa Pine Forests (Island Press: Washington).

National Research Council of the National Academies (2009). A New Biology for the 21st Century. (National Academies Press: Washington). http://books.nap.edu/openbook.php?record_id=12764&page=R1

Noss, R. F. (1996). The naturalists are dying off. Conservation Biology 10, 1–3.

Soulé, M. (1985). What is conservation biology? BioScience 35, 727–734.

Western, D & Pearl, M. C. (1989). Conservation for the Twenty-first Century (Oxford Univesrity Press: New York).

Western, D. (1989). Overview. pp. xi–xv in Western & Pearl (1989).

Robert L. Wallis
School of Science & Engineering,
University of Ballarat, Australia
r.wallis@ballarat.edu.au

BIOLOGY, COMMUNITY AND HIGHER EDUCATION

How can biology education directly contribute to the development of local communities and empower stakeholders? Closely tied to this issue, is how higher education in biology can incorporate realistic contexts for learning, and prepare students to apply scientific concepts that will directly impact their communities and societies. These issues are explored in the 12 papers in this theme, which touch on diverse issues such as the allocation of scarce water resources, the challenges to sustainable agricultural production, biodiversity conservation, and the search for alternative oil supplies.

Josefino R Castillo's paper, *"Research as an integral component of biology education in Philippine schools"* focuses on the integrated research component of the curriculum of the University of Santo Tomas. Undergraduate students are required to undertake experimental research under the supervision of a faculty member, and then present the findings to a panel as a requirement for graduation. Castillo also identifies the factors that are impeding the progress of research and development and biology education in the country.

Another study looks at how Biology education can be made interesting and relevant even for non-majors.

In *"Biology for Non-Majors at the University of the Philippines Diliman Extension Program in Pampanga (UPDEPP): Learning Sexually Transmitted Diseases Minus the Squirms"*, Nenita M Dayrit focuses on a course dealing with reproductive health and Sexually Transmitted Diseases (STD) that was offered at The University of the Philippines. Using power point slides and video presentations, the course evolved into peer teaching with the approval of instructors.

Another possible way to improve the learning process is examined in the paper *"Using Metacognition as a tool to advance Reading Comprehension in a Science Class"*. This study tested the reading comprehension of 14 sophomore biology students on three separate occasions. It found that all the participants lacked vocabulary. They were then taught strategies to improve their reading comprehension. Jocelyn D Partosa highlights the importance of using metacognition to help students in monitoring their reading comprehension.

With an eye to empowering students to be effective decision makers outside the confines of the biology classroom, Anne Wallis *et al.* explore a visualization tool called WINDSCREEN in environmental science classes to enhance learning. WINDSCREEN helps students assess the trade-offs that communities make as they allocate water for different uses, under different water supply situations. It utilizes Adobe Flash Player, incorporates photo-realism in a simple user interface designed to look like a car dashboard. A pilot study of 26 first year environmental science students was conducted to investigate their views on water allocation and the effectiveness of a visualization tool on their learning experience. The experiment found that as water supply decreases, students shifted towards allocating water to farms or environmental flows. Student receptivity to the visualization tool was also captured in an anonymous survey. These are presented in *"A Visualisation Tool for Experiential Learning in Environmental Science: Using Football Fields, Agricultural Fields and Waterways to Illustrate the Implication of Different Water Allocation Decisions"*.

Rosalinda Mercedes E Castillo also focuses on how the college curriculum can make a tangible difference to local communities. Her paper *"An Assessment of the Pantabangan Reforestation Livelihood and other Community Involvement Projects of La Consolacion College of Manila, Philippines"* explores the effectiveness of community projects undertaken by La Consolacion College of Manila. These include a tree-planting project that aimed to plant and nurture one million native trees by 2011. Student volunteers who participated in this project reported a sense of satisfaction in protecting the environment for future generations. Other projects included mobilizing students to record their electricity consumption in kilowatt-hours, and then practicing energy conservation measures for one month in order to reduce energy consumption. The results of questionnaires showed high ratings for both effectiveness and satisfaction level by both participants and beneficiaries. Castillo concluded that education is a powerful tool to achieve sustainable development, and inspire students to continue taking concrete action to promote environmental protection.

Special focus is also given to the question of how to empower millions of small farmers in Asia who face severe challenges in food production, given rising populations, declining availability of water and production land per capita. Jan Willem Ketelaar and Alma Linda Abubakar from the FAO chronicle how Integrated Pest Management (IPM) strategies were developed for a range of important crops during the last two decades. Specifically, the focus is on adult-education-based Farmers Field Schools that empower Asian farmers to be ecology-literate and better managers. This has been successful for a number of reasons, including the use of experiential and discovery-based approaches to learning, as supported by the concept of andragogy and the Critical Theory Framework. Important policy lessons learnt are presented in the paper, *"Sustainable Intensification of Agricultural Production: The Essential Role of Ecosystem-Literacy Education for Smallholder Famers in Asia"*.

Shifting the focus from empowering stakeholders to assessing the state of environmental protection, the paper *"Extent of Escherichia coli contamination of Cagayan de Oro River and factors Causing Contamination"* looks at the extent of fecal contamination of the Cagayan de Oro River. By sampling upstream, midstream and downstream areas using the Multiple Tube Fermentation Technique, the study found that average coliform values exceeded acceptable limits set by the Department of Environment and Natural Resources. Results also suggest that sources of contamination are prevalent. The study by Lesley Casas

Lubos and Lalevie Casas Lubos also explores the factors that contributed to the high fecal contamination and other environmental issues.

The ecological status of two major Manila eseros was the focus of the study by Glorina P. Orozco and Macrina T. Zafaralla. Their paper *"Biophysico-chemical and Socioeconomic Study of Two Manila Esteros"* showed that the estero waters fall under Class D water quality criterion and recommended heavy metal analysis of fishes and water samples for future studies. The survey revealed that respondents had grown accustomed to living in estero communities despite the dirty surroundings but also showed a willingness to cooperate in rehabilitation projects. The paper reported that more than 100 groups from the government, private sector, local and foreign groups have responded to the call to rehabilitate the Pasig River and its esteros. The authors examined some initiatives as possible approaches towards effective rehabilitation and sustainability of Manila esteros and concluded that environmental education is a promising way of involving the community to rehabilitate the estero system.

Moving from water quality to biodiversity conservation in the Philippines, the paper *"Indigenous Knowledge and Taxonomy of Bats in Loboc Watershed Forest Reserve, Bohol, Philippines"* reports studies on the current status of bat populations found in the Loboc watershed forest reserve in Bohol. Reizl P Jose *et al.* assess the level of community awareness on the importance of bats and bat conservation. The watershed is a secondary growth forest and supports endemic as well as threatened species of bats. The conservation program has significant implications on the potential of eco-tourism in the area.

Meanwhile, the search for alternative fuel sources is examined in the paper *"Anatomical Characterization of Oil Cells and Oil Cavities in Jatropha curas L using Light and Electron Microscopy"*. Milarosa L. Luibrea and Vivian Tolentino stated that the search for alternative fuels so as to attain self-sufficiency is a top priority in the research agenda of the Commission on Higher Education. This study is a pioneering attempt in that direction to find a new biofuel. It studies the anatomical characterization of oil secretory cells in the fruits and seeds of *Jatropha curcas*. It aims to identify the exact location of oil secretory structures in the tissues of fruits and seeds. A significant general finding is that oil cell count is inversely proportional with the oil cavity count.

In a similar study presented in *"Oil Producing Plants as Alternative Source of Energy for Sustainable Development"*, five species of plants were identified for their oil producing characteristic. The study by Vivian S. Tolentino *et al.* reported on the identification, distribution and location of oil cells in the plant, in the hope that a cost-efficient extraction of oil might be possible, hence contributing to self-sustainability in the Philippines.

The issues discussed in Theme 2 present a compelling challenge to biology educators in institutions of higher learning to consider how they can impart scientific knowledge to students in such a way as to tangibly improve the lives of communities beyond the classrooms. Engaging and empowering biology students with the paradigm of sustainability in higher education has obvious strategic values given that many will become decision-makers and leaders of their generation in biological research and enterprises. Another question worth pondering is how to create contexts in which empowering collaborative long-term relationships can be developed amongst educators, students and stakeholders to positively impact environmental and developmental outcomes.

ANNE WALLIS, MICHELLE GRAYMORE, TY MATTHEWS
AND SUSAN BYRNE

7. A VISUALISATION TOOL FOR EXPERIENTIAL LEARNING IN ENVIRONMENTAL SCIENCE: USING FOOTBALL FIELDS, AGRICULTURAL FIELDS AND WATERWAYS TO ILLUSTRATE THE IMPLICATION OF DIFFERENT WATER ALLOCATION DECISIONS

ABSTRACT

Environmental education challenges educators to provide students with activities that cover complex societal issues, enhance critical thinking and to promote interdisciplinary and holistic learning. A further challenge is to convey this information so that it provides a solid foundation for participatory decision making. For example, effective management of water resources requires consideration of the social, economic and environmental consequences of various water allocation decisions together with an understanding of the possible conflicts that arise from these decisions, particular under scenarios of limited water supply. Well designed visualisation tools can enhance teaching and understanding of difficult concepts. For example, they can be designed to allow students to participate in hypothetical decision making and to visualise the potential implications of their decisions under a range of scenarios. A review of the published literature revealed that several visualisation tools have been developed for use in science education, but few provide the option for students to participate in integrated environmental decision making. This paper presents a visualisation tool, called WINDSCREEN, that has been introduced into environmental science classes to enhance student learning. The tool focuses on water resources and requires students to think about how they would allocate available water supplies for social, economic and environmental uses. An overview of the challenges associated with water allocation decisions, together with the role that visualisation tools can play in environmental education are also discussed.

KEYWORDS

Environmental Decision Making, Environmental Education, Visualisation Tool, Water Allocation

Mijung Kim and C. H. Diong (Eds.), Biology Education for Social and Sustainable Development, 73–86.

INTRODUCTION

Globally, aquatic ecosystems continue to exhibit a net reduction in available potable water. Water allocation decisions are frequently met with conflict (Gleick, 2000; Gopalakrishnan *et al.*, 2005; Molle and Berkoff, 2009; Rowland, 2005), particularly where water resources are shared across political boundaries and access to clean drinking water forms the basis for hostility (Marcus & Onjala, 2008; Rowland, 2005; Syme *et al.*, 1999; Wurbs, 2004). Demand for various uses including domestic supplies, primary industries, energy generation and environmental flows, put pressure on decision makers to allocate water equitably (Wurbs, 2004). Effective management of water resources requires consideration of the social, economic and environmental sectors together with an understanding of possible conflicts that may arise from different allocation decisions, particularly when water supply is limited. Determining appropriate allocations, particularly under conditions of low availability, is a task of significant responsibility that requires ethical consideration, often without any prospect of satisfying all recipients within a community or region. Resource allocation triage and conflict resolution are considered important prerequisites for those faced with allocation dilemmas. Clearly, environmental educators have an interest in the integration of the complexities of such resource allocation decisions into their teaching programs and visualisation is one possible means of achieving this goal.

The use of visualisation tools to assist with strategic decision making is becoming increasingly commonplace. For example, landscape planning and military training utilise visualisation tools to represent different scenarios and to facilitate decisions that can have significant social, environmental or economic repercussions (Bishop and Rohrmann, 2003; Bowe *et al.*, 2000; Pettit *et al.*, 2004; Sheppard, 2008). The opportunity for visualisation to assist with complex environmental decisions have been realised in climate change projection models (Sheppard, 2005; O'Neill, 2009), and more recently in water resource planning and management (Jankowski, 2009; Larson and Edsall, 2010). However, its application for education associated with water allocation decision making appears to be non-existent.

If current generations of students are to become the environmental decision makers of the future, it is vitally important that some components of the university curricula include exercises in experiential learning about the consequences of resource management decisions (Wallis & Laurenson, 2004). Sheppard *et al.* (2008) considers that urban and regional planners are the 'natural' choice for making difficult water allocation decisions. However, these decisions are currently made in various professions, and decision making processes continue to involve greater community participation (Tan, 2006, Ball *et al.*, 2007 and Jankowski, 2009). Effective environmental management requires that graduates are sufficiently informed about current, critical environmental issues and the impact of actions on the future welfare of the environment. Thus, environmental educators need to provide practical ways to enable their students to envisage potential futures based on the decisions made (Hicks, 1996). Visualisation tools used in environmental science curricula may assist with studies of complex environmental problems. However, there is limited evidence of existing visualisation tools contributing to the teaching of environmental decision making in schools or tertiary institutions. The aim of this paper is to discuss the potential role of visualisation tools in enhancing student learning within environmental science education. More specifically it will:

– highlight the challenges faced by water allocation management;
– explore interactive visualisation tools and their current use within the environmental educational setting; and
– discuss how preliminary trials with a new interactive visualisation tool, called WINDSCREEN, have been used to engage students and to provide experiential learning that enhances student awareness of water allocation decision making and some potential consequences of these decisions.

WATER ALLOCATION CHALLENGES

There are 261 international river basins that encompass at least two nations (Wolf et al., 1999; Wurbs, 2004) challenging these nations to agree on water allocations. According to Syme et al., (1999), water resources have been over-allocated, and problems of reallocation are emerging. Allocation of water in many river basins has already reached or exceeded its limits. Marginal additional sources, such as desalination, often provide very costly alternatives and new projects can at times reallocate water that is already appropriated for human or environmental uses (Molle and Berkoff, 2007). In Australia, as in other parts of the world, environmental managers face issues of declining water quality, over-allocation of surface and ground water supplies and degradation of aquatic environments (Syme and Nancarrow, 2006). Australia is the driest inhabited continent with highly variable rainfall. This, together with a three tier system of government and potential changes in rainfall patterns due to climate change add to the difficulties associated with water allocation decision making.

The term 'equitable' is poorly defined and usually ambiguous, yet it is a term frequently used in water allocation discussions (Wegerich, 2007, Syme et al., 1999). Criteria for equitable distribution are particularly difficult to determine in global water conflicts, due to the ambiguity and often contradictory nature of international law (Wolf, 1999). Competing sectoral interests and scarcity invariably means that any resulting allocation tends to favour one sector to the detriment of another prompting a need for 'fairness' and 'justice' in resolving contentious environmental issues (Seligman et al., (1994). However, because there are multiple uses and therefore multiple participants who claim a stake in decisions around water allocation (Nandalal and Hipel, 2007) conflict has become an intrinsic complication in developing strategies for distributing water. However, Syme and Nancarrow (1992) showed that the perceived fairness of the process is at least as important as the direct outcomes thereby illustrating that participatory decision making is vital for reducing conflict.

It is clear that water allocation decisions, typical of issues in environmental management, present a significant source of ongoing conflict and dissention. This challenges teachers of environmental science to provide students with activities that cover complex societal issues, enhance critical thinking, promote interdisciplinary and holistic learning while also providing a foundation for participatory decision making. Education practitioners are in need of tools to assist with this task and visualisation tools can successfully convey complex information and facilitate critical thinking and decision making (Larson and Edsall, 2010).

THE ROLE OF INTERACTIVE VISUALISATION TOOLS

By definition, interactive multimedia (or visualisation) is the use of a computer to control and present combinations of media such as text, graphics, video and sound (Newhouse, 2002). Visualisation offers significant diversity in educational application including presentation of complex subject matter, research support in behaviour and perceptions, landscape planning, strategic or risk evaluation training and immersive entertainment. Visualisation tools also offer the opportunity to investigate 'what if' scenarios and explore alternative futures (Bunch and Lloyd, 2006) in a way that is motivating and compelling and can use complex information to convey strong messages in real time (Nicholson-Cole, 2005). The advantages of visualisation tools are that visual images are commonplace, are already a familiar form of communication with the public and have the ability to condense complex information into a simple means of communication that is instantaneous and easy to recall (Nicholson-Cole, 2005). Three categories of visualisation tools have been identified (Kalawsky, 1993; Yusoff *et al.*, 2010):

- Fully-immersive based on virtual technology, where the users feel present in a virtual world (i.e. computer generated virtual space that enables real time interactivity in three dimension systems) (Lawless and Coppola, 1996);
- Semi-immersive – where users are partially immersed in a virtual environment; and
- Non-immersive – an environment that presents images on a normal monitor and allows the user to interact with computer generated images.

Most computer based learning currently used in schools consists of text, static graphics, audio, 2D animation and video (Yusoff *et al.*, 2010). In the past, such 3D technology has been restrictively expensive. However, affordable personal computers and conventional input devices have made this type of visualisation more accessible to a wider audience (Yusoff *et al.*, 2010). Evidence suggests that these forms of photo realism and immersion are limited in their effectiveness (Larson and Edsall, 2010) and that less complicated 2D visuals take less time for users to interpret (Mak *et al.*, 2005).

Successful educational visualisation tools need to be attention grabbing, easy to relate to, personally applicable both spatially and temporally, offer authentic and relevant scenarios that are scientifically realistic and contain applied pressure situations that force users to act and offer replay-ability (Aldrich, 2004; He, 2003; Nicholson-Cole, 2005). Therefore, a visualisation tool with real photos of areas that are familiar to the user should be more engaging to users. However, no single image will appeal to all users and differences in experience and understanding will result in different messages being taken away (Nicholson-Cole, 2005; Larson and Edsall, 2010).

This overview of water allocation, decision making and visualisation tools along with the need to investigate new approaches to experiential learning in environmental education provides the context for: reviewing interactive visualisation tools; exploring their use in environmental educational settings; and introducing WINDSCREEN and discussing how this tool engages students and provides experiential learning that enhances their understanding of water allocation decisions and the potential consequences of these decisions. The tool also collates water allocation decisions made by students under a range of different water supply scenarios.

INTERACTIVE VISUALISATION TOOLS FOR ENVIRONMENTAL EDUCATION

There are a plethora of visualisation tools available. We found 20 visualisations tools in the published literature, which revealed that school science programs, urban and regional planning, defence training, community awareness campaigns and artificial intelligence programs all use visualisation technology (Table 1). Of the tools investigated, eleven were primarily used in educational settings, seven in planning and decision making and two, ABC Catchment Detox and the Jasper adventure trip planning tool, were applicable for use both in educational settings and decision making learning.

Public consultation in urban and regional planning incorporates the use of interactive visualisation tools for the development of proposals in built (Pettit et al., 2004; Rohrmann & Bishop, 2002) and natural environments (Bell, 2001). Interactive visualisation tools are also used to raise awareness about environmental issues and change behaviour. For example, the Ocean Project (see http://www.theoceanproject.org), an extensive worldwide collaborative of zoos, aquariums and museums dedicated to ocean conservation, have developed the watershed-to-ocean visualisation project that aims to provide a learning experience where participants can explore and be compelled to act in protection of watersheds and the ocean environment. This interactive visualisation tool is intended to change participants perception of their 'eco-address' by highlighting their awareness of how people are connected to the aquatic environmenttogether with how their activities can have both positive and negative impact on the aquatic environment.

Interactive visualisation tools are mainly used in secondary and tertiary educational institutions, however primary schools are increasingly advocating the incorporation of computer technology into their curricula and the use of these tools may appear in a relatively simplistic form. Tertiary institutions use interactive visualisation tools across several disciplines. The majority of these tools are found in information technology and urban planning, however medicine, forestry, geography, social and environmental sciences also have representation. Other uses of interactive visualisation tools include trade-specific applications, such as in engineering. ABC Catchment Detox (http://www.catchmentdetox.net.au/home/) is an example of an educational application that engages students at all levels in environmental decision making and demonstrates the impacts of those decisions on the health of river basins.

WINDSCREEN – A VISUALISATION TOOL TO FACILITATE WATER ALLOCATION DECISION MAKING

We are currently trialling a visualisation tool for community water allocation decisions to assess the effectiveness of an interactive games-based tool. The tool is designed to inform users of the trade-offs between social, economic and environmental sectors that are associated with difficult water allocation decisions under a range of water availability scenarios. The computer tool, 'WINDSCREEN,' is an interactive visualisation tool developed to assist water authorities in their understanding of community attitudes towards different water uses, and to assess the trade-offs that communities make between uses under different water supply conditions. It uses Adobe Flash Player for its graphic capabilities and accessibility and, incorporates photo-realism via photographs of local conditions in a simple user interface based on a car dashboard (Figure 1). Before the user can begin a driver's licence is required, enabling demographic data to be collected. The dashboard consists of a set of dials; one showing the total quantity of water available for allocation and three showing the quantities allocated to social (an Australian Rules Football field: *footy*), economic (agricultural production: *fields*), and environmental (waterway levels: *flows*) sectors. Users can allocate water using the up and down arrows under the dials. The numbers on the dashboard represent four water availability scenarios based on historic water availability data (scenarios 0 = highest water availability, 1 = average water availability and 2 = last 10 years under drought conditions) and climate change predictions (scenario 3) for the Wimmera region of western Victoria, Australia. Once the various allocation scenarios are selected by the user, the windscreen shows a visual representation of the impact of the water allocation decisions made using local photos of a football oval, agricultural field and flows to local waterways taken during periods of dry, moderately dry and wet conditions. The rear vision mirror contains a happiness indicator, which is a scale used to gauge how happy participants are with their allocation decisions (Figure 2).

In an educational setting, WINDSCREEN is an experiential 'hands on' interactive visualisation tool where students experiment with hypothetical decision making for varying levels of water supply scarcity. It provides them with an opportunity to increase their understanding of the impact their decisions will have on the local conditions.

Figure 1. In WINDSCREEN a dashboard interface is used for making water allocation decisions. This particular scenario represents the outcome for a user's allocation decision based on a period of water scarcity (see low water level on dial directly left of steering wheel)

Figure 2. Level of happiness with decisions made is indicated by selecting one of the happy/sad face symbols.

DETERMINING STUDENT'S WATER ALLOCATION PREFERENCES

We have trialed WINDSCREEN during a pilot study ($n = 26$ 1st year environmental science students) to investigate student views on environmental issues, with particular regard to the availability of water resources, their preferences for water allocation and whether a visualisation tool engages them and adds to their learning experience.. The pilot results suggest that student's allocation priorities change with increasing water scarcity (Figure 3). Students are showing a tendency to allocate water evenly to all water uses (*i.e. social, economic and environmental*) when there is plenty of water available. However, as water availability decreases, their preference shifts toward allocating water to farms or environmental flows. How students felt about the implications of these decisions were apparent from the happiness indicator. We plan to take this research further by conducting a survey at least 25 students from each of three faculties (Arts and Eduaction, Business and Law and Science and Tehnology) to compare decision making across students with different environmental interests.

We used an accompanying, anonymous questionnaire to ask students about the usefulness of Windscreen. Participating students described using WINDSCREEN as '*a great tool, easy to use, with simple graphics and a colourful visualisation*'. WINDSCREEN was able to demonstrate to the students the impact of climate change on water availability in their local area and what that will means for future water allocation decisions. After using the tool, students commented that it was '*difficult to decide when there is not much water*' and that they worried about the '*effects of water scarcity on the environment*'. Students also commented that their use of the tool taught them about the value of water, and the impact water allocation has when water is scarce on farms and the environment. It also prompted them to think about their priorities for water allocation and make trade-offs between water uses when there was little water available.

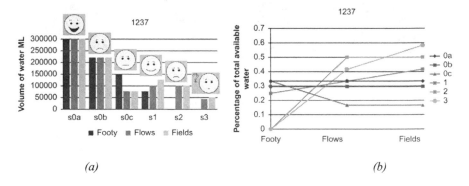

Figure 3. An example of the results of a student's water allocation decisions showing, (a) water volumes allocated to social, economic and environmental sectors together with whether they were satisfied with their decisions, and (b) proportion of supply allocated under each scenario.

FUTURE DIRECTIONS

Environmental education is considered relevant for inclusion in broad vocational fields (Shepard *et al.*, 2009). Students are being prepared for professions that may require strategic decisions to be made over critical environmental issues. Climate change and sustainability education have been identified as particularly relevant in school and university curricula (Wals and Jickling, 2002; Hurlimann, 2009; Shepard *et al.*, 2009) and water resource management is strongly tied to both of these broad areas. Thus, it is recommended that the social, environmental and economic implications of water resource allocation be taught, in order to prepare prospective students likely to be involved in such decision making either as professionals or as community members that are interested in environmental decision making. Interactive visualisation tools such as WINDSCREEN can facilitate this learning in that decision outcomes can be visually depicted in simulations that help students to evaluate alternative futures.

Virtual worlds, 2D and 3D visualisation displays, are showing promise in their ability to engage and motivate students with sometimes complex subjects, particularly in the maths and science streams. Newhouse (2002) found students who use computers to support their learning are generally more responsible, independent, cooperative, collaborative, directive and negotiative. There is a demand for carefully constructed learning experiences in educational institutions to respond to increases in professional demand for environmental education (Hurlimann, 2009). Interactive visualisation tools have significantly enhanced the learning experience of students in maths and science subjects. The development of tools such as WINDSCREEN provide further opportunity to enhance experiential learning in environmental education by allowing students to grapple with complex, cross disciplinary subject matter in a way that is engaging and motivational. The strengths of WINDSCREEN as an educational tool include a simple dashboard interface that is readily visible on a small screen, is easily uploaded onto a computer and is not time consuming to run from start to finish. Furthermore, the use of real, familiar images in WINDSCREEN was able to convey potential consequences of allocation decision to students, not only engaging them, but helping them to understand of multidimensional environmental issues (Mak *et al.*, 2005; Larson and Edsall, 2010).

It should be noted that not all visualisation tools are received favourably by students. It is clear that the development of new interactive visualisation tools to aid teaching must be thoroughly tested before general adoption is encouraged. There are a number of design improvements that would enhance the use of WINDSCREEN. For example, pop-up instructions could improve navigation within the various components of the tool, such as for moving from the historic water chart back to the dashboard; and real-time responsiveness of the photos so that they change instantaneously as the amount of water allocated is changed. However, most students found using WINDSCREEN intuitive and had little difficulty using the tool as in its current form.

The tendency for students to allocate water as equitably as possible when using WINDSCREEN is not an unusual finding. A study by Seligman *et. al.* (1994) revealed that people agree on a common set of ethical principles in making water allocation decisions. Management for future generations, water being owned by everyone and regarded as a public good, the rights of the environment and how efficiently water is being used were principles afforded the highest importance. A collective sense of ownership of the resource and its efficiency of use is supported by Cohen (1991). These common values tend to become less significant when personal livelihood and income are impacted by water allocation decisions adding further complexity to the decision making process. This is a dimension not included in WINDSCREEN in its current form and such complicating situations may be worth considering in discussion with students after they have used the tool.

CONCLUSION

The United Nations has set 2005–2014 as the Decade of Education for Sustainable Development (DESD) (UNESCO, 2008). During this time, the aim of the DESE program is to seek new behaviours and practices that promote sustainability through education promoting interdisciplinary and holistic learning, values based learning, critical thinking, multiple methods approaches and participatory decision making using locally relevant information (Hurliman, 2009). Visualisation is one method in the tool box that can help educators achieve this aim. The preliminary trials using WINDSCREEN are promising (e.g. the tool is engaging and easy to use), but further testing is needed using a greater number of students across a range of academic disciplines and backgrounds. The additional advantage of this tool is that it can be used to educate students while at the same time collecting data relating to students' attitudes and values toward the environment. It is also possible to adapt the program to address other environmental concerns, such as climate change, by altering the images and scenarios (e.g. CO_2 emissions).

Table 1. Interactive visualisation tools and their relevance in education institutions

Interactive Visualisation Tool	Use	Reference
FOR EDUCATION		
CI Space	Tertiary level study of Artificial Intelligence via Java applets	Amershi *et al.* (2005)
STArt program	Primary/secondary level study of molecular structure	Halpine, (2004)
Lichens as bioindicators PBL-GIS	Secondary level GIS unit measuring air quality using tree lichen data	Baker & White (2003)
Geowall 3D	Tertiary level study of structural geology	Boese *et.al.* (2009)
Earth Systems Visualiser	Tertiary level study of global weather via overlays of space-time data	Harrower *et.al.* (2000);
CoVis	Collaborative virtual geoscience museum for middle and high schools – teaches real-time weather, historic climate and global greenhouse data exploration	Pea (2002)
3D/VR cold front learning system	Secondary level simulation of temperature distribution subject to cold fronts	Lin & Chang (2005)
Connected Chemistry	Secondary level study on the science of pressure.	Kim (2005)
GLOBE Project	Kindergarten to secondary level study of local environmental data	Lawless & Coppola (1996); Means (1998)
Draw Your Line	Anti-bullying campaign using GIS online program for empowerment and reporting.	www.athinline.org
US Air Force Academy cadets	Compulsory engineering mechanics unit using PowerPoint FEM-based colour stress plots	Bowe *et al.* (2000)
FOR DECISION MAKING		
Jewell Station Neighbourhood Project	Urban planning tool for community engagement in planning decisions.	Pettit *et al.* (2004)

GMCRII	Decision support model for conflict resolution and community engagement.	Gopalakrishanan *et al.* (2005)
SmartForest	GIS/CAD landscape virtual reality planning tool for community engagement in sustainable forest plans	Orland (1994)
CALP research program	Local climate change landscape projections using geomatics and visualisation for community engagement and policy support.	Sheppard *et. al.*, (2008)
Entlebuch Biosphere Reserve Switzerland	Provides 3D aerial views, climate change projections	Schroth *et al.* (2006)
Local Climate Change Visioning Project – Delta, B.C. (Canada)	3D visualisation tool for local climate change landscape projections	Burch *et al.* (2010)
Computer walk-through simulation of Camberwell Junction, (Australia)	Urban landscape planning research to measure cognitive and affective response	Rohrmann & Bishop (2002)
EDUCATION & DECISION MAKING		
ABC Catchment Detox	Online game; user in charge of the whole catchment; decides what activities to undertake to avoid environmental problems	(http://www .catchmentdeto x.net.au/home/)
Jasper Adventure Player software	Solution prompting tool to a Jasper adventure trip planning scenario	Crews *et al.* (1997)

ACKNOWLEDGEMENTS

We thank the Environmental Sustainability Faculty Research Cluster for financial support, which enabled the preliminary trial of WINDSCREEN. We also thank students who willingly participated in the pilot trial of this tool and the colleagues who helped develop WINDSCREEN including Brad Mitchell, Peter Vamplew, Pam McRae-Williams and Kevin O'Toole.

REFERENCES

Amershi, S., Arksey, N., Carenini, G., Conati, C., Mackworth, A., Maclaren, H. & Poole, D. (2005) Fostering student learning and motivation: an interactive educational tool for AI. *Tech. Rep. TR-2005–06*, University of British Columbia.

Aldrich, C. (2004) Simulations and the future of learning: An innovative (and perhaps revolutionary) approach to e-learning. Pfeiffer Publishing, San Francisco, CA.

Baker, T.R. & White, S.H. (2003) The effects of GIS. on student's attitudes, self-efficacy, and achievement in middle school science classrooms. *Journal of Geography 102*, 243–254.

Ball, J., Capanni, N. & Watt, S. (2007). Virtual reality for mutual understanding in Landscape planning. *International Journal of Human and Social Sciences 2*(2), 78–88.

Bishop, I.D. & Rohrmann, B. (2003). Subjective responses to computer simulations of urban environments – a comparison. *Landscape and Urban Planning, 65*, 261–277.

Bell, S. (2001) Landscape pattern, perception and visualisation in the visual management of forests. *Landscape and Urban Planning 54*, 201–211.

Boese, M.J., Sheng, H. & Salam, M.A. (2009) Evaluating the use of 3D visualisation technology in geology education. AMCIS 2009 Proceedings, Paper 7. http://aisel.aisnet.org/amcis2009/7 accessed 28/02/2011.

Bowe, M., Jensen, D., Feland, J. & Self, B. (2000) When multimedia doesn't work: an assessment of visualisation modules for learning enhancement in mechanics. Institute for Information Technology Applications (IITA) research publication 3: education series. June 2000 – HQ USAFA/DFPS, Colorado.

Bunch, R. L. & Lloyd, R. E. (2006) The cognitive load of geographic information. *The Professional Geographer 58*(2), 209–220.

Burch, S., Sheppard, R. S. J., Shaw, A. & Flanders, D. (2010) Planning for Climate Change in a flood-prone community: municipal barriers to policy action and the use of visualizations as decision-support tools. *Journal of Flood Risk Management 3*, 126–139.

Cohen, R.L. (1991) Justice and negotiation. *Research in Negotiation in Organizations 3*, 259–282.

Crews, T., Biswas, G., Goldman, S. & Bransford, J. (1997) Anchored Interactive Learning Environments. *International Journal of Artificial Intelligence in Education 8*(2), 46–52.

Fishman, B.J. & D'Amico, L.M. (1994) Which way will the wind blow? Networked computer tools for studying the weather. Paper presented at the conference on Educational Multimedia and Telecommunications – Vancouver, B.C. pp. 209–216.

Gleick, P. (2000) Water conflict chronology. Internet electronic text. http://worldwater.org/conflict.html accessed 25/02/2011.

Gopalakrishnan, C., Levy, J., Li, K.W. & Hipel, K.W. (2005) Water allocation among multiple stakeholders: conflict analysis of the Waiahole water project, Hawaii. *Water Resources Development 21*(2), 283–295.

Halpine, S.M. (2004) Introducing molecular visualization to primary schools in California: the STArt! teaching science through art program. *Journal of Chemical Education 81*(10), 1431–1436.

Harrower, M., MacEachren, A. & Griffin, A.L (2000) Developing a geographic visualization tool to support earth science learning. *Cartography and Geographic Information Science, 27*(4), 279–293.

He, C. (2003) Integration of geographic information systems and simulation model for watershed management. *Environmental Modelling & Software The Modelling of Hydrologic Systems 18*(8–9), 809–813.

Hicks, D. (1996) Envisioning the future. *Environmental Education Research 2*(1), 101–110.

Hurlimann, A.C. (2009) Responding to environmental challenges: an initial assessment of higher education curricula needs by Australian planning professionals. *Environmental Education Research 15*(6), 643–659.

Jankowski, P. (2009) Towards participatory geographic information systems for community-based environmental decision making. *Journal of Environmental Management 90*, 1966–1971.

Kalawsky, R.S. (1993) *The Science of Virtual Reality and Virtual Environments* Addison-Wesley, Wokingham, Berks, pp. 432.

Kim, H.S. (2005) Learning with computer modelling software in a high school chemistry class: a study of conceptual growth and transfer. *In:* C.-K Looi *et.al* (eds.), *Proceedings of the 2005 Conference on Towards Sustainable and Scalable Educational Innovations Informed by the Learning Sciences:Sharing Good Practices of Research, Expermentation and Innovation IOS Press Amsterdam, The Netherlands.*Larson, K.L. & Edsall, R.M. (2010) The impact of visual information on perceptions of water resource problems and management alternatives. *Journal of Environmental Planning and Management 53*(3): 335–352.

Looi, C., Jonassen, D.H., & Ikeda, M. (2005) *Towards Sustainable and Scalable Educational Innovation Informed by the Learning Sciences*, pp. 740-743. IOS Press, Netherlands.

Lawless, J.G. & Coppola, R. (1996) Global Learning and Observations to Benefit the Environment (GLOBE): an international environmental science research and science education program. *Proceedings of Eco-Informa '96, 10*, 503–507.

Lin, M.C. & Chang, C.Y. (2005) The development of a 3D visualisation tool on the topic of cold front. *In: Looi, C., Jonassen, D.H. & Ikeda, M. (eds), Towards Sustainable and Scalable Educational Innovations Informed by the Learning Sciences,* pp. 740–743. IOS Press, Netherlands.

Mak, A., Lai, P., Kwong, R. & Leung, S. (2005) To much or too little: visual consideration of public engagement tools in environmental impact assessment. *In:* S. Bres & R. Laurini (eds). *VISUAL 2005, lecture notes in computer science.* LNCS 3736, pp. 189–202.

Marcus, R.R. & Onjala, J. (2008) Exit the state: decentralization and the need for local social, political, and economic considerations in water resource allocation in Madagascar and Kenya. *Journal of Human Development 9*(1), 23–45.

Means, B. (1998). Melding authentic science, technology, and inquiry-based teaching: Experiences of the GLOBE program. *Journal of Science Education and Technology, 7*(1), 97–105.

Molle, F. & Berkoff, J. (2007) River basin development and management. In D. Molden (ed.) *Water for food – Water for life, Comprehensive Assessment of Water Management in Agriculture,* pp. 585–624. EarthScan, London.

Molle, F. & Berkoff, J. (2009) Cities vs. agriculture: a review of intersectoral water re-allocation. *Natural Resources Forum 33,* 6–18.

Nandalal, K. D. & Hipel, K.W. (2007) Strategic decision support for resolving conflict over water sharing among countries along the Syr Darya River in the Aral Sea Basin. *Journal of Water Resources Planning & Management 133*(4), 289–299.

Newhouse, C.P. (2002) The impact of ICT on learning and teaching. A literature review for the Department of Education, Western Australia.*Environment and Urban System,* 29:255-273.

Nicholson-Cole, S. (2005) Representing climate change futures: a critique on the use of images for visual communication. *Computers, Environment and Urban System, 29,* 255–273.

O'Neill, S & Nicholson-Cole, S. (2009) Fear won't do it: promoting positive engagement with climate change through visual and iconic representations. *Science Communication, 30*(3), 355–379.

Orland, B. (1994) Smart forest: a 3-D interactive forest visualisation and analysis system. *Proceedings of Decision Support – 2001.* Combined events of the 17th Annual Geographic Information Seminar and the Resource Technology '94 symposium, Toronto: pp. 181–190.

Pea, R.D. (2002) Learning science through collaborative visualization over the internet. *Nobel Symposium: Virtual museums and oublic understanding of science and culture,* May 26-29, 2002, Stockholm: Sweden (2002)

Pettit, C., Nelson, A. & Cartwright, W. (2004) Using on-line geographical visualisation tools to improve land use decision-making with a bottom-up community participatory approach. *In:* J.P. van Leeuwen and H.J.P. Timmermans (eds.), 53-68. Kluwer Academic Publishers, Netherlands.

Rohrmann, B. & Bishop, I. (2002) Subjective responses to computer simulations of urban environments. *Journal of Environmental Psychology 22,* 319–331.

Rowland, M. (2005) A framework for resolving the transboundary water allocation conflict conundrum. *Ground Water 43*(5), 700–705.

Schroth, O., Wissen, U., Schmid, W. A. (2006) Developing New Images of Rurality – Interactive 3D Visualizations for Participative Landscape Planning Workshops in the Entlebuch UNESCO Biosphere Reserve. DISP, 166/3, 26–34.

Seligman, C., Syme, G.J. & Gilchrist, R. (1994) The role of values and ethical principles in judgements of environmental dilemmas. *Journal of Social Issues, 50*(3), 105–119.

Sheppard, S.R. (2005) Landscape visualisation and climate change: the potential for influencing perceptions and behaviour. *Environmental Science & Policy, 8,* 637–654.

Shephard, K., Mann, S., Smith N. & Deaker, L. (2009) Benchmarking the environmental values and attitudes of students in New Zealand's post-compulsory education. *Environmental Education Research, 15*(5), 571–587.

Sheppard, S.R., Shaw, A., Flanders, D. & Burch, S. (2008) Can visualisation save the world? – Lessons for landscape architects from visualizing local climate change. In Procs. Digital Design in Landscape Architecture 2008, 9th International Conference on IT in Landscape Architecture. Dessau/Bernburg, Germany: Anhalt University of Applied Sciences, May 29–31 2008.

Syme, G.J. & Nancarrow, B.E. (2006) Perceptions of fairness and social justice in the allocation of water resources in Australia. Perth, CSIRO, Division of Water Resources, Consultancy Report 92/38.

Syme, G.J. & Nancarrow, B.E.(2006) Achieving sustainability and fairness in water reform. *Water International, 31*(1), 23–30.

Syme, G.J., Nancarrow, B.E. and McCreddin, J.A. (1999) Defining the components of fairness in the allocation of water to environmental and human uses. *Journal of Environmental Management, 57,* 51–70.

Tan, P. (2006) Legislating for Adequate Public Participation in Allocating Water in Australia. *Water International,* 31(4): 455–471.

United Nations Educational Scientific and Cultural Organisation (UNESCO) (2008) *Education for sustainable development. United Nations Decade (2005–2014).* UNESCO, Geneva.

Wallis, A., Block, J., Graymore, M.L.M., Vamplew, P., O'Toole, K., McRae-Williams, P. & Mitchell, B. (In Press) WINDSCREEN: A tool for assessing community water allocation trade-offs?

Wallis, A & Laurenson, L. (2004) Environment, resource sustainability and sustainable behaviour: exploring perceptions of students in south-west Victoria. *Asian Journal of Biology Education, 2,* 39–49.

Wals, A.E. & Jickling, B. (2002) Sustainability in higher education: from doublethink and newspeak to critical thinking and meaningful learning. *International Journal of Sustainability in Higher Education, 3*(3), 221–232.

Wegerich, K. (2007) A critical review of the concept of equity to support water allocation at various scales in the Amu Darya basin. *Irrigation Drainage Systems, 21,* 185–195.

Wolf, A.T. (1999) Criteria for equitable allocations: the heart of international water conflict. *Natural Resources Forum, 23,* 3–30.

Wolf, A.T., Natharius, J.A., Danielson, J.J., Ward, B.S. & Pender, J.K. (1999) International river basins of the world. *International Journal of Water Resources Development, 14*(4), 387–427.

Wurbs, R.A. (2004) Water allocation systems in Texas. *Water Resources Development 20*(2), 229–242.

Yusoff, M.F., Zulkifli, A.N. & Mohamed, N.F. (2010) Virtual environment as aids in persuading users in learning process. *Proceedings of Regional Conference on Knowledge Integration in ICT,* Putrajaya, Malaysia, June 1, 2010.

Anne Wallis (Corresponding Author)
Environmental Sustainability Research Centre,
School of Life and Environmental Science, Deakin University, Warrnambool, Australia, PO Box 423, Warrnambool, Victoria, 3280, Australia
anne.wallis@deakin.edu.au

Michelle Graymore
Horsham Campus Research Precinct, University of Ballarat, Horsham, Australia

Ty Matthews
Environmental Sustainability Research Centre, School of Life and Environmental Science,Deakin University, Warrnambool, Australia.

Susan Byrne
Environmental Sustainability Research Centre, School of Life and Environmental Science, Deakin University, Warrnambool, Australia.

JOCELYN D. PARTOSA

8. USING METACOGNITION AS A TOOL TO ADVANCE READING COMPREHENSION IN A SCIENCE CLASS

ABSTRACT

This study aimed to examine and identify reading comprehension problems among biology majors; improve their reading comprehension, reading strategies and promote metacognition in classroom teaching. Fourteen sophomore biology students in Plant Systematics were assigned 3 articles on separate occasions. A reading survey was conducted and data analyzed showed all participants lack vocabulary. Participants demonstrate reading strategies like reading aloud, writing questions, re-reading, note taking or a combination of these. Several participants identified factors that delay their rate of comprehending articles and learned new strategies to improve their reading. The use of metacognition in classroom teaching is thus important to develop participants' awareness and skills in monitoring their reading comprehension.

KEYWORDS

Reading Survey, Comprehension Problems, Strategies, Metacognition, Biology

INTRODUCTION

Metacognition is an awareness and management of one's own thoughts, as thinking about one's own thinking and relating to self-monitoring and reflection on learning (Kuhn and Dean, 2004; Bauseman and Block, 2005; Donovan and Bransford 2005). Most students need direct instruction, ample coaching and opportunities for guided practice to develop self-reflective abilities on their own (Burke, 2000). Several reports show that using metacognition in reading comprehension showed the necessity of explicit instruction, explanation, modeling, discussion and systematic direct instruction of metacognitive strategies as means to facilitate reading comprehension across all levels of education, from children (e.g. Eilers & Pinkley, 2006; Boulware-Gooden et al., 2007; Allan and Hancock, 2008) to adult learning (Cubukcu, 2008).

It has been observed that college students are not necessarily good readers. Despite reading advanced academic material, it does not mean they always comprehend the information (Taraban, 2000). Many college teachers also fail to recognize that teaching reading skills to students is necessary (Lei et al., 2010). It is

Mijung Kim and C. H. Diong (Eds.), Biology Education for Social and Sustainable Development, 87–96.

often a common assumption among college teachers that students have developed proper reading skills from previous academic years. According to Lei *et al.* (2010) however, comprehending and identifying key information in textbooks, scholarly books and research journal articles can be difficult for college students.

Using metacognitive teaching strategies can help students achieve deeper and more durable scientific understanding (Abell, 2009). There are various ways to develop metacognition in the classroom. One is through reading. According to White (2004), reading is needed in all academic disciplines and one key component of the learning outcomes of education is the ability to comprehend reading. It is evident that metacognition can support students' learning in understanding many subjects (Abell, 2009). The use of metacognition in developing reading comprehension in Science class shows that students develop meaningful learning and sound scientific understanding. According to Abell (2009), researchers point to the effect of metacognitive instruction on the transfer and durability of conceptual understanding in science.

How does metacognition support science learning? In particular, how does metacognition improve reading comprehension and reading processes in science class? One suggested strategy is using instructional strategies which include inquiry, collaboration and mental models to improve self-regulation in the science classroom. A study by Partosa (2009) on models and modeling involving all year levels of BS Biology students showed that most used analogies in modeling their understanding of concepts. When asked their modeling behavior, most reported to review their models before final submission. The senior students were more elaborate and confident and demonstrated integration and reflective thinking in their work. The juniors (first and second year) had simple and superficial treatment of their analogies and had not developed skills in integration and reflective thinking. It was apparent that the juniors had problems in reading comprehension and thus, difficulty in articulating their ideas. The above findings provide the impetus for a study to enhance metacognition among biology students, particularly the second years.

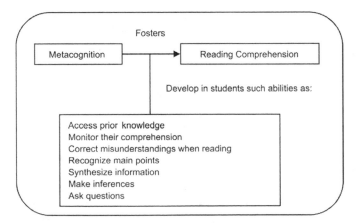

Figure 1. Metacognition in Reading Comprehension.

This study aims at facilitating reading comprehension and using metacognition as a tool to develop reflective thinking in second year BS Biology students. The foci were to examine and identify reading comprehension problems among biology majors; improve their reading comprehension, reading strategies and promote metacognition. Reading comprehension refers to the students' ability to access prior knowledge, monitor their comprehension, correct misunderstandings when reading, recognize main points, synthesize information, make inferences and ask questions (Figure 1). Reading strategies refer to the students' attempts – cognitive or behavioral – to solve or address difficulties met with reading to achieve reading comprehension. The relevance of this study is two-fold. First, it aims to improve reading comprehension and reading strategies among those students using metacognition as a tool. Second, it promotes metacognition among students.

METHODOLOGY

Research Design

This study was conducted in the first semester of calendar year 2009–2010 at Ateneo de Zamboanga University, Philippines. Plant Systematics or Botany 202 is one of the major subjects of second year BS Biology students. Fourteen students (12 females) participated in the survey. Eleven were second year students, 1 was in third year and 2 were in fourth year. Participants were given reading assignments on three journal articles on three separate occasions during the semester.

Research Instrument

A reading survey (Joseph, 2006) was modified for the purpose of this study. Two features were integrated in the survey: the reading assignment guidelines and the rubrics for some items in the reading survey (Appendix A). The guidelines are a set of instructions meant to facilitate reading by the students. Items in the reading survey are generally grouped into: time spent on reading, rate of reading comprehension and note taking of the actual reading process. Also, the items are meant to provide information on students' reading behaviors and strategies. In addition to the reading survey, students were also asked to complete a reading log each time they complete one reading assignment. The reading log consists of each student's comments and observations in response to certain guide questions found in the reading assignment guidelines.

Data Gathering Procedure and Analysis

As a preliminary activity, the article on Plant Systematics was discussed in class to guide the participants in their reading to give them ideas as to how to go about the reading process for the remaining two articles. Table 1 shows the reading survey of the 3 reading assignments. Participants' observations included the written transcripts from their journal entries in Table 2. Table 2 shows respondents' reading comprehension problems, reading behaviors and reading strategies.

RESULTS

Results showed that the pre-reading time for this group of participants took 13.2 minutes on the average; reading time took 54.8 min with 3 students' reading ranging from 81 to 102 minutes (Table 1). This averages more than one hour to finish reading and suggests they might not be concentrating or could have too many distractions and interruptions. On the other hand, a reading time of less than 25 min suggests participants may not have taken enough time to work through the article (Joseph, 2006). Table 2 showed some of the distractions as follows: respondents stopped to use a dictionary or searched online; paused to note down synthesis after reading the relevant paragraph; hesitated as that statement was not understood. This suggests the factors could be a distraction.

Results reported that the self-ratings of 6 participants vary between average comprehension for articles 1 and 3 to very good comprehension for article 2. This showed that they recognized some parts of articles 1 and 3 as difficult to follow and were occasionally distracted with new terms. The other participants, A and K self-rated very good reading rate for articles 2 and 3 but poor and average rate of reading for article 2, respectively. Except for participants C and D everyone self-rated very good reading rate for article 2. Many participants thought article 2 was interesting, easy to understand even during pre-reading and participants could relate to it.

Seven out of 10 students appreciated article 2 and self-rated it as very enjoyable. The article was very interesting, relevant and presentation is clear and simple. There were minimum negative feelings experienced. However, others found the article technical and difficult to follow and felt frustration, boredom while reading. Results varied between little and average reading enjoyment of articles 1 and 3. For example, respondents B and I found both articles boring, irrelevant and technical. Generally, reading was more of a drag than fun. Participants attributed the inability to focus while reading due to the length of article, technicality of the material and inadequate vocabulary.

Maximum reading effort was self-rated by five participants. This is evident that the participants had observed the guidelines in completing the reading assignments. In addition, despite difficulty of the text, they tried their best to understand each article by looking up the meaning of new terms and recalling of some previous lessons to help them understand the terms. The rest of the respondents self-ratings varied between average and maximum (A, B & D), poor and average (I) and poor and maximum (F). This suggest participants with self-ratings of average and poor might have skipped some guidelines in reading to look for the meaning of terms or read without understanding.

Table 1. Reading Survey of the 3 reading assignments. Participants are denoted as letters in place of their real names

Partici-pants	Pre Reading (in min)				Reading Time (in min)				Rate of Comprehension			Rate of Enjoyment			Rate of Effort		
	A1	A2	A3	Mean	A1	A2	A3	Mean	A1	A2	A3	A1	A2	A3	A1	A2	A3
A	36	8	20	21	120	14	33	56	1	10	10	5	10	5	10	10	5
B	22	10	12	15	180	15	47	81	5	10	5	1	10	1	10	5	10
C	25	25	13	21	40	40	18	33	5	5	5	5	5	5	10	10	10
D	16	20	10	15	230	45	30	102	5	5	10	1	5	5	5	10	5
F	27	8	8	14	35	20	92	49	5	10	5	5	5	1	1	10	1
H	27	7	10	15	48	12	40	33	5	10	5	5	10	5	10	10	10
I	23	5	5	11	75	10	40	42	5	10	5	1	10	1	1	5	5
J	15	4	6	8	150	31	90	90	5	10	5	1	10	5	10	10	10
K	6	7	2	5	28	15	27	23	5	10	10	5	10	10	10	10	10
L	6	5	10	7	32	25	60	39	5	10	5	5	10	10	10	10	10

*Data are from 10 students with complete entries.
*Rate of comprehension   [VG – 10, Ave – 5, Poor – 1]
*Rate of enjoyment   [VE – 10, Ave – 5, LE – 1]
*Rate of effort exerted   [Max – 10, Ave – 5, Poor – 1]
*Qualitative descriptions in Appendix A

Table 2. Summary of students' reading comprehension problems, reading behaviors and reading strategies

Reading comprehension problems	Reading behaviors	Reading strategies
Inability to focus or concentrate as a result of emphasizing meaning-making of new, unfamiliar and technical terms	Preference for a particular reading position as in lying in bed while reading	Note taking of important points or highlights of the article
Distractions from noise, frequent stops during reading to refer to dictionary or other references, feelings of boredom, lethargy and discomfort owing to small font size of articles, single spacing and little if no interest in the article.	Appreciates pictures in articles as these are helpful in reading and adds to the fun side of the activity	Writing questions for clarification purposes
	Easily distracted by noise, feelings of boredom and lethargy, perceived difficulty of the article	Referencing of dictionary and or related materials from the internet
		Asking their classmates at times
	Reading aloud Writing questions and attempting to answer the same	Synthesizing or reading aloud to be more focused
Inadequate vocabulary Lack of background or limited background on reading material		Finding a quiet and comfortable place before reading and as much as possible outside one's room to refrain from possibly sleeping
Inability to connect past lesson with concepts from the article	Attachment to particular comfort zones like reading in the room	Resort to a combination of re-reading the part they find confusing, look for meaning in the text, dictionary or the Internet.
Length and complexity of articles and generally, not the usual reading materials of interest	Forming pictures in their mind Eating, drinking iced tea, stretching	Attempts at overcoming boredom include eating, stretching
	Forcing oneself to read for fear of getting a low mark	

Participants' reflection notes collected indicated improved reading strategies from their self-evaluation inputs. For example, some participants reflected they were able to identify factors slowing their reading rate and thereafter used strategies taught to improve their reading comprehension.

In addition to developing their self-monitoring ability, this study proved useful in developing respondents' metacognitive skill; skills in analysis, writing summary and connecting prior knowledge to present readings. Table 3 shows the number of respondents reported to learn or strengthen their metacognitive skills. For example, it developed respondents' ability to access prior knowledge (45.5%), developing metacognitive skills such as making inferences (54.5%) and developed skills in asking questions and correcting misunderstandings when reading (63.6%). However, some admitted they need improvement in the skills mentioned.

Table 3. Respondents' self-evaluation on their meta-cognitive skills On the use of metacognition and development of metacognitive skills

Metacognitive skills	Respondents who learned or strengthened the skill		Respondents who need improvement	
	No.	%	No.	%
Access prior knowledge	5	45.5	2	18.2
Monitor comprehension	6	54.5	1	9.1
Correct misunderstandings when reading	7	63.6	4	36.4
Recognize main points	6	54.5	-	-
Synthesize information	3	27.3	3	27.3
Make inferences (implications, conclusions)	6	54.5	2	18.2
Ask questions	7	63.6	2	18.2

Note: Data were from 11 students who submitted their self-evaluation

DISCUSSION

The reading comprehension problems are generally of cognitive and affective origin, with all participants pointing to inadequate vocabulary as their most challenging. According to the National Institute of Child Health and Human Development (2000), vocabulary plays a critical role in comprehension. Comprehension entails constructing meaning while interacting with text (Courtney and Montano, 2006). This mostly explains why students expressed reading difficulty following articles 1 and 2 for their lack of vocabulary, encountering new and technical terms for the first time and experiencing various forms of distractions.

The limited prior knowledge of participants made their attempts to relate to past lessons with the article useless. Distractions like noise, frequent stops during reading, lethargy, discomfort and presentation of article, impaired their focus. Articles not relevant to participants also increased the time taken to complete reading. Comprehension is not only a cognitive process but a function of the affective as well. This is consistent with what Israel *et al.,* (2005) said of metacognitive experiences to consist of any cognitive or affective experiences that accompany and pertain to any intellectual task, such as reading. The participants' reading behaviors crucial or insignificant to their reading comprehension problems vary from one participant to another. Some highlighted that reading aloud helps while others find it disturbing. Some have a preference for a particular reading position.

The same can be said of reading behaviors like writing questions or appreciating pictures in the article which participants admitted were contributory to comprehension. Reading strategies included consulting the dictionary, re-reading, note taking or a combination of these. A study by Wade *et al.* (1990) involving 67 college volunteers who read a 15-page passage at the 11th grade level was followed by a recall test. Fourteen strategies were identified and classified into three types; note taking tactics, mental tactics and reading tactics. Note taking tactics included highlighting, underlining, circling, copying key words, phrases or sentences, outlining or diagramming. Mental tactics included imaging, relating information to background knowledge and reading tactics included skimming and re-reading (Cubukcu, 2008). Hence, reading comprehension requires good vocabulary, background knowledge, and strategic readers—which in this study were uncommon among the participants.

A review of literature in reading and metacognition showed that successful comprehension does not happen automatically (Cubukcu, 2008). It depends on directed cognitive effort, known as metacognitive processing, which as Cubukcu (2008) describes, consists of knowledge about and regulation of cognitive processing. Strategies which are "procedural, purposeful, effortful, willful, essential, and facilitative in nature" with "the reader purposefully or intentionally invoking those strategies" are expressions of metacognitive processing that occur during reading (Alexander and Jetton, 2000). This leads to the question of whether metacognition did improve the reading processes or strategies and reading comprehension among biology students in this study. The present study does not quantitatively establish how successful metacognition was at improving reading comprehension. However, metacognition as evidenced by students' reports, did develop their ability to monitor their strengths and weaknesses and the development of the self-monitoring process. Metacognitive knowledge about individual cognitive strengths and weaknesses, besides the process of active mediation, positively affects a student's ability to accurately monitor text comprehension (Flavell, 1979; Schraw & Dennison, 1994; Kuhn, 2000).

Metacognition is crucial in strategic reading as it emphasizes the readers' active participation. It is diagnostic of their comprehension problems, behaviors and strategies and offers an alternative to traditional methods of teaching. Therefore, this study proved explicit instruction involving metacognition in improving reading comprehension was useful. When metacognitive strategies for comprehending all text are explicitly taught, comprehension improves (Eilers and Pinkley, 2006).

Despite the small number of participants involved, the findings that metacognitionshowed a significant and valuable tool in advancing reading comprehension among biology students cannot be undermined. This is crucial not only in advancing a common learning outcome such as reading comprehension but also in making metacognition or reflective thinking as an integral part of developing critical thinking among students. This has pedagogical implication whereby using metacognition can be an alternative to traditional teaching methods. Students learnt strategies to reading comprehension such as re-reading but it is not common to learn self-monitoring of one's reading behaviours and factors impeding reading comprehension. A study to find out if participants' vocabulary improves and a monitoring their comprehension in specific academic area other than Biology could be explored.

REFERENCES

Abell, S. (2009). Thinking about thinking in science class. Science and Children. February, p. 56–57.

Allen, K. D & Hancock, T. E. (2008). Reading comprehension improvement with individualized cognitive profiles and metacognition. Literacy Research and Instruction. 47(2), 124–139.

Boulware-Gooden, R., Carreker, S., Thornhill, A., Joshi, R. M. (2007). Instruction of metacognitive strategies enhances reading comprehension and vocabulary achievement of third-grade students. The Reading Teacher. 61(1) pp. 70–77.

Courtney, A. M. & Montano, M. (2006). Teaching comprehension from the start: one first grade classroom. Young Children. 61(2) pp. 68–74.

Cubukcu, F. (2008). Enhancing vocabulary development and reading comprehension through metacognitive strategies. Issues in Educational Research. 18(1), pp. 1–11.

Eilers, L. H. & Pinkley, C. (2006). Metacognitive strategies help students to comprehend all text. Reading Improvement. 43(1), pp. 13–29.

Hobson, E. (2008). The role of metacognition in teaching reading comprehension. Metacognition in teaching.htm. Date Retrieved. May 26, 2010.

Israel, S. E., Bauserman, K. L. & Block, C.C. (2005). Metacognitve assessment strategies. Thinking Classroom. 6(2), pp. 21–28.

Joseph, N. (2006). Strategies for success: Teaching metacognitive skills to adolescent learners. New England Reading Association Journal. 42(1), pp. 33–39.

Kuhn, D. & Dean, D. Jr (2004). Metacognition: A bridge between cognitive psychology and educational practice. Theory and Practice. 43(4), pp. 268–273.

Lei, S. A, Rhinehart, P. J., Howard, H.A & Cho, J.K. (2010). Strategies for improving reading comprehension among college students. Reading Improvement. 47(1), pp. 30–42.

Partosa, J. (2009). Use of models among biology majors: implications for critical thinking development. Unpublished work. pp. 1–33.

APPENDIX A. THE READING SURVEY (ADOPTED FROM JOSEPH, 2006)

1. How much time did you spend on pre-reading? _____ minutes
2. How much time did you spend on the reading assignment? _____ minutes
3. Rate your comprehension of the reading: Very Good = 10 Average = 5 Poor = 1
4. Rate your enjoyment of the reading: Very enjoyable = 10 Average = 5 Little enjoyment = 1
5. Rate the effort you devoted to the reading: Maximum = 10 Average = 5 Poor = 1
6. Were you confused by anything you read? _____ What did you do when you became confused?
7. When you were reading, did you form pictures in your mind?
8. Did you write down any questions or mark any passages when you were reading?
9. Did you stop when reading to think about what the author was saying?
10. Did you make connections between something from the reading and ideas from class discussions?
11. Did you make connections between something from the reading and an experience in your own life?

Note: For items 3–5, refer to the rubrics below:

On Comprehension:

Very Good – No difficulty encountered in reading, there was facility of terms and little, if any, distraction occurred.

Average – Some parts of the article were difficult to follow, most terms were new and occasional distractions occurred.

Poor – For the most part, the article was difficult, terms are generally hard to understand and little, if any, consideration was made on student's background.

On Enjoyment:

Very Enjoyable – Article was very interesting, relevant and presentation was clear and simple. Little, if any, negative feelings was experienced.

Average – Article was interesting, relevant and presentation was technical and difficult to follow at times. Some feelings of frustration, dislike or boredom were felt at some points while reading.

Little Enjoyment – Article was boring, irrelevant and the entire presentation was technical and boring. Reading was dragging than it was fun.

On Effort:

Maximum Effort – I observed the guidelines in accomplishing my reading assignment. Despite the difficulty of the text, I tried my best to understand it by looking up the meaning of new terms or terms I had difficulty understanding. I recalled some lessons in the past which I thought could help me understand the text.

Average – I skipped some guidelines in accomplishing my reading assignment. On some occasions, I looked for the meaning of terms or tried to recall some past lessons.

Poor – I read the article for the sake of reading without care for understanding it. I found the task boring and taking up too much of my time.

For items 6–11, please elaborate or describe your answer further. Do not stop with answering yes or no.

Jocelyn D. Partosa
Ateneo de Zamboanga University, Zamboanga City, Philippines
ojdpartosa@yahoo.com

MARIA CRISTINA A. BORDALLO

9. DE LA SALLE-COLLEGE OF SAINT BENILDE IN THE PHILIPPINES: MAKING A DIFFERENCE IN SUSTAINABLE DEVELOPMENT

ABSTRACT

This paper examines and describes students' learning of sustainable development in De La Salle-College of Saint Benilde, Philippines. As part of their Environmental Chemistry course, students engaged in projects that will help reduce global warming. The two projects highlighted are tree-planting and energy conservation. Students would help reduce the amount of carbon dioxide in the atmosphere by planting seeds into small bags to develop into seedlings. Seedlings would then be transplanted to selected sites. Students also learned the ecological and economic importance of the species they planted. The goal of the tree-planting project: Green for LIFE: One Million Trees and Beyond is to plant and maintain one million trees by the year 2011. Energy conservation is another project students carried out in their own households. Students monitored their home electricity consumption at the start of school term and recorded a list of appliances which consumed electricity. Thereafter, they involved and encouraged other members of their households to conserve electricity. Students compared electric consumption and bill before and after the school term to evaluate the effectiveness of their energy conservation measures. The energy conservation project resulted in a total savings of 1883 kilowatt-hours of energy, or a 27% reduction in electricity consumption during the period.

KEYWORDS

Education For Sustainable Development, Global Warming, Tree-Planting, Energy Conservation

INTRODUCTION

"Sustainable development seeks to meet the needs of the present without compromising those of future generations... Education for sustainable development aims to help people develop the attitude, skills and knowledge to make informed decisions for the benefit of themselves and others, now and in the future, and to act upon these decisions." (UNESCO, 2010). To educate students in sustainable development, recycling programs, waste segregation and tree-planting activities in schools are insufficient. Breiting (2009) stated these initiatives are valuable for learning only if they are planned as student projects.

Mijung Kim and C. H. Diong (Eds.), Biology Education for Social and Sustainable Development, 97–100.

At De La Salle-College of Saint Benilde (DLS-CSB), the concept of education for sustainable development is embedded in its educational philosophy which states that "awareness of environmental concerns, service to the community, and concern for the common good" are believed to be integral components of education. One of the core values expected of graduates is social responsibility. Students at the DLS-CSB enroll in Environmental Chemistry and Ecology courses as part of their general education. These courses aim to promote students' awareness in environmental problems and issues by determining the causes and effects of the problem and proposing solutions. One example of the environmental problems discussed in the Environmental Chemistry course is global warming. Students learn that greenhouse gases such as carbon dioxide trap heat that results in increased global temperatures. In addition, they learn that plants remove carbon dioxide from the atmosphere during photosynthesis. Students would eventually identify tree-planting and energy conservation as two ways to reduce global warming.

This paper examines and describes the learning of sustainable development as part of the curriculum in the Environmental Chemistry course at DLS-CSB and engages students in projects that will help reduce global warming. The two projects highlighted in the paper are tree-planting and energy conservation.

TREE-PLANTING PROJECT: ONE MILLION TREES AND BEYOND

The Green for LIFE: One Million Trees and Beyond is a project by the Lasallian Family through the Lasallian Institute for the Environment (LIFE). Launched in September 2006, the project aims to plant and nurture one million native trees by the year 2011. It is supported by funds contributed by business and civic organizations, individuals and grants. Seedling preparation, actual planting and nurturing are done by volunteers. As of August 2010, 745,374 seedlings have been planted in over 40 sites all over the Philippines (Lasallian Institute for the Environment, 2009).

On August 21, 2010, students in Environmental Chemistry joined the One Million Trees and Beyond project as volunteers. Poor weather conditions at the time prevented them from doing the actual tree-planting activity on site. Instead, the students planted seeds in small bags. Sixty-five students prepared a total of 550 small bags (Figures 1a, b). These would be transported and transplanted at the site when the seedlings grow. The actual planting on site would be done at the end of the rainy season, usually at the end of the year to first quarter of the following year.

Most students had not planted seeds before. Besides knowing the role of plants in global warming, students also learned the medicinal properties of *Bauhinia malabarica* which they planted. They expressed satisfaction of helping the environment in a simple way. Furthermore, they realized their responsibility to protect the environment for future generations. The statements typify the reflections of the students: we learned experientially that planting trees was planting life for future generations; we are proud to be able to do something meaningful to help the environment. Besides the sense of accomplishment and social responsibility, the students also learnt the value of cooperation and teamwork.

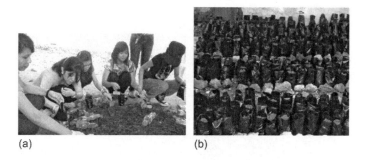

(a)   (b)

Figure1. (a) An improvised shovel made from plastic bottles was used to fill the plastic bag with soil, (b) A total of 550 bags of soil with seeds were prepared by the volunteers.

ENERGY CONSERVATION PROJECT

Energy conservation project was another project as part of Environmental Chemistry students to help reduce carbon dioxide emissions. Fifteen students participated in this project. Before the start of the one-month project, students recorded their electricity consumption in kilowatt-hours. During the month, students practiced energy conservation measures. For example, reducing the use of electrical appliances, unplugging appliances that were not being used and, posting reminders to members of the household to conserve energy. At the end of the month, students presented their electricity bills to show a reduction in the amount of electricity consumed. The energy conservation practices implemented in the fifteen households resulted in a total savings of 1,883 kilowatt-hours of electricity (Table 1). This represents a reduction in electrical consumption by 27% in that month. Reducing energy consumption would decrease carbon dioxide emissions and reduce global warming.

Other positive outcomes are reported. Energy conservation measures require students and members of the household to adopt good habits and a healthier lifestyle such as engaging in reading and sports instead of using the computer and television for hours. This project showed the significance of energy conservation and highlighted the importance of students and members of their households to maintain lower electrical consumption to reduce global warming.

CONCLUSION

Education is a powerful tool to achieve sustainable development. At the De La Salle-College of Saint Benilde, students take simple but concrete actions that help in the reduction of carbon dioxide, a greenhouse gas that leads to global warming. As part of their Environmental Chemistry course at De La Salle-College of Saint Benilde, engaging students in tree-planting activities and energy conservation gives them a sense of fulfillment in knowing that their actions will go a long way towards creating a sustainable environment. The positive feedback from these experiences shall inspire students to continue their actions and make a difference in the environment not only for the present, but also for the future generations.

Table 1. Electrical Consumption in fifteen households Before and After Energy
Conservation Measures

| Household | Electricity Consumption (kwh) | | Savings (kwh) | % Reduction |
	Before Conservation	After Conservation		
1	37	33	4	11
2	255	245	10	4
3	271	253	18	7
4	271	239	32	12
5	323	318	5	2
6	393	162	231	59
7	404	335	69	17
8	492	60	432	88
9	528	379	149	28
10	535	453	82	15
11	541	462	79	15
12	607	326	281	46
13	669	407	262	39
14	750	627	123	16
15	840	734	106	13
TOTAL	6916	5033	1883	27

ACKNOWLEDGEMENTS

I wish to thank Ms. Analyn Morales, Mr. Maynard Tamayo and Mr. Mitchel Osa for coordinating the seed-planting activity.

REFERENCES

Breiting, S. (2009, June 29). Education for sustainable education for child development and schools. Retrieved from http://educationforsustainabledevelopment.com/blog/?p=10

De La Salle-College of Saint Benilde. (2010). Student handbook. Manila: De La Salle-College of Saint Benilde. Lasallian Institute for the Environment. (2009). Green for life: One million trees & beyond. Retrieved from http://1milliontreesandbeyond.com/one/index.php?option=com_content&view=frontpage&Itemid=1

UNESCO (2010). Education for sustainable development. Retrieved from http://www.unesco.org/en/esd/).

Maria Cristina A. Bordallo
De La Salle-College of Saint Benilde
2544 Taft Avenue, Manila, Philippines 1004
tinbordallo@yahoo.com

VIVIAN S. TOLENTINO, MILAROSA L. LIBREA, MARK JOSEPH
SIBAL, EMMANUEL ESPINEDA AND WENDEL T. MARCELO

10. OIL PRODUCING PLANTS AS ALTERNATIVE SOURCE OF ENERGY FOR SUSTAINABLE DEVELOPMENT

ABSTRACT

Five species of plants were identified for their oil producing characteristics in the Philippines. They are *Pittosporum resiniferum Hemsl.*, *Jatropha curcas* L. *Calophyllum inophyllum*, *Pongamia pinnata*, and *Moringa oleifera*. The distribution and anatomical characterization of oil cells were also identified. This study reports on the identification, distribution and location of oil cells in the plant which may lead to cost efficient extraction of oils, and the isolation of intact oil cells highly valuable as alternative sources of energy and self-sustainability in the Philippines.

KEYWORDS

Oil-Producing Plants, Oil Cells, Philippines, Energy Source

INTRODUCTION

According to *Oil and Gas Journal* (OGJ), the Philippines had 138 million barrels of proven oil reserves in January 2006. The country's oil production is limited, averaging just over 25,000 barrels per day (bbl/d) during the first nine months of 2006. Between 1996 and 2000, the Philippines had no oil production. During the last several years, production has increased primarily due to the development of new offshore deepwater oil deposits. However, with human population projected to reach 120 million by 2020 (UN, 1996), the current levels of oil production is insufficient to meet oil demands.

The Philippines has alternative sources of energy. Hydroelectric sources made up approximately 2,900 MW of the Philippines' installed electricity generation capacity, or 19 percent of the total in 2004. But the country has not seen a significant expansion in hydroelectric capacity during the last two decades (Energy Information Agency, 2004). Agriculture, including forestry and fisheries, plays a dominant role in the Philippine economy. About 70% of the Philippine population is involved in agriculture and grows cash crops, including coconut, sugarcane and bananas. There is agricultural land available

Mijung Kim and C. H. Diong (Eds.), Biology Education for Social and Sustainable Development, 101–104.

to high oil-yielding plants of economic importance as alternative sources of energy for self-sustainability of this resource. The purpose of this study is to characterize the oil cells and identify the tissue locations of the oil-producing plants.

MATERIALS AND METHODS

Different histological methods such as paraffin technique were used to section tissues of the fruits and seeds. Histochemical tests on fresh and processed tissues were performed using different lipohylic stains, such as Sudan dyes and Nile Blue to test for the presence of oils in the oil cells. Light, scanning and transmission electron microscopy were used for anatomical descriptions.

RESULTS AND DISCUSSION

Five species of plants were identified for oil producing characteristics in the Philippines. They are *Moringa oleifera* (Moringaceae), *Jatropha curcas* (Euphorbiaceae), *Pongamia pinnata* (Fabaceae), *Pittosporum resiniferum* Hemsl. (Pittosporaceae) and *Calophyllum inophyllum* (Calophyllaceae). The distribution and anatomical characterization of oil cells were also identified.

In *M. oleifera*, the middle-aged and mature embryos of the seeds had thick walled oil cells (Figure 1). Oil cells are present in the seeds of *Jatropha curcas*, but they occur in the endosperm. Oil cells were also present in middle-aged and mature seeds of *Jatropha curcas*. These cells occur as either individual thick-walled cells of spherical shape or as clusters of two to three cells. In *J. curcas*, the endosperm of middle-aged and mature fruits showed oil cavities and thick-walled tripartite oil cells.

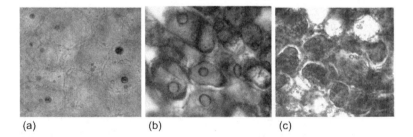

(a)   (b)   (c)

Figure 1. Accumulation of oil droplets in parenchyma cells of Moringa oleifera after histochemical test with Sudan IV. (a): cross-section of an embryo from a middle-aged fruit (400x); (b) and (c): cross-section of an embryo from and green mature fruit (400X).

In *Pongamia pinnata*, two types of oil containing cells were identified. One is an irregularly shaped parenchyma cell and the other, a relatively large idioblastic oil cell in the cotyledons of the seed (Figure 2). In contrast, only oil containing parenchyma cells were observed in *C. inophyllum.*

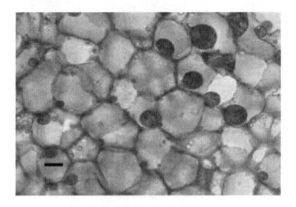

Figure 2. Pongamia pinnata seed section showing ordinary parenchyma cells with single oil droplets in each cell. Scale ‒ 20 μm.

In *P. pinnata*, the cotyledons of all ages showed irregularly-shaped parenchyma cells with oils and large idioblastic oil cells. Cotyledons of *C. inophyllum* of all ages showed ordinary parenchyma cells with oils.

The mesocarp of mature fruits of *P. resiniferum* Hemsl showed tabular-shaped epithelial cells surrounding the resin duct. The resin ducts, the source of the fruit oils, are most abundant and fully developed in the mesocarp of the fruit of *P. resiniferum.* The resin duct in the mesocarp of the fruit is lined with tabular shaped epithelial cells accompanied by vascular tissues (Tolentino *et al.*, 2002). Histochemical tests for the presence of oils in all of the aforementioned plants tested positive with Sudan dyes and Nile blue.

CONCLUSION

The study showed that the five oil-producing plants, *Moringa oleifera, Jatropha curcas, Pongamia pinnata, Pittosporum resiniferum* Hemsl., and *Calophyllum inophyllum* can potentially offer an alternative source of energy to further diversify the energy needs in the Philippines. Studies on the developmental anatomy and distribution of the oil cells in different plant structures are essential to enable a more efficient and cost effective method of extracting the oils. Further research can be done on the extraction of whole intact oil cells. The next step would be to optimize the growth and production of these oil-producing plant species in order to harvest maximum oil yield annually. Understanding the biology and physiology of the oil producing, such as their life span, susceptibility to diseases would also be important. A more immediate step in realizing the potential of these plants as an alternative source of energy would be to persuade farmers to grow the oil-producing plants, which may take a longer time to grow, over the economically lucrative cash crops, such as sugar cane and bananas.

REFERENCES

Ang, R. P., Gonzalez, C.T., Liwag, E. C., Santos, B. S., Vistro-Yu, C. P. (2001). Elements of Student Centered Learning.Office of Research and Publications, Loyola Schools, Ateneo de Manila University.

Tolentino, V. S. & Zamora, P. M. (2002). Morpho-Anatomy of the Fruit of Pittosporum resiniferum Hemsl.(Petroleum Nut). *The Philippine Scientist. 39,* 48–55.

Energy Information Agency. "Energy profile of Philippines". In: Encyclopedia of Earth. Eds. Cutler J. Cleveland (Washington, D.C.: Environmental Information Coalition, National Council for Science and the Environment).

Espineda, E. R. & Marcelo, W. T. (2008). Developmental anatomy and Histochemistry of Oil Containing Cells in the Seed of Pongamia pinnata (L.) Merr.and Calophyllum inophyllum (L). B. S. Thesis, Biology, Ateneo de Manila University, Loyola Schools, Quezon City, Philippines.

Librea, M. L. (2008). Anatomical Characterization of oil Cells and Oil Cavity in the Fruit and Seed of Jatropha curcas L. M/S. Thesis. Biology, Ateneo de Manila University, Loyola Schools, Quezon City, Philippines.

2006. Oil and Gas Journals. Tulsa. Ok.

Sibal, M. J. (2010). Developmental Morpho-Anatomy of the Oil Cells of Moringa oleifera Lam. And its Implications to the Fruit, Seed and Embryo. B. S. Thesis, Biology, Ateneo de Manila University, Loyola Schools, Quezon City, Philippines.

United Nations. (1993). World Population Prospects. New York.

Vivian S. Tolentino, Mark Joseph Sibal, Emmanuel Espineda, Wendel T. Marcelo
Department of Biology, Ateneo de Manila University,
Loyola Schools, Katipunan Road, Loyola Heights 1108, Quezon City, Philippines,
Email: vtolentino2001@yahoo.com

Milarosa L. Librea
Ateneo High School, Ateneo de Manila University, Katipunan Road,
Loyola Heights, 1108, Quezon City, Philippines

JOSEFINO R. CASTILLO

11. RESEARCH AS AN INTEGRAL COMPONENT OF BIOLOGY EDUCATION IN PHILIPPINE SCHOOLS

ABSTRACT

This paper examines the progress of Biology education in the Philippines over two decades. A lack of laboratory equipment and funds were some factors students had to contend with. The study highlights current Philippine colleges and universities which place a high premium on performance rating measured in terms of outputs in academic and professional organizations. One example was the University of Santo Tomas which had integrated research into the curriculum. Under-graduate students are required to undertake experimental research under the supervision of faculty members and to present the research work to a panel, as a requirement for graduation. Most studies focus on the testing medicinal plants against parasites, and human diseases, such as diabetes, hypertension, and cancer. Other fields for student project work include allergy, immunology, molecular systematics, and bioinformatics. Insufficient number of animal models and small sample size for a statistically robust research are factors impeding the progress and development of research and development and Biology education in the country.

KEYWORDS

Animal Models, Curriculum, Integration, Research Project, Supervision

INTRODUCTION

In the 1950s, Philippines enjoyed the distinction of being second only to Japan in East Asia in terms of socio-economic and science and technology (S&T) development. More than 50 years later, the country has remained underdeveloped scientifically, technologically and economically, overtaken by its East Asian neighbors with the exception of Vietnam, Myanmar, Laos and Cambodia. According to Posadas (2009), in his analysis of the low performance in S&T development, he outlines the most important international measure of S&T supply subsystem including (i) the country's number of full-time equivalent (FTE) researchers per million population, and (ii) the country's world share of internationally recognized or ISI publications. In the most recent UNESCO (2010) report, the Philippines has only 81 FTE researchers per million of its population in

Mijung Kim and C. H. Diong (Eds.), Biology Education for Social and Sustainable Development, 105–112.

2005. It has dropped from 155 FTE per million in the 1990s. This was below the 380 FTE target set by the UN for developing countries in 1980. In terms of ISI publications, Philippines was ahead in the number of publications in the 1980s but now ranks behind Indonesia and Vietnam (Figure 1a).

Lacanilao (2009) pointed out that the Philippines has the lowest scientific productivity and growth rate. The country has an education policy and development programmes in science. However, the quality of information disseminated through resources such as extension materials, books, and review articles may affect the desired outcomes of science education. This will in turn affect the country's state of scientific development. To ensure the quality of educational materials and resources, Lacanilao emphasized the need for an increase of ISI publications, especially in areas of scientific research.

Drastic measures in educational reforms on Philippines' research progress have to be initiated immediately to catch up with other East Asia countries. There are several neighbour-models to choose from. A landmark example of enriching research capabilities is seen in China where research is greatly emphasized by the government in the form of the growth in the grants-in-aid system, international collaborations, growth of high-tech enterprises, cutting-edge facilities and succession training of young scientists to replace older scientists (Mervis, 1995; Mervis and Kinoshita, 1995). If these models could be applied to the Philippine setting, this could provide the impetus to boost S&T capabilities and jumpstart the lethargic state of science and technology development.

BIOLOGY EDUCATION IN PHILIPPINES BEFORE THE 1990'S

Biology students, hampered by the lack of proper equipment and funding, have to resort to research work which are mere compilations of previous work done.

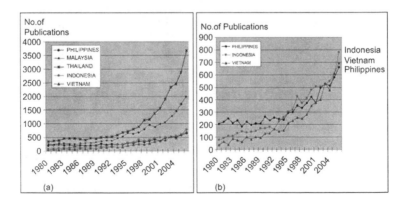

Figure 1(a). Publications of five ASEAN countries, (b) Close up of the last three, Philippines, Indonesia, and Vietnam. Note that the Philippines was ahead of Indonesia and Vietnam from 1980, but was last in 2006. (Posadas, 2009).

In short, students wrote reviews instead of doing original research. No scientific data were collected, no progress was made and no breakthroughs in research developments occurred. These factors in part explain the steady decline in the country's research and scientific publications. Where experiments were conducted, the available apparatus were limited to ordinary glassware and culture media. In addition, students rushed to complete college to start a living. Colleges and universities had to cut short their courses resulting in the truncation of 5-year college courses to a compact 4-year course.

BIOLOGY EDUCATION IN PHILIPPINES IN THE 1990'S AND BEYOND

Educational institutions in the Philippines are well aware of the need to address the dismal performance of their graduates in the international arena. This is the reason for a clamor to increase the number of years spent in elementary and high school from 10 to 12 in a bid to increase global competitiveness of graduates. This incurred additional expenses for the government and parents who are hard-pressed to pay for their children's tuition.

Import liberalization and lower taxes imposed on educational institutions' new equipment and apparatus boosted research capabilities in Philippine schools. Figure 2 shows government institutions like the Department of Science and Technology (DOST) were able to allocate funds for research through many scholarship programs, from basic research, to research on marine and aquatic resources, agriculture, advanced science and technology, health, industry and energy through its different councils (Yumul, 2010). Furthermore, DOST facilitates students' applications to secure foreign scholarships, notably the Japan Society for the Promotion of Science and the Japan International Cooperation Agency.

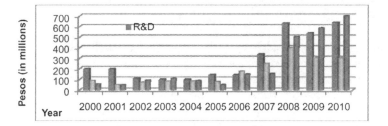

Figure 2. Department of Science and Technology (DOST) – Grant-in-Aid Budget (In million Php) for Research and Development (R&D), Technology Transfer, and S&T HRD and Services.

International organizations are promoting research in the region. The UNESCO Inter-University Post-Graduate Course in Biotechnology was offered by Osaka University for over three years until 2007 and was held in four different cities this year. Bangkok, Hanoi, Manila, and Yogyakarta were chosen in view of the large number of alumni. The objective is to collect inputs from biotechnology experts in the region towards the design of a new regional biotechnology program that would emphasize more strongly the role of biotechnology as a valuable tool for addressing sustainable development issues (UNESCO, 2010).

BIOLOGY EDUCATION IN PHILIPPINES: THE UNIVERSITY OF SANTO TOMAS (UST) EXPERIENCE

At the University of Santo Tomas (UST), the academic year consists of two semesters and a 2-month summer break. Biology Research is taken as a 3-unit course spread over three semesters at 1-unit per semester starting in the students' third year second semester and culminating in the second semester of his senior year. The course was initially conceived as a seminar-style research orientation for students to: (i) be aware of the current topics in biology, (ii) complete an assignment on a given topic, and (iii) present the research work in class to a panel of at least three faculty members with expertise in the field of interest. In the 1990s, the student projects centered mostly on antimicrobial and anti-helminthic properties of medicinal plants, with a few projects on genetics. With an increasing number of students and faculty members of various disciplines, the research interests have since expanded.

At present, students in their third year are required to think of an experimental study that can be done within one school year, taking into consideration the facilities available in the University and other research institutions where support services are available. Two faculty members handle each section enrolled in the course. Since there are more than 200 senior Biology students per academic year, it is not feasible for individual research. During the summer break, students are assigned in groups with approved topics and an academic adviser knowledgeable in the field of study. Research work commence as soon as an adviser is appointed.

RESEARCH PROJECTS

Students are allowed to select their preferred field of study when equipment and reagents can be purchased from local sources. A Student Research Laboratory is designated for their experimental setup, if necessary. Thus far, proposed studies cover a wide array of fields from biodiversity, bioremediation to freshwater biology. Most common topics center on testing medicinal plants for anti-helminthic, antidiabetic, anti-angiogenic, or anti-tumorigenic activity. With the purchase of new attachments for the department's PowerLab® unit, students can now measure the effects of certain substances on muscle contraction, nerve conduction velocity and hypertension in animal models, using frogs or rats. Its molecular biology laboratory is likewise provided with electrophoresis and PCR equipment for DNA/RNA isolation, purification and amplification. DNA sequencing is outsourced to other institutions. Field work, whenever necessary, is allowed only if accompanied by the faculty adviser.

The existence of a multidisciplinary collaborative research endeavor at the UST – Research Center for the Natural Sciences provides students with specialized laboratories and possible funding. The Medical Biotechnology section undertakes diagnostic procedures for allergy, cancer and asthma. It is also involved in development of assays. The Environmental Biotechnology section does bioremediation/phytoremediation studies, The Aquaculture Biotechnology section is primarily involved in host-pathogen interaction in shrimps, while the Molecular Plant Systematics group uses molecular techniques to establish phylogenetic positions of various plant families, genera and species (Nonato, 2010).

LIMITATIONS OF RESEARCH PROJECTS

The lack of test organisms is one of the primary limitations faced by the student–researchers. Only pure-bred rats (one strain) and mice (two strains) can be secured either from two to three government research institutions or from a private university albeit at a higher price. In addition, disease models are not available and had to be sourced from as far as Taiwan. Student-researchers resort to inducing disease-related conditions using pancreatic beta-cell destroying alloxan or streptozotocin to induce diabetes, or carcinogens using MNU or DMBA to induce cancer, or the more invasive renal stenosis to produce hypertensive rats.

The secondary limitation comes from the Institutional Animal Care and Use Committee under the UST which ensures humane treatment of animals in all research done by members of the academic community. It is authorized by the Department of Agriculture – Bureau of Animal Industry which mandates a maximum of three test animals per treatment especially for invasive procedures. The UST-IACUC has managed to convince the BAI that the number is statistically unacceptable. Eventually, they settled for six animals. This still poses a large problem for Philippine researchers as many international journals require a statistically larger sample size.

There was no suitable venue for oral or poster presentations. Information gathered or generated by more than 50 groups per academic year are stored away in the shelves. The UST College of Science, in recent years, organized a poster contest for its students during its College Week celebrations. UST–RCNS similarly conducts a University–wide S&T Research Colloquium for undergraduate students at the end of each academic year to improve the quality of the student research work through peer review.

ACADEMIC AND PROFESSIONAL ORGANIZATIONS HEED THE CALL

There is a need for student-researchers to present their research data. It is now easier for students to gain access to conferences held at the end of the school year or summer vacation. Such conferences are also useful to recruit new researchers. The following are research papers, articles or education articles published in a variety of research fields. Professional organizations in other fields of science now collaborates with student-researchers to provide more research experience and exposure, an increased avenue for information dissemination and a greater chance of peer review for most current S&T development in the country.

BIOTA.

Established in 1966, the *Biology Teachers' Association of the Philippines, Inc.* counts among its members the biology teachers from both secondary and tertiary level throughout the country. Students are allowed to participate in the Young Biologists' Forum (YBF) wherein selected student researches from participating schools compete for top honors. Peer-reviewed articles are published in the *Philippine Biota,* the official publication of the BIOTA – Philippines.

PSBMB.

Formerly known as the Philippine Biochemistry Society (PBS) established in August 1973 by a group of biochemistry educators to foster the development of biochemistry in the country, the *Philippine Society for Biochemistry and Molecular Biology* launched the *Young Scientists' Forum* (YSF) in 1995 as a competition for outstanding undergraduate student research work.

NPSP.

In honor of National Scientist Dr. Alfredo C. Santos who pioneered in phytochemistry in the Philippines, the *Natural Products Society of the Philippines* initiated the Dr. Alfredo C. Santos Lecture on Natural Products to honor him and continue his mission of promoting natural products research. Now on its 20th year, the NPSP invites young researchers (35 years old and below) to submit papers for oral presentation. As an incentive, the NPSP waives the registration fee of selected participants.

ASBP.

The *Association of Systematic Biologists of the Philippines* was founded in 1982, put up its official publication, the *ASBP Communication,* 2 years after its inception but hibernated in the late 90s. It was revived on 31 May 2003 with its official publication relaunched in 2007 as the *Philippine Journal of Systematic Biology* that went online two years after. It has since been listed in the *Thomson Reuters Master Journal List.* Students doing research on biodiversity, conservation and systematic are invited to present their papers either orally or as posters in its annual convention every May.

PSCB.

The *Philippine Society for Cell Biology*, officially organized in 2008, was conceived with the vision of providing avenues for sharing results of scholarly work on cell biology done locally or abroad by Filipino scientists and researchers. Students doing research on cell biology and physiology are highly encouraged to participate.

NIMBUS.

The *Network for Integrative Multidisciplinary Bioinformatics Utilization Strategies*, intended to promote the science of bioinformatics in the Philippines, was initiated in 2003. Bioinformatics practitioners from the academe and industry gather on October of every year. Students get to present their work during the conference.

IMPACT ON QUALITY OF EDUCATION

The Department of Biological Sciences in UST was recently awarded the Center of Excellence in Biology by the Commission on Higher Education. UST was cited among others as a strong research foundation. This honor is enjoyed by only four other universities in the Philippines, two units of a state university, a second state university and one sectarian school. In addition, UST was ranked in the top 200 universities in Asia with only four Universities from Philippines.

In conclusion, the slow progress and development of research and development (R&D) and education promoting science as a research pillar of the country is the result of a number of infrastructural and funding issues the country is facing. The government, its people and the academia must co-operate to address pressing issues in the country before proceeding to enhance the research capabilities of students. It is with hope that rapid progress in R&D will drive the economy of Philippines to catch up with other countries in Asia.

REFERENCES

Lacanilao, Flor. (2009). "*Doing research for development.*" Keynote address at the 27th Meeting of the Association of Systematic Biologists of the Philippines, National Museum, Manila, 29–30 May 2009. Available at:

Mervis, Jeffrey, (1995). "Science Policy: The Long March to Topnotch Science". *Science, 270*(5239), 1134–1137.

Mervis, Jeffrey & June Kinoshita. (1995). "Science in China: a great leap forward." *Science, 270,* 1131.

Nonato, Maribel G. (2010). "Biotechnology Research at the University of Santo Tomas." Proceedings of the UNESCO Manila Conference on Capacity – Building in Life Science, 6 February 2010, Manila, Philippines.

Posadas, Roger D. (2009). "Scientific and technological capabilities and economic catch-up," *Philippine Management Review, 16,* 1–14.

UNDP Human development report (2009). "Overcoming barriers: Human mobility and development". UNDP, New York.

UNESCO. (2010). Proceedings of the UNESCO Manila Conference on Capacity – Building in Life Science, 6 February 2010, Manila, Philippines.

UNESCO Institute for Statistics (2010). Accessed on September 1, 2010 at: http://stats.uis.unesco.org/unesco/reportfolders/reportfolders.aspx

Yumul, Graciano P. Jr., (2010). "DOST Research and Development Programs: Tapping the Resources," Symposium held at the University of Santo Tomas, July 16, 2010.

J. R. CASTILLO

Josefino R. Castillo
Department of Biological Sciences, College of Science
University of Santo Tomas
Manila, Philippines
jrcast327@yahoo.com

NENITA M. DAYRIT

12. BIOLOGY FOR NON-MAJORS AT THE UNIVERSITY OF THE PHILIPPINES DILIMAN EXTENSION PROGRAM IN PAMPANGA (UPDEPP): LEARNING SEXUALLY TRANSMITTED DISEASES MINUS THE SQUIRMS

ABSTRACT

The University of the Philippines pioneered the Revitalized General Education Program (RGEP) to allow students to choose from a menu of General Education courses. One such course is Biology 1– Contemporary Topics in Biology which deals with Reproductive Health and Sexually Transmitted Diseases. Instead of the conventional teaching methods using power point slides and video presentations, the teaching was supplemented with the creativity of students who suggested peer teaching through role play and quizzes. To ensure effective peer teaching, the course professors had to provide guidelines on acceptable behaviors pertaining to subjects like sexuality and STDs. This teaching model provided a highly interactive and engaging learning environment and encouraged teachers and students to be partners in the learning process.

KEYWORDS

Biology, Student Presentations, Role Play, STD, HIV, Extension Program

The Revitalized General Education Program (RGEP) of the University of Philippines Diliman was the university's distinct pioneering undergraduate extension program. Prior to the RGEP, there was the regular General Education Program (GEP) with compulsory courses applicable to all students. Although the new RGEP adapted the old GEP's objectives and framework, the difference between the two lies in the approach. The RGEP allowed students to choose courses that were more relevant to their chosen career paths and their needs and interests.

When RGEP was implemented in the University of the Philippines Diliman Extension Program in Pampanga (UPDEPP), a new course called Biology 1 – Contemporary Topics in Biology (Bio 1 for short) – was introduced under the Science and Technology Domain. A carry-over from the Institute of Biology from the Diliman campus, the course content of the syllabus runs as follows:

Mijung Kim and C. H. Diong (Eds.), Biology Education for Social and Sustainable Development, 113–120.

Course Number: Biology I
Course Title: Contemporary Topics in Biology

EXPLORING LIFE (3 meetings)
Topics: 1.   The Concept of Life
        2.   Manifestations of Life
        3.   Life: Structure, Function and Control
        4.   Methods in the Study of Biology
REPRODUCTION (7 meetings)
Topics: 1.   Asexual and Sexual Reproduction: cloning
        2.   Sex and Diversity of Life
        3.   **Reproductive Health and Sexually Transmitted Diseases**
                 [AIDS, Gonorrhea, Chlamydia, Syphilis, Jock Itch, Yeast, Infection,
                 Hepatitis B., Herpes simplex, Human Papillomavirus, Molluscum,
                 Pubic
                 Lice, Scabies and Trichomoniasis]
        4.   Assisted Reproductive Technology
        4.1.   In vitro Fertilization
        4.2.   Artificial Insemination
        4.3.   Sperm Cryopreservation
        4.4.   Embryo Transfer
        5.   Development and gene action stem, cells, aging
GENETICS (5 meetings)
Topics: 1.   Laws of inheritance
        2.   Patterns of Inheritance
        3.   Genome Projects: Human and Fish
        4.   Familial Diseases and Genetic Counseling
        5.   Gene Technology
        5.1.   Gene Therapy
        5.2.   Genetically Modified Organisms
EXAM I (1 meeting)
EVOLUTION (5 meetings)
Topics: 1.   Concepts of Species
        2.   Mechanisms and Evidence of Evolution
        3.   The Darwninian Theory: Model for Explaining the History and
                 Diversity of Life.
        4.   Scientific Creationism, Punctualism vs. Gradualism
        5.   Human Evolution: Biological and Cultural
        6.   Evolution of Sex
ECOLOGY (5 meetings)
Topics: 1.   Ecosystems: Structure and Processes
        2.   Anthropogenic Impact
        3.   SustainableNatural Resources: Management and Bioremediation
        4.   Biodiversity Conversation
        4.1.   Endangered species
OTHER CURRENT TOPICS (5 meetings)

Cancer Biology
Emerging pathogens and diseases
Biological warfare
Others

EXAM II (1 meeting)

The course turned out to become one of the favorites amongst students. One of the major topics listed, as can be glimpsed from the syllabus, was Reproductive Health and Sexually Transmitted Diseases. Given the current realities in UPDEPP, the offering of Bio 1 was very timely for two reasons: (i) the university is located near the night clubs and bars frequented by male foreigners and Filipinos alike, and (ii) the age bracket (approximately 16–20 yrs) of the students at the tertiary level jibed with their psychological developmental tasks of curiosity about sex. Thus, the knowledge that the students obtain from the course will be most helpful and useful to them.

The course was typically taught with power point slides and video presentations and further supplemented with lecture-discussions. No matter how sophisticated students may think of themselves, the visuals on diseased reproductive organs were repulsive and often induced screams and squirms from the students. Interestingly, the students eventually "demanded" to take over some portions of the lessons, to add variety to the lessons. And that was how they came up with some interesting original learning modes!

Formed into learning groups where the size of a group depends on the number of students in the class, students regaled the class (and their Professors) with the following theater presentations and games.

1) Mr. and Miss STD Beauty Pageant.

A hilariously funny pageant, this was always a "sell-out".
Part I
To the tune of rock and roll, the student actors entered the classroom with their hilariously outrageous costumes and painted faces. They each wore placards bearing the descriptions of the STDs they were representing on them. Then, one by one, they introduced their names. Instead of enticing and charming the audience with their pulchritude, they would try to outdo each other in convincing the audience and the judges how obnoxious and dangerous they are to the human race.
Part II
Each student actor would be called on stage by the emcee for the question and answer session. Through the interactive question and answer session, students would obtain information on how the diseases were contracted and the preventive measures against them. The winners of the role playing skit would be decided by a panel of judges.

Part III

The student actors would do another walk on stage. The winners would be bestowed with ribbons and simple tokens. As usual, the constant winner who got the crown was androgynous Acquired Immune Deficiency Syndrome. (Note: A 45- minute presentation.)

2) Mini-drama Presentation.

A couple was having a discussion in the privacy of the bedroom. The wife complained of some unpleasant symptoms in her reproductive organ and cried with unabated tears blaming her husband's nocturnal activities for her condition. (This scandalous crying always elicited laughters from the audience). The couple then approached a doctor for advice. During the consultation, the doctor explained the symptoms of certain STDs and how preventable they were if some precautions were followed. Hubby swears that he was 'clean'! After 6 months, bedroom scene was repeated. Wife was shown to be very pregnant with a "basketball" belly and the contented hubby beaming with pride. To be more attractive to the audience, roles were played with appropriate attire.

3) Quiz Show

What am I? The class was divided into two groups. In the tradition of "Family Feud", 2 groups of 5 members were each pitted against one another. The group which had the most number of correct answers won. Points were tallied to determine the winner. Simple tokens were awarded to the smarter group. Sample questions were lined up below:

− What is the most deadly virus causing STD?
− Name the 3 types of organisms causing STDs.
− An opportunistic disease caused by AIDS is abbreviated KS. What does KS mean?
− Identify the particular WBC which is the main target of HIV.
− Are pregnant women susceptible to STDs?
− Enumerate at least 7 tips to help prevent STD.
− What are the common symptoms of STD that should immediately alert persons at risk?
− Some STD doctors do not recommend douching for women. Why?
− How is HIV transmitted?
− In syphilis, the earliest symptom is a painless open sore. Where may they appear in the human body?
− Is Penicillin, an old antibiotic, still effective against some STDs?
− Can STDs caused by virus be cured?
− Name some STDs caused by virus.
− Pubic lice or crabs are not only transferable by sexual contact. By what other means could they be passed on?

- What are the treatments for genital warts?
- What STDs are caused by:
- Neisseria sp.
- *Treponema pallidum*
- HIV
- What does ELISA mean?
- Differentiate STI from STD.
- Give the meaning of HAART.
- Name 3 STDs treatable with antibiotics.

4) "Bring Me" Game.

The Emcees would ask the class a series of questions regarding reproductive health. Contestants (the whole class) would write the correct answer in paper provided to them. The first hand to be raised gets to answer the query. A student who gets the most number of correct answers is gifted with a prize. The sample questions of the Game Show can also be applied here.

Variations of these student-initiated leaning methodologies were continuously churned out by students with vivid and wealthy imaginations every semester. Consequently, Biology non-majors always find it interesting and refreshing to take up Bio 1 and be educated with smiles and laughter, minus the squirms.

But here is the caveat. Can teachers trust students to take over some lessons in class to educate their classmates? This is one of the accepted teaching modes called peer teaching. A word of caution though. Before students were given the go ahead to manage the teaching-learning process, they ought to be instructed on the aim and learning outcomes of a particular activity. It must be purposeful and it must have a sense of direction. The objective is to learn the subject matter, concepts, the knowledge and facts as delineated in the syllabus and to foster the development of values which is an integral part of holistic education. Students who are engaged in the aforementioned teaching activities should be instructed on what they can or cannot do and the limits of their instructional activities, without violating proper and acceptable behavior.

In this aspect, the University of the Philippines (UP) learners are trustworthy and can be relied upon to follow closely the professor's instruction on what to accomplish and the extent to which he could alter the lessons to catch the audience's attention. This is an advantage of the UP over the other state colleges and universities, including private learning institutions. The UP learner is the product of an intensive and extensive screening of prequalification entry criteria, of a robust and discriminatory college admission test that attracts over 65,000 high school graduates of which only 12,000 freshmen are selected. UP learners are highly motivated and have shown they are able to deliver good and structured presentations as specified by their professors.

Role play is a teaching technique widely used by teachers to enliven learning. For teachers whose classes follow the learning curve – few above average students and below average students are in the extreme ends of the bell curve with a majority of students, the average ones, in the middle of the curve – the bright ones could be tasked as leaders to organize the learning activity. But can a class of mostly average learners handle such issues like sexuality and STDs? This is where the professor's realistic assessment of his or her learners becomes critical to determine the teaching strategy. It is the "sine qua non" of effective teaching.

How does one evaluate and mark student-initiated learning activities like games, quiz shows, mock pageants, theatrical presentations and other activities? In UP, as in other Philippine tertiary institutions, no particular type of assessment is recommended by the administration but some professors rely heavily on summative evaluation, the final examinations for giving grades or marks to students. However, more professors like the author uses both summative and formative forms of evaluation. For student presentation, the formative type of assessment is suitable and works well. The questions in Table 1 below can help assess the usefulness of student presentations for whole class learning.

Table 1. Suggested list of guide questions and tasks for student presentations

Guide Questions	Suggested Tasks
How effective were the students-performers in the delivery of knowledge relative to the lesson and how adeptly were they absorbed by the student-audience?	Give quizzes to find out the acquisition of knowledge in the next class meeting.
How may a change in behavior be affected by the student-presentation?	Give a reaction paper on an ethical dilemma, e.g. regarding reproduction and STDs. From the answers, the professor will have a basis to reform questionable choices to fit the society's norms. There may be no wrong or right answers, papers will be unmarked, but kept for future reference during consultations.
Which student-presentation, from the point of view of the student-audience was the most effective in the delivery of facts, ideas, concepts and principles and in the acquisition of human values that will give them respectability, dignity and honor?	Hand out pieces of paper where individual students would vote for the presentation they liked best. The class could tally the votes on the board to determine the most favored to the least. The no. of votes could be given corresponding rating scale. This could serve as a guide for the eventual grading of the student presentation.

In conclusion, in the day-to-day classroom interactions between professors and students, the mentor is not always the fountainhead of ideas and concepts for a more vibrant and effective teaching-learning situation. Amazingly, students can be valuable sources of innovative teaching ideas and presenters of the teaching ideas as well. With their enthusiasm, students could change a staid classroom atmosphere into a sparkling arena of fun and laughter for learning. Students can work alongside their busy professors to plan some teaching topics more imaginatively. Student resources should be tapped because they are keen to be involved. This writer could read it from the students' faces when novel ideas enter the student's minds, while, for example, viewing power point presentations of ghastly STD realities: "We love to learn those things from you but we would like to learn it our way." Let them learn it their way under an academic's guidance, and be glad you did as a mark of professionalism in teaching, recognizing that teachers and students are partners in learning.

REFERENCES

Elevazo, Aurelio & Rosita Elevazo, (1995). Philosophy of Philippine Education. Metro Manila: National Book Store, Inc.

Gearheart, Bill R., Mel W. Weighahm & Carol J. Gearheart. The Exceptional Student in the Regular Classroom, 5th Ed. New York: Macmillan Publ. Co.

Joyce, Bruce, Martha Weil & Emily Calhoun, (2000). Models of Teaching, 6th Ed. Needham Needham Hts. MA: Allyn and Bacon.

Letter to Dr. Julieta C. Mallari, Director of UPDEPP, from the Dean of the College of Science and informing Dr. Mallari of the approval to offer Bio 1 Contemporary Topics in Biology in the UPDEPP, November 2002.

McMillan, James H., Von Wergin, (2010). Understanding and Evaluating Educational Research. New Jersey: Pearson Education, Inc.

Merther, Craig A. & C. M. Charles, (2005). Educational Research. USA: Pearson Education, Inc. Polloway, Edward, James R. Patton, James S. Payne & Ruth Anne Payne, 1989. Strategies for Teaching Learners with Special Needs. Ohio: Merrill Publ. Co

Price, Kay, Karna L. Nelson, (2003). Planning Effective Instruction. Belmont, Ca. USA: Thomson Thomson Higher Education

RGEP Introduction

http://www.upd.edu.ph/~ovcaa/rgep/bginfo01.html

4/22/2003

RGEP Framework Arts & Humanities 02

RGEP Framework 03

Science and Technology 04

Permanent Substitution 06

Syllabus of Biology 1, Institute of Biology, College of Science, UP Diliman.

What is the RGEP of UP?

http://www.upd.edu.ph/~ovcaa/rgep/fag_main.html

4/22/2003

Nenita M. Dayrit
University of the Philippines Diliman
Extension Program in Pampanga,
Clarkfield, Pampanga, Philippines
dayritnitz@yahoo.com

ROSALINDA MERCEDES E. CASTILLO

13. AN ASSESSMENT OF THE PANTABANGAN REFORESTATION, LIVELIHOOD AND OTHER COMMUNITY INVOLVEMENT PROJECTS OF LA CONSOLACION COLLEGE OF MANILA, PHILIPPINES

ABSTRACT

The study assesses the effectiveness of community projects organised by La Consolacion College Manila and the level of satisfaction of the beneficiaries. It also reports on the extent of involvement of La Consolacion College Manila (LCCM) with its partner community and how it can lead to improved projects to increase the level of effectiveness and satisfaction on existing and new projects. Several projects involved the livelihood of communities such as fish culture, production of barbecue sticks, while others were a dental-medical mission and reforestation programmes. The project implementation is in line with the mission of LCCM to reach out and help the less fortunate members of society. A survey was conducted to assess all programmes. Through questionnaires, project-implementers-participants and beneficiaries-participants rated the projects on a scale. Results showed both ratings for effectiveness and satisfaction level as *outstanding* (4.44 and 4.42 out of 5.00, respectively). However in the study, many prioritized projects were not assessed. It is recommended that the problems identified and enumerated be addressed and follow–up activities instituted for projects which were not sustained.

KEYWORDS

Community Beneficiaries, Livelihood, Sustainable, Education.

INTRODUCTION

Since 2002, the "*National Service Training Program Law*" or RA 9163 integrated college curriculum encourages students to perform community work. In 2004, La Consolacion College (LCCM) in Manila submitted a five-year strategic plan for membership to the UNESCO-Associated Schools Project (ASP). It was a fruitful year for LCCM; it initiated many programmes and projects to help the adopted community in West Poblacion, Pantabangan, Nueva Ecija (Suliguin, 2007). The aim of the implementation was to promote education towards sustainable living as part of the students' curriculum in the college. It was one of the thrusts of LCCM to preserve and protect the environment through a holistic approach on sustainable

Mijung Kim and C. H. Diong (Eds.), Biology Education for Social and Sustainable Development, 121–126.
© *2012 Sense Publishers. All rights reserved.*

development. This was in line with the mission of LCCM to reach out and help the less fortunate members of society. The college's Community Relations and Extension Services (CRES) coordinated with residents of the community. Pantabangan was adopted as the first partner community on March 12, 2004 (Memorandum of Agreement, 2004).

Prioritized projects initiated in 2004 included, making soap, atsara, tocino, preservation of mangoes, goat farming, and construction of sari–sari stores. To date, several programmes have been implemented, such as: the construction and maintenance of backyard piggeries (initiated in 2005), fish culture, extraction of virgin coconut oil, construction of branches of Botika ng Bayan (initiated in 2006), and production of barbecue sticks (initiated in 2007) (MRBPC, 2008). In addition, with the help of the municipal and barangay officials, the reforestation project, training workshops for the different livelihood projects and the creation of Basic Ecclesial Communities (BEC) to uplift the moral and spiritual aspect of the community were implemented. Definitions of some terms are provided in Appendix 1.

SIGNIFICANCE OF THE STUDY

The study is significant as it assesses the effectiveness of community projects organised by La Consolacion College Manila and the satisfaction level of the beneficiaries. In addition, it reports on the extent of involvement of LCCM with its partner communities and how it can lead to improved projects to increase the level of effectiveness and satisfaction on existing and new projects.

METHODOLOGY

The study used a purposive survey. Two sets of questionnaires in Filipino, after consultation with RES Consultant Dr. Divina M. Edralin, were prepared. One set was for project-implementers-participants (both LCCM and community leaders) and the other for beneficiaries-participants. Different sets of questionnaires were administered depending on the extend of involvement of the participants. Project-implementers-participants and beneficiaries-participants rated the programmes separately. All participants' responses were tabulated according to the following ratings:

(a) 4.38 – 5.00 = *Outstanding*;
(b) 3.75 – 4.37 = *Very Satisfactory*;
(c) 3.13 – 3.74 = *Satisfactory*;
(d) 2.50 – 3.12 = *Unsatisfactory*; and
(e) Below 2.49 = *Very unsatisfactory*.

Data were analyzed to determine the effectiveness of the programmes. Twenty–five project-implementers-participants of LCCM and community leaders from Pantabangan, Nueva Ecija participated. A majority were involved in livelihood projects (52%), followed by medical and dental missions (28%) while the rest were involved in BEC (12%) and reforestation (8%). 113 beneficiaries-participants were involved. Medical and dental missions had the most beneficiaries (28%), followed by BEC and barbecue stick making (13%), then goat farming (12%), fish cage construction (11%) to other smaller beneficiaries.

RESULTS

Questionnaire survey data showed project-implementers-participants believed the service they provided had met the needs of the community. A *very satisfactory* rating was achieved for the objectives of the project (Table 1). However, the results showed there was room for improvements. An *outstanding* rating was achieved for the project implementation. However, the results also showed the project participants did not start on time, did not have sufficient time to finish the project or lacked the necessary materials for the full implementation of the project.

Project-implementers-participants reported there was coordination between LCCM participants and the community and therefore, a high degree of satisfaction. Proper coordination between LCCM and the community achieved the highest rating of 4.57 and was rated *outstanding* in this criterion (Figure 1a).

Survey data of the beneficiaries-participants showed the medical-dental programme/service was rated as *outstanding* at 4.41, together with reforestation programme at 4.42, and BEC at 4.52. Livelihood projects, however, only obtained a *very satisfactory* rating (Table 2). The means of all project areas are summarized in Figure 1b.

Table 1. Average scores of project-implementers-participants by area

		Total	Respondents	Mean	Interpretation
A	Objectives of the program/services				
	1	95	22	4.32	Very satisfactory
	2	92	22	4.18	Very satisfactory
	3	92	22	4.18	Very satisfactory
	4	97	21	4.62	Outstanding
Average (A)				*4.33*	*Very satisfactory*
B	Implementation of the program/services				
	1	92	22	4.18	Very satisfactory
	2	94	20	4.70	Outstanding
	3	97	22	4.41	Outstanding
	4	98	21	4.67	Outstanding
	5	102	21	4.86	Outstanding
	6	95	24	3.96	Very satisfactory
	7	90	21	4.29	Very satisfactory
	8	94	21	4.48	Outstanding
Average (B)				*4.44*	*Outstanding*
C	Coordination between community & LCCM				
	1	90	21	4.29	Very satisfactory
	2	97	21	4.62	Outstanding
	3	106	22	4.82	Outstanding
Average (C)				*4.57*	*Outstanding*
Overall average				*4.44*	*Outstanding*

Table 2. Average scores of beneficiaries-participants by project area

		Total	Respondents	Mean	Interpretation
A	Medical – Dental Mission				
	1	178	38	4.68	Outstanding
	2	172	39	4.41	Outstanding
	3	156	35	4.46	Outstanding
	4	167	39	4.28	Very satisfactory
	5	156	37	4.22	Very satisfactory
Average (A)				*4.41*	*Outstanding*
B	Reforestation				
	1	150	34	4.41	Outstanding
	2	135	31	4.35	Very satisfactory
	3	135	30	4.50	Outstanding
Average (B)				*4.42*	*Outstanding*
C	Basic Ecclesial Communities				
	1	144	33	4.36	Very satisfactory
	2	149	34	4.38	Outstanding
	3	138	32	4.31	Very satisfactory
	4	157	34	4.62	Outstanding
	5	141	30	4.70	Outstanding
	6	147	31	4.74	Outstanding
Average (C)				*4.52*	*Outstanding*
D	Livelihood projects				
	1	154	34	4.53	Outstanding
	2	126	30	4.20	Very satisfactory
	3	137	31	4.42	Outstanding
	4	138	33	4.18	Very satisfactory
	5	148	34	4.35	Very satisfactory
Average (D)				*4.34*	*Very satisfactory*
Overall average				*4.42*	*Outstanding*

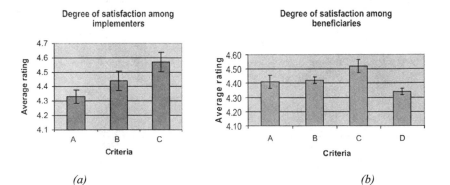

Figure 1. (a) Graph of mean responses of project-implementers- participants, (b) Graph of mean responses of beneficiaries-participants.

Non-empirical data of the study reported the lack of assistance from the Bureau of Fisheries and Aquatic Resources (BFAR) and the on-and-off production of virgin coconut oil (VCO) from project-implementers-participants. Lack of funds for logistics and planning of community projects were also highlighted. Continued support for the projects was recommended by project-implementers-participants so that the community programmes would be able to attain self-sufficiency and be sustainable in the long term. In that way, the community need not be totally dependent on La Consolacion College Manila (LCCM). One participant suggested a shift in focus to livelihood projects to provide more income to the beneficiaries. Another suggested autonomy to the community service department and to give credit to performance of employees involved in the projects.

Data from beneficiary-participants reported a lack of permanent jobs and insufficient income. The lack of communication from their leaders and unaccounted income from their livelihood projects were also highlighted. Some beneficiary-participants requested training in areas such as the making pickled papayas and candies for sale. They reported they were grateful for the support from LCCM. For example, LCCM repaired their houses and provided potable water.

CONCLUSIONS AND RECOMMENDATIONS

The study showed that La Consolacion College Manila (LCCM), through its Community Relations and Extension Services (CRES), had successfully implemented most of the community programs in West Poblacion, Pantabangan, Nueva Ecija. The implemented projects were successful are effectively carried out with community involvement to the high satisfaction of the project-beneficiaries. However, many prioritized projects were not assessed in the study because they did not continue for long, e.g. tocino making, and mango preservation. In the case of the Mother Consuelo Barceló Ecological Park slated for SY 2007–2008 (Montallana, 2007), the project has not been constructed as of date. It is recommended that the problems enumerated above be addressed and follow–up activities be instituted for projects which were not sustained. Education is important to promote such community awareness among students so that the projects can be sustainable in the longer term with community participation and collaboration. With the assistance that the college gives, several programs and projects targeted to serve the community will allow others including government agencies to draw expertise from such activities and to provide welfare support to their people.

REFERENCES

Montallana, J.N. (2007). "Mother Consuelo Barceló Ecological Park", *LCCM First Board of Trustees Meeting, SY 2007 – 2008*, pp. 21–22.
Memorandum of Agreement (2004). In: Self-survey report (2008). "Appendix B, Area VIII – Social Orientation and Community Involvement." *BS Tourism Accreditation*, Feb 18 – 19, 2008.

MRBPC (2009). "Mother Rita Barceló Pastoral Center List of Livelihood Projects" In: Self-survey report (2008). "Appendix A, Area VIII – Social Orientation and Community Involvement." *BS Tourism Accreditation*, Feb 18 – 19, 2008.

Suliguin, G.C. Jr. (2006). "Making it work – A Multi-stakeholders Approach towards environmental protection and stewardship: The case of LCCM's Pantabangan Project." *LCCM Research Journal. 17*(1), 41–50.

APPENDIX 1

Definition of Terms.

Basic Ecclesial Communities (BEC). This is the new way of "being the Church" as described in the 2nd Plenary Council of the Philippines.

CWTS. The Citizen Welfare Training Service which is a component of the NSTP.

NSTP. The National Service Training Program as embodied in Republic Act 9163.

RA 9163. Otherwise known as the NSTP Law.

UNESCO-ASP. The UNESCO-Associated School Project which places emphasis on reinforcing the four pillars of learning for the 21st Century.

West Poblacion, Pantabangan. The pilot area situated on the northeastern part of the municipality bounded on the North by Barangay Conversion, South by Fatima, East by the reservoir and West by San Jose City and Carranglan.

Rosalinda Mercedes E. Castillo
La Consolacion College Manila
Manila, Philippines
lyndy_312@yahoo.com

REIZL P. JOSE, MARINA A. LABONITE, RUMILA C. BULLECER,
AGUSTIN B. ANCOG, NIDA G. BUTRON AND
RICARDO P. BULLECER

14. INDIGENOUS KNOWLEDGE AND TAXONOMY OF BATS IN LOBOC WATERSHED FOREST RESERVE, BOHOL, PHILIPPINES

ABSTRACT

The island of Bohol is one of the least biologically explored in the Philippines. Faunal explorations in the island are few as compared to other islands in the country. This paper aims to taxonomically assess the current status of bat populations in the Loboc Watershed Forest Reserve (LWFR) in Bohol. In addition, the level of community awareness on the importance of bats and bat conservation was determined. Mist netting was used to sample bat species at the various sampling sites. A survey through interviews using a prepared questionnaire was also conducted. A total number of 15 bat species were recorded, namely: *Cynopterus brachyotis, Eonycteris spelaea, Haplonycteris fischeri, Ptenochirus jagori, Rousettus amplexicaudatus, Emballonura alecto, Megaderma spasma, Hipposideros diadema, Hipposideros obscurus, Hipposideros pygmaeus, Rhinolophus arcuatus, Rhinolophus rufus, Miniopterus australis, Miniopterus schreibersi,* and *Scotophilus kuhlii*. The most commonly caught and recorded bat species in all sites was *C. brachyotis*. The Loboc Watershed is known to be a secondary growth forest, hence, the abundance of this fruit bat in the area. The watershed also supports the endemic species as well as *Nearly Threatened* bats. This is an encouraging sign and thus protection and conservation of their habitats should be clearly taken into account. The greatest threat that most bat species face is the destruction of habitats which include deforestation and other land use practices. Continued hunting is another main threat to the bat populations. The local communities within the study area have inadequate knowledge about bats.

KEYWORDS

Conservation, Endemic, Bats, Tropical Ecosystem, Threatened, Sustainable Development, Dipterocarp Forest

Mijung Kim and C. H. Diong (Eds.), Biology Education for Social and Sustainable Development, 127–144.

INTRODUCTION

Bohol Island is among the many places in the Philippines requiring immediate attention for conservation efforts. It is one of the major karst (limestone) areas of the Philippines and has the highest percentage of karst (approximately 60%) of any island in the country (SWCF, 2007). Since the island is characterized with Karst, the region has many caves and because the cave features are attraction to the general public, it is also important to protect the resources in caves, particularly the bats. The island has also been very heavily deforested wherein less than 50% forest-cover remains and much of this is not in good condition. Therefore there is an urgency to study the flora and fauna of the island before they further threatened with extinction.

Of the major faunal groups in tropical ecosystems, bats often comprise more than half of all mammal species. Their biomass, in some places, may be equal to that of all other mammals combined. In the Philippines, bat fauna is very diverse, with 78 species recorded, of which 24 species are endemic to the country (Ingle and Heaney, 1992). Bats are one of the most fascinating mammals in the world and are the only mammals that can fly. Generally, bats undertake a range of important ecological functions in the tropical rain forest. They are responsible in balancing the ecosystem; they are pollinators of many night-blooming flowers, dispersers of seeds that are economically important and they also act as natural controllers of many night flying insects that are serious pests of agricultural crops of farmers. Despite their ecological importance, populations of bats appear to be declining almost everywhere in the world. Several species have become extinct and other species considered abundant have experienced declines. The declining population of bats is due to extensive deforestation and exploitation of animals for food. The on-going forest destruction and other environmental issues that cause a rapid loss of natural habitat is of increasing concern. Many species of bats, especially endemics, depend primarily on forests. Loss of habitats due largely to traditional timber harvesting practices and conversion of forests to agricultural lands have had serious consequences on other species as well (Kunz and Pierson, 1994).

Approximately 94% of the Philippine land area was once covered by forest. That figure had been reduced to 40% at the end of World War II and current estimates of forest cover ranges from 25% to less than 20% depending in part on the amount of degraded forest that is included. In making sure that development in Bohol is sustainable, the Provincial Government and local people have formulated an environmental code in order to protect, manage and develop the natural landscapes and seascapes of the island in such a way that will safeguard the functional capacities of these ecosystems and their sustainable use (RSPL-GMP, 2007). A portion of the forest reserve site of Bohol is the Loboc Watershed Rehabilitation Project.

The Loboc Watershed is an ideal site for this study. The area has a secondary forest and is known as the only remaining well-stocked timber forest in the region with many disturbing anthropogenic activities like hunting, illegal and legal cutting of trees and conversion of forests to agricultural lands. These have threatened the bat species diversity and their populations especially endemic species in the area. Information from faunal studies like the current study on bats will not only provide a sound basis for faunal conservation programs but also an improved management of forests and other ecosystems as well as the sustainable utilization of the various resources therein. It is equally important to raise the awareness of local communities on the important roles of animals like bats for ecosystems to be healthy and productive, thus engaging them more in cooperative and concerted conservation efforts. This paper presents the diversity of bats in LWFR of Bohol Island Province in central Philippines. Specifically, it identifies fruit and insect bats to species level, describes the ecological status of the bats in terms of relative abundance, species richness and diversity, and the existing threats to bats in the area. Local knowledge, utilization practices and prevailing attitudes toward bat conservation are also contained in this report.

METHODOLOGY

Description of the Study Area

The study area is a forest reserve of Loboc Watershed that covers the two municipalities of Sevilla and Bilar covering six villages namely: Bayawahan, Magsaysay, Roxas, Campagao, Dagohoy, and Zamora. The portion of these forested areas, under the management of Bohol Island State University (BISU) – Forest Academic Research Area (FARA) and the Department of Environment and Natural Resources (DENR), amounts to 3,020 hectares. The area is covered with secondary dipterocarp forest of approximately 2,945.86 hectares, with patches of forest gaps, brushlands and grasslands. Upland farms and agroforestry plantations totaled about 74.14 hectares (BISU-FARA Management and Development Plan, 2008).

The survey area is a mature dipterocarp forest on limestone substrate. The area is hilly, mountainous with elevation ranging 200 to 380 m above sea level. Slopes are steep in areas dominated by karst. Topsoil varies depending on their physiography. In relatively flat areas, top soil could reach half a meter. In the hills, the soils are often loose, rarely exceeds 20 mm in depth and are considered extremely fertile and highly erosive (Urich, 1995). Approximately 350 species of plants are recorded in the BISU- FARA (BISU-FARA Management and Development Plan, 2008). Binangbang (2007) and Reyes (2007) documented the presence of at least 10 dipterocarp species, one conifer, seven species of palms, 30 species of shrubs, 56 erect and climbing herbs, 15 creeping vines, 16 creeping and erect grasses, 7 sedges, and 5 ferns and fern allies. Emergent trees mostly comprise white lauan *Shorea contorta*, dagang *Anisoptera aurea*, and palosapis *Anisoptera thurifera*. Canopy trees and sub-scanopy trees are mostly composed of Hasselt's panau *Dipterocarpus hasseltii*, manggachapui *Hopea acuminata*, guisok-guisok *Hopea philippinensis*, *Hopea quisumbingiana*, manggasinoro

Shorea assamica, Shorea contorta, guijo *Shorea guiso,* mayapis *Shorea palosapis* and narig *Vatica mangachapoi* (BISU- FARA Management and Development Plan, 2008).

RESEARCH PROCEDURE

Prior Informed Consent: Coordination with Concerned People and Agencies

Prior to the conduct of the study, the researchers obtained permission from the municipal mayor and Barangay chairmen of the chosen sites. The local detachment of the Philippine army was also informed for safety purposes. In addition, selected men in each village who were knowledgeable of the forests were hired as local guides.

Reconnaissance Survey and Field Sampling

A reconnaissance survey was conducted in each sampling site to determine the amount of work to be done as well as the equipment and materials that were needed. The largest forested area in each village was chosen. Mist nets were used to sample bats during the fieldwork in the two municipalities. Selection of the net locations was done by ocular inspection considering the presence of fruit trees, existence of water systems, such as creeks and canals as these habitats are known to be the foraging and roosting sites of bats. For convenience, some nets were set in a series of two to three nets. Nets were left open at night to capture as many bats as they can. Nets were inspected in the early evenings since insect-eating bats are active at this time, and every hour thereafter, to minimize stress to bats that were caught in the nets. Each bat was placed in separate cloth bags.

Measurement and Identification of Each Bat

Captured bats were identified to species level using the key to the bats of the Philippine (Ingle and Heaney, 1992). Biometrics data were recorded (mm), such as length of forearm (FA), hind foot (HF), ear (E), tail vent (TV), and total length (T). Bat species identified and examined were marked using indelible ink on their wing membranes, after which they were released back to the forest.

Data Processing and Analysis

Relative Abundance This quantifies the abundance of one bat species relative to the other bat species existing within a particular site. It is expressed in percentage when multiplied by 100, thus giving a range of 0 to 100. The greater the numerical value, the more abundant is a particular species relative to the others within a site. The number of individuals in a given area was computed for each species using the formula, Relative Abundance $= Ni / N_T \times 100$, where $Ni =$ the number of individuals per species, $N_T =$ the total number of individuals.

Species Richness The simplest measure of species richness is the total number of species (S) present in a sample of individuals or the number of species found in an area. The number of species recorded generally increase with sample size. Thus, as more individuals are captured or when a larger the area is surveyed, the greater is the number of species likely to be encountered. Species diversity was computed using the formula:

Richness = $\dfrac{S - 1}{\ln nr}$

where:
S- number of bat species within site
nr- total number of individuals for all bat species in a particular site
ln- natural log

SPECIES DIVERSITY (SHANNON-WEINER DIVERSITY INDEX)

Theoretically the Shannon-Weiner (S-W) index requires that the sample is both random and representative, i.e. it contains all species. The index is however less sensitive to sample size than many other diversity measures. The index is normally calculated from:

$H' = -\Sigma pi \ln pi$ ⟵ this is equals to ni/Ni where ni is the number of individuals of species i and N is the total number of individuals in the sample.

Since the logarithm of each proportional pi will be negative, this negative sign ensures that the final index has a positive value.

Descriptive Normative Survey Tool

One-on-one and grouped interviews using a structured questionnaire were conducted. The number of respondents or sampling intensity was 10% of the total number of households in a village. At least 10% of the total adult population in immediate villages in the research site were selected using non-probability (purposive) sampling. Questionnaires were worded in the Visayan dialect.

RESULTS AND DISCUSSION

Species Account

A total of 15 species of bats in six families were recorded in the six barangays of Loboc watershed-forest reserve (Table 1). Five fruit bat species (Megachiroptera) and 10 insect bat species (Microchiroptera) were identified. Of the 78 bat species presently known in the Philippines (Heaney *et al.*, 1987), 19% were recorded in the inventoried areas. The results showed a low percentage of bats present in the sampling sites compared to previous records in the Philippines. However, the site is a secondary forest with a relatively small area and can still support a good number of bat species, including endemic species. These species are fully accounted in terms of distribution, status, size and some important notes of their habitats, as presented in Table 1 and species account that follows.

Table 1. The distribution and status of the fruit and insect bats recorded in six sites

FAMILY	SCIENTIFIC NAME	COMMON NAME	DISTRIBUTION (Heaney et al. 2010)	STATUS (IUCN, 2006)
Pteropodidae	Cynopterus brachyotis	Common Short-nosed Fruit Bat	Widespread	LC
	Eonycteris spelaea	Common Nectar Bat	Philippine Endemic	LC
	Haplonycteris fischeri	Philippine Pygmy Fruit Bat	Philippine Endemic	LC
	Ptenochirus jagori	Musky Fruit Bat	Philippine Endemic	LC
	Rousettus amplexicaudatus	Common Rousette	Widespread	LC
Emballonuridae	*Emballonura alecto*	Philippine Sheath-tailed Bat	Widespread	LC
Megadermatidae	*Megaderma spasma*	Common Asian Ghost Bat	Widespread	LC
Hipposideridae	*Hipposideros diadema*	Diadem Roundleaf Bat	Widespread	LC
	Hipposideros obscurus	Philippine Forest Roundleaf Bat	Philippine Endemic	LC
	Hipposideros pygmaeus	Philippine Pygmy Roundleaf Bat	Philippine Endemic	NT
Rhinolophidae	*Rhinolophus arcuatus*	Arcuate Horseshoe Bat	Widespread	LC
	Rhinolophus rufus	Large Rufous Horseshoe Bat	Philippine Endemic	NT
Vespertilionidae	*Miniopterus australis*	Little Bent-winged Bat	Widespread	LC
	Miniopterus schreibersi	Common Bent-winged Bat	Widespread	LC
	Scotophilus kuhlii	Lesser Asian house bat	Widespread	LC

Legend: LC- Least Concern; NT- Nearly Threatened

Cynopterus brachyotis (Muller, 1838)   The Short-Nosed Fruit Bat was the most abundant species in most of the areas surveyed. The species was commonly caught in open fields especially in areas that have agricultural lands and forest edges but they were never found in a good forest. This species has wide tolerance to both non-forest and secondary forest areas. Its total length (T) measured 89–99mm, tail vent (TV) 5–10mm, ear (E) 16–18mm, and forearm (FA) 58–65mm. According to Heaney *et al.*, (2010), this bat is widespread with a stable population and is common in secondary forests.

Eonycteris spelaea (Dobson, 1871)   The Common Nectar Bat was caught and recorded in all sites surveyed. It was abundant in areas near fruiting trees like Balete sp., forest areas near agricultural lands, and caves. The bats measured 123–142mm (T), TV 13–17, E 20–23mm, and FA 69–80mm. This is considered a widespread species with a stable population; however, according to Heaney *et al.*, (2010), this bat is heavily hunted in caves and is now vulnerable.

Haplonycteris fischeri (Lawrence, 1939)   The Philippine Pygmy Fruit Bat was very rarely netted during the sampling periods. This endemic species is only common in the primary forest and it is rare in secondary forest and absent in agricultural areas (Heaney et al., 2010). Yet this species can still be found in secondary areas like BISU-FARA where there are cleared forests replaced with agricultural lands. The population has declined in recent decades due to habitat destruction by logging and the species is listed in International Union for the Conservation of Nature and Natural Resources (IUCN) as Vulnerable. However, this species was recently categorized as Least Concern, maybe because the bat is adapting to forest disturbance. The bat measured 65–75mm (T), E 13–16mm, FA 48–50mm. This species is a good indicator of the quality and type of the forest.

Ptenochirus jagori (Peters, 1861)   The Musky Fruit Bat was one of the most commonly caught bats during the sampling periods in all sites. It was commonly netted near agricultural fields, forest edges and in the secondary forest. The result was not anticipated because this endemic bat is abundant in primary forest and occasionally present in agricultural areas near forests (Heaney *et al.*, 2010). According to Utzurrum (1992), the species has large stable populations, but has been threatened with continuing habitat destruction. The total length ranged from 124–145mm, TV 8–18mm, E 20–24mm, and FA 78–87mm.

Rousettus amplexicaudatus (Geoffroy, 1810)   The Common Rousette Bat was also one of the most fruit bats recorded in all study sites, especially in areas that are open, near caves, and in the secondary forest. The total length ranged from 128–151mm, TV 14–24mm, E 18–23mm, and FA 82–90mm. This widespread species are known to roost in caves (Heaney *et al.*, 2010) and is locally abundant and stable in agricultural areas, but has been subjected to intense hunting at some cave roosts (Utzurrum, 1992).

Emballonura alecto (Eydoux and Gervais, 1836)   The Philippine Sheath-Tailed Bat was recorded in all sampling areas. The occurrence of caves in the site explains its presence. Based on the observation, this species is very sensitive to habitat disturbance and its existence can be threatened further by their fragile habitats. The total length measured from 57–66mm, TV 9–12m, E 12–15mm, and FA 44–45mm. This is a widespread species (Heaney *et al.*, 2010).

Megaderma spasma (Linnaeus, 1758)   Very few individuals of the Common Asian Ghost Bat was caught during the sampling period. The species was only found in one village. Its low abundance could be due to its ability to echolocate thus enabling them to evade the mist nets or perhaps, its population is already very small or the study area was not a suitable habitat for the bat. It is noteworthy to mention that this "false vampire bat" is the only species in the Philippines that eats small frogs and lizards. The total length ranged from 72–85mm, E 36–40mm and FA 58–62mm. This species is widespread and locally common to uncommon in the primary forest and secondary forest (Heaney *et al.*, 2010).

Hipposideros diadema (E. Geoffroy, 1813)   The Diadem Roundleaf Bat was captured in all sites. During the sampling periods, retrieval of the bats were challenging as they have the ability to cut the nets easily using their sharp teeth thereby freeing themselves. As an alternative, mist nets were set near caves to determine the number of individuals. The total length ranged from 138–147mm, TV 40–50mm, E 29–33mm, and FA 78–88mm. According to Heaney *et al.*, (2010), this widespread species can be found in disturbed lowland areas, hence, the presence of this species in BISU-FARA was expected.

Hipposideros obscurus (Peters, 1861)   The Philippine Forest Roundleaf Bat was found to be common in the municipality of Sevilla only. This species is dependent on forest and perhaps in caves since the records were from the caves and areas near a cave. The total length ranged from 70–76mm, TV 18–23mm, E 18–20mm, and FA 42–46mm. This species is only found in the Philippines. It is locally common to uncommon in the primary and disturbed forest. (Heaney *et al.*,2010).

Hipposideros pygmaeus (Waterhouse, 1843)   The Philippine Pygmy Roundleaf Bat was only recorded in the village of Magsaysay, Sevilla. Its presence in the area could be due to the presence of a good cave. According to Heaney *et al.*, (1998), this bat is commonly found in caves, however the species is seemingly rare because it is probably strongly impacted by the destruction of cave habitats, just like what we observed in most of the caves we visited at BISU-FARA. Its total length ranged from 62–70mm, TV 22–26mm, E 12–14mm, and FA 38–40mm. This Philippine endemic insect bat (Heaney *et al.*, 2010) is considered under threat as cited by the IUCN (2006).

Rhinolophus arcuatus (Peters, 1871)   The Arcuate Horseshoe Bat was recorded in all sites but very few individuals were captured. According to Heaney *et al.* (1998), this widespread species is lacking in data on its population status, perhaps due to the mist netting technique that may not provide an accurate representation of its population. This species was not thought to be found in Bohol, however, a study conducted by Jose *et al.* (2007) revealed its presence in the island. Its total length measured 69–72mm, TV 17–23mm, E 20–21mm, and FA 43–45mm.

Rhinolophus rufus (Eydoux and Gervais, 1836)   The Large Rufous Horseshoe bat seemed to be very rare during the sampling as very few individuals were captured. Being endemic, they could not have adapted to the habitat destruction in the site. Its body measurements were 110–127mm (T), TV 31–32mm, E 34–36mm, and FA 70–73mm. The population status of this endemic bat was is not well known because there is little information on the species (Heaney *et al,.*2010).

Miniopterus australis (Tomes, 1858) *and Miniopterus schreibersi* (Kuhl, 1817) The Little Bent-Winged Bat and Common Bent-Winged Bat were netted in most of the sites. Their presence was due to the existence of caves in all sites where they could thrive well. According to Heaney *et al.* (2010), these widespread species are considered common but dependent on caves (Heaney *et al.*, 1998). The total length of *M. asutralis* ranged from 82–90mm, TV 35–42mm, E 10–11mm, and FA 34–38mm, while *M. schreibersi* measured 103–110mm (T), TV 47–55mm, E 11–13mm, and FA 43–46mm.

Scotophilus kuhlii (Leach, 1822)   Only one individual of the Lesser Asian House Bat was found in Dagohoy village. This bat is probably common in all areas since all sites are surrounded by agricultural lands. However it was not captured using the mist nets. They measured 112(T)mm, TV 42mm, E 14mm, and FA 49mm. According to Heaney *et al.* (2010), this widespread species commonly roost in buildings and in "tents" formed from modified palm fronds. They forage in urban and agricultural areas and secondary forests.

Relative Abundance of Bats

In all, a total of 3,144 individuals of the 15 species were recorded. Based on the total number of individuals captured per species, the common Short-Nosed Fruit Bat *Cynopterus brachyotis* was the most common, with 826 individuals found in the six villages (Figure 1). It was the most commonly observed in each of the villages surveyed. The bat is a non-forest fruit bat and can be expected to tolerate disturbance in forests, enabling it to exist in both non-forest and forest areas. According to Heaney *et al.* (1999), the roosting sites of this species were constructed from the leaves of palm trees that were common in agricultural area.

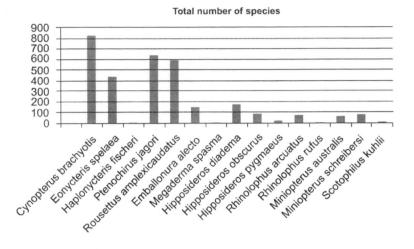

Figure 1. Total number of individuals captured per species.

Table 2. The number of individuals per species/per site with its relative abundance

Scientific Name	Site 1 Bayawahan		Site 2 Magsaysay		Site 3 Campagao		Site 4 Roxas		Site 5 Dagohoy		Site 6 Zamora	
	NI	RA	NI	RA	NI	RA	NI	RA	NI	RA	NI	RA
C. brachyotis	168	0.227	210	0.235	140	0.363	65	0.186	102	0.284	141	0.337
E. spelaea	117	0.158	134	0.150	39	0.101	14	0.040	55	0.153	80	0.191
H. fischeri	1	0.001	3	0.003	0	0	1	0.002	2	0.006	0	0
P. jagori	148	0.2	160	0.179	79	0.205	87	0.249	68	0.189	92	0.220
R. amplexicaudatus	140	1.189	158	0.177	72	0.187	57	0.163	76	0.212	88	0.211
E. alecto	34	0.046	48	0.054	10	0.026	30	0.086	22	0.061	0	0
M. spasma	0	0	2	0.002	0	0	0	0	0	0	0	0
H. diadema	34	0.046	52	0.0583	20	0.052	34	0.097	23	0.064	10	0.024
H. obscures	48	0.065	22	0.025	0	0	13	0.037	0	0	0	0
H. pygmaeus	0	0	21	0.023	0	0	0	0	0	0	0	0
R. arcuatus	16	0.022	24	0.027	10	0.026	12	0.034	6	0.017	5	0.012
R. rufus	0	0	0	0	0	0	3	0.008	4	0.011	2	0.005
M. australis	12	0.016	30	0.034	16	0.0415	6	0.017	0	0	0	0
M. schreibersi	22	0.030	28	0.0314	0	0	27	0.077	0	0	0	0
S. kuhlii	0	0	0	0	0	0	0	0	1	0.003	0	0
Total	740		892		386		349		359		418	

Legend NI – Number of Individuals; RA – Relative Abundance

The presence of this species can be attributed to the vegetation in the area which consists of secondary growth forest cummunities. The total number of individuals captured per species was followed by three more fruit bats, namely: *Ptenochirus jagori, Rousettus amplexicaudatus* and *Eonycteris spelaea.* It was observed that fruit bats were more abundant than insect eating bats. This may be attributed to the capacity of the fruit bats to thrive successfully in almost all types of habitat. The presence of large number of fruit trees and the structural complexity of the forest would also contribute to their success in invading all the sites sampled. Insectivorous bats were relatively few, probably because of their ability to echolocate, they were able to evade the mist nets. Furthermore, in the event that these bats are captured in mist nets, they have the ability to cut the nets with their sharp teeth, thereby freeing themselves. Table 2 presents the number of individuals per species/ per site and their relative abundance.

Species Abundance, Diversity and Richness

Based on the total number of individuals recorded per site, Magsaysay had the highest number of individual bat species (Figure 2a), followed by Sevilla. These two villages are under the municipality of Sevilla. The availability of a wide variety of food resources in this area is probably a factor that makes it a favorable foraging site for the bats. The presence of suitable cave habitats in the area could also be the reason for the abundance of bats.

The number of species recorded in each village is shown in Figure 2b. Magsaysay had the highest number of species compared to other sites, with a species diversity 0.91, followed by Roxas (0.905), Bayawahan (0.864) and Dagohoy (0.782). Species diversity is shown in Figure 3a. There is little difference in the number of species that was observed in all sites. In terms of species richness, Roxas had the highest index of 4.32, followed by Magsaysay (4.06), and Dagohoy (3.52) (Figure 3b).The six villages did not differ much in their elevations and vegetation types, hence, bats can easily move from one area to another. The higher or lower number of individuals and number of species in the six sites could be attributed to the availability of suitable foraging habitats and the presence of fruit trees in the area. Moreover, the highest evenness index in Roxas indicates that bats in this sampling site were distributed more evenly or almost in proportion among the species present.

Existing Threats

Forests are critical habitat for many bat species and most of the lowland forests in Bohol have nearly disappeared. Bat population decline has been attributed mainly to human disturbances of bats and alteration of their habitats (Brady et al., 1982). This is evident in the Loboc watershed, especially in the areas surveyed. The common human activities that threatened bat populations include kaingin or slash-and-burn agriculture, small scale logging, the conversion of forests into agricultural lands, cave exploration for swift nests, guano harvesting, and the general ignorance of the threats to bat biodiversity.

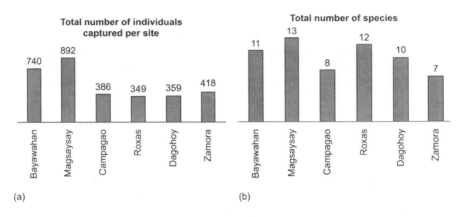

Figure 2. (a) Total number of individuals recorded per site, (b) The total number of species represented by each barangay.

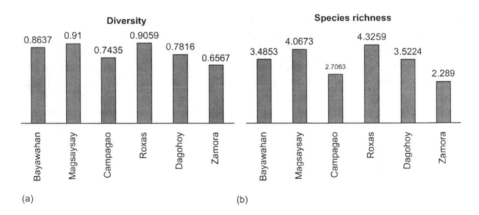

Figure 3. (a) The species diversity represented by each barangay, (b)The species richness represented by each barangay.

Socio-economic Profile of the Respondents

Table 3 shows the socio-economic profile of the 144 respondents which sheds light on the knowledge, attitudes and practices on bats and conservation. Older participants, with longer life experiences, were more knowledgeable on the species and characteristics of bats. The respondents' educational attainment, their economic status, and their dependency of natural resources also had a bearing on biodiversity conservation knowledge and practices.

Table 3. Socio-economic Profile of Respondents

Profile	Site 1	Site 2	Site 3	Site 4	Site 5	Site 6	Total	%
1. Gender:								
Male	10	10	15	21	11	9	76	53
Female	7	20	5	14	8	14	68	47
2. Age:								
13–30	3	7	6	10	7	4	37	25.7
31–50	10	18	9	12	9	15	73	50.7
51–70	4	3	5	10	1	2	25	17.4
71–85	0	2	0	3	2	2	9	6.2
3. Education								
Elem. Level	7	17	0	9	9	10	52	36.1
Hi-school	5	9	8	8	6	7	43	30.0
College	2	5	7	5	-	1	20	13.9
No answer	1	-	0	8	-	-	9	6.2
4. Occupation								
Farmer	8	4	9	9	8	4	46	32
Employee	3	-	3	3	2	5	22	15.3
Self-employed	-	1	1	1	-	1	5	3.5
None	2	6	5	4	1	1	19	13.2
H-keeper	3	17	3	9	4	10	46	32
Retired	-	-	0	2	-	-	2	1.4
5. Monthly Income (Ph Peso)								
1,000 – Below	3	12	5	2	3	6	31	2.2
1001–3000	6	7	1	9	3	6	32	22.2
3001–5000	2	3	2	3	3	5	18	12.5
6000 & above	-		2	2	-	-	4	2.8

Indigenous Knowledge on Bats

Respondents were asked to give a physical description of the bats they have known and the differences between the species, their roosting places, the bats' population trends, and the threats to their existence and conservation (Table 4). Most (57%) of the respondents believe that bats are mammals. The meanings of various English technical terms in the answer choices which could not be translated (in one word) into the dialect were explained to them. Many respondents (40%) thought that bats are birds. They were able to distinguish fruit bats from insectivorous bats. Some (73%) thought that there is only one kind or one species of fruit bat, and another 17% thought that there is one kind of insect feeding bats. Most (40%) of the respondents indicated that guyabano is the most common roosting plant for the fruit bats and forest trees (51%) for the insect feeding bats. Other respondents identified roosting trees of both bats are the coconuts, ficus (balete), lauan, silk cotton (doldol), mahogany. bay-ang, taluto, banana, jackfruit, and batiles. A number of respondents believed that bats only roost in caves.

Table 4. Indigenous knowledge on bats

Villages	Site 1	Site 2	Site 3	Site 4	Site 5	Site 6	TOTAL	%
1. Type of animal								
Reptile		1		1			2	1.4
Mammal	12	20	16	17	10	7	82	57.0
Amphibian					1		1	0.7
Bird	3	9	9	17	7	14	59	41.0
2. Number of kabog (fruit bats) known								
3 spp	4	3			1	3	11	7.6
1 sp	7	18	16	33	13	18	105	73.0
More than 5	2	3			2		7	5.0
Don't know	3	6	2	1	2	3	17	11.8
3. Number of (insect bats) species known								
1	13	14	15	28	9	14	93	64.6
2		9	3	3	5	4	24	16.7
3		2	1		1	1	5	3.5
5								

Perceived Importance of Bats and Attitude Towards Bat Conservation

Table 5 shows most of the respondents perceived that bats are useful as a source of guano fertilizer, as pollinators, and seed dispersing agents in natural forest regeneration . However, some respondents regard them as harmful because of their damage to crops. Others described bats as scary creatures due to their "horrible looks" and thought they are related to vampire bats. Most respondents were in favor of conserving the bats due to the benefits they impart and their roles in ecosystem stability. Among the conservation strategies suggested were: to just leave the bats alone, they should not be hunted, conserve them, create local policies/ ordinances which promote bat conservation, and establishment of bat sanctuaries.

Destruction of forests that threatened bat biodiversity and conservation strategies that can increase bat populations should be highlighted to the communities. A thorough inventory of the bat communities to document their diversity in the province is recommended. Such an inventory should also include information on the uses of caves by bats, and their relative abundance. A systematic study to monitor how caves are used by bat populations should also be conducted. A potential eco-tourism is possible once sustainable populations of bats in Loboc watershed in Bohol are established.

Most respondents do not eat bats mainly due to its bad taste, odor, or belief that bats are dirty creatures. Those who do eat bats hunt only the fruit bats. Only a few of the respondents hunt bats. When asked for the best conservation measures, these respondents replied that bats should be left unharmed, while some had no idea on suitable conservation measures. Most (45%) of the respondents believed bat populations are declining. The main causes cited were hunting and destruction of roosting sites. Some respondents though that bat populations are increasing because most people do not hunt them to eat. Threats to bat population include continued hunting, loss/destruction of roosting sites and the general ignorance of the people about bats.

Table 5. Importance of bats and attitude towards their conservation

Barangays	Site 1	Site 2	Site 3	Site 4	Site 5	Site 6	TOTAL	%
How do you find the bats?								
useful	9	20	13	20	10	17	89	61.8
Reasons: Food; for ecosystem balance; guano fertilizer; Control insect populations; pollinators; seed dispersal or for natural regeneration; for fun.								
Harmful	6	7	6	2	6	4	31	21.5
Reason: Feed on crops, coconuts								
Both useful and harmful	4	2	5			5	16	11.1
Useful / harmful & /also scary		1	4	3			8	5.6
Reasons: Horrible looks; maybe vampires; might eat people								
Is bat conservation important?								
Yes	14	21	15	26	12	18	106	73.6
Reasons: Source of guano; control some insect population like mosquitoes; to increase their population; it's a pity to kill them; should be given equal chance to survive like other animals; pollinators; so they won't go extinct; they aren't aggressive; useful in natural regeneration of fruit and timber trees; important in ecosystem stability; they are endangered								
No	4	8	1	6	1		20	13.9
Reasons: Bats feed on or destroy some crops; insignificant in controlling the insect population								
Benefits from Bats	Source of guano fertilizer; useful to man and the environment; helps in ecosystem balance; attraction to tourists; food; control some pests							
Suggested strategies to increase bat population	Leave them alone – should not be hunted; conserve; create local policies / ordinances which promote bat conservation; should be protected; provide them with food sources; trees should not be cut; not destroying their roosting sites; there should be a lead agency doing active bat conservation programs; ban the hunting of bats; DENR should do some protection; create a bat sanctuary; government must finance more tree projects.							

Legend: Site 1- Zamora, Site 2- Dagohoy, Site 3- Roxas, Site 4- Campagao, Site 5- Bayawahan, Site 6- Magsaysay

CONCLUSIONS AND RECOMMENDATIONS

Of the 15 species of bats, six are endemic species and two of them are considered as *Nearly Threatened*. Despite disturbances in the forest reserve, there are still endemic and threatened bats. The presence of these species in the sites surveyed is very encouraging and thus efforts should be taken to protected and conserve the populations. Destruction and human disturbance of the forest habitat still remains a major threat to the survival of the bat populations. The data gathered in the study is strong enough to support policies for the protection of all areas in this study and the conservation of the bats. On respondents' knowledge of bats, the respondents were certain only of the existence of the fruit and insect feeding bats, the roosting sites and the guano fertilizers they provide. Very few respondents were aware that bats are pollinators, seed dispersal agents, help control mosquito populations, and have other roles of ecological importance. Most of the respondents came to know of this research for the first time during the FGD sessions. Hunting, destruction or loss of roosting sites and general ignorance about bats were perceived to be the causes /threats to the declining populations of the bats. Though most of the respondents do not eat bats, they still recommend their conservation for the guano benefits and other ecological importance. Formulation of local policies /ordinances on banning bat hunting and in other conservation schemes was highly recommended. The results of the study provide scientific data for a strong recommendation to initiate bat a conservation program in the BISU-FARA barangays. Presentation of the research data to village and municipal Local Government Units is strongly recommended to enhance biodiversity conservation policy. IEC on bats should be among the immediate activities of this program.

REFERENCES

Binangbang, L. (2007). Fern Diversity in Barangay Zamora and Barangay Roxas (Portions of CVSCAFT Forest Academic Research Area, Bilar, Bohol). Undergraduate Thesis. CVSCAFT Main Campus. Unpublished.

Brady, J. T., Kunz, T. H., Tuttle, M. D., & Wilson, D. E. (1982). "Gray bat recovery plan," U.S. Fish and Wildlife Service, Denver, CO.

CVSCAFT Forest Academic Research Area (FARA) Management and Development Plan (2008). Central Visayas State College of Agriculture, Forestry and Technology, Main Campus, Zamora, Bilar, Bohol. Unpublished.

Heaney, L.R., M.L. Dolar, D.S. Balete, J.A. Esselstyn, E.A. Rickart, J.L. Sedlock, A.C. Alcala, P.A. Alviola, M.V. Duya, N. Ingle, M.L. Tabao, W. Oliver, L.M. Paguntalan, B.R. Tabaranza, Jr., R.C.B. Utzurrum, & M. Josefa Velaez. (2010). A Synopsis of the Mammalian Fauna of the Philippine Islands. The Field Museum, S. Lake Shore, Dr. IL.

Heaney, L. R., D. S. Balete, E. A. Rickart, R. C. B. Utzurrum, & P. C. Gonzales. (1999). Mammalian diversity on Mount Isarog, a threatened center of endemism on southern Luzon Island, Philippines. Fieldiana: Zoology, new series, 95, 1–62.

Heaney, L. R., D. S. Balete, M. L. Dolar, A. C. Alcala, A. T. L. Dans, P. C. Gonzales, N. r. Ingle, M. V. Lepiten, W. L. R. Oliver, P. S. Ong, E. A. Rickart, B. R. Tabaranza Jr. & R. C. B. Utzurrum. (1998). A Synopsis of the Mammalian Fauna of the Philippine Islands. Fieldiana; Zoology, New Series, 88, 1–5.

Heaney, L. R., P. C. Gonzales, & A. C. Alcala. (1987). An annotated checklist of the taxonomic and conservation status of land mammals in the Philippines. Silliman Journal, 34, 32–66.

Ingle N. & L. Heaney. (1992). A Key to the Bats of the Philippine Islands. Fieldiana. Zoology. Field Museum of Natural History, Chicago, USA. p. 69.

Kunz, T. H. & E. D. Pierson. 1994. Bats of the World : An Introduction. The Johns Hopkins University.Press, USA Ballimore and London.

Pamaong-Jose, R., S. P. Ramayla, W. G. Granert, & A. B. Carino. (2007). Conservation of Bats in Karst Areas of Bohol Island, Philippines. Bat Research News, 48(3), 99

Reyes, T. Jr. (2007). Checklist of Forest Plant Species at CVSCAFT Forest Academic Research Area. CVSCAFT Main Campus. Unpublished.

RSPL-GMP, (2007). Rajah Sikatuna Protected Landscape General Management Plan. An unpublished General Management Plan.

[SWCF] Soil and Water Conservation Foundation. (2007). Annual Report on Flora and Fauna Field Survey. Bohol, Philippines

Urich, Peter. Stress on tropical karst cultivated with wet rice: Bohol Philippines. Environmental Geology. 21:129–136. 1995

Utzurrum, R. C. B. (1992). Conservation status of Philippine fruit bat (Ptreopodidae). *Silliman Journal, 36*, 27–45

Reizl P. Jose (gzl_4@yahoo.com)
MARINA A. LABONITE,
RUMILA C. BULLECER
AGUSTIN B. ANCOG
NIDA G. BUTRON
Bohol Island State University,
Tagbilaran City, Bohol, Philippines gzl_4@yahoo.com

Ricardo P. Bullecer
University of Bohol

MILAROSA L. LIBREA AND VIVIAN S. TOLENTINO

15. ANATOMICAL CHARACTERIZATION OF OIL CELLS AND OIL CAVITIES IN *JATROPHA CURCAS* L. USING LIGHT AND ELECTRON MICROSCOPY

ABSTRACT

The country's effort on propagation of *Jatropha curcas* L. is a response to the call of the Department of Energy (DOE) to increase the use of alternative fuels as means to achieve its goal of "self-sufficiency in 2010" (Department of Energy Philippines 2006). In the same way, the Commission on Higher Education (CHED) includes the intensive research on alternative energy source in the top list of its research agenda. Thus, the need to continually explore and intensify research on alternative energy resources becomes imperative and poses an urgent challenge to scientists. This study on the anatomical characterization of oil secretory cells in the fruits and seeds of *J. curcas* is a pioneering attempt to contribute to the limited literature on the anatomy of oil secretory cell in plants. The study aims to identify the exact location of oil secretory structures in the tissues of the fruits and seeds. These structures are found both in the fruits and seeds at different stages of development. Sections were prepared using free hand technique and observed under light and electron microscopes. Tests with Sudan IV and Sudan Black prove positive for oils. Oil cells are found in the middle-aged and mature seeds of *J. curcas*. While oil cavities are present in all ages of fruits and in the middle-aged and mature seeds. Generally, oil cell count is inversely proportional with the oil cavity count. The presence of oil secretory structures suggests significant contribution in the maximum use of the plant and yield of oil.

KEYWORDS

Alternative Energy, Oil Secretory Structure, Free Hand Technique, *Jatropha curcas*

INTRODUCTION

The Philippines is currently focused on the propagation of *Jatropha curcas* L. in response to the call of the Department of Energy (DOE) to increase the use of alternative fuels as means to achieve its goal of "self-sufficiency in 2010". Likewise, private sectors are also including the intensive research on alternative energy source in the top list of their research agenda. Thus, the need to continually

Mijung Kim and C. H. Diong (Eds.), Biology Education for Social and Sustainable Development, 145–152.

explore and intensify research on alternative energy resources becomes imperative and poses an urgent challenge to scientists.

The study on the presence, location, distribution and development of oil cells at different developmental stages of fruits and seeds of *J. curcas* in different locations were confirmed through light and transmission and scanning electron microscopy. The oil cell was differentiated from neighboring cells based on complex wall structure, presence of oil sacs and cupule. The number of oil cells per field of vision at different developmental stages of fruits and seeds obtained from different collection sites varied.

The detection of oil cavities in fruits is a potential basis for extraction of oils in fruits at all ages. The presence of oil cavities along with oil cells in seeds seems to suggest that it could be an additional source of oil leading to maximum usage of the plant. Having identified two oil secretory structures in the seeds could lead to studies of the difference of chemical composition of oils secreted by the structures or even comparison of oil yield based on topographical location of the plant.

This study on the anatomical characterization of oil secretory cells in the fruits and seeds of *J. curcas* is a pioneering attempt to contribute to the limited literature on the anatomy of oil secretory cell in plants. Though this is a basic study, it is deemed invaluable in the efficient extraction, increase yield of oils and maximum use of the plant. Identifying the exact location of possible oil secretory structures in the tissues of the fruits and seeds will lessen extraction time and cost leading to increase yield of oil. The oil cells found in the middle-aged seeds of *J. curcas* indicate that oil extraction is not limited to mature seeds. In addition to oil cells, oil cavities in all ages of fruits and in the middle-aged and mature seeds are found to secrete oils suggesting significant contribution in the maximum use of the plant.

MATERIAL AND METHODS

The anatomical characterization of oil cells were performed using light and electron microscopy. Specimens were cut using the free hand technique for light microscopy. Staining with Sudan Black and Sudan IV was employed to differentiate oil cells from ordinary parenchyma cells. Oils in the oil sac of the oil cell stained red with Sudan IV. Sections were observed using BH-Olympus epifluorescence Microscope and photomicrographed with Microncam. Ultra structure characterization was done with electron microscopy at BIOTECH-UP Los Baños with the assistance of Dr. Lorelle Trinidad.

RESULTS AND DISCUSSION

Anatomy and Location of Oil Cavity in Fruits and Seeds Under Light Microscope

Oil cavities were observed in both fresh and fixed samples of young and middle-aged fruits from Talisay and Ateneo. They appeared spherical and measured from 6μ to 35 μ in diameter. Each empty cavity was surrounded by secretory cells which stained bright red with Sudan IV (Figure 1a) and black with Sudan Black (Figure 1B). They were found widely distributed on the mesocarp tissues of both young and middle aged fruits and a few were adjacent to the pericarp tissues. Oil cavities in seeds at all developmental stages appeared similar in structure with those of the fruits. However, the cavities found in seeds were smaller in size than that of the fruits (Figure 2c).

Anatomy and Location of Oil Cell in Seeds

Oil cells in both fresh and fixed middle aged and mature seeds appeared as thick-walled spherical structures with an oil sac almost filled with oil. Oil in the sac appeared as single solid dark red when stained with Sudan IV (Figure 1 a-b). These designated oil cells occurred more prominently on the endosperm tissues though some occurred as individual cells and distantly apart from each other. The presence of oil cells in seeds alone particularly on endosperm of the middle aged and mature seeds is similar to the studies on *P. americana* done by Platt and Thomson (1992) wherein oil cells were found abundant in its seed cotyledons. The oil cells detected in middle aged and mature seeds of *J. curcas,* however, did not show the "cupule" in different sections of the seeds at different developmental stages. This could be due to its restricted location that it is limited in a particular area of the cell wall. Furthermore, if present, it could be just an artifact in paraffin sections (Postek and Tucker 1983).

The oils in seed samples from Ateneo and Talisay stained red and confined in sac-like structure. This is true for almost all oil cells. Furthermore, in the study of oil cells in various species namely, *Saururus cernuus* (Tucker 1976), *Persea americana* (Platt and Thomson 1992), and *Magnolia grandiflora* (Postek and Tucker 1983), oils in the sac of these cells turned red when stained with Sudan dyes.

Scanning Electron Micrographs

Scanning electron micrographs taken in young and middle aged fruits showed no evidence of oil cells but oil cavities were observed. However, in middle aged and mature seeds, oil cells were found in the endosperm tissue. There were numerous spherical bodies scattered in the cytoplasm (Figure 3 a-b) which looked like oil bodies.

There are a limited number of literature on oil cell viewed under SEM. The only distinguishing feature seen as far as this study is concerned would be the detection of thick walls which is a characteristic feature of an oil cell. The presence of cupule is not detected since SEM can only provide the surface image of the specimen observed. It is also noted by Mariani *et al.,* (1989), that this cupule is a structure which is localized exclusively in the cell wall of an oil cell. Oil accumulations have been recently described to be present in leukoplasts, which can evolve into oil storing plastids known as elaioplasts. These elaioplasts occur usually in seeds (Lersten *et al.,* 2006). In middle aged and mature seeds of

J. curcas, oil bodies appear to occur in the endosperm. Cutter (1978), as quoted by Lersten *et al.*, (2006), reported that elaioplasts generally occur in the cytoplasm of the cells.

Transmission Electron Microscopy Images

The transmission electron microscopy images of the endosperm of middle aged seed showed an almost complete tripartite wall with suberin layer(S) which was denser than the cellulosic layers (Figure 3c-e). Electron dense bodies, which looked like oil droplets were found scattered in the cytoplasm of the oil cells in fresh mature seeds from Ateneo.

Ultrastructure of oil cells in *J. curcas* appears similar to the ultrastructure of the oil cells in the mesocarp of avocado (Platt-Aloia *et al.*, 1983). The oil cells observed in the endosperm of mature seeds of *J. curcas* appear to be mature oil cell with oil droplets (also designated as elaioplasts) scattered in the cytoplasm or in the vacuole . (Platt-Aloia *et al.*, 1983)

The cytoplasm appeared alveolar similar to the findings of Platt-Aloia *et al.*, 1983 in avocado fruits. Also, the oil cells showed well developed walls with suberin layer appearing like electron dense lines. A densely staining lamellate suberin layer has been detected in the developing oil cell of *Magnolia grandiflora* (Postek and Tucker 1983).

CONCLUSION

There are two oil secretory structures observed in the seeds of *J. curcas* from Talisay and Quezon City. Oil cells and oil cavities are present in the seeds of *J. curcas* from Quezon City and Talisay. Generally, they are seen scattered in the endosperm tissues of the middle aged and mature seeds from both locations. The detection of oil cavities in the fruits opens a possibility of investigating the feasibility of extracting oils from these plant organs. In fruits, these cavities are widely distributed in the mesocarp tissues and notably scattered on its central portion. Some are adjacent to the pericarp tissues. In seeds, they are widely dispersed in the endosperm tissues and appear smaller in size.

Oil cavity development in fruits and seeds of *J. curcas* suggests a schizogenous type of cavity formation. The intact epithelial lining all throughout the development of the oil cavity indicates schizogeny formation. The number of oil cavity in fruits and seeds seems to be not significantly affected by the location but by the ages of the plants. It is noticeable that as number of oil cells increases, the number of oil cavity decreases. This could be an indication of conversion of oil cells into secretory structure such as the oil cavities. The ultrastructural anatomy of oil cells shows thickness of walls, presence of oil droplet in cytoplasm and vacuoles. The SEM micrograph reveals resemblance to oil cell found in the mesophyll tissue of *Tasmania lanceolata* (Read and Meanry 2000) while the TEM micrograph appears similar to ultrastructure of oil cell in the mesocarp of avocado fruit (Platt-Aloia *et al.,*1983). The oil droplets are found in the cytoplasm.

Table 1. Summary of results on presence and location of oil cells in fruits and seeds at different developmental stages of J. curcas from Ateneo and Talisay, Philippines

| | | | | Structures | | Histochemical tests |
Location	Sample	Age	Plant Organ	Oil cavities	Oil Cells	Sudan IV and Sudan Black
Ateneo/ Talisay	Fresh	Young	Fruit	+	-	++
			Seed	+	-	++
		Middle Age	Fruit	+	-	++
			Seed	+	+	++
		Mature	Seed	+	+	++
	Fixed	Young	Fruit	+	-	++
			Seed	+	-	++
		Middle Age	Fruit	+	-	++
			Seed	+	+	++
		Mature	Seed	+	+	++

+ presence, - absence, ++ positive for oil

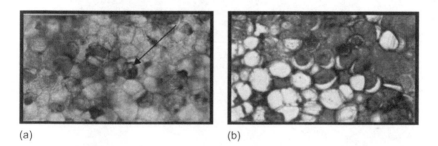

(a) (b)

Figure1. Light micrographs of oil cells in seeds of Jatropha curcas. Oil cells stained dark orange to almost red scattered on the endosperm tissues of middle aged seed, (100X).

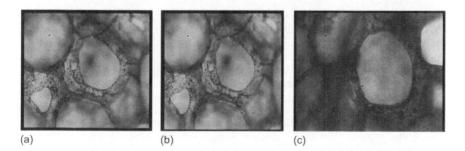

(a) (b) (c)

Figure 2. a-c Light micrographs of oil cavities in fruits and seeds of Jatropha curcas. a - oil cavity in young fruit, stained with Sudan IV, b - oil cavity in young fruit stained with Sudan Black, c - oil cavity in young seed with stained with Sudan IV.

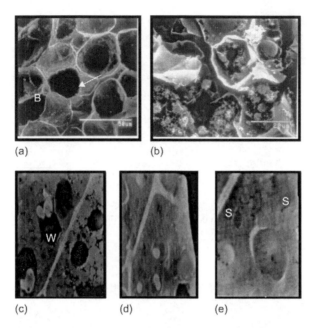

Figure 3. SEM micrographs of oil cavity and oil cell Jatropha curcas. a - oil cavity in middle aged fruit (1000x), b - oil cell in mature seed (1500x), c-e are TEM micrographs of oil cells, c-d oil droplets in the cytoplasm. Cytoplasm appears alveolar. e - oil droplet inside the vacuole. O - oil droplet, v- vacuole, W-developing wall, E suberin layer (S) more distinct indicating a more complete thickening of the wall.

REFERENCES

Heller J. (1996). Physic Nut. *Jatropha curcas* L. Promoting the conservation and use of Underutilized and neglected crops. 1. Institute of Plant Genetics and Crop Plant Research, Gatersleben| International Plant Genetic Resources Institute, Rome.

Lersten N. R. & Curtis J. D. (1998). April-June. Foliar Idioblasts in *Physostegia virginia* (Lauriacea). *Journal of the Torrey Botanical Society. 125*(2), 133–137.

Mauseth J. D. (1988). Plant Anatomy. Texas: The Benjamin/Cummings Publishing Company, Inc.; pp. 142–143.

Mauseth J. D. (2001). Plant Anatomy. Texas: Cummings and Hathaway, 141–166.

Mariani R., Cappelletti E.M., Campoccia D. & Baldan B. (1989). December. Oil Cell Ultrastructure and Development in *Liridendron tupilifera* L.. *Botanical Gazette. 150*(4), 391–396.

Pant K.S. Khosla V., Kumar D., & Gairola S. (2006). Seed oil content variation in Jatropha curcas Linn. In different altitudinal ranges and site conditions in H.P. India. Lyonia: A Journal of Ecology and Application. Internet. Available from http://www.lyonia.org/dowloadPDF.php? pdflD=390.487 .1 Accessed on 14 February 2008.

Patil V. R. (2003). "Jatropha-an alternative to Diesel" Agriculture & Industry Survey. *13*(5).

Platt-Aloia, K. A. ,Thomson W. W. & Young R. E. (1980). Ultrastructure changes in the walls of Ripening Avocados: Transmission, Scanning,and Freese Fracture microcsopy. *Botanical Gazette 141*(4), 366–373.

Platt, K. A.-Aloia, Gross, J. W. & Thomson W. W. (1983). Ultrastructure. Study of the Development of Oil Cells in the Mesocarp of Avocado Fruit. *Botanical Gazette. 144*(10) 49–55.

Platt K. A. & Thomson W. W. (1992). Idioblast Oil Cells of Avocado: Distribution, Isolation, Ultrastucture, Histochemistry, and Biochemistry. *International Journal of Plant Sciences. 153*(3), 301–310.

Postek, M. T. & Tucker, S. C. (1983). Ontogenty and Ultrasctructure of Secretory Oil Cells in *Magnolia grandiflora* L. *Botanical Gazette*, 144 (4):501–512.

Read C. & Menary R. (2000). Analysis of the contents of oil cells in *Tasmannia lanceolata* (Poir.) C. Smith (Winteracea). *Annals of Botany. 86*, 1193–1197.

Shepherd, K. A., Macfarlane, T. D. & Colmer, T. D. (2005). Morphology, Anatomy and Histochemistry of Salicornioidaea (Chenopodiaceae) Fruits and Seeds. *Annals of Botany. 95*, 917–933.

Tolentino V. S. (1995). Morpho-Anatomy of the Fruit of the *Pittosporum resiniferrum* Hemsl. (Petroleum Nut). The Philippine Scientist (39) 46–55.

Trinidad L. (2006). TEM and SEM Working Protocol. National Institute of Molecular and Biotechnology. Personal Communication.

Tucker S. C. (1964). December. The terminal Idioblsts in Magnoliaceous Leaves. American Journal of Botany. *51*(10), 1051–1062.

Tucker S. C. (1976). December. Intrusive Growth of Secretory oil cells in *Saururus cernuus. Botanical Gazette. 137*(4), 341–347.

Milarosa L. Librea
Ateneo De Manila High School, Science Area,
Loyola Heights, Philippines
milarosalibrea@yahoo.com

Vivian Tolentino
Ateneo de Manila University, Biology Department,
Loyola Heights, Philippines
vtolentino@ateneo.edu

LESLEY CASAS LUBOS AND LALEVIE CASAS LUBOS

16. EXTENT OF *ESCHERICHIA COLI* CONTAMINATION OF CAGAYAN DE ORO RIVER AND FACTORS CAUSING CONTAMINATION

ABSTRACT

The study determined the extent of fecal contamination of Cagayan de Oro River stretching along the nine river barangays. Sampling sites include upstream, midstream, and downstream areas. The Multiple Tube Fermentation Technique (MTFT) was used to identify total coliform, fecal coliform, and *Escherichia coli* in water samples. Average coliform values from sampling sites exceeded acceptable values set by the Department of Environment and Natural Resources, indicating contamination of the river water quality guidelines at 1000 fecal coliform organisms/100 ml. The factors that contribute to high fecal contamination were high proportion of riverbank dwellers using the river as public toilets, direct connection of pipes from toilets to the river, high mobility of migrant settlers, and lack of water supply for illegal settlers. Temporal variable is a critical differentiating factor in the concentrations of total coliform across sampling areas and in the concentrations of fecal coliform across sampling sites by month. The spread of coliform was similar in the upstream, midstream, downstream sections of the river, indicating that sources of contamination are prevalent.

KEYWORDS

Fecal Contamination, *E. Coli*, River Quality, Human And Animal Wastes

INTRODUCTION

Every year 700,000 people die from food or waterborne diseases in the Asia-Pacific region alone, including the Philippines (WHO,2010). A gram of human feces has 10 million viruses, one million bacteria, one thousand parasite cysts and 100 parasite eggs, thus humans and animals are not safe in contaminated rivers (DENR, 2004). Excessive exposure to the natural elements and the need for food and water are critical issues that need to be addressed. After a flood or water disaster, waterborne transmission of agents, such as *Escherichia coli*, is common and cause widespread disease (Smeltzer, *et al.*, 2008). Widespread contamination of rivers has been evident in many areas in the Philippines. As people become aware of the conditions of the environment, they also become conscious of their actions toward the environment. They begin to find time to reflect about their

Mijung Kim and C. H. Diong (Eds.), Biology Education for Social and Sustainable Development, 153–160.

relationship with nature, to think of ways and means to protect the environment, and to analyze environmental phenomenon in their local community. They become more concerned about their surroundings (Deauna and Dorado, 1996).

Cagayan de Oro City is the capital of Misamis Oriental, Philippines. To the south, the city is bordered by Bukidnon and Lanao del Norte (Iligan City). The Municipality of Opol, Misamis Oriental, borders the city on the west and Tagoloan, Misamis Oriental , to the east. To the north lies Macajalar Bay facing the Bohol Sea. Its total land area is 488.86 km² representing 13.9% of the entire Misamis Oriental. According to the 2007 census, the city has a total population of 553,966. There are 80 barangays composing Cagayan de Oro City, 14 of which are situated along the river banks.

The Cagayan de Oro River is a major river of Cagayan de Oro City and surrounding barangays. Its contribution to the growth of the city and the role it plays to sustain the city's development cannot be overemphasized. The river is rich and abundant in natural resources specifically aquatic organisms. It also serves as a means of livelihood for some people. Improper waste disposal greatly affects the river ecosystem.

Throughout the history of Cagayan de Oro City, the Cagayan de Oro River has been used for bathing, washing clothes, as food sourcing and recently, ecotourism activities, such as white-water rafting, has been recognized by many foreign and local tourists. With the increase in population of residents along the river system, as a consequence of urbanization, comes the question of proper sewage disposal and fecal contamination in the river. However, despite this growing threat and rapid developments in the city, not much attention has been given to the Cagayan de Oro River as few studies have been carried out to assess the water quality. Studies to date are concerned with the physico-chemical properties of the water (Calingin , 2000). One approach to assess water quality of Cagayan de Oro River is to determine the extent of fecal contamination in the river. This is essential in providing information on sanitation and for health-improvement.

Coliform analysis of rivers and other water systems in Misamis Oriental have been conducted, but not for the Cagayan de Oro River. This study was inspired by the study of Alvarez et al (2008) and is part of a continuing effort to assess the fecal pollution level in the river. Detection of *E. coli* provides a better understanding of the potential public health risks to barangays located along Cagayan de Oro City. This study aims to provide insights for disease prevention, health promotion, and health maintenance. Results of the study should offer awareness of disease-causing contaminants and suggestions for an effective waste management system.

The study was aimed at determining the extent of *Escherichia coli* contamination in the Cagayan de Oro River stretching along nine barangays. Specifically, this study was conducted to: (i) determine the MPN index of total coliform, fecal coliform, and *E. coli* in the water samples obtained from the river system, (ii) determine whether the MPN index of total coliform, fecal coliform, and *E. coli* is acceptable according to specific standards, and (iii) determine the possible factors that contributed to *E.coli* contamination.

MATERIALS AND METHOD

A preliminary survey was conducted along the target areas. A letter asking permission to conduct the study was given to the barangay captains. The researchers visited and explained to the barangay captains and officers the objectives of the study. One-day microbial sampling was conducted in three consecutive months with a 28-day interval as prescribed by DOST- 10 Microbial Laboratory, the agency that approved the sampling plan. The study measured the fecal bacteria indicators, including the total coliform count (MPN/100 mL), fecal coliform count (MPN/100 mL), and *E. coli* detection/enumeration (MPN/100 mL), based on the Regional Standards and Testing Center – 10. Counts were analyzed based on the acceptable value set by the DENR Administrative Order Number 34.

The study was conducted in June 2008 to May 2010. Samples were collected from the Cagayan de Oro River stretching along nine (9) river barangays ,namely Mambuaya, Dansolihon, and Bayanga (UPSTREAM) ; Lumbia, Upper Balulang, and Nazareth (MIDSTREAM); and Barangays 13(Isla de Oro), Kauswagan , and Bonbon (DOWNSTREAM). Locations where there were no previous microbial studies and which had an increase in population along the river banks were selected for the study. To detect for Escherichia coli in the river system, a cross-sectional study- the division of the river from upstream, midstream, to downstream – was used to investigate variations and contamination of the river by bacteria. Residents at sampling sites were interviewed and water samples collected from upstream, midstream, and downstream sites. A landmark was considered for sampling 25 meters away from the center point of reference. To ensure accuracy of samples, a red flag secured in a rick was placed as a marker at the sampling location. Standard sampling procedures (Eaton *et al.,* 2005) were observed to prevent any significant changes in the composition of the samples prior to analysis to ensure accurate analytical results. Factors such as time and holding temperature can affect microbial density. Water samples collected were maintained at 4–10°C and analyzed after 6 hours pursuant procedures prescribed by DOST- 10. One-way analysis of variance was used to test differences in spatial and temporal variables.

RESULTS

All sampling sites were fecally contaminated as shown by the MPN indices (Table 1, Figure 1). The safe level total count was only 1000 MPN/100mL. All area that were sampled exceeded the allowable standard, which is alarming.

Bonbon showed the highest MPN index of 16,000/100ml; the lowest index was from Lumbia (4,400/100ml). For fecal coliform count, Bonbon had the highest MPN index of 8,300/100mL and Dansolihon, the lowest (2,496 MPN/100ml). For *E. coli* count, Bonbon had the highest value of 7,066MPN/100ml, and Dansolihon (1,296MPN/100ml). In the test of difference for temporal variable, in the three sampling months (October, November, December 2008) registered significant difference in the level of concentration of total coliform (F = 8.894, p < .001), indicating that temporal variable is a critical differentiating factor in the concentrations of total coliform across sampling areas. Similarly, the test of difference for temporal variable, in the same three sampling months registered significant differences in the levels of concentration of fecal coliform (F = 14.05, p < .001), suggesting that temporal variable is a critical differentiating factor in the concentrations of fecal coliform across sampling sites by month.

Table 1. Mean MPN Values of total coliform, fecal coliform, and E. coli along the nine river barangays of Cagayan de Oro City from three samplings

Sampling mean	Total coliform count MPN/100 ml Mean	Fecal coliform count MPN/100 ml Mean	*Escherichia coli* MPN/100ml Mean
Barangay			
UPSTREAM			
1. Mambuaya	8300	5990	3420
2. Dansolihon	11833	2496	1296
3. Bayanga	8300	6933	3980
MIDSTREAM			
4. Lumbia	4400	3400	3230
5. Upper Balulang	9566	7270	5626
6. Nazareth	11833	4976	2056
DOWNSTREAM			
7. Isla de Oro	13733	6866	1730
8. Kauswagan	13733	6933	6933
9. Bonbon	16000	8300	7066

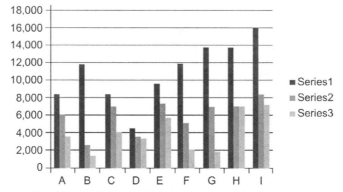

Legend: blue- total coliform, red- fecal coliform, green- E. coli. A- Mambuaya, B- Dansolihon, C- Bayanga, D- Lumbia, E- Upper Balulang, F- Nazareth, G- Isla de Oro, G-Isla de Oro, H-Kauswagan, I-Bonbon.

Figure 1. Mean MPN of total coliform, fecal coliform, and E. coli along the nine River barangays of Cagayan de Oro City.

DISCUSSION

The results showed Bonbon consistently had the highest MPN values for fecal coliform count and *E. coli* . The factor that contributes to high fecal contamination of the water is the increasing population of residents along the river banks. Most of the residents do not have toilets. They directly flush or drain human fecal wastes into the river. Bonbon is situated near the mouth of the river or downstream. This supports the contention of Pratt (1995) and Lata *et al.,* (2009) that areas near the mouth of the river or areas downstream receive large doses of pollutants.

Levels of fecal-coliform bacteria in a river can be influenced by many factors. The high fecal coliform concentrations in the different sites along the Cagayan de Oro River are contributed by human and animal (pigs, goats, cows, dogs, and chicken) wastes. This observation confirms the study of Alvarez *et al.,* (2008). The pathways these bacteria take to get into streams and rivers are varied and depend on the sources and the hydrologic conditions. Fecal-coliform bacteria from poultry houses and piggery might be washed into a stream down into the river during rainfall; pigs and dogs might defecate directly into a stream or river while feeding, and bacteria from human sources enter the water as a result of sewage spills, leaking sewer lines, malfunctioning of septic systems, or the number of comfort rooms draining into the river.

Escherichia coli is a bacterium commonly found in human and animal digestive tracts. High concentrations of fecal indicator bacteria like *E. coli* indicate an increased likelihood of pathogens being present (U.S. Environmental Protection Agency,1986). *E. coli* is a widely used indicator of fecal contamination in water bodies. External contact and subsequent ingestion of bacteria from fecal contamination can lead to harmful health effects (Money, *et al.,* 2009). A person swimming in highly contaminated water has a greater chance of getting sick from swallowing disease-causing organisms, or from pathogens entering the body through cuts in skin, the nose, mouth, or the ears. Diseases and illnesses such as typhoid fever, hepatitis, gastroenteritis, dysentery, and ear infections can be contracted in waters with high fecal coliform counts (Boothman, *et al.,* 2002). Some strains cause diarrhea, nausea and, if untreated, death (Todar, 2008).

High MPN indices indicate fecal contamination and pathogens in the water, increasing the risk of disease to people who use the river to bathe and for other activities. Ecotourism in the City will be adversely affected if the levels of disease-causing bacteria are not substantially reduced. According to Keeling (2007), contamination of drinking water by microbial pathogens, chemical compounds, or radiologic agents has the potential to affect the health of the population and may lead to severe morbidity and mortality in vulnerable population.

In general, the closer a sample is taken to the time and/or entry point of contamination, the higher the level of concentration of the bacteria. Inversely, the longer and/or further away from the point of entry, the lower the levels of the bacteria (U.S. Environmental Protection Agency) as cited by Alvarez *et al.,* (2008). Thus, it is possible that the high fecal coliform concentration obtained from the sampling sites was due to the proximity of sampling site to the point of entry. Direct disposal of human and animal feces into the river was the cause for the high level of contamination found in this study. Other factors that contribute to fecal coliform levels are dispersion of the bacteria over spatial scales, rainfall, discharge from streams, light penetration, and turbidity (Bracken and Harding, 2006).

On our test of differences in temporal and spatial variables, it can be seen that mean coliform count increased from Oct to Nov, then decreased sharply in Dec. There was a dry spell in the months preceeding the wet month of Dec. The sampling was done after the rain when the bacteria in the sampling sites were already washed away by the strong water currents. It is interesting to note that fecal coliform was higher during the rainy season, suggesting that there was a large disposal of human wastes into the river regardless of the season.

No significant differences were noted in the spatial variable, indicating that the concentration of bacteria was the same in the upstream, midstream and downstream sampling sites. This finding implies that the contamination is widespread. Animal husbandry in the upstream areas and large communities of residents in the midstream and downstream areas contributed to the river contamination.

Since Cagayan de Oro City is identified the water regulatory board as one of the urbanized areas with critical water quality , it is important for the city to maintain the quality of its water resources to safeguard public health, and to protect the ecotourism industry of the city. Improved sanitation and sewerage must be in place to prevent contamination of the water. Existing laws must be strictly implemented for the protection of the rivers for their sustainable use. The results of this study call for the relevant government agencies to share the responsibility of conserving and protecting the Cagayan de Oro River as a valuable water resource.

RECOMMENDATIONS

- Samples from seven tributaries of the Cagayan de Oro River should also be taken and analyzed since these tributaries could also be a contributory factor to the contamination of the river,
- Plan a wider study covering other river barangays, especially the upstream barangays to assess the implications of fecal contamination of the river to the city's ecotourism industry,
- Public education on river contamination and health issues for families living along the river, and proper sanitation and waste disposal procedures,
- Regular monitoring of river water quality with programs to restore and improve the river ecosystem for sustainable use,
- The findings of this study should be considered by the City Council for local legislation in the protection of the Cagayan de Oro River,
- The type of E. coli in the river must be identified,
- Conduct studies using molecular techniques to identify the source of E. coli whether from human or animal fecal wastes to aid the management of waste disposal in the river system.

CONCLUSION

High average MPN values of total coliform, fecal coliform, and E. coli exceeding the allowable values set by the DENR indicate that the Cagayan de Oro River is fecally contaminated. Among the barangays, Bonbon has the highest concentration of *E.coli* while Dansolihon has the lowest. The factors that contribute to the river's fecal contamination are the direct disposal of human wastes into the river system and the disposal of livestock manures into rivers. Total coliform and fecal coliform concentration vary spatially and temporally in the river system.

REFERENCES

Alvarez, Shane, Wedad Zainoden, Mohammad Abdullatif, Lani Marie Alamban, Sohali Laguindab, Norahinar Mamari, Dhan Michelle Itao and Haidee Modehar. (2008). *A cross-sectional study on the extent of fecal contamination of Cagayan de Oro River along five urban barangays and the factors affecting contamination.* (October 2007 – January 2008). JPAIR Journal.

Boothman, S. Mansfield, J. Weston, L. (2002). *Sources of Fecal Coliform Pollution within the Manly Lagoon Catchment.* In: UTS Freshwater Ecology Report 2002, Department of Environmental Sciences, University of Technology, Sydney. page 5

Bracken L., C. Hendricks & Anna Harding. (2006). *Apparent bias in river water inoculums following centrifuge. J. Microbiological methods.* 67(2), 304–309.

Deauna, M. C. & S. L. Dorado (1996). *Environmental science for Philippines schools* .927 Quezon Avenue, Philippines Phoenix Publishing House Inc.

Department of Environment and Natural Resources (DENR) – Region 10. *Standard methods for examination of water and wastewater.*

DOST. (1997) How to Collect Water samples for Microbiological Studies.Vol.No.2.

Eaton, A. D, S. C. Leonore, R. W. Eugene, G. E. Arnold. (2005). Standard Methods : For The Examination of Water and Wastewater.21st ed.

Evans, Doyle Jr. & Dolores G. Evans. Medical Microbiology.4th edition. The University of Texas Medical Branch at Galveston. Greenpeace. The State of water in the Philippines. 2007. p. 12

Pratt, Carl R. (1995). Ecology. Springhouse, Pennsylvania. pp 148–150.

Smeltzer, S. C., et.al., (2008). *Textbook of medical-surgical nursing* (11th Edition,Volume 2). Philadelphia: Lippincott Williams and Wilkins, a Wolters Kluwer Business. pp 2565–2566. World Heath Organization. *United Nations Environmental Programme.* 1999. Global Environmental Outlook 2000. Earthscan Publications, London, Op. cit

Lesley Casas Lubos
Research Publication Office
Liceo de Cagayan University, Liceo Arcade,
Rodolfo N. Pelaez Boulevard, Kauswagan, 9000 Cagayan De Oro City, Philippines
dawsonia@yahoo.com

Lalevie Casas Lubos
Bukidnon State University
Malaybalay City, Bukidnon Province, Philippines
lal2004love@yahoo.com

GLORINA P. OROZCO AND MACRINA T. ZAFARALLA

17. BIOPHYSICO-CHEMICAL AND SOCIOECONOMIC STUDY OF TWO MAJOR MANILA ESTEROS

ABSTRACT

Two major Manila esteros, the Estero de San Miguel and Estero de Quiapo, were studied to determine their ecological status. Analyses of physicochemical parameters of the esteros – turbidity, temperature, salinity, EC, pH, DO, BOD, COD,TKN, TP, chl-a, and oil and grease- showed the estero waters fall under Class D water quality criterion. TKN and TP values indicated hypertrophic conditions AT all stations. Low chl-a values were indicative of stressful conditions to the primary producers. Mean differences of most of the parameters differed significantly between stations and season. Four fish, *Rasbora maculata* (Kataba), *Gambusia affinis* (Mosquito Fish), *Anabas testudineus* (Climbing perch) and *Hypostomus plecostomus* (Janitor fish), with *Rasbora* and *Gambusia* inhabit the esteros. Fish communities exhibited high evenness but low in dominance and diversity. 19 phytoplankton genera - Cyanophyta (3 spp), Chlorophyta (9 spp) and Bacillariophyta (7 spp) thrived in the esteros. A socioeconomic study revealed that attitudes and actions of stakeholders to their esteros were influenced primarily by economic status, and educational and cultural background. Survey also showed the awareness of the communities on the problems of esteros and their willingness to cooperate to rehabilitate their polluted river system. Institutional initiatives such as environmental education and community-based programs were examined as possible approaches towards effective rehabilitation and attainment of sustainability of Manila esteros.

KEYWORDS

Esteros, Barangays, Rehabilitation, Sustainability

INTRODUCTION

Esteros, such as the Pasig River, are polluted creeks that drain into river systems. It is a natural type of waterway compared to man-made canals that receive wastewaters from municipalities. The Spanish term "estero" means estuary or little river and was probably coined by early Manila settlers during the Spanish era (Cojuangco, 2007). The original pristine freshwater condition of esteros have markedly deteriorated due to urbanization (Quismundo, 2004; Uy, 2006; Calumpita 2007) and many have been destroyed and are gone (Cojuangco, 2007).

Mijung Kim and C. H. Diong (Eds.), Biology Education for Social and Sustainable Development, 161–172.

Extensive pollution and clogging of esteros are causing extensive flooding in Metro Manila (Carcamo, 2007).

The worsening problem of the Pasig river, its esteros and communities, has prompted the government and private institutions to research the river system (JICA-MMDA, 2005; PRRC, 2007). There are few studies on Manila esteros (Corpuz and Librea, 1993; Parra and Socorro, 1994; Orozco and Dayao, 1996) and assessment of their current status can contribute to effective rehabilitation of these water systems. The main aim of this research were to determine the current ecological status of two major Manila esteros located in the frequently flooded university belt area. Specific objectives of the research were to: (i) determine the physico-chemical and biological parameters of two Manila esteros, (ii) assess the level of biodiversity in terms of species richness, diversity and dominance in the representative esteros, and (iii) provide baseline data and environmental information that can be used to educate and warn the public against the impending hazards brought about by the deteriorated condition of the esteros.

METHODOLOGY

(i)   *Study area and sampling sites:* The two esteros, Estero de San Miguel (2,674 m) and Estero de Quiapo (903 m) are located in the university belt area. Five sampling sites from the upstream, downstream, and three in the midstream areas were identified for the study. The study was conducted from May 2007 to May 2008. Measurements of physical parameters were done on-site. Chemical analyses (APHA, 1998) were conducted at the Institute of Chemistry, University of the Philippines at Los Baños

(ii) *Physico-chemical analysis:* Physical parameters measured on site using HORIBA Water Sampling Meter were, salinity, conductivity, turbidity, pH, temperature. Water depth and clarity were measured using an improvised Secchi Disc. Chemical parameters analyzed were chlorophyll-a (chl-*a*) by acetone extraction/ spectrophotometry, biological oxygen demand (BOD) at 5 days, 20 ^{0}C (by DOST), chemical oxygen demand (COD), total nitrogen (TN), and total phosphorous (TP), oil and grease (by ASL-Chem,UPLB). Dissolved oxygen (DO) was measured using the HORIBA sampling meter.

(iii) *Biological analysis:* Fishes were captured using fish net and sampling was done for an hour in the 10m length of the sampling area. Plankton was sampled with a plankton net. Captured fishes and plankton were preserved in 10% formalin and brought to the lab for identification and analysis.

(iv) *Statistical analysis:* Primary and secondary data were subjected to regression and correlation analysis to determine the parameters that have negative or positive impact with each other. Two-way ANOVA and DMRT were also conducted to determine if there are significant differences among the means of the physico-chemical parameters (SAS v.6.12)

(v)   *Species community indices*: Species diversity, dominance, evenness and similarity indices were measured using the formulae (Odum, 1981): Shannon index of general diversity H' = - $\sum$ Pi (log Pi), Evenness index, e = H'/ log S, index of dominance C = $\sum$ Pi^2 index of similarity , % IS = (2C/ S1+S2) x100.

(vi) *Socio economic survey:* A total of 250 structured interview questionnaires were used for the socio-economic survey. Households were randomly chosen within the study area. The survey instrument has four parts, (i) demographic and socio-economic parameters, (ii) awareness and attitude towards the esteros, (iii) uses of esteros and associated problems, and (iv) willingness to cooperate with government programs for the rehabilitation of esteros.

RESULTS AND DISCUSSION

Physical Parameters

(i) *Water depth and stream velocity:* Maximum water depth in the five sampling stations was 1.93 m at Station III during the Initial Wet sampling period (Table 1). Shallowest section was 0.5 m at Station I during the Dry Sampling season. Stream velocity was zero at Station I (Flood Gate) and very minimal at Station III (Pumping Station), (ii) *Temperature:* Differences in air and water temperatures at sampling stations were small. Average air and water temperature ranged from 27–36°C and 25–30°C. Warmer waters accelerated the growth of blue-green bacteria and could potentially stress fishes and aquatic organisms.

Table 1. Summary of physical parameters of the estero at five sampling stations during the wet and dry seasons

Parameters	Sampling Period*	I	II	III	IV	V	Mean	SD
				Stations				
Water depth (m)	IW	0.56	0.71	1.93	1.32	1.29	1.16	0.55
	CW	0.59	0.61	1.17	1.06	0.78	0.84	0.32
	DS	0.5	0.61	1.17	1.06	1.06	0.88	0.30
Stream velocity (m/s)	IW	0	0.103	0	0.12	0.12	0.07	0.06
	CW	0.00	0.07	0.13	0.29	0.32	0.16	0.14
	DS	0.00	0.10	0.05	0.09	0.08	0.06	0.04
Water temp(°C)	IW	30.63	29.33	29	29	29	29.40	0.70
	CW	26.5	25.67	25.70	25.93	25.70	25.90	0.35
	DS	32.53	28.2	31.6	30.1	30.1	30.51	1.65
Air temp (°C)	IW	36.67	38.17	36.67	35	35.3	36.37	1.26
	CW	28	27	27.00	27.33	27.00	27.27	0.43
	DS	38	33	36.00	34.00	34.00	35.00	2.00
Turbidity (NTU)	IW	30.33	25.67	24	21.33	24.3	25.13	3.30
	CW	41.33	37.67	32.33	45.00	33.67	38.00	5.27
	DS	51.33	51	32.33	71.67	40.33	49.33	14.80
SD clarity (m)	IW	0.33	0.46	0.35	0.46	0.41	0.40	0.06
	CW	0.25	0.31	0.5	0.36	0.42	0.37	0.10
	DS	0.25	0.39	0.42	0.25	0.36	0.33	0.08

*IW - Initial Wet, CW - Cold, Wet, DS – Dry Season

Table 2. Average field measurements of the chemical parameters

Parameter	Sampling Period*	Stations						
		I	II	III	IV	V	Ave	SD
Salinity (%)	CW	0.3	0.02	0.02	0.02	0.01	0.07	0.13
	DS	0.03	0.003	0.22	0.01	0.01	0.05	0.09
Conductivity	IW	15.37	0.47	14.14	0.4	0.42	6.16	7.86
(ms/cm)	CW	0.7	0.5	0.53	0.52	0.38	0.53	0.11
	DS	0.84	0.24	4.24	0.04	0.80	1.23	1.72
pH	IW	5.3	5.27	4.97	3.44	5.5	4.90	0.84
	CW	7.83	7.7	7.70	7.53	7.50	7.65	0.14
	DS	5.63	4.69	6.58	5.32	5.23	5.49	0.70
DO (mg/l)	IW	4.42	4.51	4.52	4.57	4.5	0.49	0.52
	CW	2.92	2.9	2.80	2.75	2.89	2.85	0.07
	DS	0.14	1.41	0.21	0.30	0.38	4.50	0.05
BOD (mg/l)	IW	11	19.2	18.4	19.7	19.8	17.62	3.74
	CW	12	35.6	26.8	49.8	28.7	30.58	13.76
	DS	11.7	13.3	25.1	38.3	39.8	25.64	13.30
COD (mg/l)	IW	101.44	18.01	51.19	18.49	20.86	42.00	36.03
	CW	12.06	24.13	21.34	31.32	17.63	26.10	13.53
	DS	9.56	17.21	44.93	30.59	28.2	21.30	7.20
TKN (mg/l)	IW	5.7	13.18	16.44	12.58	16.44	12.87	4.39
	CW	1.84	16.28	15.27	23.09	12.51	13.80	7.74
	DS	0.9	1.33	10	11.29	12.59	7.22	5.65
TP (mg/l)	IW	1.1	1.53	1.66	1.55	1.61	1.49	0.22
	CW	0.45	1.72	1.43	1.84	1.15	1.32	0.55
	DS	0.82	0.83	1.34	1.67	1.46	1.22	0.38
OG (mg/l)	IW	11	6.22	10	6.7	16.78	10.14	4.24
	CW	5.67	10.41	8.61	6.57	6.06	7.46	2.00
	DS	7.07	4.29	3.51	3.09	3.91	4.37	1.57
Chl-a (mg/m³)	IW	6.22	3.09	2.46	0.5	0.61	2.58	2.33
	CW	7.66	2.66	2.03	0.45	1.15	2.79	2.85
	DS	6.59	0.88	2.32	0.8	0.39	2.20	2.56

(iii) *Turbidity & Clarity:* Turbidity is a function of at least three variables, namely, dissolved chemicals, suspended particles and density of microorganisms in water, and phytoplankton blooms which make the water opaque causing light depletion (Sarokin and Schulkin, 1992). Water turbidity ranged from 25–38 NTU for the Wet Sampling season and increased to 49 NTU for the Dry Season.

Clarity is a measure of water transparency using Secchi Disk (SD). The highest reading was recorded at Stations II & IV and the lowest, at Station I .Station I, a flood gate that was kept closed, was the dirtiest sampling station. This explained why Station I had the highest turbidity and lowest transparency readings due to the high concentration of wastes and scum trapped in the flood gate.

Chemical Parameters

(i) *Salinity*: The salinity standards for fresh water and brackish water are < 0.05% and < 0.05% to 3%, respectively (WQM, 2007). Stations I and III had high salinity, indicative of a brackish water condition probably due to its proximity to Pasig River which runs into Manila Bay. (ii) *Conductivity*: Conductivity measured at Stations I and III was high. (iii) *pH*: Average pH of the esteros was 4.9, ranging from pH 3.44 at Station IV to pH 5.5 of Station V. The lower pH probably results from decomposition of wastes and fecal materials in the esteros. (iv) *Dissolved oxygen*: Dissolved oxygen concentration measures the assimilation capacity of water to dissolve oxygen from air and from aquatic photosynthesis. DO readings fall between the criteria values of 5.0 mg/l and 3.0 mg/l for Class C and D waters, respectively. Other studies on esteros have shown very low DO readings in different sampling stations (PRRC, 2007; Orozco and Dayao, 1996; Parra and Socorro, 1994; and Corpuz and Librea, 1993). (v) *Biological oxygen and chemical demand*: BOD and COD measure the relative oxygen-depletion effect of a waste contaminant and are widely adopted as measures of pollution. In shallow waters, excessive BOD and COD can cause oxygen depletion and deprived organisms of oxygen (LLDA, 2007). Average COD of 21 – 42 mg/l indicates Class C waters, BOD of 17–30 mg/l fell beyond Class D waters. Water quality criteria (DAO 34; Zafaralla, *et.al.*, 2005) are as follows: For DO: Class C = 3–5 mg/l; For BOD: Class C =5–10 mg/l , Class D =10–15 mg/l, below than D > 15 mg/l; For COD: Class C =25–50 mg/l, Class D =50–75 mg/l , below D > 75 mg/l; For Total N: Class D = 3–10 mg N/ l , below D > 10 mg N/ l, Hypertrophic > 0.3 mg/l; For Total P: Class C = 0.2–0.4 mg P/l, Class D > 0.4 mg P/l, Hypertrophic > 0.10 mg/l; For Chl-a : Class B < = 25 ug/l (mg/m^3) , Oligotrophic: 0–4 mg/m^3; For Oil & Grease: Class D > 5mg/l. (vi) *Total nitrogen:* Total nitrogen (TN or TKN) combines all ionic forms of nitrogen and those fixed in the tissues of living organisms and organic debris. It measures the amount of nitrogen incorporated in organic biomass (Zafaralla, *et.al.*, 2005). Average TKN ranged from 7–13 mgN/ l which fell beyond the classification of Class D waters. High levels of nitrogen is a confirmatory indicator of the extensive inputs of domestic sewage and other nitrogen sources in the esteros. (vii) *Total phosphorous*: Total phosphorous (TP) is the combined phosphorous (P) and fixed (P) in the bodies of living and dead organisms. Average TP of 1.2 – 1.5 mgP/l fell beyond the limit of 0.4 mgP/ L for Class D waters and is indicative of hypertrophic waters (Zafaralla *et al.,* 2005). (viii) *Oil and grease*: Average oil and grease ranged from 4–10mg/l indicative of Class D waters. Stagnant waters at the Station V, the dead end of the esteros, accounted for the high oil and grease value. High tides in Manila Bay cause the normal river flow to reverse its direction, and polluted waters drain back to the river tributaries and Laguna Lake (ADB, 2007). (ix) *Chlorophyll-a*: Chl-*a* measures the relative amount of algal biomass in the esteros. It is one of the parameters used to describe the trophic state of a body of water (Zafaralla *et al.,* 2005). Observed mean chl-a of 2.6 mg/m^3, with a range of 0.5 – 6.22 mg/m^3 in the stations, is indicative of a low potential of producers in the estero to provide plankton-based nourishment for fishes.

There was significant positive correlation between the following sets of parameters: salinity, conductivity, COD; depth, TP,TN; velocity, clarity; and BOD,TP,TN, chl-a. Significant negative correlation was found for these sets of parameters: salinity, velocity, chl-a; chl-a,TP, TKN, BOD; and DO, turbity, oil and grease. ANOVA and DMRT showed significant mean differences of most of the parameters per station and sampling season. The levels of parameters noted were indicative of a worse than Class D water; these waters were very polluted and were therefore not used unless it has undergone natural filtration via a vegetated buffer zone. TKN and TP results show The esteros pose a threat to eutrophication and organic pollution in the Pasig River which they feed, as borne out by the TKN and TP results.

Biological Parameters

Four species of fish were found in the esteros. The smaller number of fish species in Estero de Quiapo does not appear to be the result of the more degraded nature of the estero as indicated by the Class D water quality based on the physico-chemical analysis. Community indices showed that fish diversity in Estero de San Miguel and Estero de Quiapo were similar; Evenness Index was higher in the first estero with only two fish species. Dominant fish were the mollies and mosquito fishes. Index of dominance is higher in the first estero. Index of Similarity of the two esteros was moderate, with a value of 67%, implying that the number and species of fish in most of the stations were mostly similar.

Biological diversity was higher in Estero de San Miguel than in Estero de Quiapo, and lower during the dry season. Evenness index showed a greater apportionment of individuals per species in Estero de San Miguel than in Estero de Quiapo, with values of 0.280 and 0.106 respectively. Lower evenness index was observed during the dry season. However, the index of dominance was higher during the dry season with values ranging from 0.93 to 0.96, and slightly lower, 0.85 to 0.90, during the wet season. This may be due to some of the more resilient species of cyanophytes that tend to dominate and out-number the less resilient chlorophytic species. Index of similarity is also higher during the dry season as many of the less resilient species had died off.

SOCIO-ECONOMIC STUDY: DEMOGRAPHIC AND SOCIO-ECONOMIC CHARACTERISTICS

The study area covers two adjacent municipalities of Manila, namely Quiapo of District III and San Miguel of District VI . Draining the area are Tow esteros, Estero de San Miguel and Estero de Quiapo, drained the area. San Miguel has 12 barangays and a total population of 16,798 in 3,589 households. Quiapo has 16 barangays and a population of 24,616 in 5,153 households (MCLUPZO, 2005).

Table 3. Average count of estero fishes and their community indices

Fishes per Sampling Period	Average Count of Fishes		Community Indices*	
	San Miguel Stations (I & III)	Quiapo Stations (IV–V)	Estero San Miguel	Estero de Quiapo
Initial Wet				
Anabas testudineus	10	0	H' = 0.30	0.30
Hypostomus plecostomus	2	0	e = 0.50	0.99
Rasbora maculata	236	662	C = 0.56	0.50
Gambusia affinis	550	700	% IS 0.67	
Total	798	1362		
Cold Wet				
Anabas testudineus	0	0	H' = 0.27	0.25
Hypostomus plecostomus	0	0	e = 0.90	0.84
Rasbora maculata	238	245	C = 0.57	0.60
Gambusia affinis	519	657	% IS 1.00	
Total	757	902		
Dry Season				
Anabas testudineus	0	0	H' = 0.30	0.30
Hypostomus plecostomus	0	0	e = 0.98	1.00
Rasbora maculata	929	384	C = 0.51	0.50
Gambusia affinis	686	348	% IS 1.00	0.30
Total	1615	732		

*Community Indices:
(1) Shannon Index of diversity
(2) Evenness Index
(3) Index of Dominance
(4) Index of Similarity

$H' = -\sum Pi\ (log\ Pi)$
$e = H'/log\ S$
$C = \sum Pi^2$
$\%\ IS = (2C/S1+S2)\ x100$

Table 4. Average count of estero phytoplankton for the wet and dry sampling periods

Species	Average Count			
	Wet Season		Dry Season	
	San Miguel	de Quiapo	San Miguel	de Quiapo
Division Cyanophyta				
Anabaena sp.	0	0	23	0
Microcystis sp.	63936	0	84809	0
Oscillatoria sp.	519	779	1145	1395
Division Chlorophyta	0	0	0	0
Cladophora	0	0	3	4
Closteriopsis sp.	12	0	0	0
Closterium sp.	6	0	0	0
Coelastrum	0	0	113	0
Crucigenia sp.	89	0	0	0
Pediastrum sp.	456	0	293	10
Scenedesmus sp.	44	0	11	0

Spirogyra	0	0	0	0
Staurastrum	0	0	6	0
Division Bacillariophyta	0	0	0	0
Coscinodiscus sp.	12	0	6	0
Melosira ap.	833	0	31	0
Navicula sp.	0	9.5	3	4
Nitzschia sp.	63	0	17	10
Stephanodiscus sp.	1264	57	1677	0
Surirella sp.	0	0	0	4
Synedra sp.	12	0	6	0
Total	67245	845.5	88144	1427
n	12	3	14	6

Among the problems in sanitation and sewage in Manila is the heavy pollution from the effluents of domestic septic tanks. World Bank (MCLUPZO, 2005) reported that the estimated amount of septic tanks in year 2000 was 125, 279 with a population septic tank ratio of 13:6. A portion of Manila's wastewater is collected by lateral interceptor pipes and are conveyed to Tondo main pumping stations through seven lift pumping stations. The ultimate sewer outfall is Manila Bay. The Manila Sewerage system serves 30% of the city, while other households discharge their sewage either into a storm drains, septic tanks or directly into esteros (MCLUPZO, 2005). In the absence of septic tanks, households have structural provisions of human excrement to drop directly to the esteros.

Respondents' Awareness and Attitude Towards Esteros

78% of respondents have houses encroached to the esteros, with a majority claiming the estero as their birthplace; 24% said they worked there and schools are close to the estero. The community were not bothered by the stinky odour and the filthy surroundings of the esteros. Respondents were well informed by the government through their barangay leaders of the hazards of living near the esteros since these are the major passageway of flood waters during rainy season. Respondents claimed they were well adapted to living in estero communities despite the filthy surroundings. Unknown, or ignored by the community, is the fact that the estero is a reservoir of harmful chemicals that can harm the human body. The water in the river system is one large culture medium of waterborne diseases tied to the esteros that receive human and animal excreta. Scarcity of algal species and their small populations, and low fish species richness and diversit are biological indicators of the impaired aquatic health of the esteros as shown by the results of physico-chemical analysis.

Institutional Initiatives

Community-based program is a key to resource rehabilitation and sustainability. More than 100 groups from the government, private sector, local and foreign groups have responded to the call to rehabilitate the Pasig River and its esteros. Some of the institutional programs include the Green Coalition and Sagip Pasig Movement that focuses on community mobilization, public information and advocacy in the context of the overall rehabilitation program.

The Pasig River Rehabilitation Commission (PRRC) under the Dept. of Environment and Natural Resources (DENR) was created under the Executive Order no. 54 (1999) to look into the problems of the Pasig River and its tributaries. Presidential Decree No. 274 (1973) pertains to the function of PRRC on the preservation, improvement and pollution control of Pasig River and its banks (Chanrobles, 2006). PRRC is currently collaborating with academic institutions, such as Far Eastern University and other schools under the Mendiola Consortium for effective rehabilitation of the river and its esteros.

CONCLUSION AND RECOMMENDATION

Physico-chemical parameters of the esteros fall under the class C and D water quality criteria, indicating a very polluted water system. TN and TP values indicate hypertrophic estero waters. However, chl-a values are within those for oligotrophic waters. Pearson's correlation analysis showed a positive correlation between TN, TP, DO, BOD, COD, turbidity, hl-a, water depth, temperature, salinity, conductivity, clarity, and stream velocity. Four fish species thrived in the esteros, with Rasbora maculata and Gambusia affinis as the dominant species. Shannon Index showed higher fish diversity in Estero de Quiapo than in San Miguel with an index of similarity of 67%. Evenness index showed higher apportionment of fishes per species in Estero de San Miguel. Previous studies (Orozco and Dayao, 1996) had reported that mudfishes were captured in other esteros and sold in wet markets. Since the fishes captured in this study were not for human consumption, it is recommended that a different sampling method be used to capture this fish. Heavy metal analysis of fishes and water samples and investigations of plankton, macrobenthos and coliform in biological analysis, are recommended for future studies.

Socioeconomic study revealed a low poverty level of the estero communities which affects their attitude and use of the esteros. Survey also showed the awareness of the communities on the problems of esteros and their willingness to cooperate in the rehabilitation of their water resource. Institutional initiatives and community-based programs are promising tools for the effective rehabilitation and attainment of sustainability of Manila esteros. Environmental education of the estero communities is a promising response. Environmental education, through the joint efforts of the Far Eastern University and other Mendiola Consortium NSTP classes, holds considerable promise and is an important initiative to involve the community in community-based resource management programs to successfully rehabilitate the estero system.

ACKNOWLEDGEMENTS

Our deep gratitude to the following: (1) The *Philippines Commission on Higher Education*, for support of the dissertation research and travel grants given to the first author for the conduct and presentation of this study, (2) Far Eastern University administration and colleagues, for their support and encouragement, (3) Dr. Maxima Flavier and the staff of the Analytical Services Lab, UPLB-Institute of Chemistry, for the loan of the HORIBA water sampling meter and allowing the first author to work in their laboratory, (3) Our families and friends for their loving support, and (4) The Lord God Almighty, for the success of this research. Unto HIM be the glory forever, amen.

REFERENCES

American Public Health Association (APHA). (1998). American Water Works Association and Water Pollution Control Federation. Standard Methods for the Examination of Water and Wastewater. APHA, Washington, DC.

Asian Development Bank (ADB). (2007). ADB Project Loan: The Pasig River System. http://www.adb.org/Documents/RRPS/PHI/rrp_phi_30308.pdf (Retrieved: April 17, 2007)

Calumpita, R. (2002). Poor Sewage treatment, sanitation costs. P67B. http://www.yehey.com/news/Article.aspx?id=131354 (Retrieved: Jan.10,2007).

Carcamo, D. (2007). MMDA Squatters causing floods. http://www.gmanews.tv/breakingnews.php?id=19530 (Retrieved: Jan.10,2007).

Chanrobles, (2006). Phil. Environmental Laws. http://www.chanrobles.com/adminstrativeorder no.3 .htm. (Retrieved: May 8, 2008).

Cojuangco, (2007). The Vanishing Esteros. The Phil. Star. Sunday Lifestyle. H-2. Sept. 2, 2007.

Corpuz, M. L. & M. Librea. (1993). Physico-chemical and Microbiological study of Estero Aviles. College of the Holy Spirit. Mla. Undergad Thesis. Unpubl.

DENR Administrative Order No. 34. Series of 1990. www.emb.gov.ph/region (Retrieved:May 8,2008).

Japan International Cooperation Agency (JICA) and Metropolitan Manila Development Authority (MMDA). March 2005. The study on the drainage improvement in the Core Area of Metropolitan Manila, Philippines.

Laguna Lake Development Authority (LLDA) –Mondrian, 2007. *http://www.llda.gov.ph* (Retrieved: Mar.15,2007).

Manila Comprehensive Land Use Plan and Zoning Ordinance (MCLUPZO). 2005–2020, Manila City, Philippines.

Odum, E. 1981. Fundamental of Ecology. Philadelphia: WB Saunders Co., USA.

Orozco, G. P. & L. Dayao. (1996). Physico-chemical analysis and Fish study of Estero Aviles. *CHS Research Monitor. 19*(1), 1–11.

Parra, E. & M. T.Socorro. (1993). Determination of the extent of pollution in various exteros around San Miguel, Mla. Centro Escolar Univ. Undergrad thesis , unpubl.

Pasig River Rehabilation Commission (PRRC). (2007). Preliminary Baseline Study: Pasig River Tributaries. Dept. of Environment and Natural Resources (DENR)-PRRC, Visayas Ave, QC.

Quismundo, T. May (2004). Manila catch basin of metropolis' trash. http://www.inq7.net/met/2004/may/26/met_3-1.htm (Retrieved: Mar.15,2007).

Sarokin , D. & J. Schulkin 1992. The role of pollution in aquatic populations. *Environment Science and Technology. 26*(8), 1476–1483.

Uy, Veronica. (2006). Recto: RP must say 'sayonara' to Japanese waste. http://www.inq7.net/ (Retrieved: Mar.15, 2007).

Water Quality Monitoring. (2007). http://www.fivecreeks.org/monitor/sal.html (Retrieved: Jan 10, 2007).

Zafaralla, M et. al. (2005). Water Resources of Laguna Lake. Ecosystems and People. The Philippine Millennium Ecosystem Assessment: Sub-global Assessment. College of Forestry and Natural Resources. Univ. of the Phil. Los Baños.

Glorina P. Orozco
Far Eastern University,
Nicanor Reyes Street, Manila, Philippines
Email: orozcogp@yahoo.com

Macrina T. Zafaralla
University of the Philippines at Los Baños
Institute of Biological Science, College of Arts and Science
Philippines

JAN WILLEM KETELAAR AND ALMA LINDA ABUBAKAR

18. SUSTAINABLE INTENSIFICATION OF AGRICULTURAL PRODUCTION: THE ESSENTIAL ROLE OF ECOSYSTEM-LITERACY EDUCATION FOR SMALLHOLDER FARMERS IN ASIA

ABSTRACT

FAO estimates that farmers will have to produce twice as much food as they do today as to feed the expected 9.2 billion global population by 2050. With declining availability of water and production land per caput, lower productivity, stress induced by climate change and changing consumer patterns, farmers will have to *intensify* agricultural production. The challenge will be for them to do so *sustainably*. Inefficient use of agro-chemicals, both pesticides and fertilizers, remains prevalent among smallholder farmers in Asia. Vital ecosystem services provided by natural biological control and pollination are compromised as a result. Enduring and new concerns over farmer health, environmental pollution and food safety caused by indiscriminate use of agro-chemicals call for safer and more sustainable crop intensification and protection strategies. FAO has been working with Asian governments to develop robust Integrated Pest Management (IPM) strategies for a range of economically important crops during the last two decades. This paper will detail case studies of successfully employed IPM farmer education strategies, making optimal use of the innovative and adult-education-based Farmers Field Schools. The paper will make the case that it is of vital importance for achieving global food security that the millions of Asian farmers become ecology-literate and better managers through access to quality education. The paper will also highlight policy lessons learned, at national and global level, with regards to the pivotal role that farmer education plays for sustainable intensification of agricultural production.

KEYWORDS

Sustainable Crop Intensification, Integrated Pest Management, Farmers Field Schools, Ecology-Literacy Training

INTRODUCTION

FAO estimates that farmers will have to produce twice as much food as they do today as to feed the expected 9.2 billion global population by 2050. With declining

Mijung Kim and C. H. Diong (Eds.), Biology Education for Social and Sustainable Development, 173–182.

availability of water and production land per caput, lower productivity gains, changes in land-use patterns (e.g. increased use of land for bio-fuel crop production instead of food crops), stress induced by climate change (drought, floods, pest and disease yield reducing factors) and changing consumer patterns (increased meat and dairy consumption by the growing affluent urban population in the rising economies, particularly in Asia), farmers will have to *intensify* agricultural production. The challenge will be for them to do so *sustainably*.

Much of global food production is in the hands of smallholder farmers, many with landholdings equal or less than 1 ha per farmer. These farmers are the custodian of vital ecosystem services provided by natural biological processes, such as biological control, pollination and nutrient cycles. Intensification of agricultural production will require smallholder farmers to manage these important biological processes (FAO, 2010). Unfortunately, many farmers remain ignorant of good agricultural practices for sustainable management of these biological processes, vital for crop production. Smallholder farmers across Asia, often encouraged by government supported agricultural intensification programs, continue to increase the use of chemical inputs (e.g. inorganic fertilizers and pesticides) in order to boost crop yields. In 2010 global pesticide sales were expected to exceed US$ 40 billion. Herbicides represent the largest market segment whereas the share of insecticides has shrunk and that of fungicides has grown of the last 10 years (Rana, 2010). Intensive use of pesticides compromises vital ecosystems services, leading to increased risk of pest and disease outbreaks and subsequent crop failures. Intensive use of agro-chemicals, most notably pesticides, cause domestic and international food safety concerns and jeopardizes trade. Pesticides are also known to cause serious health concerns among often ill-prepared and highly exposed applicators, although most pesticide poisoning cases go unreported. Increasingly, there are calls for global food production to move away from the dominant model of high-input based crop intensification through increased use of agro-chemicals. In recent years, governments are encouraged to promote and educate farmers to manage and make better use of agro-ecological processes for sustainable intensification of agricultural productions (De Schutter, 2010; FAO, 2011).

Awareness raising in tandem with knowledge and skill development on the management of agro-ecological processes among the millions of smallholder farmers will thus be of vital importance as to secure global food security. Global investments in the agriculture sector have diminished substantially in recent decades and most rural extension systems have been neglected and are under-funded. Despite of this, FAO, over the last two decades, supported the development of innovative rural education efforts to promote understanding and good management of agro-ecological processes. Millions of smallholder farmers have benefitted from participation in Farmers Field Schools and obtained direct benefits in terms of higher yields and economic returns. This paper will explain and outline the underlying educational principles of the Farmers Field School and include case studies on the successful employment of this education tool for training smallholder farmers in Integrated Pest Management and more productive crop management making optimal use of the vital ecosystem services mentioned above. The paper will conclude with a couple of important lessons learned and policy level recommendation, with focus on making the case for increased investments in rural education and ecosystem literacy training for Asian smallholder farmers in particular.

FARMERS FIELD SCHOOLS: EFFECTIVE EDUCATION TOOLS FOR ECOSYSTEM-LITERACY TRAINING

Integrated Pest Management: The Development, Spread and Diversification of Farmers Field Schools

Integrated Pest Management can be defined as a knowledge-intensive management approach for keeping crop insect populations and disease pathogens below economically-damaging levels. Various extension methods have been used in the past to promote IPM among smallholder farmers, from World Bank promoted Training &Visit (T&V) based strategic extension campaigns to more participatory, non-formal education based approaches. No method has been proven as successful in the promotion of -and education of farmers about- Integrated Pest Management as has been the Farmers Field School.

Originally invented by FAO and piloted among rice farmers in Indonesia in the late 1980s/early 1990s, the FFS-approach was rapidly applied to IPM education programs supported by FAO and other donors in countries throughout Asia during the early-mid 1990s and from 1995 onwards piloted in Africa and elsewhere. What made the Farmers Field School so successful and geographically-wide applied was the realization that farmers learn best about knowledge-intensive management techniques/approaches through adult-education based discovery learning. The Farmers Field Schools promoted group-based learning through exchange of experience, field-based experimentation and application of management recommendations based on field observations and analysis thereof. Farmers meet on weekly basis throughout a cropping season, grow a crop from seed to harvest and learn how to make well-informed crop management decisions (Figure 1). Conventional management approaches are

Figure 1. Lao farmers learn about Bean Integrated Pest Management in a Farmers Field School (Source: Ketelaar, J.W.H).

compared with IPM management approaches and impact thereof on yields and net returns. Farmers Field Schools-based education programs in recent years have diversified to educate farmers about other knowledge-intensive management approaches such as land and soil ecology, integrated crop and nutrient management, conservation agriculture, farming systems, animal husbandry, agro-forestry and watershed-management. The FFS is now internationally recognized for its potential for agricultural extension reform (IAASTD, 2009) and as the most effective educational approach for educating farmers about *knowledge-intensive* natural resource management approaches (Swanson and Rajalahti, 2010). FFS-based discovery learning methods have also been used to inform and educate school children in rural areas, and through them their parents, about biology education, agriculture and vital importance of ecosystem services for sustainable development (Bartlett and Jatiket, 2004).

Adult Education Concepts and Theories and Application in Farmers Field Schools

Farmer Field School alumni not only address plant production and protection issues in their own fields with confidence but they also help other farmers learn and apply IPM. FFS alumni continue to work in groups and actively seek solutions to other broader community concerns that impact on their lives, e.g., irrigation issues and pesticide-related community environmental problems. The empowerment resulting from learning in Farmer Field Schools can be attributed to processes learners go through that are based on key concepts and theories of adult non-formal education (FAO, 2002). Learning is defined as the process whereby knowledge is created through the transformation of experience and all activities in the FFS follow the experiential learning cycle that allows for concrete experience, observation and reflection, generalization and active experimentation (Kolb, 1984). For that matter, the FFS employs experiential and discovery-based approaches because adults tend to attach more meaning to learning they gain from experience rather than passive means. The concept of andragogy, the art of teaching adults, recognizes that human beings become ready to learn when there is a need as to cope with problems faced in real life (Knowles, 1968) and is optimized when they are placed in control of their learning (Rogers, 1969). This explains why FFS participants design their own location-specific curriculum and experiments based on their field problems. This concept is supported by the *Critical Theory Framework* that explains how humans approach knowledge with an "orientation toward technical control, mutual understanding in the conduct of life, and emancipation from seemingly 'natural' constraint" (Habermas, 1971). The *Critical Theory Framework* also explains the importance of interaction and communication to arrive at consensual agreement demonstrated in FFS through the process of small and plenary group discussions aimed at consultation and arriving at agreed management decisions to employ in crop management and field experiments. Likewise, FFS activities are designed around the concept that adult learners see education as a process of developing increased competence to achieve their full potential in life.

CASE STUDIES: ECOSYSTEM-LITERACY TRAINING IN RURAL COMMUNITIES FOR PROMOTION OF INTEGRATED PEST MANAGEMENT AND PESTICIDE RISK REDUCTION FOR SUSTAINABLE CROP PRODUCTION INTENSIFICATION.

Sustainable Intensification of Rice Production and the Vital Role of Ecosystem-literacy Training Through IPM Farmers Field Schools in the Philippines

The development and promotion of Integrated Pest Management among rice farmers in the Philippines has a long history of success and failure. The International Rice Research Institute, based in Los Banos, Philippines, played a key role in the development of rice Integrated Pest Management, based on field research in the early 1980s. This research was prompted by increased reports of rice pest outbreaks, most notably Brown Plant Hoppers (*Niloparvata lugens*), following calendar-based applications of broad-spectrum pesticides by smallholder farmers across Asia, including in Philippines. Under normal, non-disturbed rice ecological conditions throughout much of Asia, rice pest populations are kept in check through biological control by a variety of parasitoids and predators. Pesticide applications eliminate these vital ecosystem services and encourage pest resistance build-up (Gallagher *et al*, 2005).

The Philippine government extension services initiated Strategic Extension Campaigns and Training and Visit (T&V) based training programs for extension workers and farmers to learn about IPM. However, despite of considerable efforts and resources employed for these T&V based extension efforts, rice farmers were not convinced and continued their practice of calendar-based pesticide applications in their attempts to keep pest problems under control. It was only when the non-formal education based Farmers Field School was introduced in the Philippines, that rice farmers, nation-wide, started to learn about IPM and make use of the vital ecosystem services provided by natural biological control. Figure 2 illustrates the frequency of pesticide applications and use of pesticide active ingredient per hectare used in rice production in Central and Southern Luzon in the Philippines from 1966 to 2007. The figure shows a steady increase of frequency and pesticide active ingredient throughout much of the 1966–1990 period, during the heydays of the Green Revolution. Whereas IPM T&V based extension campaigns were initiated in earnest during the mid-1980s it was only from the early 1990s onwards that, with the development and up-scaling of Farmers Field Schools, Philippine rice farmers started to reduce on-farm use of pesticides. During the 1994–2007 period rice farmers reduced pesticide application frequency and active ingredient per hectare with over 70% and increased yields per hectare with over 12%. Rice yield obtained by IPM-trained farmers were also much more stable over seasons (15%) compared to those obtained by non-IPM trained farmers. During the same period, total national rice production increased over 60% from 10.5 MMton in 1994 to 16.8 MMton in 2007.

The IPM and ecosystem literacy training provided to rice farmers nation-wide through the Department of Agriculture's National IPM/Farmers Field School Training Program KASAKALIKASAN was instrumental in obtaining these impressive results. The case of successful rice production intensification in the

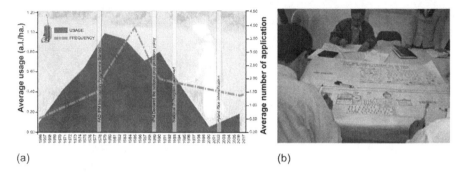

(a)   (b)

Figure 2. (a) Pesticide application frequency and use of active ingredient per hectare by Philippine Rice Farmers and initiation of IPM policy and training programmes during period 1966–2007 (Source: Jesse Binamira, Coordinator, Philippine DA's National IPM/Farmers Field School Programme KASAKALIKASAN, adapted from Rola & Pingali, 1993; Mataia, Jamora, Maya & Dawe, 2009; Warburton, Palis & Pingali, 1995; Dawe, 2006; IRRI, 2007), (b) Vietnamese community stakeholders prepare Map on Pesticide Flow in the Community in a Curriculum Development Workshop for Farmer Field School on IPM and Pesticide Risk Reduction (Source: Do, K.C.).

Philippines described above clearly shows that total national rice production output can be raised substantially in tandem with considerable reductions in use of pesticides. In other words, successful cases of *sustainable* intensification of crop production exist in Asia and lessons learned should be shared and taken on board when other countries in Asia embark on new efforts to intensify crop production in the years/decades to come.

Community Education for Pesticide Risk Reduction in Vietnam

During the past decade, the Government of Vietnam has emphasized a commodity based agricultural approach aimed at securing domestic food security while maintaining a high level of export growth. The need to adhere to prevailing quality standards as a requirement to secure stable exports and in response to increasing concerns among domestic consumers over food safety it has become even more important to strengthen Integrated Pest Management (IPM) and Good Agricultural Practices (GAP) farmer training programs. In tandem with such training efforts, there was a need to develop sustainable pest and pesticide management policies, to strengthen the regulatory framework to control the distribution and use of pesticides, and to enhance capacity for implementation of these policies and enforcement of pesticide legislation. These were the premises on which the Vietnam National IPM Program with support from the FAO, designed the

Community Education Programs on Pesticide Risk Reduction in two pilot communes (Hanoi and Thai Binh) in Vietnam in recent years. The Programs were designed to strengthen community ownership in planning, management and implementation of pesticide risk reduction efforts. The pilot areas were selected based on their high pesticide use and the willingness and agreement of local leaders, farmers, pesticide sellers, representatives from the public health sector and social organizations to volunteer and participate actively in the program.

At inception of the project, all concerned stakeholders were involved in a Community, Environmental and Household Mapping exercise to determine the status of current crop production, pesticide use and management in the communities. The information was used to prepare Community Action Plans to address pesticide risks and design the training curricula and activities. The stakeholders involved local leaders, farmers, pesticide sellers, representatives from social organizations (e.g., Women's Union, Farmer's Union, Youth Union, etc.), local environment agency, public health sector and pesticide inspectors. The results of the survey were consolidated in a Community Planning Meeting where the stakeholders also developed the long-term Community Pesticide Risk Reduction Plan. These Plans included ecology-literacy training for farmers through IPM Farmer Field Schools with a fortified Pesticide Risk Reduction curriculum. A multiple-year Impact Assessment Study done by Hanoi Agriculture University (HAU) and completed in December 2010 revealed positive impacts at community and farmer levels (Do et al, 2010). For example, pesticide sellers showed marked increases in awareness and knowledge of pesticide policies and regulations, which resulted into more thorough and frequent inspections of pesticide stores (by 53% in Hanoi and 73% in Thai Binh compared to baseline). Consequently, three shops were forced to close because they had no license or they were selling poor quality pesticides.

Communities adopted IPM and reduced use of pesticides in crop production. The annual consumption of pesticides was reduced by 4.9 kg/ha in Hanoi and 4.3 kg in Thai Binh (-69% and -60%, respectively, relative to control). Communities also took action on organizing the proper disposal of empty pesticide containers to reduce environmental contamination and prevent contact with children, livestock and wildlife. In the two project communes in Vietnam, 11 new pesticide collection tanks were constructed, four of which with funds from local social organizations, i.e., Cooperative, Women's Union, Farmers' Union, Youth Union. In Thai Binh, the gathering of empty pesticide containers increased by 59%. The FAO supported Pesticide Risk Reduction Community Education Programs also has had an extraordinary impact on national pest management policy reform.

The Vietnamese government has enacted Directive No. 1504-BNN-BVTV dated on 3rd June 2009 on Strengthening Pesticide Management. This policy required the involvement of the community in pesticide risk reduction and the use of Good Agricultural Practices, including IPM for production of safe vegetables. The enactment of MARD's Circular No. 2388-BNN-BVTV on Pesticide Management in Vegetable Production indicates the policy impact of the program. At the provincial level, the model of pesticide risk reduction is being extended to many other communes using local resources. The Vietnam Government now actively pursues policies and provides funding for upscaling of *sustainable* crop intensification programs. Experiences, challenges faced and lessons learned should be shared with other countries in Asia as they embark on renewed efforts for crop intensification and as they will face similar challenges to do so *sustainably*.

Policy Lessons Learned

Below follows a summary of some key lessons learned with concrete reference to the subject matters discussed at the 23rd Biennial Conference of the Asian Association for Biology Education (AABE) on Biology Education for Social and Sustainable Development, held in Singapore in 2010.

– Sustainable Intensification of Crop Production requires smallholder farmers in Asia to understand and responsibly manage agro-ecosystems. Conservation and sustainable utilization of vital ecosystem services provided by natural biological control, pollination and soil fertility/nutrient cycles is central to sustainable intensification.
– Smallholder farmers have a right to quality non-formal education on agro-ecology and skill development for sustainable management of natural resources. Participation in season-long Farmers Field Schools allows them to master key agro-ecological concepts and apply these in crop management.
– Today's rural youth will be the farmers of tomorrow. Formal education systems (primary & secondary education, vocational schools & agricultural universities) could benefit from a re-orientation towards non-formal education and learning-by-doing methods. Formal education curricula should include field-based training in agro-ecology as to prepare rural youngsters for the knowledge-intensive management of ecosystem services for sustainable crop intensification.

REFERENCES

Bartlett, A. & Jatiket, M. (2004). Growing up in the REAL world. LEISA Magazine, June 2004
De Schutter, O. 2010. Annual Report Human Rights Council, presented to the UN General Assembly on 17 December 2010, New York.
Do, K. C., Kim, T. D., Do, T. N., Nguyen, T. S. & Nguyen, T. P. (2010). Impact Assessment on Pesticide Risk Reduction in Vietnam: Case Studies on Vegetable Production in Hanoi and Thai Binh Province. Hanoi.
FAO, (2002). From Farmer Field School to Community IPM: Ten Years of IPM training in Asia, by J. Pontius, R. Dilts & A. Bartlett, eds. Bangkok.
FAO, (2010). Sustainable crop production intensification through an ecosystem approach and an enabling environment: Capturing efficiency through ecosystem services and management. Rome.
FAO, (2011). Save and Grow: A policymaker's guide to the sustainable intensification of smallholder crop production. Rome.
Gallagher, K., Ooi, P., Mew, T., Borromeo, E., Kenmore, P.E. & Ketelaar, J. (2005). Ecological basis for low-toxicity: Integrated Pest Management (IPM) in rice and vegetables. In: J. Pretty, ed. The Pesticide Detox, pp. 116–134. London, Earthscan.
IAASTD. (2009). Agriculture at the crossroads, by B. D. McIntyre, H. R. Herren, J. Wakhungu & R. T. Watson, eds. Washington, DC.
Habermas, J. (1971). Knowledge and Human Interests. Boston: Beacon Press, USA.

Knowles, M. (1968). The Adult Learner: A Neglected Species. Second edition. Gulf Publishing Company, Houston.

Kolb, D. A. (1984). Experiential Learning. Prentice Hall, Englewood Cliffs, NJ, USA.

Rana, S. (2010). Global agrochemical market back in growth mode in 2010. Agrow (www.agrow.com)

Rogers, C. (1969). Freedom to Learn. Merrill, Columbus, Ohio, USA.

Swanson, B. E. & Rajalahti, R. (2010). Strengthening agricultural extension and advisory systems: Procedures for assessing, transforming, and evaluating extension systems. Agriculture and Rural Development Discussion Paper 45, Washington, DC, The International Bank for Reconstruction and Development and World Bank.

Jan Willem Ketelaar
FAO Regional Office for Asia and Pacific in Bangkok
Thailand
Johannes.Ketelaar@fao.org

Alma Linda Abubakar
FAO Regional Office for Asia and Pacific in Bangkok
Thailand
Almalinda.Abubakar@fao.org

TEACHING PRACTICE & STUDENT
LEARNING OF BIOLOGY
AND THE ENVIRONMENT

How are scientific concepts best learnt? What are some best teaching practices in Biology instruction? What resources could improve students' learning of scientific concepts? These and other issues are explored in the 13 papers under this theme.

Baojun Yao and Yuhong Huang examine how biological concept is formed in the classroom using the hypothesis testing model. The model suggests that the character of biological concept formation is to begin at a higher level and infers there may be a threshold in concept formation, and that different concepts have different thresholds. Their findings are presented in *"An Exploration of Biological Concept Formation in the Classroom"*

Another study by Thasaneeya R. Nopparatjamjomras, *"Developing a Social Constructivist Teaching and Learning Module on DNA for High School Students in Thailand"*, examines the current situation in the teaching and learning of genetics concepts in four schools in Bangkok. Nopparatjamjomras reports that a learner-centered approach is an important feature in Thailand's national education. Subsequently, the DNA module was developed based on the social constructivist approach, with an emphasis on allowing peer interaction and teachers adopting the role of a facilitator. There were three stages of learning – orientation, focus and conclusion, incorporating hands-on activities, small group discussions and whole class discussions.

The importance of timely and targeted feedback on student learning is highlighted in *"Importance of Lecture Feedback in H2 Biology Lecture in a Junior College"* by Woon Keat Foo-Lam *et al*. By using post-lecture feedback, the researchers evaluated if main concepts taught in a lecture have been conveyed to students, and if any major concepts confused a significant proportion of the lecture group. Surveys conducted since 2007 have shown a positive correlation in the use of feedback with students' ability to grasp concepts, and provided evidence that students improved in their capability to make connections between related themes. For example, nearly 80% of students surveyed reported a link between effectiveness of lecture feedback with the enhancing and consolidation of main points from a previous lecture, before moving on to new content. Another positive finding was that students found lecture feedback as a good way of interacting with the lecturer that might otherwise be difficult in large lecture groups. These findings were further substantiated in the use of pre and post-lecture tests in which students from the "lecture feedback group" did better than the control group.

Another attempt to improve learning outcomes is explored in Narenda D Deshmukh's study, *"Designing and Field Testing of Remedial Material to Rectify Students' Misconceptions in Biology at the Secondary School Level"*. This paper looks at the common misconceptions secondary students have about biological concepts. It was found that across grade levels in rural and urban India, misconceptions about respiration, vitamins, blood circulation and gas exchange persist. Remedial materials were then developed taking into account the nature of these misconceptions and their sources. This material was then tried in a sample of rural and urban students, and was found helpful in rectifying some of the misconceptions.

In *"The Development and Evaluation of an Inquiry-Based Lesson on Plants"*, Sheau-Wen Lin examines the effectiveness of an inquiry-based lesson that employed a backward design to teach elementary students about plants. The findings showed that the experimental group performed better on attitudes towards science, metacognition and concept understanding than did the control group. In *"Correlates of Achievement Test Performance in Biology 1 of Second Year Students in the Philippine Science High School-Central Visayas Campus, Argao , Cebu from 2007–2010"*, Sherry P Ramayla looks at the factors that contribute to the achievement test performance of the abovementioned students. The findings suggest that there is a strong correlation between the grade and IQ of the students. Less relevant were the teacher's experience and whether students graduated from private or public elementary schools.

In *"Improving Science Learning through Learning-To-Write Strategy: Writing Claim and Evidence in Classroom Teaching"*, Hang Chuan Teng *et al.* qualify and quantify the effects of using writing-to-learn science for a group of Primary 5 students. The research investigates how writing claims and evidence statements can support learning of science concepts and ideas. The study highlights the important role teachers play in supplying rhetoric and writing structures, and by pointing out critical aspects of the object of learning.

A quasi-experimental design was also conducted in two 6th grade classes to study the effectiveness of using concept map strategies for science learning. It was found that students in the experimental group scored higher in both the achievement test and attitudes towards science than the control group that had no exposure to the concept map teaching strategy. These findings are presented in *"Effectiveness of Concept Map Strategies for Science Learning in 6th Grade"* by Ching-San Lai and Chi-Yao Ni.

Apart from writing strategies, the influence of cues and prompts in facilitating students' thinking processes was also examined. First, students visited dinosaur exhibits at the Gwacheon National Science Museum in Seoul, Korea, and were asked to explain what they saw and understood. Then teachers provided prompts related to the exhibits and asked students to revise their explanations. It was found that students exhibited inferential thought in the second instance, when they were given prompts, which functioned as cognitive supports. For example, a student was asked if he knew the environment of "The Cretaceous Period in Korea" represented in an exhibit. He successfully linked the palm trees he saw to a warm climate and inferred that the dinosaurs would have lived in a hot environment because they did not have fur. The researchers conclude that prompts served as cognitive supports for students' thinking processes. These findings are reported in *"The Influence of Prompts on Students' Thinking Processes in Dinosaur Exhibits"* by Eunhee Kang, Jane Jiyoung Lee and Heui-Baik Kim.

Another paper *"A study of 1st Graders' Science Learning on Biodiversity at Taipei Zoo, Taiwan"* by Ching-San Lai looks at the impact of incorporating zoo resources into science teaching and biodiversity issues. Over 400 elementary 1st graders participated in a study, which included classroom teaching on animals and biodiversity issues, and a one-day field trip to the Taipei zoo. Results showed that close to 60% of students had a greater understanding on animals, and over 50% were willing to visit the zoo again in the near future.

Apart from relevant field trips, what other resources could improve students' learning of science concepts? The paper *"A Designed-and-Developed Biology Laboratory Kit for Rural High School Students in Philippines"* explores the effectiveness of a designed and developed science laboratory kit in increasing students' academic achievement and laboratory skills competency. It includes a manual, the teacher's guide and materials for use. Topics were identified using the learning competencies in the Biology curriculum provided by the Department of Education. Experimental activities were then designed based on the topic. Melindam M Garabato and Manuel B Barquilla conducted a pilot test and found that the experimental group registered improved marks achievement and experimental skill competency as seen from pre and post-test scores, and recommends that the kit be used in more schools. Further study is also necessary to refine the design of the laboratory kit for students in other grades.

The role of student participation is also investigated in a few papers. In *"Exploring Middle School Students' Attitudinal Changes Towards Science through Participation in Club Activities in Creating and Publishing a Science Magazine"*, Minjoo Lee and Heui-Baik Kim examine the impact of student participation in creating and publishing a science magazine on their interest and attitudes towards science. The findings shed light on the factors that promote students' understanding and highlights implications on how to improve students' attitudes towards science and science learning.

Another study provided students with an opportunity to collaborate in environmental problem solving. It explores how students with different knowledge and skills communicate to collect data and make decisions throughout their investigative fieldwork and problem solving process. Based on students' discussions, fieldwork reports, and reflection notes, this research highlights the importance of knowledge integration and decision-making, amongst other attributes, as important qualities in science learning. These are presented in *"Students' Knowledge Integration and Decision Making: Learning from Collaboration during Environmental Field Study"* by Mijung Kim and Hoe Teck Tan.

From using creative laboratory resources to teaching focused writing strategies, concept maps, providing timely feedback, and informal contexts of science learning, the papers in this theme present practical suggestions for improving learning outcomes in the science classroom. Beyond that, giving students practical avenues to apply scientific concepts in real-life settings has also been found to enhance the learning process and students' interest in science.

HANG CHUAN TENG, JASHANAN KASINATHAN, VIVIANNE LOW,
MOSBERGEN IRVING BRIAN AND ASIIRI B. SHUKRI

19. IMPROVING SCIENCE LEARNING THROUGH WRITING-TO-LEARN STRATEGY: WRITING CLAIM AND EVIDENCE IN CLASSROOM TEACHING

ABSTRACT

This paper draws on an action research into the use of writing-to-learn strategy and claim and evidence in the teaching of science lessons on the human circulatory system, and the cell system. This study seeks to qualify and quantify the effects of using writing-to-learn science for a lower and middle performing group of students. The research describes how writing claims and evidence statements support learning of science concepts. Students were taught to organize claims and evidence in their writing. Pre-and-post tests were conducted to assess students' performance in topics taught and applications of writing strategy. Interviews were conducted with teachers on how the writing strategy was implemented and the challenges they encountered. The study found that young students can develop complex understandings using claims and evidence writing-to-learn science method. The rhetoric and writing structures used by the teachers in real-life examples were important. The study points to a relationship between writing-to-learn science and students' learning of life science topics.

KEYWORDS

Primary Science, Life Science, Writing-to- Learn, Claim-and-Evidence

INTRODUCTION

Writing has been advocated as a tool for science and mathematics concept learning by researchers and educator (Koeller, 1982; National Council of Teachers of Mathematics (NCTM), 1989; Sturtevant, 1994). However, there is also a need to improve the kinds of writing experiences of students, not just in the amount of writing students produce (Rillero et al., 1995). According to Kober (1993) when students are asked to write about their observations, results, reasoning processes or attitudes, they pay attention to details, organize data more logically, and structure their arguments in a more coherent way. In so doing, they clarify their own understanding of science and hone their communication skills. However, there is

Mijung Kim and C. H. Diong (Eds.), Biology Education for Social and Sustainable Development, 187–196.

anecdotal evidence to support the learning through writing-across-curriculum (Moore, 1993). No doubt that history, science and mathematics educators have supported that writing activity does contribute to students' learning in these content subjects (Wadlington *et al.*, 1992; Audet *et al.*, 1996) and language educators believed that students can think critically and even construct new knowledge through writing to understand the difficult content (Emig, 1977; Spivey, 1990; Newell, 1998), there is still a lack of information on the cognitive processes of students when they learn by writing. There is a need to research on the links between writing-to-learn, conceptual change, and critical thinking before any assertion on the effectiveness of using the writing-to-learn strategy in learning scientific concepts can be made.

There are research results that show positive relationship of writing on students' recall and comprehension of text and lecture materials (Horton *et al.*, 1985; Hinkle & Hinkle, 1990; Wiley & Voss, 1996), but the question of how writing contributes to learning has only been addressed by few researchers (Newell, 1984; Marshall, 1987; Penrose, 1992). In the humanities and social sciences disciplines, the impact of literacy on students' cognitive processes has been controversial (Goody & Watt, 1968; Harris, 1989; Olson, 1996). There are inconsistencies in the empirical results of studies on writing-to-learn, with some research reporting positive results and others, positive and null findings (Newell, 1984; Langer & Applebee, 1987; Boyles *et al.*, 1994).

The writing process helps shape ones thoughts. A review of writing-to-learn in science indicates that writing can enhance science learning when: (i) teachers plan for lesson goals, (ii) students have the requisite meta-cognitive knowledge, and (iii) the teaching environment encourages promotes scientific literacy and conceptual understanding (Rutherford & Ahlgren, 1989). Students are usually encouraged by teachers to be engaged in a writing task or to pen down something they have learnt. In most cases, writing is done for either data recording or for assessment purposes. By doing this, students attempt to integrate new information with prior knowledge (Newell, 1983). Writing-to-learn strategies can vary according to how they are implemented. Some can be done in class, as homework or on-going projects, and even essay writing. Writing can also be done in the form of entrance or exit slips given to pupils at the beginning or end of the class.

Primary school students are engaged in writing in English and Mother Tongue language lessons more than in science. In many Science lessons, students are encouraged to begin their discovery of the topic with questions or trigger that would spark their curiosity. They will then go through activities and exercises that are targeted to grasp the scientific concepts. During the activities, students develop science process skills, habits of the mind, attitudes and ethics necessary for scientific inquiry and content mastery. The holistic approach in developing the pupils is evident in the school culture. Students are encouraged to apply what they have learnt in different situations or contexts.

Current emphasis on 5E curriculum and innovative Science lesson is driven by the notion that discrete knowledge should not be learned for its own sake. Students are encouraged to use scientific skills and their inquiring mind to understand the surrounding world and in solving meaningful problems. Writing in the form of answering structured questions are seen as an end-product as well as a grading tool for student performance. Writing is rarely used as a learning task. Students used activity books for their science activities. All science activities are planned in line with the learning outcomes from the Ministry of Education. The science teachers will usually carry out the science activities using strategies like investigation, construction of concept maps, problem solving. Throughout these activities, students do not need to write. Probably, the most extensive writing is done when pupils write short notes at the end of selected activities. Much of our experience talking with Science teachers reveals lower and middle ability students have great difficulties in answering open-ended questions. The answers given are usually incoherent, not related to the questions being asked at all and in many cases left blank.

Writing-to-learn and its repertoire of strategies are believed to stimulate students' interest in learning, encourage writing and more importantly, help students to become better writers of science. But more research needs to be carried out to support the effectiveness of these strategies on the cognitive processes of students' learning. There is also a need to provide data from a variety of perspectives through both qualitative and quantitative studies (Rivard, 1994). In this action research, we seek to support, with both qualitative and quantitative studies, the effectiveness of writing-to-learn (claim and evidence) in the learning of Science in elementary students.

PURPOSE OF STUDY

The purpose of this action research is to investigate the role of "claim-and-evidence", a method of writing-to-learn science strategies in the learning of science. "Claim-and-evidence" can be considered a modified genre approach where students use scientific genre as a questioning and exercise tool in mastery of science concepts. The effect of this approach on the learning of human circulatory system and cell system will be assessed after 8 weeks of cumulative learning and revising of science topics covered as part of the Primary 5 syllabus. The topics include all Primary 4 syllabuses and the current Primary 5 curriculum on human circulatory system and cells.

The null hypothesis that framed the quantitative part of the study is: There would be no significant difference in the effect size of 3 science tests that can be attributed to treatment 1, 2 and 3 over a period of time (claim and evidence approach). We expect that students who used the writing-to-learn "claim-and-evidence" approach learn science in a greater depth and retain their understanding better compared to students using traditional inquiry science approach. We also expect that the patterns of differences among the experimental group would vary according to time. The qualitative component is framed by two questions: How did the use of "claim-and-evidence" method helps influence students in knowing what to include, knowing what to exclude and how to organize claim and evidence in their writing? A second question address from the teachers' view of the strategy: How was the "claim-and-evidence" being used in your instructions?

RESEARCH METHODOLOGY

The action research was carried out in a series of science activities and lessons in a regular classroom context. No special prior arrangements were made in selecting the students. Two control classes were selected based on relative examination performance in the previous year. Teachers in the experimental groups have to use "claim-and-evidence" during classroom discussions, science activity and rounding up lessons while control groups do not deliberately use different teaching strategies. The format of each lesson and students' written entries can vary but the core feature is that students need to write down the claims and evidence statement as indicated by the teachers.

All students had learnt organ systems in human (digestive, respiratory, circulatory, skeletal and muscular) in the Primary 4 curriculum in school. They would be able to identify the major organs and describe their functions. A quasi-experimental design was used to collect data. The experimental groups (low and middle ability students) were compared with the control with almost similar performance the previous year. The quantitative component is a pre- and three post-tests design. Two post-tests were administered immediately after the students have completed the topics and the last post-test was based on results extracted from three structured questions found in the mid-year semester assessment. Students answered structured questions in all the tests based on the two topics taught. The effect size calculation was used to provide a quantitative perspective of treatment. Effect size calculation was performed by calculating the Cohen's d value (Meier, 2006). The impact of treatment determined by Cohen's d effect size calculation is: an effect size of 0.20 is small, 0.50 is medium and 0.80 is large. Teachers from the experimental groups were interviewed. Feedback and reflections of the teachers provide insights of the teacher's views of using writing-to-learn strategy and its usefulness. The second qualitative element of the raw data was students' answers in all three post-tests.

RESULTS

Analysis of Quantitative Data

Tables 1 and 2 show the post-test results, unpaired t-test, and effect size for $p < 0.05$ unless otherwise indicated, of experimental and control groups. Unpaired *t*-test showed that there was no significant difference in means scores of post-tests that could be attributed to the treatment. Effect size for the post-tests for low ability group suggests that the treatments were small (effect size for low ability < 0.2). Effect size (0.52) for the middle ability suggests a positive trend from post-test 1 to post-test 3. It is worth noting that effect sizes for the middle-ability students increased over a period of time.

Table 1. Results of post-tests 1, 2, 3, Unpaired t-test and effect size for p< 0.05, two-tailed, for low ability students

	Post-test 1		Post-test 2		Post-test 3	
	Experimental	Control	Experimental	Control	Experimental	Control
Mean	2.21	2.14	5.33	4.79	2.13	2.00
	(n = 12)	(n = 14)	(n = 12)	(n = 14)	(n = 12)	(n = 14)
SD	1.23	1.46	2.47	2.19	1.61	0.96
p-value	0.9037		0.5546		0.809	
Signifi cance	not sig.		not sig.		not sig.	
Effect size	0.04		0.25		0.13	

Table 2. Results of post-test 1, 2, 3, Unpaired t-test and effect size for p < 0.05, two-tailed, for middle ability students

	Post-test 1		Post-test 2		Post-test 3	
	Experimental	Control	Experimental	Control	Experimental	Control
Mean	4.97	6.48	9.07	8.06	4.52	3.84
	(n = 29)	(n = 25)	(n = 29)	(n = 25)	(n = 29)	(n = 25)
SD	1.86	2.04	2.07	3.29	1.50	1.30
p-value	0.0063		0.1779		0.0854	
Signifi cance	sig.		not sig.		not sig.	
Effect size	-0.74		0.31		0.52	

ANALYSIS OF TEACHERS' FEEDBACK ON THE USE OF THE STRATEGY

Lower Ability Experimental Group

Resources used for the "claim-and-evidence" practice were textbooks, teachers' guide, student's activity books, and the writing-to-learn student portfolios. Questions directed at students were structured and guided. Instead of using the word 'claim' and 'evidence', 'claim' was replaced with 'believe' or 'belief' and 'proof' replaced 'evidence' for easier understanding. Writing was done with modeling. Teachers modeled the writing of claim and evidence by first discussing with students, then modelling, using sentence starter "I believe..." or "I do not believe...". Students referred to their portfolio to fill in the evidence statement for a claim made in the initial lessons. During the claim and evidence writing, students were engaged in teacher-student dialogues to scaffold their phrasing and rephrasing of claim and evidence statements, and to decide whether to include the information as evidence or not.

Students were delighted and thrilled when their claims matched the evidence. They felt they had gained more confidence and were more vocal in science lessons. Teachers felt that the claim and evidence writing had helped the students to think through their learning experiences and to link relevant answers or ideas to inquiry questions in the lessons. It is a strategy for pupils to organize information from their reading or learning activities.

Middle Ability Experimental Group

The Know-Want to know-Learnt (KWL) strategy was used to start the lessons. Students wrote and complete the columns under "What we know", "What we want to know" and "What have we learnt" at the end of each science lesson. Mind map was used to help students organize the writing. Claims were written in the "K" and "W" segments and students suggested relevant evidence to show whether their claims were right or wrong. In subsequent lessons, students carried out the science activities, and related their learning to the KWL chart to re-look at their claims. After each activity, the students wrote down what they had learnt in the portfolio. The cycle was repeated for subsequent activities and in the topic on cells. Teachers scaffold his students to search for the evidence. Students were taught explicitly what to observe. In general, the students understood the idea of claim and evidence after a few rounds of explanations. However, students did not use the strategy actively. It was observed students had to discuss and think as they searched for evidence, but they were enthusiastic in sharing their responses with their peers. Occasionally, students commented on statements that were not the evidence to match the claim. Writing of claim-and-evidence had helped students to organize their writing.

DISCUSSION

Results of the study indicated that the use of "claim-and-evidence" writing-to-learn strategy is beneficial for students in the low and middle performance bands to understand science concepts. However, the strategy benefited students with average ability more in the way they answered test questions. This study highlights an important trend when implementing writing-to-learn science strategies. There is a positive impact for middle ability students but not the low ability group. The results confirm writing-to-learn studies that the impact of writing-to-learn science increases over time when students had multiple experiences in the use of writing-to-learn strategies.

Students' post-test results and teacher's comments showed support and learning value of writing-to-learn science activities. It was observed that when students clarified their meanings further for themselves and others in the "claim-and-evidence" exercises, they became more motivated to learn and were able to master the contents. Teachers knowingly or unknowingly used the forward and backward search when they used the claim and evidence method. As described by the teachers, these search methods helped students to clarify understanding of key concepts and stayed focused on their activities or writing tasks. Students and teachers were able to focus on relevant contents that enabled them to make informed judgments about their progress.

The study also shows how teachers use the writing-to-learn strategy in teaching and learning activities. Lesson planning was important for the strategy to succeed. In this study, the teachers applied the claim and evidence strategy in more than one way, in either KWL or science inquiry, and continued using the prescribed method in in their lessons. Teachers were able to engage the students in writing claim and evidence with confidence and provided effective transition from writing claim and evidence, to carrying out activities, to textbooks, or in any effective sequence. The writing exercise (claim-and-evidence or summary statement) enabled students to consolidate and organize their knowledge of key concept and relationships between concepts. Writing for lower and middle ability students have to be executed with prudence, and writing-to-learn tasks should take into account of students' language and writing abilities. Teachers' scaffold in thinking aloud and modeling writing were used in the claim and evidence method.

This action research also incorporated teacher-designed generic templates to guide students to structure their writing. Teachers and students found these additional support useful in organizing ideas, and hence their comments provide further support for the validity of genre-based theories on how writing serves learning. The templates did not specify sentence structure (linguistic features) for students to incorporate or to express their ideas into proper sentences. The study also found that students who participated in repeated writing tasks achieved learning gains. This improved performance can be seen in the post-tests within one month, suggesting possible cumulative learning benefits of using the claim and evidence method.

The study suggests that claim and evidence (writing genre) can be integrated into science inquiry and KWL strategies to provide a plausible framework for interpreting how writing serves learning. Future research should address task sequences and the number of tasks that will optimize learning opportunities for students. It is evident that students and teachers had gained from the experience and there is a heightened awareness of the use of writing-to-learn strategies in the teaching of science. Although the results for lower-ability group are not significant, this study should spur further studies on how teachers can modify or use other writing-to-learn science strategies.

REFERENCES

Ary, D. Jacobs, L. C. Razavieh, & A. Sorensen. C. (7th ed.). (2006). Introduction to Research in Education. Thomson, Wadsworth.

Abell, S. (1992). Helping science methods students construct meaning from text. Journal of Science Teacher Education, 3(1), 11–15.

Ackerman, J. M. (1993). The promise of writing to learn. Written Communication, 10, 334–370.

Audet, R., H., Hickman, P., & Dobrynina, G. (1996). Learning logs: A classroom practice for enhancing scientific sense making. Journal of Research in Science Teaching. 33, 205–222.

Beins, B. C. (1993). Writing assignments in statistics classes encourage students to learn interpretation. Teaching of Psychology, 20, 161–164.

Bereiter, C., & Scardamalia, M. (1987). The psychology of written composition. Hillsdale, NJ: Lawrence Erlbaum Associates, Inc.

Berninger, V., Yates, C., Cartwright, A., Rutberg, J., Remy, E., & Abbott, R. (1992). Lower-level developmental skills in beginning writing. Reading and Writing: An Interdisciplinary Journal, 4, 257–280.

Boyles, M. P., Killian, P. W., & Rileigh, K. K. (1994). Learning by writing in introductory psychology. Psychological Reports, 75, 563–568.

Butler, G. (1991). Science and thinking: The Write Connection. Journal of Science Teacher Education, 2(4), 106–110.

Copeland, K. A. (1987, May). The effect of writing upon good and poor writers' learning from prose (Tech. Rep.). (ERIC Document Reproduction Service No. ED 276 993).

Davis, B. H.,Rooze, G. E., & Runnels, M. K. T. (1992). Writing-to-learn in elementary social studies. Social Education, 56, 393–397.

Emig, J. (1977). Writing as a mode of learning. College Composition and communication, 28, 122–128.

Flower, L., & Hayes, J. R. (1981). A cognitive process theory of writing. College Composition and Communication, 32, 365–387.

Flower, L., & Hayes, J. R. (1980). The cognition of discovery: Defining a rhetorical problem. College Composition and Communication, 31, 21–32.

Flower, L., Stein, V., Ackerman, J., Kantz, M. J., McCormick, K., & Peck, W. C. (1990). Reading-to-write: Exploring a cognitive and social process. New York: Oxford University Press.

Foos, P. W. (1995). The effect of variation in text summarization opportunities on test performance. Journal of Experimental Education, 63,89–95.

Galbraith, D. (1992). Conditions for discovery through writing. Instructional Science, 21, 45–72.

Goody, J., & Watt, I. (1968). The consequences of literacy. In J. Woody (Ed.), Literacy in traditional societies (pp. 27–68). New York: Cambridge University Press.

Hand, B. Hohenshell, L. & Prian, V. (2004) Exploring Students' responses to conceptual questions when engaged with planned writing experiences: A study with Year 10 science students. Journal of Research in Science Teaching, 41(2), 186–210.

Harris, R. (1989). How does writing restructure thought? Language and Communication, 9, 99–106.

Hayes, D. A. (1987). The potential for directing study in combined reading and writing activity. Journal of Reading Behaviour, 19, 333–352.

Hinkle, S., & Hinkle, A. (1990). An experimental comparison of the effects of focused freewriting and other strategies on lecture comprehension. Teaching of Psychology, 17, 31–35.

Horton, P. B., Fronk, R. H., & Walton, R. W. (1985). The effect of writing assignments on achievement in college general chemistry. Journal of Research in Science Teaching, 22, 535–541.

Klein, P. D., (1999b). Reopening inquiry into cognitive processes in writing-to-learn. Educational Psychology Review, 11, 203–270.

Kober, N. (1993). EDTALK: What we know about science teaching and learning. Washington, DC: Council of Educational Development and Improvement. (ERIC Document Reproduction Services No. ED 361 205).

Koeller, S. (1982). Expository writing: A vital skill in science. Science and Children, 20(1), 12–15

Konopak, B. C., Martin, S. H., & Martin, M. A. (1990). Using a writing strategy to enhance sixth-grade students' comprehension of content material. Journal of Reading Behaviour, 22, 19–37.

Langer, J.A., & Applebee, A.N.(1987). How writing shapes thinking: A study of teaching and learning. Urbana, IL: National Council of Teachers of English.

Liss, J. M., & Hanson, S. D. (1993). Writing-to-learn in science. Journal of College Science Teaching, v(n), 342–345.

Marshall, J.D. (1987). The effects of writing on students' understanding of literacy text. Research in the Teaching of English, 21, 30–63.

McCrindle, A. R., & Christensen, C. A. (1995). The impact of learning journals on metacognitive and cognitive processes and learning performances. Learning and Instruction, 5, 167–185.

Meiers, M. (2007). Writing to learn. NSWIT Research Digest, (2007). Retrieved April 14, 2010, from http://www.nswteachers.nsw.edu.au.

Moore, R. (1993). Does writing about science improve learning about science? Journal of College Science Teaching, 22(4), 212–217.

Nash, J. G., Schumacher, G. M., & Carlson, B. W. (1993). Writing from sources: A structure-mapping model. Journal of Educational Psychology, 85, 159–170.

Newell, G. E., & Winograd, P. (1989). The effects of writing on learning from expository texts. *Written Communication, 6*, 196–217.

Newell, G. E. (1984). Learning from writing in two content areas: A case study / protocol analysis. *Research in the Teaching of English*, 18, 265–287.

Olson, D. R. (1996). Towards a psychology of literacy: On the relations between speech and writing. *Cognition, 60*, 83–104.

Olson, V. L. B. (1990). The revising process of sixth grade writers with and without peer feedback. *Journal of Educational Psychology, 84*, 22–29.

Ong, W. J. (1982). Orality and literacy. New York: Methuen.

Penrose, A. M. (1992). To write or not to write: Effects of task and task interpretation on learning through writing. *Written Communication, 9*, 465–500.

Rivard, L. P. (1994). A review of writing to learn in science: Implications for practice and research. *Journal of Research in Science Teaching, 31*(9), 969–983.

Rutherford, F. J., & Ahlgren, A. (1989). Science for all Americans: A project 2061 report on literacy goals in science, mathematics and technology. Washington, DC: American Association for the Advancement of Science.

Schumacher, G. M., & Nash, J. G. (1991). Conceptualizating and measuring knowledge change due to writing. Research in the Teaching of English, 25, 67–96.

Spivey, N. N. (1990). Transforming texts: Constructive processes in reading and writing. Written Communication, 7, 256–287.

Sturtevant, E. G. (1994). Reading, writing and experience in high school social studies and science. Contemporary Education, *65*(2), 95–98.

Sturtevant, E. G. (1992). Content literacy in high school social studies: Two case studies in multicultural settings. Doctoral dissertation, Kent State University.

Van Nostrand, A. D. (1979). Writing and the generation of knowledge. Social Education, *43*(79),178–90

Wadlington, E., Bitner, J., Partridge, E., & Austin, S. (1992). Have a problem? Make the writing-mathematics connection! *Arithmetic Teacher, 40*, 207–209.

Wiley, J., & Voss, J. F. (1996). The effects of "playing historian" on learning in history. *Applied Cognitive Psychology, 10*, S63–S72.

Wood, K. D. (1992). Fostering collaborative reading and writing experiences in mathematics. *Journal of Reading, 36*(2), 6–103.

Young, R., & Sullivan, P. (1984). Why write? A reconsideration. In R.J. Conners, L. S. Ede, & A. A. Lunsford (Eds.), Essays on classical rhetoric and modern discourse (pp. 215–225). Carbondale: Southern Illinois University Press.

van Gelderen,A. (1997). Elementary students' skills in revising: Integrating quantitative and qualitative analysis. Written Communication, *14*, 360–397.

Hang Chuan Teng
Jashanan Kasinathan,
Vivianne Low,
Mosbergen Irving Brian,
Ashri B. Shukri
Si Ling School
Woodlands Avenue 1, Singapore 739067,
teng_hang_chuan@moe.edu.sg

EUNHEE KANG, JANE JIYOUNG LEE AND HEUI-BAIK KIM

20. THE INFLUENCE OF PROMPTS ON STUDENTS' THINKING PROCESSES IN DINOSAUR EXHIBITS

ABSTRACT

The purpose of this study was to identify the influence of prompts for scientific reasoning on students' thinking processes in dinosaur exhibits at the Gwacheon National Science Museum in Seoul, Korea. First, students visited the exhibitions without any prompts and were asked to explain what they saw and understood. Then, we provided questions and cues as prompts related to the exhibits and asked the students to revise their explanations. Fourteen third and fourth grade students participated in this study and explored the exhibits either alone or in a group. Dialogues between students and researchers were recorded, transcribed, and analyzed. Without prompts, students were able to describe only the information of exhibits and their prior knowledge, and failed to link the exhibits, labels, and previous knowledge to their explanations. On the other hand, when either questions or cues were provided, they were able to connect the exhibit information to their prior knowledge through inferential thinking. Prompts functioned as cognitive supports, which facilitated students' reasoning by encouraging students to recall and confirm their prior knowledge, analogize using related knowledge, and consider various points of view through reflection. These additional supports were necessary to complement the exhibits' limitations, and to help students understand the exhibits in science museums meaningfully.

KEYWORDS

Reasoning, Cognitive Support, Questioning, Informal Learning

INTRODUCTION

The importance of supplementing formal science education with museum visits is acknowledged not only by schools and institutions, but also by museums themselves. Falk and Dierking (2000) considered learning as both the process and product of the interactions between an individual's personal, sociocultural and physical contexts. Stocklmayer and Gilbert's(2002) study showed that visitors apply their prior scientific knowledge and experience to interpret exhibits and generate ideas from them. Hein(1996) considered that establishing connections between exhibits and ideas (or explanations) can be quite a difficult task for less knowledgeable museum visitors. Explicit support, Hein posited, is necessary to form such links.

Mijung Kim and C. H. Diong (Eds.), Biology Education for Social and Sustainable Development, 197–204.

The meaningful connections between exhibits, prior knowledge, and explanations result in desirable learning in science museums. Hence, exhibits in either science museums or educational programs supporting such exhibits should help visitors to construct scientific ideas or explanations by actively using the exhibits, as well as providing facts about natural phenomena.

The aim of this study was to investigate the interactions between students and exhibits in a science museum and to identify the kinds of instructional supports that are needed. The study addressed these questions: (i) What are the characteristics of students' thinking processes when they construct their own meanings and explanations based on the exhibits?, (ii) How do students' thinking processes change when prompts are given? and (iii) What do prompts function in students' thinking processes?

METHOD

Selected Exhibit and Participants

The research was carried out at the Gwacheon National Science Museum in Korea. Two dinosaur exhibits (one of the most interesting subjects for elementary students) were selected for the study. One exhibit, entitled, "Various Dinosaurs", shows bone fossils of dinosaurs; the second, "The Cretaceous Korea", displayed various dinosaurs, plants, and Korea's environment in the Cretaceous Period (Figure 1). Exhibits labels describe the names of the dinosaurs and their meanings, and the appearances, dietary habits (carnivore or herbivore) and the environment of the dinosaurs at that geological era.

Researchers asked elementary students entering the dinosaur exhibitions to participate in the research study, which included an interview. Fourteen third and fourth grade students took part in this study.

Students' Activities

In this study, the participants engaged in activities in which they constructed their own explanations about the exhibits and explored them either alone or in a group. Students' activities were composed of two steps. In the first step, students were asked to explain what they saw and understood through the exhibit. Then, we provided questions and specific cues as prompts related to the exhibits and asked the students to revise their explanations. Prompts given to students did not include direct information related the exhibits, but were provided to enable the students to focus on various aspects of the exhibits, such as "What was the dinosaurs' disposition like?", "What was the weather like in that period of time?" Questions, such as, "Why do you think so?" also encouraged students to support their explanations with certain evidence as prompts for their reasoning. Dialogues between students and researchers were recoded, transcribed and analyzed.

(a)   (b)

Figure 1 (a) Bone fossils of the "Various Dinosaurs" exhibit and (b) the diorama "The Cretaceous Korea".

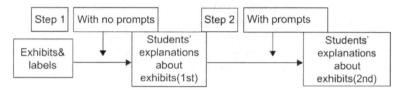

Figure 2. Schematic representation of the procedures for the student participants' activities.

ANALYSIS OF STUDENTS' THINKING PROCESSES

Students' thinking processes were analyzed based on their explanations about the exhibits. We tracked the source of evidence of the explanations (e.g., information presented by the exhibits, students' prior knowledge and prompts provided by researchers) and identified the connections between diverse pieces of information in their explanations. We categorized the information related to the exhibits into 'object', 'event', and 'system', according to the properties of the information. We then examined what the students reported they saw in the exhibits (Table 1), together with their prior knowledge into 'direct knowledge' about dinosaurs and 'indirect knowledge'. Connections between these various types of information were assorted into 'confirmation', in which students simply described their prior knowledge related the exhibits without reasoning processes, and 'reasoning', in which they reasoned using exhibit information combined with their prior knowledge.

Table 1. Property of exhibits and their labels

Category	Content
O (Object)	Name, appearance
E (Event)	Connection between objects, dietary habits, disposition, locomotion
S (System)	Connection between events, organisms-environment, events-events

FINDINGS

We first present our findings and then discuss students' thinking processes that were represented in their explanations both without prompts and with prompts. Then, we describe how prompts function in influencing students' thinking processes.

Students' Thinking Processes Without Prompts

When students were asked to explain what they saw and understood in the step 1 activity, their explanations about the exhibits were limited and fragmentary. The excerpt below describes a student's account of exhibits, sources of information, and connections between information. He only described names of dinosaurs that were written on the exhibit labels and the events, such as a simple scene which could be identified directly, with no analytical process required.

S: *Brachiosaurus* father and son are feeding on trees and *Megalosaurus* is having an eye to them. **(Exhibit O, E).** I think *Jinzhousaurus* was hurt by *Dromaesauruses*, and *Hypsilophodon* is playing. Turtle and crocodile are seeing that scene peacefully. **(Exhibit E)**

(Exhibit "The Cretaceous Korea", S5)

The majority of students' thinking processes are depicted in Figure 3. Students only described either the objects or the exhibit events (e.g., appearances of dinosaurs and eating habits), and failed to focus on the systemic aspects of the exhibits, such as the environment. In addition, students were neither able to use prior knowledge nor to connect their knowledge with the exhibits to formulate their own explanations (Figure 3a, b). Some students tried to link the exhibits with previous other knowledge, but they ended up simply recalling and confirming their prior knowledge through the exhibit observations with no complex reasoning (Figure 3c). Other students only used simple reasoning (e.g., disposition and eating habits of dinosaurs) to complete their explanations. Although the exhibits and their labels contained many types of information, students struggled to see and meaningfully learn from the exhibits without additional assistance or support.

Students' Thinking Processes with Prompts

When we provided prompts (e.g., cues or questions) for students in the step 2 activity, students were able to connect the information embedded in the exhibits to their prior knowledge through reasoning abilities. The excerpt below includes a student's explanation of information sources and their connections when we presented related questions. The student constructed his own explanation using the exhibits' palm trees and his prior knowledge about palm trees and dinosaurs. Furthermore, he tried to establish the connection between them. This allowed him to infer the environment of "The Cretaceous Period in Korea" represented in the exhibit.

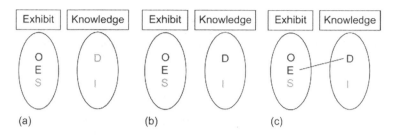

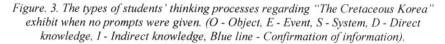

Figure. 3. The types of students' thinking processes regarding "The Cretaceous Korea" exhibit when no prompts were given. (O - Object, E - Event, S - System, D - Direct knowledge, I - Indirect knowledge, Blue line - Confirmation of information).

I: Do you have any idea about the climate or weather, environment of "The Cretaceous of Korea"?

S: I think the temperature of that period of time was very high. That kind of palm trees lives only in tropical region. **(Exhibits O-Knowledge I-Exhibit S)**

I: Do you think it fits the condition for dinosaurs to live?

S: Yes, I think they liked warm weather because they didn't have furs to protect them from cold weather. **(Knowledge D-Exhibit S)**

(Exhibit "The Cretaceous Korea", S3)

The diagram in Figure 4 represents the majority of students' thinking processes when prompts were provided. Students used diverse information from the exhibits (e.g., the number of trees, the shape of leaves, dinosaurs' walks, and volcanic eruptions on the wall paintings) while they were inferring the environment of that cretaceous period. They constructed their own explanations based on this evidence. Some students made inferences about the system involved in the exhibits based on the exhibit events (Figure 4a), and others constructed their explanations using their own prior knowledge in addition to the exhibit information (Figure 4b, c). Students often used previous knowledge that was not directly related to dinosaurs that helped them to construct well-grounded explanations. This shows that it is possible for students to reason and make their own explanations based on the exhibits and additional prompts even though they lack direct knowledge about dinosaurs.

The Functions of Prompts in Influencing Students' Thinking Processes

We found that prompts, in our study, helped students to focus more intently on the exhibits as well as actively link the exhibits with their prior knowledge. This facilitated the students' thinking by making them confirm and recall existing knowledge, analogize using related knowledge, and consider various points of view through reflection. Prompts functioned as cognitive supports for students' thinking processes, bridging between the exhibits and students' prior knowledge, as follows:

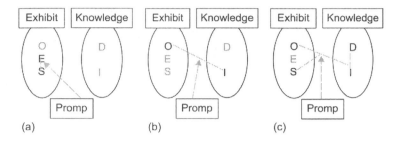

Figure. 4. The types of students' thinking processes about the "The Cretaceous Korea" exhibit with prompts. (O - Object, E - Event, S - System, D - Direct knowledge, I - Indirect knowledge, Red dotted line: Denotes Inference of information).

Recall and Confirmation of Prior Knowledge

When students had prior knowledge related to the exhibits, prompts triggered the recollection of such knowledge, allowing recall. Prompts also allowed students to confirm this previous knowledge through use of the exhibit. In such cases, however, there is neither reasoning nor other complex thinking processes.

I: What was the dinosaur's disposition like?
S: It was violent. I saw it in the comic book. **(Knowledge D)** But in this exhibit, it seems to be gentle. **(Exhibit O)** Although not shown in exhibit ..., but if there is a rustle, it will swing its tail and threaten. **(Knowledge D)**

(Exhibit "Various Dinosaurs", S7)

Clarification and Expansion of Prior Knowledge

When students' prior knowledge was unclear or inactivated, they had a tendency to use the information of the exhibits as a stepping stone to activate their prior knowledge. This led them to clarify and articulate their knowledge. In such instances, prompts induce and elaborate upon students' prior knowledge by making them actively observe the exhibits and find the evidence that connects them to their knowledge.

I: How did you know that it (*Stegosaurus*) was a herbivore?
S: Well... Herbivore is... There were herbivorous dinosaurs and carnivorous dinosaurs.... **(Knowledge D)**
I: What do herbivores usually eat?
S: Grass.
I: Then, how do we know whether *Stegosaurus* were grass-eaters or not?
S: Ah~! It used four legs to stand. **(Exhibit O)** Herbivorous dinosaurs walked with four legs and the arms of carnivorous dinosaurs were short and with two long legs. **(Exhibit E-Knowledge D)**

(Exhibit "The Cretaceous Korea", S9)

Facilitation of Reasoning

When clues were provided, students attempted to construct their explanations through reasoning although they lacked prior knowledge about dinosaurs. Their reasoning was based on particular features of the exhibits and prior, relevant knowledge. Prompts facilitated students' reflection, permitting them to connect the exhibit information to their existing knowledge. Two types of reasoning were evident.

    -Deductive reasoning. Several students developed their own opinions and conclusions based on premises as reasons to support them and accepted these as true. Although their conclusions or premises may be neither scientific nor true, their reasoning processes seemed reasonable.

I: What do you think it ate?
S: Grass. **(Conclusion)**
I: How did you know that?
S: Because body color of the dinosaur on the label is green. **(Premise 2)** Green colored dinosaurs were herbivorous. **(Premise 1) (Exhibit O-Exhibit E)**
(Exhibit "The Cretaceous Korea", S14)

-Analogical reasoning. Several students also attempted to understand the exhibits and construct explanations using analogies. They selected similar and familiar cases, either from their everyday lives or from prior knowledge, and applied them to new cases in the target exhibit.

I: What do you think *Pteranodon* ate?
S: As you can see, its' beak is long. **(Exhibit O)** I think it is suitable to pick worms. As its beak is small just like beak of crane, it seems like it couldn't eat meat. **(Exhibits O-Knowledge I)**
(Exhibit "Various Dinosaurs", S6)

CONCLUSION

In terms of informal science learning in natural history museums, it is important to consider the interactions between students and science museum exhibits. The exhibits are designed to provide scaffolding for students' thinking processes and students are expected to use this information to formulate their own scientific explanations. Our results indicate that students had difficulties constructing explanations regarding the dinosaurs, since the exhibit labels were neither sufficient nor adequate to facilitate students' reasoning and thinking process. Students also failed to use the exhibit information and to link such information to prior knowledge. Prompts that focused on the exhibits and which were given to facilitate reflective thinking, functioned as cognitive supports for students' thinking. They promoted students' reasoning by making students confirm and recall their previous knowledge, analogize using related knowledge, and consider various points of view through reflection. These additional supports complement the exhibit's limitations, and thereby foster students' understanding of the exhibits in the science museum in a meaningful way.

REFERENCES

Falk, J. H., & Dierking, L. D. (2000). Learning from museums: Visitor experiences and the making of meaning. Walnut Creek, CA: AltaMira, USA.

Hein, G. E. (1996). Constructivist learning theory. In G. Durbin (Ed.), Developing museum exhibitions for life long learning. London: The Stationery Office.

Stocklmayer, S. & Gilbert, J. K (2002). New experiences and old knowledge: Towards a model for the personal awareness of science and technology. International Journal of Science Education, 24(8):835–858.

Eunhee Kang,
Jane Jiyoung Lee,
Heui-Baik Kim
Seoul National University
599 Gwanak-ro, Gwanak-gu, Seoul, Korea 151–742
chukbai@hanmiail.net

SHEAU-WEN LIN

21. THE DEVELOPMENT AND EVALUATION OF AN INQUIRY-BASED LESSON ON 'PLANTS'

ABSTRACT

This study presented the development and evaluation of an inquiry-based lesson that employed a backward design aimed at enhancing student learning on the subject of plants. The researcher used a quasi-experimental design to determine the effects of the inquiry-based lesson. Two hundred and eighty five fifth grade students from six elementary schools in Kaohsiung city were selected as subjects. The student scores for 'Attitudes toward Science', 'Meta-Cognition', and 'Conceptual Understanding of Plants I and II' were collected and analyzed using One-way ANCOVA. The findings showed that the experimental group performed significantly better on attitudes toward science ($\eta2 = 0.02$), meta-cognition ($\eta2 = 0.07$), and concept understanding ($\eta2 = 0.143, 0.188$) than did the control group students. This study highlights the potential of using inquiry-based lessons with the backward design as a means to help elementary students learn biology.

KEYWORDS

Curriculum Development And Evaluation, Elementary Student, Inquiry, Plant

INTRODUCTION

Recent years have seen educational reforms call for students to focus on the development of intellectual ability over the accumulation of knowledge in order to meet the challenges of their future lives (Ministry of Education [MOE], 2002; National Research Council [NRC], 1996). As a result, it has been widely recommended that learning approaches shift from teacher-centered to student-centered models. Inquiry is critical to the study of science and it is believed that through inquiry one can construct the most meaningful understandings (NRC 2000). Both inquiry teaching and learning methods affect student performance in the realms of problem solving, reflecting on work, drawing conclusions, and generating predictions. Many studies have explored the effectiveness of inquiry-based instruction and found it more effective than traditional approaches in enhancing student performance, process skills, and attitudes toward science (Shymansky *et al.*, 1983; Minner *et al.*, 2010).

As the first step to deep science learning, inquiry at the elementary level is of critical importance. However, in Taiwan, little progress has been made in a real

Mijung Kim and C. H. Diong (Eds.), Biology Education for Social and Sustainable Development, 205–212.

teaching context with respect to the inquiry process at the primary level (Wang & Lin, 2009). Despite the obvious benefits of more open and mind-on inquiry instructions, many science instructors perceive or implement guided hand-on activity (Jeanpierre 2006, Roth *et al.*, 1998) as inquiry. These obstacles to the incorporation of inquiry may be in part due to (1) teachers inability to direct student inquiry, (2) a perception that open inquiry is too time intensive, and (3) a lack of evidence that point to improved student outcomes (Settlage 2007).

In response, the "backward design" (Wiggins and Mctighe 1998) was considered as a possible approach to facilitating the teacher as designer to address the concerns associated with inquiry. This study was undertaken to determine whether this approach is suitable for building science as inquiry environment to allow students to develop deep understandings of science concepts while leaving them with better attitudes toward science at the elementary level. Three elementary teachers were invited to cooperate with the author in using the backward design approach to design inquiry-based science units aimed at increasing its feasibility in the real teaching context. "Plants" was used as a case because the context is relevant to everyday student life and is an important topic of elementary textbooks in Taiwan.

The purpose of this study was to develop and evaluate an inquiry-based lesson to enhance the study of life science course-plants in elementary students. The research questions were as follows: (i) Can the inquiry-based plant unit assist the students in improving their attitudes toward science? (ii) Can the inquiry-based plant unit assist the students in a deep understanding of plant concepts?

LITERATURE REVIEW

Constructivism

Constructivism informed the design of the plant course in this study. From a constructivist perspective, learning is viewed as a process in which the learner constructs understanding on the basis of existing knowledge and in a social context (Duit and Treagust 1998). Thus, science teaching strategies based on constructivism should focus on providing students with learning experiences that induce students to actively engaged with others in an attempt to understand and interpret science phenomena. The science learning activities with support by group learning will challenge learners' prior conceptions and encourage learners to recognize their science frameworks (Driver *et al.*, 1994, Palmer 2005).

Inquiry-Based Approach

Inquiry-based learning refers to a pedagogical strategy that uses general processes of scientific inquiry as its teaching and learning methodology. This approach emphasizes student questioning, investigations, and problem solving similar to the process scientists use to conduct their inquiries (Bybee 2004; DeBore 2004). There are five core components of inquiry based teaching and learning: a student engages in scientifically oriented questions, a student gives priority to evidence in responding to questions, a student formulates explanations from evidence, a student connects explanations to scientific knowledge, and student communicates and justifies explanations (NRC 2000).

Why does the author consider the "backward designs" approach in this study? Curriculum is used as a means to an instructional end. However, many teachers begin with textbooks rather than deriving those tools from targeted goals or standards. Wiggins and Mctighe (1998) advocate for the reverse: A teacher starts with the goals or standards-and then derives the curriculum from the evidence of learning called for by the goals or standards. This backward approach to curricular design also calls for teachers to transform instructional goals or standards into terms of assessment evidence as they begin to plan a unit or course, rather than creating assessments near the conclusion of a unit of study,. Greater coherence among instructional goals, key learning evidences, and teaching and learning experiences leads to better student performance.

METHODS

Study Design

This study was designed as a quasi-experimental design-nonequivalent group/ pretest-posttest control group design with the goal of examining the effectiveness of the inquiry-based approach unit. The participants of the study comprised ten classes of 5th grade students (N = 285) from six elementary schools in the Kaohsiung area (experimental group = 148, control group = 137). These ten classes were randomly divided into experimental and control groups.

Inquiry-Based Plant Unit

The curriculum and lesson plan was designed using a student-centered approach to the backward design model (Wiggins and Mctighe 1998). Three elementary science teachers cooperated with the author to design an inquiry –based science unit for Plants. They also implemented these lessons in some of their own science classes and employed the teacher-centered approach simultaneously in other classes. The objectives of the inquiry-based plants unit involved gaining an understanding of a plant's structure ad function. The multiple assessment activities provided evidence for the students' explanations of the structure and function of plants, interpretations of seed dispersal and transpiration, applications of their knowledge to classify different plants, perspectives of managing a botanic garden, empathy of challenge and crisis, and comparisons and summaries of the learning process (as illustrated in Figure 1). This twelve-lesson unit encouraged students to formulate questions, plan and conduct their own experiments, share ideas with peers, and solve problems. Teachers acted as facilitators during the class. Standards for teaching for understanding were used to check the validity of the teaching plan. In the twelve-lesson unit control group, teacher-centered and textbook-driven lessons were prominent. The teachers controlled all the space and steps of student learning, and students followed directions from their teachers.

Data Collection and Analysis

Four tools were administered to students before and after the teaching-learning process: Attitude toward Science (Wu and Tsai 2005), Meta-cognition (Ho *et al.*, 2004), and Conceptual Understanding Tests I and II. Meta-cognition questionnaire and Conceptual Understanding Tests were selected or designed to address the second research question which asks whether an inquiry-based unit can improve the deep understanding of a student in alignment with the six facets of understanding that guide the plan of instruction. The Attitude toward Science and Meta-cognition questionnaires included five point Likert scales: almost always, often, sometimes, seldom, and almost never. The Concept Understanding of Plants Tests was developed from the five facets of understanding: explanation, interpretation, application, perspective, and empathy. Twelve open-ended questions on plant structure and function (Test I), and ten open-ended questions about transpiration (Test II) were written. The questions were verified by three experts for content reliability and validity. Student answers were classified by three science educators in accordance with the levels of correctness from 0 to 1 or 2.

Analysis

The data were analyzed with an analysis of covariance (ANCOVA) for posttest scores (from Attitude toward Science, Meta-cognition questionnaire, and Conceptual Understanding tests). The pretest (Attitude toward Science and Meta-cognition) and student science scores served as the covariate for determining any significant differences between the experimental group and the control. The assumptions of ANCOVA (homogeneity of regression) were first checked to ensure they met in the analysis of covariance for the study. A significant level of 0.05 was considered appropriate for this study.

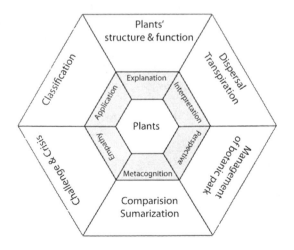

Figure 1. Assessment: evidence of understanding.

RESULTS

As a result of the ANCOVA in Table 1, a significant difference was found between the adjusted total posttest scores of groups for Attitudes toward Science [F = 4.811(P = .029<.05)], Meta-cognition [F = 22.564(P = .000 < .05)], Conceptual Understanding Test I [F = 32.907(P = .000 < .05)] and Conceptual Understanding Test II [F = 42.269 (P = .000<.05)]. This showed that students' achievement was related with the group they belong. When the adjusted total posttest scores of the groups are considered, the mean scores of the treatment group (For Attitudes toward Science, M = 42.45; for Meta-cognition, M = 45.76; for Conceptual Understanding Test I, M = 7.06; and for Conceptual Understanding Test II, M = 4.54) were found to be higher than the mean scores of the control group (For Attitudes toward Science, M = 41.06; for Meta-cognition, M = 42.53; for Conceptual Understanding Test I, M = 5.14; and for Conceptual Understanding Test II, M = 2.97). This indicates that the performance level of students in the treatment group for Attitudes toward Science, Meta-cognition, Understanding Tests I and II was higher than that of the students in the control group. On the other hand, when eta squared effect size values [for Attitudes toward Science, η^2 = 0.017, f = 0.13(small to medium); for Meta-cognition, η^2 = 0.074, f = 0.28 (medium to large); for Conceptual Understanding Test I, η^2 = 0.143, f = 0.41(large); and for Conceptual Understanding Test II, η^2 = 0.188, f = 0.48 (large)] were considered, it can be stated that the instruction of the treatment group had a small to large effect on the development of student Attitudes toward Science, Meta-cognition, and Conceptual Understanding.

Table 1. Comparison of the group posttest scores for attitude toward science, meta-cognition and conceptual understanding

Questionnaire	Group	Mean	SD	Mean dif.	df	F	eta squared
Attitude toward Science	Exp.	42.45	5.50	1.39	1,282	4.81*	.02
	Control	41.06	5.22				
Meta-cognition	Exp.	45.76	6.80	3.23	1,284	22.56*	.07
	Control	42.53	7.90				
Conceptual Understanding I	Exp.	7.06	2.75	1.92	1,283	32.91*	.14
	Control	5.14	2.25				
Conceptual Understanding II	Exp.	4.54	1.81	1.57	1,283	42.27*	.19
	Control	2.97	1.49				

ps. * <.05

DISCUSSION AND IMPLICATION

This study found that the experimental group scored significantly better for Attitudes toward Science, Meta-cognition, and Conceptual Understanding on Plants than did the control group. These results support the previous work (Shymansky et al., 1983, Minner et al.,2010) that has determined that inquiry-based instruction has a positive effect on science achievement. The experimental group exposed to supportive learning environment that emphasized formulating questions and explanations, connecting knowledge, and communicating and justifying explanations achieved a deeper understanding of science knowledge and a better attitude toward science than did the control group. This had a considerable effect on the development of concept understanding. It was concluded that student-centered practices that both provide support and emphasize learning evidence environments enhance student attitudes toward science as well as deep conceptual understanding.

The participant teachers that adopted this design approach indicated that the process that "thinking like an assessor" about the evidence of learning not only helped them to clarify their objectives but also resulted in a more effective learning experience for their students. In addition, the teachers expressed the feeling that the six facets of understanding were a bit ''nebulous'' because they needed to make sure that the meanings were easily understood before others could adopt and implement them.

It is therefore suggested that students can learn science through inquiry and that the backward approach is an effective one. Science teachers may design and implement inquiry-based instruction cooperatively in their classrooms to effectively manage their designing and teaching time. It is expected that in the future the difference between these findings can be better understood and the strategies of implementation can be improved.

REFERENCES

Bybee, R. W. (2004). Scientific inquiry and science teaching. In L. B. Flick, & N. G. Lederman (Eds.). Scientific inquiry and nature of science (pp.1–14). Netherlands: Kluwer academic publishers.

DeBore, G. E. (2004). Historical perspectives on inquiry teaching in schools. In L. B. Flick, & N. G. Lederman (Eds.). Scientific inquiry and nature of science (pp.17–35). Netherlands: Kluwer academic publishers.

Driver, R., Asoko, H., Leach, J., Mortimer, E., & Scott, P. (1994). Constructing scientific knowledge in the classroom. Educational Researcher, 23(7), 5–12.

Duit, R., & Treagust, D. (1998). Learning in science- From behaviorism towards social constructivism and beyond. In B. A. Frazier, & K. C. Tobin (Eds.), International Handbook of Science Education: Part One (pp. 3–25). Dordrecht: Kluwer Academic Publishers.

Ho, W. Y., Hsieh, C. S., & Shih, K.Y. (2004). A study of meta-cognition for creative problem posing. Journal of Pingtung University of Education, 21, 37–68.

Jeanpierre, B. (2006). What teachers report about their inquiry practices. Journal of Elementary Science Education, 18(1), 57–68.

Minner, D. D., Levy, A. J., & Century, J. (2010). Inquiry-based science instruction-What is it and does it matter? Results from a research synthesis years 1984 to 2002. Journal of Research in Science Teaching, 47(4), 474–496.

Ministry of Education (MOE) (2002). Curriculum guideline for 1 to 9. Taiwan: Minister of Education.

National Research Council (NRC). (1996). National science education standards. Washington, DC: National Academies Press.

Palmer, D. (2005). A motivational view of constructivist in formed teaching. International Journal of Science Education, 27(15), 1853–1881.

Roth, W-M., McGinn, M. K. & Bowen, G. M. (1998). How prepared are preservice teachers to teach scientific inquiry? Levels of performance in scientific representation practices. *Journal of Science Teacher Education, 9*, 25–48.

Settlage, J. (2007). Demythologizing science teacher education: conquering the false ideal of open inquiry. Journal of Science Teacher Education, *18*, 461–467.

Shymansky, J. A., Kyle, W. C. & Alport, J. M. (1983). The effects of new science curricula on student performance. *Journal of Research in Science Teaching, 20*, 387–404.

Wang, J. R. & Lin, S. W. (2009). Evaluating elementary and secondary school science learning environments in Taiwan. *International Journal of Science Education, 31*(7), 853–872.

Wiggins, G. & McTigue, J. (1998). Understanding by Design. ASCD.

Wu, Y.-T. & Tsai, C.-C. (2005). Effects of constructivist-oriented instruction on elementary school students' cognitive structures. Journal of Biological Education, *39*(3), 113–119.

Sheau-Wen Lin
Graduate Institute of Mathematics and Science Education,
Pingtung University of Education, Taiwan
linshewen@mail.npue.edu.tw

CHING-SAN LAI AND CHI-YAO NI

22. EFFECTIVENESS OF CONCEPT MAPPING STRATEGIES FOR SCIENCE LEARNING IN 6TH GRADE

ABSTRACT

The purpose of this study was to determine the effectiveness of using concept mapping strategies for science learning in 6th grade. A quasi-experimental design was conducted on two classes. One class was assigned the experimental group and the other the control. Students in the experimental group attended science lessons using the concept mapping strategies while the control attended lessons without exposure to the teaching strategy. The study was carried out using the unit on animal reproduction. Two research tools used included the two-tier science achievement test and a Likert scale to measure students' attitudes toward science. In addition, qualitative data such as concept maps and study sheets were collected to determine the learning effectiveness of the students from the experimental group. Results were summarized as follow: students in the experimental group scored higher in both the achievement test and attitudes toward science than the control group. It can be concluded science learning using concept mapping strategies had a significant influence on the learning of elementary 6th graders.

KEYWORDS

Animal Reproduction, Attitudes Toward Science, Concept Mapping, Science Achievements

INTRODUCTION

Concept maps are graphical representations of human knowledge, consisting of a set of concepts and their relationships that are interconnected to encode propositions in the form of natural-language sentences (Reichherzer, 2009). They are intended to represent meaningful relationships between concepts in the form of propositions (Novak and Gowin, 1984). Novak and Gowin (1984) argued that "the most important point to remember about sharing meanings in the context of educating is that students always bring something of their own to the negotiation; they are not a blank tablet to be written on or an empty container to be filled". By using concept maps, it will help students negotiate meanings with their teachers. Once students learn how to prepare concept maps, their maps can be used as powerful evaluation tools. Developed in the 1970s by Joseph D. Novak from Cornell University, concept

Mijung Kim and C. H. Diong (Eds.), Biology Education for Social and Sustainable Development, 213–218.

mapping has been widely used in educational settings to enable students to externalize their knowledge for examination and aid them in constructing new knowledge by linking new, observed concepts to those already known.

DNA sequencing, Genetic Modified, and Bioinformatics are the major topics of study in genetics recently. These new biotechnology techniques have contributed economic benefits economic and improved health services to humans. The topic reproduction in biology is an important theme in genetics. The importance of reproduction is highlighted by the component of "reproduction and heredity" and related concepts in NSES (National Research Council, 1996). NSES states all students should experience quality science instruction rooted in inquiry-based authentic experiences (National Research Council, 1996). Inquiry instruction refers to any teaching method focused on developing science understanding and scientific inquiry. Hence, concept map is a powerful tool for teachers and science educators to evaluate students' science understanding even though it was stated by Chattopadhyay (2005) that international studies reported a poor understanding of reproduction, genetics and genetic technologies, with widespread misconceptions at various levels by students. Thus, much more efforts need to be done in helping students understand the concepts in animal reproduction. Students' science learning on concepts in animal reproduction using concept mapping strategies are explored in this study.

OBJECTIVES

The purpose of this study was to evaluate the effectiveness of concept mapping strategies for elementary school 6th graders' science learning in the unit on animal reproduction. The specific objectives of the research were (i) to investigate the effects of using concept mapping strategies on the achievements of 6th graders, and (ii) to determine the effects of concept mapping strategies on the attitudes of 6th graders toward science.

METHODOLOGY

A quasi-experimental design was conducted in two classes. One class was assigned the experimental group and the other the control. Pupils in the experimental group attended science lessons using the concept mapping strategies while the control group attended lessons without exposure to the teaching strategy, over the same period. Two research tools used included the two-tier science achievement test and a Likert scale to measure students' attitudes towards science. The purpose of the achievement test was to evaluate students' concepts on animal reproduction. The test had two levels of response types that include 'choose answers' and 'reasons for selection' (Treagust, 1995, 1996) and four sub-tests with a total of 25 items covering themes such as: (i) the meaning and importance of reproduction (4 items), (ii) the concept of animal mating and feeding (7 items), (iii) animal reproduction (8 items), and (iv) animal genetic (6 items). The reliability coefficients (KR_{21}) of the four sub-tests were 0.49, 0.78, 0.82, 0.59, respectively, and the reliability coefficients of the full test was 0.90.

The purpose of the attitude scale was to determine students' attitudes towards science before and after learning. It was a 4-point Likert type scale that consisted of three subscales with a total 24 items, including: (i) attitude toward science courses (8 items), (ii) motivation in science learning (8 items), and (iii) attitude toward science learning strategies (8 items). The reliability coefficients (Cronbach α coefficients) of 3 sub-scales were 0.83, 0.81, 0.88, and the reliability coefficients of the full scale was 0.93. Validity of these instruments was assessed by 3 science educators. Qualitative data such as concept maps and study sheets were also collected to determine the learning effectiveness of the students from the experimental group.

RESULTS AND DISCUSSION

Learning Outcomes of Two-tier Science Achievement Test

Table 1. Mean and SD of Achievement Test Scores by Groups

	Experiment group (N = 33)		Control group (N = 32)	
	Mean	SD	Mean	SD
Pre-test	25.03	8.42	25.53	6.09
Post-test	38.94	6.84	35.59	7.66

Table 2. ANCOVA of Achievement Test Scores

Source	SS	df	MS	F
Between	215.557	1	215.557	7.207**
Error	1824.456	61	29.403	

Learning outcomes of the two-tier science achievements test showed a significantly higher score from students in the experimental group than control (F = 7.207, p < .01) (Tables 1, 2). This result indicated that science teaching integrated with concept mapping strategies had a significant influence on elementary 6th graders on the concepts of animal reproduction.

Learning Outcomes of Students' Attitudes Toward Science

Table 3. Mean and SD of Attitudes Toward Science Scores by Groups

	Experimental group (N = 33)		Control group (N = 32)	
	Mean	SD	Mean	SD
Pre-test	61.59	5.30	63.37	5.30
Post-test	77.94	3.64	72.53	3.23

Maximum and minimum of test score = (96, 24).

Table 4. ANCOVA of Attitudes toward science scores by groups

Source	SS	df	MS	F
Between	467.64	1	467.64	39.4***
Error	735.84	62	11.86	

Outcomes of attitudes toward science showed a significantly higher score for students in the experimental group than control (F = 39.40, p < .001) (Tables 3, 4). This result indicated science teaching integrated with concept mapping strategies had a significant influence on 6th graders' attitude towards science learning. Hence, students in the experimental group had a more positive attitude toward the learning of science.

Qualitative Findings from Experimental Group

After comparing students' pre- and post- concept maps in the experimental group, post-concept maps revealed their concept representations were more fruitful. This result further indicated that science teaching integrated with concept mapping strategies had a significant influence on students in the experimental group. However, the study found that the teaching the concept mapping tool was time consuming. Students generally required around 20 to 30 minutes to learn concept mapping skills. As they became familiar with concept mapping skills, they were able to spend less time creating concept maps. Educators using the concept mapping strategies in their teaching practice must provide time buffer for students to first learn the concept mapping skills.

CONCLUSION

The results of this study are summarized as follows: students in the experimental group scored significantly higher in both the achievement test and attitudes toward science than the control in the instructional unit on animal reproduction. These results indicated science learning using concept mapping strategies had a significant influence on learning among elementary 6th graders.

REFERENCES

Chattopadhyay, A. (2005). Understanding of genetic information in higher secondary students in northeast India and the implications for genetics education. Cell Biology Education, 4(1), 97–104.

National Research Council (1996). The national science education standards. Washington, DC: National Academy Press.

Novak, J. D., & Gowin, D. B. (1984). Concept mapping for meaningful learning. *In*: Learning how to learn (pp. 15–54). NY: Cambridge University Press.

Reichherzer, T. R. (2009). A concept map-based approach to document indexing and navigation. (Doctoral dissertation, Indiana University).

Treagust, D. F. (1995). Diagnostic Assessment of Students' Science Knowledge. *In*: S. M. Glynn, & R. Duit (Eds.). Learning science in the schools: Research reforming practice. New Jersey: Lawrence Erlbaum Associates.

Treagust, D. F., Duit, R., & Fraser, B. J. (Eds.) (1996). Improving teaching and learning in science and mathematics. New York: Teachers College Press.

Ching-San Lai
National Taipei University of Education,
Taipei, Taiwan
clai@tea.ntue.edu.tw

Chi-Yao Ni
Chung-Hu Elementary school,
Taipei County, Taiwan
twnicy@gmail.com

CHING-SAN LAI

23. A STUDY OF 1ST GRADERS' SCIENCE LEARNING ON BIODIVERSITY AT THE TAIPEI ZOO, TAIWAN

ABSTRACT

The purpose of this study is to promote students' science learning and understanding on biodiversity by integrating zoo resources and biodiversity issues into learning activities. A total of 439 elementary 1st graders participated in this study. Teaching activities include classroom discussions on the topics, animals and biodiversity issues, and a one-day field trip to the Taipei Zoo, Taiwan to enable students to gain experiential insights on biodiversity. Results of the study were as follows: 97.3% of students were satisfied with the field trip, 58.8% obtained a greater understanding on animals, and 54.9% on biodiversity; 55.8% of students were willing to re-visit the Taipei Zoo in the near future. The top five favourite animals identified were the elephant, panda, giraffe, koala, and zebra. Students were able to demonstrate their strategies for the biodiversity conservation of these animal groups. The results of the study indicated that science teaching integrated with zoo resources and biodiversity issues had significantly influenced the learning outcomes of 1st graders in a positive way.

KEYWORDS

Biodiversity, Field Trip, Informal Science Learning, Science Education, Zoo

INTRODUCTION

In recent years, the trend of the world's science education reform has focused on hands-on and minds-on science learning. In addition, informal science education has received much attention for improving students' science learning (e.g. Knapp, 2000; Pugh & Bergin, 2005; McCoy *et al.*, 2007). Zoos and other informal science education sites can provide students with different learning opportunities and experiences. Lind (1995) indicated that a trip to a zoo can be a terrific way for young children to learn about animals, especially using planned learning experiences. Teaching activities at a zoo allow children to develop knowledge about animals and environmental awareness in a safe environment while fostering the development of social skills (Pringle *et al.*, 2003).

Anderson *et al.*, (2003) pointed out that learning experiences outside school should be understood and fully appreciated by science educators. Kisiel (2006) argued that most teachers struggle with finding a way to connect that learning with

Mijung Kim and C. H. Diong (Eds.), Biology Education for Social and Sustainable Development, 219–224.

their classroom curriculum. Some strategies have been used by teachers and science educators to help students' learning at zoos, but much more efforts should be done for the teaching and learning at zoos.

The year 2010 is proclaimed by the United Nations as the International Year of Biodiversity (Taiwan Biodiversity Information Network, 2009). It is a celebration of life on earth and of the value of biodiversity for our lives. This year's theme is "Biodiversity is life, biodiversity is our life". A zoo is a wonderful place with rich educational resources to allow students to explore the natural world and promote development of concepts about animals, ecology, and biodiversity. Students' scientific learning and science inquiry should begin in the zoo. The purpose of this study is to promote students' science learning and biodiversity understanding by integrating zoo resources and biodiversity issues into learning activities.

METHODOLOGY

A total of 15 classes of 1st graders participated in this study. Teaching activities include classroom discussions on the topic, animal and biodiversity issues, and a one-day field trip to the Taipei Zoo, Taiwan to allow pupils to gain more experiential insights on biodiversity. Students were guided by teachers and volunteer parents. Instruments used were questionnaire on students' learning at Taipei Zoo and study sheets. During their post-visit, students were asked to fill up the questionnaire.

The questionnaire consists of eight questions to gather information such as the number of visits to the Taipei and other zoos, and the students' level of their learning at the Taipei Zoo. The study sheets have three open-ended questions about their learning of animal and biodiversity conservation at Taipei Zoo. A total of 439 copies of the data sets were judged valid for the study.

RESULTS AND DISCUSSION

Results of Questionnaire Survey at Taipei Zoo

212 of the 439 1st graders were males. Tables 1 and 2 show the number of visits to Taipei Zoo and other zoos.

Table 1. The number of visits to Taipei Zoo by 1st graders

No. of Visits	1st time	2–6 times	7–10 times	11 times & above
Male (n)	42	133	24	13
%	67.7	44.3	48.0	48.1
Female (n)	20	167	26	14
%	32.3	55.7	52.0	51.9
Total (n)	62	300	50	27

The lowest frequency of visits to Taipei Zoo is between 2 to 6 times for both boys (44.3%) and girls (55.7%) while the highest is 11 times and above (Table 1).

Boys and girls visit Taipei Zoo mostly between 2 to 6 times and very few visit the Taipei Zoo more than 11 times. Table 2 shows most boys have not visited the other zoos while most girls have visited other zoos at least once.

Table 2. The number of visits to other zoos by 1st graders

No. of Visits	0 time	1~3 times	4~5 times	6 times & above
Male (n)	97	92	10	13
%	48.7	46.7	50.0	56.5
Female (n)	102	105	10	10
%	51.3	53.3	50.0	43.5
Total (n)	199	197	20	23

Table 3 shows the results of the feedback on the questionnaire at the Taipei Zoo. 331 students (75.4%) were strongly satisfied with the visit with only 3 (6.8%), strongly dissatisfied. Both the boys and girls understood about animals (n = 212, 94.3%) and biodiversity (n = 227, 96.9%). Only 4.7% boys and 3.1% girls did not understand about animals and 6.6% boys and 3.5% girls did not understand about biodiversity. 55.8% of the boys and girls were willing to re-visit the Taipei Zoo again and only 4.8% did not want to re-visit the zoo.

Table 3. Questionnaire survey results on students' learning outcomes, by gender, after their visit to the Taipei Zoo

	Satisfaction of Visit				Understanding about animals			Understanding about Biodiversity			Willingness to Re-visit		
	Strongly satisfied	Sati-sfied	Dissat-isfied	Strongly dissatis-fied	Gained a lot	Gained some	No gain	Gained a lot	Gained some	No gain	Definitely	Maybe	No
Male (n)	154	52	3	3	119	81	12	106	92	14	117	85	10
%	46.5	54.2	50.0	50.0	46.1	50.0	63.2	44.0	52.3	63.6	47.8	49.1	47.6
Female (n)	177	44	3	3	139	81	7	135	84	8	128	88	11
%	53.5	45.8	50.0	50.0	53.9	50.0	36.8	56.0	47.7	36.4	52.2	50.9	52.4
Total	331	96	6	6	258	162	19	241	176	22	245	173	21

Feedback to the open-ended questions on learning at the Taipei Zoo are as follows: many students expressed positive thoughts on animal conservation concepts; most students expressed satisfaction with the visit and had a lot of fun with their friends. This finding is similar to the results of Davidson *et al.* (2010). The results indicate that integrating zoo resources and biodiversity issues into teaching activities significantly contributed to the first graders' learning about animals and biodiversity.

Qualitative Results from Students' Study Sheets

Students' study sheets were collected and analyzed. The results are as follows: the top five most popular animals in order were elephants (n = 206), panda (n = 197), giraffe (n = 122), koalas (n = 113), zebra (n = 99), and the least popular, in order, were fish (n = 17), peacock (n = 15), raccoon (n = 15), beetles (n = 13), flamingo (n = 12). This finding revealed the animals that were popular among students represent a wide range of species – the concept of biodiversity they have learnt at the Taipei Zoo. Several study sheets reflected students' understanding of biodiversity conservation and what they would do to care for animals. For example, some students stated that there should be no abuse to animals, while others stated that the public should not buy ivory products.

CONCLUSION

The results of the study were summarized as follows: (i) 97.3% of students were satisfied with the field trip to the Taipei Zoo for learning the science concepts, (ii) 58.8% of students understood more about animals, (iii) 54.9% of students understood biodiversity more after the zoo visit, (iv) 55.8% of students were willing to re-visit the Taipei Zoo again, (v) the top five species of animals students like the most were the elephant, panda, giraffe, koala, zebra, and (6) students have been able to demonstrate their strategies for the biodiversity conservation of various animal groups. These results indicated that science teaching integrated with zoo resources and biodiversity issues had significant influenced the science leaning outcomes of elementary 1st graders.

For a successful informal science education experience at a zoo, Summers (2004) mentioned the importance of prior preparation of intended learning outcomes by teachers before visits to out-of-school informal science learning institutions. Teachers should structure the student leaning by asking questions to guide students in meaningful learning and integrate activities in different fields of teaching to further promote more effective learning at the zoo (e.g. Engstrom et al., 2004; Wilcox & Sterling, 2008). Furthermore, Trainin et al. (2005) reported the outdoor activities that promote observation and inquiry can enhance students' motivation and boost their interests in learning situations to strengthen their understanding on concepts about animals.

To sum up briefly, Davidson et al. (2010) suggests that: (i) in order to empower the effectiveness of teaching during students' visit to the zoo, teachers should make clear learning objectives about the field trip, plan activities that connect to classroom curriculum, and include pre-visit and post-visit activities to reinforce science learning, (ii) to ensure students' social interaction, teachers should allow students to freely form their groups to facilitate group work at the zoo, (iii) teachers are to give encouragement to students to motivate them during their visit at the zoo. Last but not least, Lederman & Lederman (2008) argued for assessment of the learning at the zoo if teachers want students to acquire some knowledge. They suggested multiple methods of assessment for informal science assessment, such as: observing how students learn, oral tests, writing assignments, presentations, problem solving, planning, home work, team work, interviews, achievement tests, and keeping a portfolio. Appropriate methods of assessment can be used to evaluate learning outcomes of students at zoos.

ACKNOWLEDGEMENTS

This study was funded by the National Science Council, Taiwan, under contract no. NSC-98-2515-S-152-002. Opinions expressed in this study do not necessarily reflect the positions or policies of NSC.

REFERENCES

Anderson, D., Thomas, G. P., & Ellenbogen, K. (2003). Learning science from experiences in informal contexts: The next generation of research. *Asia-Pacific Forum on Science Learning and Teaching, 4*(1), 1–6.

Cherif, A. H., Verma, S., & Somervill, C. (1998). From the Los Angeles zoo to the classroom: Transforming real cases via role-play into productive learning activities. *American Biology Teacher, 60*(8), 613–617.

Davidson, S. K., Passmore, C., & Anderson, D. (2010). Learning on zoo field trips: The interaction of the agendas and practices of students, teachers, and zoo educators. *Science Education, 94*(1), 122–141.

Engstrom, D. E., Boulton, J. L., & Wurzelbacher, L. (2004). From old 2 new. *Teaching Pre K-8, 34*(6), 56–57.

Hofstein, A. & Rosenfeld, S. (1996). Bridging the gap between formal and informal science learning. *Studies in Science Education, 28*, 87–112.

Kelly, J., Stetson, R., & Powell-Mikel, A. (2002). Science adventures at the local museum. *Science and Children, 39*(7), 46–48.

Kisiel, J. (2006). More than lions and tigers and bears-- Creating meaningful field trip lessons. *Science Activities, 43*(2), 7–10.

Knapp, D. (2000). Memorable experiences of a science field trip. *School Science and Mathematics, 100*(2), 65–72.

Lederman, N. G., & Lederman, J. S. (2008). *Integration of assessment and evaluation into previously created curriculum materials.* Keynote speech at International conference on informal science education. Taipei, Taiwan.

Lind, K. K. (1995). A trip to the zoo. *Science and Children, 32*(8), 37–38.

McCoy, M. W., McCoy, K. A., & Levey, D. J. (2007). Teaching biodiversity to students in inner city and under-resourced schools. *The American Biology Teacher, 69*(8), 473–476.

Pringle, R., Hakverdi, M., Cronin-Jones, L., & Johnson, C. (2003). *Zoo school for preschoolers: Laying the foundation for environmental education.* (ERIC document no.ED475663)

Pugh, K. J. & Bergin, D. A. (2005). The effect of schooling on students' out-of-school experience. *Educational Researcher, 34*(9), 15–23.

Slack, A. (2010). Who's in the zoo? *Science Teacher, 77*(3), 38–42.

Summers, S. (2004). Museums as Resources for Science Teachers. *Science Scope, 27*(9), 28–29.

Taiwan Biodiversity Information Network (2009). *The international year of biodiversity.* Retrieved September 10, 2009, from http://www.biodiv.org.tw/jsp/index.jsp

Trainin, G., Wilson, K., Wickless, M., & Brooks, D. (2005). Extraordinary animals and expository writing: Zoo in the classroom. *Journal of Science Education and Technology, 14*(3), 299–304.

Wilcox, D. R., & Sterling, D. R. (2008). Bring the zoo to you. *Science and Children, 45*(8), 42–45.

Worch, E. A., Scheuermann, A. M., & Haney, J. J. (2009). Role-play in the science classroom. *Science and Children, 47*(1), 54–59.

Ching-San Lai
National Taipei University of Education, Taipei, Taiwan
clai@tea.ntue.edu.tw

SHERRY P. RAMAYLA

24. CORRELATES OF ACHIEVEMENT TEST PERFORMANCE IN BIOLOGY 1 OF SECOND YEAR STUDENTS IN THE PHILIPPINE SCIENCE HIGH SCHOOL-CENTRAL VISAYAS CAMPUS, ARGAO, CEBU FROM 2007-2010

ABSTRACT

The aim of this study is to examine the different factors that might contribute to the achievement test performance of students in the Biology 1 course. Key findings of this investigation showed that there is a substantial correlation between the grade and IQ of the students to the performance in achievement test. Other results showed that the teacher's number of years in teaching the subject and the educational backgrounds do not affect the achievement test results. There is no difference on the achievement test results between students who graduated in private and public elementary schools. This shows that the student intrinsic factor plays an important role in the academic performance. However, it cannot be concluded that only such factor is accountable for the academic achievement of the students when multiple factors could be responsible for the observed outcome.

KEYWORDS

Correlates, Achievement Test, Academic Achievement

INTRODUCTION

This research was initiated from the article of Popham (1974), "Why Standardized Tests Don't Measure Educational Quality". Historically, classroom teachers used evaluation only in relation to the grading of students. Tyler (1930) viewed evaluation not as the appraisal of students but appraisal of the educational program's quality. It determines the degree to which the objectives of an educational program had been attained.

Student academic performance is shaped by multiple factors. McLaughlin and Drori (2000) created a model of student's achievement as related to four factors: student background, school organizational features, teacher's professional characteristics and school behavior climate. In addition, Walberg (1974) explained that standardized test correlates with heredity, home environment and schooling. Student's background includes intrinsic and extrinsic factors. Student's behavior and IQ are examples of intrinsic factors while extrinsic factors include family background, socioeconomic status, and community of the student. Both intrinsic and extrinsic factors contribute to the academic performance of students. According to Anderson and Walberg (1974), IQ generally accounts for more than 16% of the variance in learning while learning environments account for between 13% – 46%. The learning environment or school organizational features especially on class sizes greatly affects the performance of the student. Finn and Archilles (1990) confirmed the link between reduced class size and greater student learning. It is being assumed that greater attention was given to the student if class size is small. Brophy (1974) also stressed that uncrowdedness of rooms increases the opportunity to learn.

Teacher's qualification may also affect the academic performance of the student. Walberg (1974) elucidated that good teachers may cause high student achievement, or high achieving students may attract good teachers to their schools, or more likely both of these factors may affect one another and causally interact with other factors. However, the review of Rosenshine (1970) showed that teacher effectiveness in producing student learning gains is not a stable "trait", that a teacher who produces large gains in his students this year is not necessarily going to do the same the next year. Furthermore, the study of McLaughlin and Drori (2000) shows a weak correlation between a teacher's experience and the student's achievement.

The problem of why standardized test do not measure educational quality was addressed in this study. Among the factors mentioned above, this study focused on two factors that might affect the scores of the student in a given test. These factors are the student's background and teacher's professional characteristics. The student background factors include IQ, grades in Biology 1 and the previous school attended by the student. According to Sax (1974), intelligence and achievement test scores correlates highly with one another. Several studies also reveal that IQ is the best indicator of academic performance. On the other hand, Walberg (1974) correlates high student achievement to teacher's capacity. Although Glass (1974) pointed out that no matter how stable the traits of the teacher it may not guarantee the stability of producing students with high academic performance. For the benefit of verifying this aspect, teacher's academic background and the number of years in teaching the subject were included in this study. Background of student such as the previous school where he attended was also included. Some schools may provide curriculum that was already advanced in science and this too will contribute to the present academic performance of the student.

METHODOLOGY

Research Subjects

Biology 1 course is offered to second year students in Philippine Science High School System (PSHSS). They have taken the National Competitive Exam (NCE) during their last year in elementary. This is the entrance exam of PSHSS. The top 240 students will be admitted to the main campus in Diliman and the top 90 students in each region will be admitted to the regional campuses. Qualifiers to take the NCE were the top students of their class.

The research subjects are said to have a high aptitude in Science and Mathematics. Three batches of students were included in the study. The first or pioneering batch took the Biology subject in SY 2007–2008; the second had their Biology 1 in SY 2008–2009; and the third batch had it in SY 2009–2010.

Data Collection

Data used in this research were taken from Philippine Science High School – Central Visayas Campus with the permission from the Campus Director last April 2010. IQ test administered last 2008 to the students were extracted from the guidance counselor while background information about the student such as previous elementary school graduated, Biology 1 grade and Achievement test result were taken from the school registrar. The rest of the information was supplied by the author of this study.

Statistical Analysis of the Data

The data was analyzed using Pearson Product-Moment Correlation Coefficient (r) for correlation analysis of Achievement test scores to the student's IQ, grade in Biology 1, the teacher's number of years in teaching Biology 1 subject and trainings and seminars attended by the teacher. To check if there are really correlations on the factors mentioned above, a test was computed of each data. Analysis of Variance (ANOVA) was also used to test the relationship between Achievement test scores to the teacher's educational background. T-test was employed in testing the relationship between the scores in Biology 1 achievement test and the previous elementary school attended by the student. All computations were done using Statistical Package for the Social Sciences (SPSS) software.

RESULTS AND DISCUSSION

IQ of the Student in Three Batches from 2007–2010

The computed value of r using SPSS for the correlation between the achievement test score in Biology 1 and the IQ of the student in batch 2007–2008 and batch 2008–2009 is 0.596 and 0.737 respectively at 0.01 level of significance (as shown in Table 1). According to Guilford's (Sprinthall, 1997) suggested interpretation for the values of r, the correlation between achievement test scores and IQ for batch 2007–2008 is moderate or there is a substantial relationship between the two variables. For batch 2008–2009, the correlation is also moderate achievement test scores and IQ of the student.

The correlation result for batch 2009–2010 is 0.305 at 0.05 level of significance (Table 1). This value means that there is a low correlation or a definite but small relationship between the achievement test scores and IQ of this batch of students.

The result on the first and second batches conforms to the idea of Walberg (1974). According to him, performance of the student to standardized test is correlated to heredity which includes IQ of the student. Hartlage and Steele (2006)

227

also find that there is a strong correlation between IQ of the student to achievement test measures among American students. However, the result from the third batch does not conform to the idea of Walberg and Hartlage and Steele.

Table 1. Correlation between achievement test scores to the IQ of the student in the third batch 2009–2010

	Correlations	Achievement test score	IQ
Achievement test score	Pearson Correlation	1.000	.305
	Sig. (2-tailed)		.059
	N	39	39
IQ	Pearson Correlation	.305	1.000
	Sig. (2-tailed)	.059	
	N	39	39

Student's Grade in Biology 1

To test if there was correlation between the achievement test scores and the grade of the students in Biology 1 subject, the Pearson Product-Moment Correlation Coefficient was computed using SPSS. Value of r is -0.737 for the first batch; -0.755 for the second batch and -0.694 for the third batch at 0.01 level of significance shown in Table 2. Using Guilford's (1956) suggested interpretation for the values of r (Sprinthall, 1997), these values mean that there is a high correlation or marked relationship between the achievement test scores and the grade of the student in Biology 1 in all three batches. This further means that the achievement test score in Biology 1 can be partly explained or predicted using the grade of the students in Biology 1. The study of Hartlage and Steele (2006) on correlates of academic achievement revealed that grades of the student may be one of the predictors on the achievement test scores and this was supported by the current result of this study.

Table 2. Correlation between Achievement Test scores and the Biology 1 grade of the three batches of students

		Batch 2007–2008		Batch 2008–2009		Batch 2009–2010	
	Correlation	Achiev-ement test score	Grade in Biology 1	Achievement test score	Grade in Biology 1	Achieve-ment test score	Grade in Biology 1
Achievement Test score	Pearson Correlation	1.000	-.737**	1.000	-.755**	1.000	-.694**
	Sig. (2-tailed)		.000		.000		.000
	N	25	25	33	33	39	39
Grade in Biology 1	Pearson Correlation	-.737**	1.000	-.755**	1.000	-.694**	1.000
	Sig. (2-tailed)	.000		.000		.000	
	N	25	25	33	33	39	39

**. Correlation is significant at the 0.01 level (2-tailed).

Teacher's Number of Years in Teaching Biology 1

The teaching experience of the teacher in teaching a particular subject may or may not affect the student performance. In order to check this, the correlation between the number of years in teaching Biology 1 and the achievement test score was computed using SPSS. The computed value of r is 0.027. Following the Guilford's interpretation of the value of r, this means that there is slight correlation or almost negligible relationship between the numbers of years of the teacher in teaching Biology 1 to the achievement test scores of the students. This finding agrees with the review of Rosenshine (1974) that the teacher is not a gauge in the achievement test performance of the student. McLaughlin and Drori (2000) also stressed that teacher's experience correlates to student's achievement but the correlation is weak.

Trainings and Seminars Attended by the Teacher

Teacher's attendance to trainings and seminars may enhance the knowledge and skills in her chosen field. To check if attendance to trainings and seminars affects the performance of the students in PSHS-CVisC, Pearson Product-Moment Correlation Coefficient was computed using SPSS. The value of the computed $r = 0.044$. This means that there is a slight or almost negligible relationship between the two factors following Guilford's interpretation.

Educational Background of the Biology 1 Teacher

To test if there is a relationship between the educational background of the teacher to the achievement test performance of the student, Analysis of Variance (ANOVA) was computed using the SPSS. The critical value of F for $\alpha = 0.01$ is 3.11. Since the computed value of $F = 0.283$, it means that there is no relationship between the educational background of the teacher to the achievement test performance of the student.

The result of this study contradicts the study of Vlaardingerbroek and Neil Taylor (2003) on teacher education variables as correlates to primary science ratings. Their result showed that there is a higher ranking on the scores of the primary student with teacher's having good educational background and trainings in sciences. According to the old axiom teachers' competence in primary science arises largely from their own mastery of scientific concepts. Hammond *et al.*, (2001) also find a strong and consistent evidence of higher performance in student having teachers that hold standard certifications. This present study may not be a manifestation of this factor since there is only one teacher that handles the subject and there is no point of comparison with other teachers who also teach the subject.

Elementary School Previously Attended by the Student

Previous elementary school of the students may or may not contribute to the current educational performance of the student. In this study, the type of school (public or private), has been investigated if it contributes to the achievement test score of the student.

A *t*-test was computed using SPSS to check if there was a significant difference on the achievement test score between public and private schools in three different batches from 2007–2010. The computed value of $t = -0.472$ (equal variances not assumed) for batch 2007–2008, $t = -1.105$ for batch 2008–2009, and $t = -1.342$ for batch 2009–2010. These values of t are lower than the critical values of t at 0.05 level of significance; this means that there is no significant difference on the achievement test scores of the student who graduated from public elementary school to the student who graduated in private elementary school in all three batches.

According to the study of Jimenez and Lockheed (1995), there is really a difference in achievement test performance between public and private schools in developing countries. Contributing factors to the achievement test score difference are the mean salary of the teacher in public and private schools, class size and also the gender. Teachers with high salaries both in public and private schools tend to produce students with high scores in achievement test. Students in large class in private schools excel in achievement test compared to public schools with large class. Moreover, gender may also contribute to the achievement performance. Male performs better in private school but not in public schools. In the Philippines, students from private schools perform better than students in public schools. The socioeconomic of the student plays an important role in the academic performance of the student. Students enrolled in private schools come from more advantage background and are more expose to media and other amenities that might contribute to the academic performance of the student. However, in this study, relationship between the achievement test performance of the student coming from private and public school is not significant.

CONCLUSION

As presented in the findings, it can be concluded that IQ and grades of the students correlated to the achievement test scores of the students. This means that the achievement test score can be predicted using the IQ and Biology 1 grade of the student. Other factors studied in this paper have shown insignificant relationship with the achievement test scores.

REFERENCES

Barclay, J. R. (1974). Needs assessment. In H. J. Walberg (ed). Evaluating educational performance: a sourcebook of methods, instruments and examples. McCutchan Publishing Corporation, USA.

Brophy, J. E. (1974). Achievement correlates. In H. J. Walberg (ed) Evaluating educational performance: a sourcebook of methods, instruments and examples. McCutchan Publishing Corporation, USA.

California Physical Fitness Test. (2005). A Study of the Relationship Between Physical Fitness and Academic Achievement in California Using 2004 Test Results

Gay, L. R. & P. Airasian. (2000). Educational Research: Competencies for Analysis and Application (6th ed).Pearson Education, New Jersey.

Popham, W. J. (Ed.) (1974). Evaluation in Education: Current Applications. American Educational Research Association, USA.

Popham, W. J. (1988). Education Evaluation. Prentice Hall, New Jersey.

Sax, G. (1974). The use of standardized test in evaluation. In W. James Popham (Ed) Evaluation in Education: Current Applications. American Educational Research Association, USA.

Scriven, Michael. (1974). Evaluation Perspective and Procedures in Evaluation. In W. James Popham (Ed) Evaluation in Education: Current Applications. American Educational Research Association, USA.

Sprinthall, Richard C. (1997). Basic Statistical Analysis 5th ed. Allyn & Bacon A Viacom Company, Needham Heights, MA.

Stufflebeam, D. L. (1974). Alternative Approaches to educational Evaluation: A self-study guide. In W. James Popham (Ed) Evaluation in Education: Current Applications. American Educational Research Association, USA.

Stufflebeam, D. L. (1974). Evaluation according to context, input, process, product CIPP Evaluation Model. In W. James Popham (Ed) Evaluation in Education: Current Applications. American Educational Research Association, USA.

Walberg, H. J. (Ed.) (1974). Evaluating educational performance: a sourcebook of methods, instruments and examples. McCutchan Publishing Corporation, USA.

On-Line Sources

Hammond, L., B. Berry & A. Thoreson (2001). Does Teacher certification matter? Evaluating the evidence. Educational evaluation and policy analysis. Vol. *23*(1), 57–77.
http://epa.sagepub.com/cgi/content/abstract/23/1/57

Hartlage, L.C. & C.T. Steele 2006. WISC and WISC-R correlates of academic achievement. Psychology in the schools Vol. *14*(1), 15–18.
http://www3.interscience.wiley.com/journal/112421733/abstract

Jimenez, E. & M. E. Lockheed (1995). Public and Private Secondary Education in Developing Countries: A Comparative Study. The International Bank for Reconstruction and Development/THE WORLD BANK, Washington D. C., USA.
http://books.google.com.ph/books?id=Of6VywrbiccC&pg=PA41&lpg=PA41&dq=achievement+test+s cores+in+public+and+private+schools&source=bl&ots=qmWybeNtgz&sig=Cy94MZThN0nPe90C oyFjuNuv21U&hl=tl&ei=PsUATPrgMom-rAfp8KnhDg&sa=X&oi=book_result&ct=result&resnum=4&ved=0CCMQ6AEwAw#v=onepage& q=achievement%20test%20scores%20in%20public%20and%20private%20schools&f=false

Thomas-Bratley, Betty. 1988. The Relationship between Self-Esteem and Academic Achievement in a Group of High, Medium, and Low Secondary Public High School Achievers
http://www.eric.ed.gov/ERICWebPortal/custom/portlets/recordDetails/detailmini.jsp?_nfpb=true&_&E RICExtSearch_SearchValue_0=ED323486&ERICExtSearch_SearchType_0=eric_accno&accno=E D323486

U.S. Department of Education. National Center for Education Statistics. School-level Correlates ofAcademic Achievement: Student Assessment Scores in SASS Public Schools, NCES 2000–303, by Donald McLaughlin and Gili Drori. Project Officer: Michael Ross. Washington DC: 2000

Vlaardingerbroek, B & T.G. Neil Taylor 2003. Teacher education variables as correlates of primary science ratings in thirteen TIMSS system. International Journal of Educational Development Vol 23(4):429–438.
http://www.sciencedirect.com/science?_ob=ArticleURL&_udi=B6VD7-48M7R7R-7&_user=10&_coverDate=07%2F31%2F2003&_rdoc=1&_fmt=high&_orig=search&_sort=d&_do canchor=&view=c&_searchStrId=1352096435&_rerunOrigin=google&_acct=C000050221&_versi on=1&_urlVersion=0&_userid=10&md5=9e94b712c208862a7a8968a825a2f69d

http://www.pshs.edu.ph
http://mailer.fsu.edu/~slynn/popham.html
http://nces.ed.gov/pubs2000/2000303.pdf

Sherry P. Ramayla
Philippine Science High School-Central Visayas Campus and
University of the Philippines of the Visayas Cebu Campus
platenae@yahoo.com

THASANEEYA R. NOPPARATJAMJOMRAS

25. DEVELOPING A SOCIAL CONSTRUCTIVIST TEACHING AND LEARNING MODULE ON DNA FOR HIGH SCHOOL STUDENTS IN THAILAND

ABSTRACT

The purpose of this study is to develop a social constructivist teaching module on DNA for high school students in Thailand. The first phase of the study in the teaching and learning of genetics concepts was studied. A social constructivist teaching module on DNA was developed in the second phase. The survey in Phase I was conducted with five high school biology teachers and thirty-one high school students from four schools in the Bangkok Education Service Area Office. Data from interviews were analyzed using content analysis. Results showed most teachers surveyed acknowledged the genetics concepts for students' understanding were moderately difficult, which was supported by the poorer performance in most students' answers. Both the teacher and student groups highlighted 'DNA Properties and DNA Synthesis' and 'DNA and RNA in Protein Synthesis' as difficult concepts in genetics. The DNA module in Phase II was developed based on the social constructivist approach. Each of the units consisted of an 'Orientation' phase, a 'Focus' phase, and a 'Conclusion' phase. Hands-on activities, small group discussions and whole class discussions were introduced into the class. The module included 'DNA Properties and DNA Synthesis', 'DNA and RNA in Protein Synthesis', and 'Chemical Structure of DNA'.

KEYWORDS

Genetic Concepts, Social Constructivist Approach, DNA Teaching And Learning Module

INTRODUCTION

DNA, an important topic in genetics, is taught in the biology curriculum at high school level in Thailand. In 2002, the Institute for the Promotion of Teaching Science and Technology (IPST) published the Handbook for Learning Management in the Section of Science. It shows the outcome of science education at the end of high school. IPST included genetics in living organisms

Mijung Kim and C. H. Diong (Eds.), Biology Education for Social and Sustainable Development, 233–240.

for Grades 10–12 that involve describing and discussing the genetic transfer process, variation, mutation and the causes of biodiversity. Thus, after studying life science in Grades 10–12, students should have the ability to investigate, describe and discuss genetic materials, chromosomes, transfer of genetic traits, genetic variation, mutation, and benefits and disadvantages of the results of inherited genetic traits. The process and intended outcomes of science education are as follows: an understanding about living organisms and living process; biodiversity; relationships between living organisms and the environment; using the investigative process to learn science; problem solving in science learning by hands-on experience; investigations, and researching from a variety of learning sources and the Internet, and presenting the knowledge to other people (IPST, 2002).

Learning reforms and a learner-centered approaches are important themes in Thailand's national education. The rationales for learning reforms are: the improvements to the quality of life of the Thai people, strengthening of the Thai society, service to others in harmony with the learning culture in the age of globalization, service to the needs of learners, teachers, parents and the Thai society, and fulfillment of the law (Office of the National Education Commission, 2000). The rationales aim to motivate educators and science teachers in Thailand to prepare students for living in a global society.

Constructivist teaching and learning are based on learning reforms in Thailand. It also relates to the learner-centered approach. Teaching and learning pedagogy in science classrooms focus on the 'construction of meanings', and the role of the science teacher is to facilitate and mediate the construction of knowledge (Jones, 1997). In addition, based on a social constructivist perspective, teaching and learning pedagogy corresponds with the spirit and intent of sections 22 and 24 of the National Education Act (1999, 2002) (Office of the National Education Commission, 2002), in which teachers as facilitators should encourage students to realize their abilities.

Contributions of peers are significant to promote students' learning. According to Vygotskian, whose perspective as social constructivism is well known in educational development in teaching and learning, the child is the focus in a social context, where everyday concepts are integrated into the learning of concepts through interactions, negotiations, and sharing. According to him, knowledge develops through appropriation of the culture, through social interaction between the children who are more capable. He argued that concepts could not grow without social interaction. An item in the appropriation of the culture is the development of an ability to use societal tools, especially language, for mediating intellectual activity, an ability that can be acquired through interactions with more capable peers (Howe, 1996). Thus, teachers need to plan activities where students can participate effectively with more capable peers (Hodson and Hodson, 1998).

Therefore, the teaching strategies for developing students' understanding of genetic topics in this research place an emphasis on social constructivism, in which learners can construct their knowledge by participating with peers, with teachers taking on the role as learning facilitators. In science teaching, the implementation of social constructivist strategies requires that students use their existing knowledge as the starting point for change to scientifically acceptable concepts (Hand *et al.*, 1997). Driver and Oldham (1986) presented stages of constructivist teaching as follows:

1. Orientation – where students are given the opportunity to develop a sense of purpose and motivation for learning the topic;
2. Elicitation – when students make their current ideas on the topic of a lesson clear. This can be achieved by a variety of activities such as group discussion, designing of posters, or writing;
3. Restructuring of ideas – this being the heart of the constructivist lesson sequence consists of a number of stages, including:
   3.1 Clarification and exchange of ideas – during which time students' understandings and language may be sharpened by contrasting or conflicting ideas held by other students, or by ideas contributed by the teacher;
   3.2 Construction of new ideas arising from the above discussions and demonstrations. Students begin to see that there are a variety of ways of interpreting a phenomenon or evidence;
   3.3 Evaluation of the new ideas either experimentally or by thinking through their implications. Students should try to figure out the best ways of testing the alternative ideas. Students may at this stage feel dissatisfied with their existing conceptions;
4. Application of ideas where pupils are given the opportunity to use their developed ideas in a variety of situations, both familiar and novel;
5. Review – this is the final stage in constructivist teaching in which students are invited to reflect on how their ideas have changed by drawing comparisons between their thinking at the start of the lesson sequence, and their thinking towards the end of the lesson.

Cosgrove and Osborne (2001) suggested different stages of constructivist teaching. The difference is the 'Application' phase' of Cosgrove and Osborne (2001) is similar to both 'Application of Ideas' and 'Review in the Final Stage' of Driver and Oldham (1986) who used their ideas in a number of situations and compared their ideas before and after learning a learning episode.

The important stage of constructivist teaching argued in science education is the activity. The activities are given in the 'Elicitation' phase (Driver and Oldham, 1986) but in the 'Focus' phase of Cosgrove and Osborne (2001), and in the 'Restructuring of Ideas' in Driver and Oldham (1986) but in the 'Challenge' phase of Cosgrove and Osborne (2001). Windschitl (1999) supported using questions and activities, while Osborne (1996) argued that activities were composed of structured exercises and they require group activity work, such as group discussion.

Many educators in social constructivist teaching argued for activities to be done within a group. Driver and Oldham (1986), Osborne (1996), and Colburn (2000) are example of this school of thought.. Stanbridge (1990) suggested using only small groups. Hand *et al.* (1997) argued using both small and larger group work.

Constructivist learning was stated in a number of papers. The Generative Learning Model (GLM) of Cosgrove and Osborne (2001) stated that teaching and learning should be composed of a 'Preliminary' phase, 'Focus'phase, 'Challenge' phase, and an 'Application' phase. The learning activities were used in the last three phases. 'Focus' phase uses materials to explore concepts, asks questions related to the concepts, and presents students' views in group or class discussions. 'Challenge' phase considers other students and compares scientist's views with the class's views. 'Application' phase discusses and debates the merits of solutions, solves practical problems using the concept as a basis, and presents solutions to others in the class.

For this study, the researcher used the indicators for social constructivist teaching in the genetics classroom as follows: 'Orientation' stage to check students' prior knowledge; 'Focus' stage included inquiry, small group discussion, or investigation; and 'Conclusion' stage included whole class discussion. In the orientation stage, the teacher invites students into the lessons by referring to the previous lessons or to some social issues. To check students' prior knowledge is a way to explore the existing knowledge of students and to begin the zone of proximal development of each student. In the focus and conclusion stages, students have opportunities to participate with their peers and teacher in discussions. To use inquiry, small group discussion or investigation is a strategy to promote students' thinking and participation between students and the teacher, or among peers. To encourage students in the whole class discussion is a strategy to help form the students' idea and also to promote classroom participation.

The objectives of the Phase 1 study were to determine the current situation of teaching and learning genetics to high school science students in the Bangkok Education Service Area Office 1. The objective of the Phase 2 study was to develop a DNA module based on social constructivist approach.

METHODOLOGY

Subjects

Five biology school teachers and thirty-one high school students from four schools in the science program in Bangkok Education Service Area Office 1 volunteered for the interviews. All teachers were females. Four out of five were more than 50 years of age and the others, 35 years. Four of them had a major in science with two of them, a Bachelor's degree and the other two, a Master's degree. The remaining teacher had a Doctoral degree. All five had more than 10 years of teaching experience in biology. Only the youngest teacher was trained in genetics. The high school students were between 16 to18 years and 15 were males.

Instruments

A Teachers' Questionnaire Form and a Students' Questionnaire Form were used to survey current teaching and learning of genetics in high school science students in the Bangkok Education Service Area Office 1. The instruments comprises a questionnaire about teaching and learning genetics for teachers (Teachers' Questionnaire Form) and another one for students. The Teachers' Questionnaire Form consisted of 16 questions with open-ended and closed-ended questions using a Likert scale. It had two parts; Part A surveyed the background information of teachers including age, gender, teaching experience, experience in professional development, and their duties in school; Part B focused on the difficulties of teaching genetics topics, how to problem-solve in genetics, teaching strategies with instructional materials, assessment and evaluation methods that teachers had used successively; and suggestions for teaching genetics in high school classrooms in Thailand. The Students' Questionnaire Form consisted of 10 questions with open-ended and closed-ended questions using a Likert scale. It had two parts; Part A surveyed the background of students including the students' gender, age, grade, and favourite subjects; Part B focused on experiences in learning genetics, the difficulties of genetics, problems and problem-solving in learning genetics, suggestions for learning genetics and using genetics knowledge in their daily lives.

Data Collections

Data were collected from four schools in the Bangkok Education Service Area Office 1. The first phase was done in 2009 after all the participants had finished learning genetics. The DNA module of the second phase was developed in 2010.

Data Analysis

For this research, data analysis was separated into two main categories. The first was using data with Likert scales, which were coded and analyzed in percentages and described. The second set of data from the open-ended questions were categorized, grouped and analyzed by interpretation.

RESULTS

The results showed most students liked learning science, with eight of them having a preference for the subject biology. The most common reason why students liked to study biology was that 'biology is related to daily life'. Most teachers surveyed acknowledge that it was not easy for the students to understand the topic of genetics. It is consistent with most students' answers. Table 1 shows the number of students' response to the level of difficulty of each genetic concept.

Table 1. Number of student responses to the level of difficulty of each genetics concept for learning (N = 31)

Genetic concepts	Number of Responses			
	MD*	D*	M*	E*
Genetic Traits	-	1	25	5
Dominant and Recessive	-	3	14	14
Homozygous and Heterozygous	-	3	18	10
Genotype and Phenotype	-	4	17	10
Law of Segregation and Law of Independent Assortment	-	15	12	4
Alleles	1	9	18	3
Multiple Genes or Polygenes	3	14	13	1
Chromosome	-	6	20	5
Relationship between Gene and Chromosome	1	10	17	3
Chemical Structure of DNA	2	7	17	5
DNA Properties and DNA Synthesis	4	15	11	1
DNA and RNA in Protein Synthesis	6	15	10	-
Genetic Codes	2	14	11	4
DNA in Prokaryote and Eukaryote	4	8	13	6
Mutation	-	13	14	4
Genetic Engineering and Applications	2	15	14	-

*Most difficult = MD, Difficult = D, Moderate = M, Easy = E

Results in Table 1 revealed most students surveyed highlighted 6 of the 16 concepts were difficult. For example, 48.4% of students selected 'Law of Segregation and Law of Independent Assortment', 'DNA Properties and DNA Synthesis', 'DNA and RNA in Protein Synthesis', and 'Genetic Engineering and Applications' as the most difficult concepts.

The results also showed some agreement with the teachers' responses in which 'DNA Properties and DNA Synthesis' and 'DNA and RNA in Protein Synthesis' were identified as difficult concepts for teaching genetics.

The teachers taught by explaining and asking questions coupled with other teaching strategies such as teacher demonstrations, and using CAI for most of the teaching and learning. Most instructional materials used were powerpoint slides. Most students were assessed by tests. When they had problems with understanding genetics concepts, the students read up additional books, asked teachers or discussed their learning difficulties with their peers.

In the second phase of the study, the DNA module was developed based on the social constructivist approach. The module included 'DNA Properties and DNA Synthesis', 'DNA and RNA in Protein Synthesis', and 'Chemical Structure of DNA' as these were important fundamentals. Each genetics unit was based on the social constructivist approach and the current science teaching curriculum in the Bangkok Education Service Area Office 1. Each unit consisted of an 'Orientation' stage, a 'Focus' stage, and a 'Conclusion' stage. Hands-on activities, small discussions and whole class discussion were also introduced into the class.

DISCUSSION

Teachers are the most important asset in the classroom. Effective learning cannot take place in classroom if teachers did not prepare themselves before coming to the class. This study reported the current situation of teaching and learning genetics to high school science students in the Bangkok Education Service Area Office 1. It allowed the researcher to understand the biology course in each school and to analyze the difficulties in the teaching and learning of genetics in the Area Office 1. In addition, the finding has helped in the development of a DNA module for the school teachers based on the social constructivist approach to fit the school curriculum. The approach focused on encouraging students in small groups to carry out investigations in biology and to conduct peer discussions. It is important for researchers to survey both teachers and students in the teaching and learning of science subjects in order to enhance students' understanding of the subjects.

REFERENCES

Colburn, A. (2000). Constructivism: Science Education's 'Grand Unifying Theory'. The Clearing House, 74(1), 9–12.

Cosgrove, M., & Osborne, R. (2001). Lessons Frameworks for Changing Children's Ideas. pp. 101–111. In Roger Osborne and Peter Freyberg (eds.). Learning in Science: the implications of children's science. Hong Kong: Heinemann.

Donald, D.; Lazarus, S., & Lolwana, P. (2002). Educational Psychology in Social Context. South Africa: Oxford University Press Southern Africa.

Driver, R., & Oldham, V. (1986). A Constructivist Approach to Curriculum Development in Science. Studies in Science Education, 13(-), 105–122.

Hand, B., Lovejoy, C., & Balaam, G. (1991). Teachers' Reaction to a Change to a Constructivist Teaching/ Learning Strategy. The Australian Science Teachers Journal, 37(1), 20–24.

Hand, B., Lovejoy, C., & Balaam, G. (1991). Teachers' Reaction to a Change to a Constructivist Teaching/ Learning Strategy. The Australian Science Teachers Journal, 37(1), 20–24.

Hand, B., Treagust, D. F., & Vance, K. (1997). Student Perceptions of the Social Constructivist Classroom. Science Education, 81(5), 561–575.

Hodson, D., & Hodson, J. (1998). From Constructivism to social constructivism: a Vygotskian perspective on teaching and learning science. School Science Review, 79(-), 33–41.

Vygotskian perspective on teaching and learning science. School Science Review, 79(-), 33–41.

Howe, A. C. (1996). Development of Science Concepts within a Vygotskian Framework. Science Education, 80(1), 35–51.

Institute for the Promotion of Teaching Science and Technology (IPST). (2002). Handbook for Learning Management in the Section of Science. Bangkok: Krurusapha Ladprao.

Institute for the Promotion of Teaching Science and Technology (IPST). (2003). Handbook for Learning Management in the Section of Science (2nd ed.). Bangkok: Krurusapha Ladprao.

Jenkins, E. W. (2001). Constructivism in School Science Education: powerful model or the most dangerous intellectual tendency?. Science and Education, 9(6), 599–610.

Jones, M. G. (1997). The Constructivist Leader. pp. 140–149. In J. Rhoton and P. Bowers (eds.). Issues in Science Education. VA (U.S.): The National Science Teachers Association.

Office of the National Education Commission (ONEC). (2000). Learning Reform: a learner-centered approach. Bangkok: Watana Panit Printing & Publishing

Office of the National Education Commission (ONEC). (2002). National Education Act:B.E. 2542 (1999) and Editing (2nd ed.). Bangkok: Prig Wan Graphic.

Osborne, J. F. (1996). Beyond Constructivism. Science Education, *80*(1), 53–82.
Stanbridge, B. (1990). A Constructivist Model of Learning Used in the Teaching of Junior Science. The Australian Science Teachers Journal, *36*(4), 20–28.
Windschitl, M. (1999). A Visio Educators Can Put into Practice: portraying the constructivist classroom as a cultural system. School Science and Mathematics, *99*(4), 189–196.

Thasaneeya Ratanaroutai Nopparatjamjomras
Institute for Innovative Learning, Mahidol University
999 Phuttamonthon 4 Road, Nakhon Pathom 73170
Thailand
iltrt@mahidol.ac.th

MELINDAM M. GARABATO AND MANUEL B. BARQUILLA

26. A DESIGN-AND-DEVELOP BIOLOGY LABORATORY KIT FOR RURAL HIGH SCHOOLSTUDENTS IN THE PHILIPPINES

ABSTRACT

The study aims to determine if the use of a design-and-develop science laboratory kit to enhance the learning of science concepts increases students' academic achievement and science laboratory skills in rural high schools in the Philippines. The kit contains resources created from indigenous and recyclable materials and a manual for teachers' use in teaching Biology concepts. The study is composed of three phases, namely: Developmental Phase, Pilot Testing Phase, and Evaluation and Utilization Phase. Participants from Odiongan and Kalipay National High School (NHS), Gingoog City Division, Philippines, participated in the Evaluation and Utilisation Phase and were divided into experimental groups with the kit and control groups without the kit. Results showed an improvement in marks and experimental skill competency from participants' pre- and post-test scores with the kit. It is evident the developed kit resources are effective and can improve participants' scores. Concepts developed among participants include reproduction and genetics and science experimental skills such as observation, classification, inference, prediction, comparison and interpretation skill. Thus, the kit is recommended for use and it is hoped that the developed-and-tested laboratory kit can be used in more rural schools to contribute to enhancing students' laboratory skills and the acquisition of scientific knowledge at the same time. A further comparison of participants' results in the 2010 National Achievement Test Results between the experimental and control group could help determine the extent of the effectiveness of the kit. The use of the laboratory kit could be promoted in urban schools as well.

KEYWORDS

Biology Concepts, Laboratory Kit, Achievements, Experimental Skills

INTRODUCTION

According to Haury et al., 1994, hands-on science is defined as any science laboratory activity that allows the student to handle, manipulate or observe a scientific process. It involves the child in a total learning experience which enhances the child's ability to think critically. The child must plan a process to test

Mijung Kim and C. H. Diong (Eds.), Biology Education for Social and Sustainable Development, 241–248.
© 2012 Sense Publishers. All rights reserved.

a hypothesis, put the process into motion using various hands-on materials, see the process to completion and then be able to explain the results. Laboratory activity is a "hands-on-learning" in science education and "hands-on-learning" is learning by doing activities.

In Gingoog City, in particular Misamis Oriental, however, most rural secondary schools lack the facilities, equipments and apparatus in their Science laboratory necessary for the study in Biology. Students are unable to carry out Science laboratory experiments due to insufficient resources. Teachers teach Science lessons to students using the descriptions and drawings of science diagrams. As a result, students find difficulties in the learning of Science concepts, which is one of the reasons why rural students in Misamis Oriental do not perform well in national evaluation. Gingoog City is ranked bottom for their performance in the National Achievement Test.

The study addresses this issue by determining if the use of a design-and-develop science laboratory kit to enhance the learning of science concepts increases students' academic achievement and science laboratory skills competency in Philippines' rural high schools. The kit contains resources created from indigenous and recyclable materials and a manual for teachers' use in teaching Biology concepts. The kit is tested in a pilot school and thereafter, in rural high schools, where students' results in a pre- and post-test would be compared with schools without the laboratory kit. The results in terms of participants' marks and experimental skill competency would be compared. Figure 1 shows the conceptual paradigm of the study, a possible relationship between the developed laboratory kit and high school students' achievement and enhancement of laboratory concepts and skills.

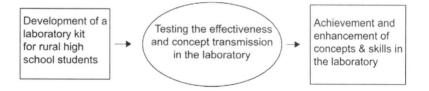

Figure 1. Relationship of concept variables in the paradigm.

MATERIALS AND METHODS

A quasi-experimental design was carried out to determine the performance of the students during the pre-and-post achievement and skills test with the aim of evaluating the effectiveness of the laboratory kit through formative and summative evaluation.

In Phase I, topics were identified using the Learning Competencies in Biology curriculum provided by the Department of Education. They were chosen based on the competencies during the Third Grading Period. Experimental activities were then designed based on the need of the topic to have a laboratory activity. These activities and the identified topics were compiled to form a manual which serves as a guide for students in the laboratory. It includes a Preface, Table of Contents and Definition of Keywords. In addition, the Teacher's Guide was planned according to the activities to provide a set of instructions for teachers using the laboratory manual. Resources in the kit were created using indigenous or recyclable materials. Some of the apparatus had been assembled while some were put together as a kit according to its use in the Laboratory Activity. The designed activities and resources were validated by an expert from the Division of Gingoog City and two from MSU-IIT. Readability of Laboratory Activities was tested through Fry Readability Test. A test run had been conducted earlier on students of the workers to ensure that the kit could be used to run a pilot test and for a laboratory activity in the participating school.

In Phase II, Formative Evaluation was given to the pilot school. A group of participants used the kit to carry out experiments. They were given a pre-laboratory Activity or a pre-test to assess the relevance of the kit with regards to the given topics. In Phase III, half the participants from Odiongan and Kalipay NHS carried out Science activities 1 to 5 with the laboratory kit while the other half carried out activities 6 to 10 without. On the other hand, participants in Kalipay NHS carried out activities 1 to 5 without the kit and activities 6 to 10 with it. Both schools were given a summative pre- and post-test using the Achievement Questionnaire and Skills Development Questionnaire. In between the summative tests, i.e. the Third Grading Period, students used the kit for their laboratory activities. Their formative laboratory skills were observed and students were classified into fast, moderate and slow learners. Forty and forty-seven second-year students participated in the summative test and formative kit evaluation respectively. For pre-test and post-test average, mean was used. Comparison of the performance of the two schools tested was done through paired t-test and correlation. All statistical analysis was done using SPSS version 9.2.

RESULTS AND DISCUSSION

The Content and Face Validity of the Designed Laboratory Kit in Phase II of Study

Table 1 shows an improved result in participants' performance in the summative evaluation in the Phase II pilot test when the Laboratory Kit was used. The Laboratory Kit improved learning among students in the pilot school. From feedback contributed by teachers and students in the pilot test, the sequence of the designed laboratory activity was shifted to the beginning of the lesson, instead of the middle. Some materials were replaced and indicated in Appendix Table 1. Appendix Table 1 shows the indigenous and recyclable materials used for every developed activity in the laboratory kit, as well as comments and suggestions from the Division of Gingoog City and MSU-IIT. Appendix 1 Table 2 shows the evaluation of the developed Laboratory Kit for the designed manual, teacher's guide, the reusability of the resources and its feasibility in rural high schools. The evaluation serves to further improve the functionality and reusability of the kit.

Table 1. Formative evaluation - Significant difference in the Pre- and Post-Achievement Test during Pilot Testing in Phase II of study

	Pre-Test	Post Test	D	t-test
Pilot Testing	3.76	6.04	2.28	1.0327*

*Significant at α 0.05

Odiongan and Kalipay NHS in Phase III of Study

Figures 2(a) and (b) show participants' performances in the post-test were higher in both groups with the Laboratory Kit and without, in Kalipay NHS. However, results for the group without the laboratory kit were lower, compared to the students with the kit. Figures 3(a) and (b) show participants' performances in the post-test were higher in both groups with the kit and without in Odiongan NHS. However, the difference in their achievement from pre- to post-test is small, compared to participants with the kit.

Table 2 presents results of the paired t-test of groups with and without the kit. The results indicate that the designed laboratory kit helped participants improve their Biology learning in their third grading lessons. In both phases, the data shows that there is significant difference in the pre- and post-test, with or without the kit.

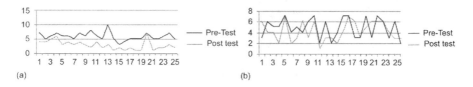

Figure 2. a) Achievement of participants in Kalipay NHS with the laboratory kit (First phase), b) Achievement of participants without the kit (Second phase).

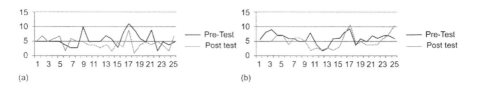

Figure 3. a) Achievement of participants in Odiongan NHS without the Laboratory Kit (First phase), b) Achievement of participants with the kit (Second phase).

Results in Table 3 imply that there is a positive increase in the scientific skills developed by those with laboratory kit. Students with the kit developed an increase in scientific skills compared to students without, as indicated in the difference of their pre- and post-test, a significant difference of 0.005. Table 4 shows the correlation between participants' achievement and the laboratory kit, as well as participants' improved scientific skills. The significant correlations suggest that the use of laboratory kit affects the achievement of the students and the development of scientific skills in students. The use of the laboratory kit reports an enhanced learning in rural high school students.

Table 2. The mean difference and paired t-test of pre- and post-achievement of participants with Laboratory Kit and those without the kit

	With kit (mean)			Without kit (mean)		
	Pre-Test	Post-Test	d	Pre-Test	Post-Test	D
First phase	2.88	5.84	2.96	4.56	5.6	1.04
Paired t-test	1.49*			0.0835*		
Second phase	4.64	6.08	1.44	3.8	4.68	0.88
Paired t-test	0.00027*			0.143*		

Table 3. t-test of scientific skills participants developed when using the kit and those without

Scientific skills	First phase (computed t-values)		Second phase (computed t-values)	
	With kit	Without kit	With kit	Without kit
Observing	0.637*	0.802*	0.00023*	0.000131*
Classifying)	0.548*	0.008*	0.057*	0.966*
Inferring	0.265*	0.046*	0.00119*	0.0210*
Predicting	0.0133*	0.185*	0.116*	0.00744*
Comparing	0.118*	0.832*	0.037*	0.000724*
Describing	0.273*	0.649*	0.000133*	0.000623*
Manipulating	0.023*	0.111*	0.228*	0.0234*
Interpreting	0.327*	0.574*	0.00311*	0.0290*
Analytical Skill	0.229*	0.824*	0.0013*	0.119*
Associative Skill	0.073*	0.133*	0.0383*	0.021*

*Significant at $\alpha = 0.05$

Table 4. Correlation between participants' achievement and the Laboratory Kit, as well as scientific skills development and Laboratory Kit

	With kit (mean difference)	Without kit (mean difference)	Correlation
Achievement	1.48	0.44	0.399*
Scientific skills	2.86	2.06	0.571*

*Significant at $\alpha = 0.05$

CONCLUSIONS AND IMPLICATIONS

The study shows that the laboratory kit for learning Biology can be developed using indigenous and recyclable materials for students' use in rural areas for the Third Grading Period.. The kit contains the manual, teacher's guide and materials for use. The Laboratory Manual and Teacher's Guide is readable even at lower levels and has been validated by the experts. There is significant difference between the achievement and skills development among participants with the laboratory kit and those from the usual laboratory classrooms in Biology. Participants with the kit achieved more, compared to participants without. The kit has brought about an improved test achievement and experimental skill competency from participants' pre- and post-test scores. It is evident the developed curriculum resources in the kit are effective and can improve participants' scores. Concepts developed among participants include reproduction and genetics and science experimental skills such as observation, classification, inference, prediction, comparison and interpretation skills. Thus, the kit is recommended for use and it is hoped that the developed-and-tested laboratory kit be used in more rural schools to contribute to enhancing students' laboratory skills and the acquisition of scientific knowledge at the same time.

The study has demonstrated the use of the designed Laboratory Kit using native and environmentally friendly materials. It is strongly encouraged that teachers constantly innovate and use commonly available resources to cater to the learning needs of students in Biology lessons for academic achievement and to promote lifelong interest in the subject. Similarly, facilities and equipment in a laboratory experiment can be innovated to suit the learning needs of the students to facilitate lifelong learning.

RECOMMENDATIONS

A further comparison of participants' results in the 2010 National Achievement Test Results between the experimental and control group could help determine the extent of the effectiveness of the kit. The use of the Laboratory Kit could be promoted in urban schools as well. In addition, further study is needed to refine the design of the biology Laboratory Kit to include lessons for students in the first, second and fourth grades. More experimental activities and resources could be designed for other grading periods to aid teachers in teaching biology concepts and skills..

REFERENCES

Haury, David L. & Rillero Peter (1994) Perspective on Hands-On-Teaching. Date Accessed: July 10, 2008. Retrieved from:(http://ncrel.org/sdrs/areas/issues/content/cntareas/science/eric.htm)

Jarantilla, Ellen L. (2008). Development of Laboratory Activity Manual for the Do-it-Yourself (DIY) Chemistry Equipment. *Thesis*. College of Education, MSU-Iligan Institute of Technology.

APPENDIX 1

Table 1. Design of Laboratory Kit using indigenous or recycled materials

Topics	Activities	Indigenous and recycled materials used	Experts comments and suggestions
Mitosis	Simulating Mitosis	Coconut Mat	The process of mitosis will be discussed by the teacher after the activity Let the students construct their own objectives Let the students label their model Specify how meiosis can be visualized
Meiosis	Simulating Meiosis	Coconut Mat	Same comments and suggestions with Activity 2
Asexual Reproduction	Observing Asexual Reproduction in Some Organisms	Kangkong, Kataka-taka Bread mold, Rhizome of Ginger, Carabao Grass Potato Tuber, Rose Cutting/Parpagayo, Fern Frond, Cover Cellophane with a drop of water	Let the students describe the specimen one by one Indicate what is to be examined Use tables to describe asexual reproduction of some organisms
Sexual Reproduction	Observing Sexual Reproduction	Live Animals	No comments
Population Growth	Population Growth	Record of Population Growth in the Barangay	No Comments
DNA Replication	Simulating DNA Replication	Zipper Drinking Straw	No Comments
Monohybrid Inheritance	Monohybrid Inheritance	Yellow Corn Seeds White Corn Seeds Wide-Mouthed Jar	No Comments
Dihybrid Inheritance	Dihybrid Inheritance	Type of Hair Type of Earlobe	No Comments
Incomplete Dominance	Incomplete Dominance	Blue Crayon Red Crayon	P1 should be indicated as First parental generation.
Multiple Alleles	Multiple Alleles	Blood Type	No comments

Table 2. Evaluation of the developed Laboratory Kit from the Division of Gingoog City and MSU-IIT based on provided rubric

Experts	Laboratory manual		Teacher's guide		Materials	
	Rating		Rating		Rating	
1	2.75	Good	2.75	Good	2.75	Workable
2	2.60	Good	2.60	Good	3.05	Workable
3	3.48	Very Good	3.48	Very Good	3.48	Very Workable
Average	2.94	Good	2.94	Good	3.09	Workable

Melindam M. Garabato
Odiongan National High School,
Odiongan, Gingoog City, Philippines

Manuel B. Barquilla
Department of Science and Mathematics Education
College of Education, MSU-Iligan Institute of Technology
Iligan City, Philippines

MINJOO LEE AND HEUI-BAIK KIM

27. EXPLORING MIDDLE SCHOOL STUDENTS' ATTITUDINAL CHANGES TOWARDS SCIENCE THROUGH PARTICIPATION IN CLUB ACTIVITIES IN CREATING AND PUBLISHING A SCIENCE MAGAZINE

ABSTRACT

The interest in and the attitude towards science are areas which need special attention in secondary science education from the perspective of a student's subject choice and career decision. Based on this viewpoint and on an ethnographic perspective, this study was designed to explore how learners' autonomous participation develop if provided with opportunities for various scientific practices and publications in the form of creating and publishing a science magazine as an extra-curricular club activity and what kinds of influence the participation has on learners' attitudes and interest towards science. A qualitative study was done for 14 months and the participants were the instructor and fourteen 8th grade students who voluntarily took part in the club activities. Based on practices like observations of organisms around the school, scientific investigation of everyday life, and meeting with scientists, articles for the magazine were written while operating a web site. Data from participant observations, in-depth interviews with students, and documents were used to extract common characteristics of the practices. The learners' change was categorized into 3 stages in terms of participation in the learning community, the science magazine club: peripheral participation, transitional participation, and full participation. The findings of this study provide a deep understanding of the factors promoting students' participation and suggest several implications for the influence that improved the attitude towards science and on science learning.

KEYWORDS

Participation, Attitude Towards Science, Interest Development, Learners' Community, Apprenticeship, Science Magazine

INTRODUCTION

One of the main concerns currently in science education is the tendency of disinterest and relatively negative attitudes when students study science in school.

Mijung Kim and C. H. Diong (Eds.), Biology Education for Social and Sustainable Development, 249–258.

Attitudes towards science are the feelings, beliefs, and values held about an object that may be the enterprise of science, school science, and the impact of science on society or scientist themselves (Osborne, 2003). These kinds of attitudes are known to be formed and changed during adolescence. Further more, for attitudes, once formed are enduring and difficult to change (Ajzen and Fishbein, 1980). Thus, specific attention must be given to secondary-school science and learning environments of the students

SITUATED LEARNING: PARTICIPATION

Situated learning, a well-known social theory of learning by Lave and Wenger (1991), could be a theoretical framework for this study. According to Lave and Wenger, learners inevitably participate in communities of practitioners, and the mastery of knowledge and skill requires newcomers to move towards full participation in the sociocultural practices of a community. Being a full participant of a community means developing an identity as a member of the community as well as the individual's intellectual growth. Given that a science magazine club is a learner's community based on science related activities and publications, it leads to situated learning in which a novice can become an expert by legitimate peripheral participation. Students participating in some community- relevant practices can continue to do so even after they have left formal schooling. Such an approach, therefore, sets students up for lifelong participation because of the close association of participation and learning (Lave, 1993). Sfard (1998) suggested that in a community of practitioners while the learners are newcomers and potential reformers of the practice, the teachers are the preservers of the community. This study adopted the framework of participation and analyzed the development of students. The various features of students' interest towards science were also examined in accordance with the change in participation.

INTEREST DEVELOPMENT

There is a common distinction between individual and intrinsic interest and situational and extrinsic interest. The latter is stimulated by contextual factors such as good teaching that stimulates interest and engages the student (Osborne, 2003). Various Research reports on 'interest development' provide an empirically derived description of the kinds of interest for students engaged in scientific practices (Hidi & Harackiewicz, 2000; Hidi, 2006; Krapp, 2000, 2002). Furthermore, Hidi (2006) proposed a four-phase model of interest development and suggested it had the potential to support educational intervention. The first phase of interest development is a triggered situational interest. If sustained, this first phase evolves into the second phase, a maintained situational interest. The third phase, which is characterized by an emerging individual interest, may develop out of the second phase. The third phase of interest development can then lead to the fourth phase, a well-developed individual interest. Hidi particularly has argued that the role of situational interest is highly significant in the classroom or in subjects where children are disinterested in the subject at hand or academically unmotivated. In this sense, this study sought to suggest a practice for emerging and sustaining situational interest in science through a community forged by the creation of a science magazine.

DESIGN AND METHOD

Research Questions

Given the emphasis in science education on the interest towards science and on the formation of positive attitudes, we believe that studying the students' development in participation for various scientific activities and publications is a meaningful way to gain insight into the students' affective domain. Specifically, this qualitative research investigated, in depth, the factors of students' development in participation. We asked two specific questions: first, how learners' autonomous participation develops through the engagement in activities promoted by a science magazine club? And second, what kinds of factors have influence on the participation?

Context

The study population for this analysis consisted of fourteen 8th grade female students from an urban middle school which was in a lower socioeconomic area. The study was done for a period of 14 months through the use of extracurricular club activities and by creating and publishing a science magazine. Student participants volunteered for this science magazine club, but they were diverse with respect to the following factors: interest towards science, achievement in school science, the purpose of their participation, and tendency of subject preference. Once enrolled in the science magazine club, students engaged in creating and publishing a science magazine which dealt with their own curiosity related to everyday science. Some of the articles such as reports on laboratory experiments or interviews with scientists involved two or more students, whereas others were done by a single student. The types of activities were determined by the students' own willingness including laboratory experiments, observation of plants and animals around the school, and finding scientific principles encountered in everyday life. Genres had diversity too. Experimental reports, explanations, letters, scientific novels, review of science books, pictures of plants, birds, and insects, science cartoons, and science quizzes were all included. After planning what topics they would investigate, students often allocated topics to themselves based on personal interest. Practical activities followed, and articles were written describing the outcomes of their own investigation. The process of creating and publishing a science magazine was presented in Figure 1.

For better understanding, we added the comparison of a scientific report and journal and science magazine articles which were commonly written at the participants' school in Table 1.

Throughout the 14 months, students met regularly as a group with a teacher (first author) for planning and reviewing and kept a journal of their experiences, thoughts, feelings, opinions, and reflections on a message board on their own website. During the study period, the students published 3 quarterly science magazines, and twelve 7th grade newcomers joined the club as new members.

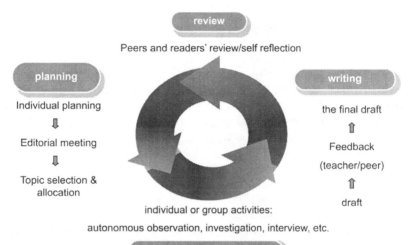

Figure 1. The process of creating and publishing a science magazine.

Table 1. Comparison of scientific reports and journal and science magazine articles in school science

	Scientific reports	Daily journal	Science magazine article
Purpose	Presentation	Daily recording	Public sharing
Genre	Report	Journal	Various genre (report, journal, explanation, argument, letter, quiz, novel)
Context	Lab activities	Instruction, Lab activities	Various activities based on real life (lab activities, Interview, observation, reading, searching, drawing)
Theme organizer	Teacher	Teacher	Student
Status of writer	Student/novice	Student/novice	Journalist/expert
Language	Scientific	Daily life	Scientific & daily life
Audience	Oneself, teacher	Oneself, teacher	Peers, family member, neighbor
Autonomy	Directed/passive	Directed/passive	Autonomous/active

Participants

Fourteen 8th grade female students had voluntarily participated in the science magazine club after public advertisement on a message board at the school. A few students already had some interest in science but most of them didn't. Two students had an interest in drawing cartoons and pictures, and therefore, they volunteered for the purpose of having their pictures published in the magazine. Some students had high scores in school achievement but had little interest in science because they thought themselves as having a tendency for liberal arts and made their career decision related to social and human sciences. They just volunteered to acquire some scientific knowledge through participation in the science magazine. For successful entrance to the university, students must have enough experiences and knowledge in various fields. There were also students who were originally disinterested in science but became interested through participation in the community due to strong relationships with classmates. The self-efficacy of the students was low in general regardless of their achievements. Some of the students' characteristics are shown in Table 2. The teacher (first author) majored in biology education and worked as a journalist for 7 years before teaching middle school. At the time of this study, she had taught full time in middle school for 7 years and was in a master's course for biology education. She had sought ways of motivating students to be interested in science, and the teaching goal for this project included providing students ways of learning from everyday science.

Table 2. Characteristics of students in the study

Name	Favorite subject	Interest in science	Purpose of participation
Sara	Biology	Intermediate	To be with best friend
Jane	English	Very low	To fill a gap in science
Helen	Math	Intermediate	By teacher's suggestion
Rose	Astronomy	High	To be more familiar with science
Marry	Arts	Intermediate	To draw pictures in science magazine
Carol	Science	High	To have an experience as journalist
Nora	English	Low	By teacher's suggestion

METHODOLOGY

The methodology for the study was action research, and the researcher conducted participant-observation from inside the community. In addition, we employed an ethnographic approach having characteristics such as prolonged and intensive observations and continuous participation in the setting (Erickson1986; Guba & Lincoln, 1989). These features allowed the in depth understanding of the students' affective domain. Giving students the opportunities to express their own interest, curiosity and opinions involved in self-publishing a science magazine within an environment of autonomous participation, the community fostered by the science magazine provided a unique context to explore students' attitudinal changes. Using media studies such as video production, a more complete story can be told from the students' views than what might be allowed by observations or interviews alone (Furman & Barton, 2006).

Data Collection and Analysis

Data from participant observations, in-depth interviews with students, and documents were used to extract common characteristics of practices. Since the main idea of the science magazine was to change students' participation and not what students wrote in their articles, the main source of data used in this study was the video and audio tapes of the students' regular meetings for planning and reviewing. Audio tapes of semi-constructed in-depth interviews with students were also analyzed as a main source of data. These sources provided critical information on the participation that occurred during the study period and how participation changed over time. Additional data sources included the teacher's field notes, students' reflective journals and written articles for the magazine. Written texts on the bulletin board on their own website and e-mails contributed additional information. Analysis of the data followed a narrative method and additional data sources were used to triangulate the data.

Findings

We found in our analysis that individual learners' characteristics varied according to their development of participation. The findings are presented in two parts: the development of learners' participation, and the factors which influenced their development. The overall finding was that the community fostered by the science magazine allowed situated learning in which a novice became an expert science journalist by legitimate peripheral participation, and there were two major factors which improved that participation. They were external scaffolding from the teacher, and the learners' internal changes induced from self-reflection and social interactions in the community.

Development of Learners' Participation

In looking at the data, we noticed changes in the pattern which reflected the students' mind and behavior in accordance with their development. As newcomers to the community, students often said they don't know what to do and how to write an article for a science magazine demonstrating low self-efficacy. Most of them were uncomfortable except some students who showed excitement as a member of the journalistic community. Students had to think of suitable topics for their articles and therefore situational interest accompanied the task. Though situational interest had been triggered, there were no visible autonomous behaviors that followed. The teacher acted as the master of the practitioners' community and the students had an apprenticeship with the teacher. During this time, the students' participation was thought to be legitimate but peripheral.

But as time goes by, the situation changed. With increased participation, the students became more interested in their practices. They read books, surfed the internet, and visited the science center by themselves for the investigation of various topics. Interactions among the community members had noticeably increased. They posted daily journals on their own website and exchanged opinions about articles and resources. Eventually when the first issue of the science magazine was published, all of them were extremely excited and completely motivated. Attitudes towards science became more positive and their self-efficacy improved. Situational interest was sustained through the circular mechanism of publishing a science magazine repeatedly. Students gradually acquired a degree of competence in themselves for science and learned the norms of a qualified article. They repeatedly wrote, read and revised the articles they had written. Some students developed individual interests even though it was just the beginning level and showed an interest in various occupations within the different disciplines of science.

It is worth noting that finally when some students became core members in the community, they exhibited an identity as a science journalist with vigorous norms for science magazine articles and showed consideration of their audience. They recognized the importance of publically sharing information and the responsibility a student science journalist has. They also were able to help the 7th grade newcomers of the community as mentors after 10months and showed a strong responsibility for the magazine to be continued after their graduation.

In this section, we categorized students' development into 3 stages in terms of participation in the learning community, the science magazine club: peripheral participation, transitional participation, and full participation. The stage of each student's participation was somewhat movable in that it could be both developed into next stage and regressed to the previous stage depending on various factors. Characteristics of the individual learners' development and features of development during the participation are presented in Table 3 and Table 4.

Factors Influencing Participation

Factors which influenced students' participation were analyzed mostly by two parts. The first one was external scaffolding from the teacher. During the participation, the teacher as a master of publishing a science magazine provided a scaffolding to the novice, which could be divided into mental support for forming an identity and methodological support for technical skills. The teacher's scaffolding for identity included facilitating self-reflection in detail, and helping students for meaning-making in their own writing practices while keeping in mind that each of them was a science magazine writer and not a passive student. It promoted student's motivation and enhanced their self-efficacy. Methodological scaffolding such as instruction on planning and investigation skills for a science magazine, technical mentoring for writing, and supporting students for collaboration with experts outside the school also made students become more familiar with the community fostered by the science magazine. As students' participation developed, the teacher's scaffolding was reduced.

Another main factor, the autonomous learners' self reflection and social interactions among the community promoted participation too. Students reflected on their own practices and writings from the viewpoint of the quality of the articles they wrote with consideration for their audience and responsibility as a journalist for the public sharing of information in a science magazine. Reflections were also found to be influenced by the teacher's scaffolding factor and provided positive feedback for the participation of students.

Table 3. Characteristics of individual learners' development

Name	Sustaining interest	Attaching value	Intertextuality	Meta-cognitive writing	Responsibility	Identity as a journalist
ara	√	√	√			
Jane	√	√	√	√		
Harry	√			√		
Rose	√	√		√	√	√
Marry	√	√	√	√	√	√
Carol	√	√	√		√	
Nora	√	√	√			

Table 4. Features of development during the participation

	Peripheral participation	Transitional participation	Full participation
Engagement	Passive	Active	Active, autonomous
Interest	Triggered situational interest	Sustained situational interest	Emerging individual interest
	- no idea or follow up behavior	- connect everyday life with Science magazine	- form one's own scientific question for article
Writing	Copy and paste in general	Knowledge telling	Knowledge transforming
Resource	Mainly singular resource	Emerging intertextuality	Increased intertextuality – thematic, organizational
Reflection	Little	Directed reflection	Self reflection
Self-efficacy	Low	Increased	High / forming new identity

CONCLUSION

The aim of this study was to explore how learners' autonomous participation developed by creating and self-publishing a science magazine and what influence participation had on learners' attitudes and interest towards science. The findings of this study suggest that students' participation developed from peripheral participation to full participation through involvement in the community fostered by the creation and publishing of the science magazine. In developing participation, students showed increased interest in science related practices and formed positive attitudes towards science. Cognitive and affective growth of the participants also appeared. We believe it is worthwhile to note that even participants who didn't become full participants showed maintenance of situational interest in science. This was believed to be related to the features of the science magazine which has a repetitive circular mechanism dealing with everyday science. The attributes of the science magazine which created a bridge between school science and everyday life were also thought to contribute to students' development of participation. Sustained scaffolding from the teacher and social interaction with community members strengthened their participation, and self reflection enriched participants' cognitive and affective growth. Within the frame work of participation, this development of participation can be interpreted as authentic learning.

There are increasing requirements for educational practices in and out of the school curriculum for the sake of students' positive attitudes towards science. This study not only suggests introducing a community which fosters the creation and self-publishing of a science magazine as an extracurricular activity as an alternative for increasing the engagement and attitudes of the students, but also raises the view that through the development of autonomous participation, students can improve authentic learning.

REFERENCES

Jean Lave & E. Wenger. (1991). situated learning: Legitimate Peripheral Participation. Cambridge University Press, Cambridge, UK.

Jonathan Osborne. (2003). Attitudes towards science. *International Journal of Science Education*, *25*(9), 1049–1079.

Melina Furman, Angela Barton. (2006). Capturing urban student voices in the creation of a science Mini-Documentary. *Journal of Research in Science Teaching*, *43*(7), 667–694.

Sfard, A.(1998). On two metaphors for learning and the dangers of choosing just one. *Educational Researcher*, *27*(2), 4–13.

Suzanne Hidi, K.Ann Renninger.(2006). The Four-Phase Model of Interest Development. *Educational Psychologist*, *4*(2), 111–127.

Vaughan Prain.(2006). Learning from Writing in Secondary Science : Some Theoretical and Practical implication. *International Journal of Science Education*, *28*(2), 179–201.

Minjoo Lee
Seoul National University, Korea
mjtree@snu.ac.kr

Heui-Baik Kim
Seoul National University, Korea
hbkim56@snu.ac.kr

NARENDRA D. DESHMUKH

28. DESIGNING AND FIELD TESTING OF REMEDIAL MATERIAL TO RECTIFY STUDENTS' MISCONCEPTIONS IN BIOLOGY AT THE SECONDARY SCHOOL LEVEL

ABSTRACT

A study was conducted to find out ideas of students from rural and urban areas about biological concepts such as respiration, reproduction, circulation, photosynthesis, nutrition and excretion. It was observed that students displayed anthropocentric and mechanistic views about these biological concepts. They understood the concepts of circulation, role of vitamins and a balanced diet but were confused with the concepts of respiration, functioning of the heart, photosynthesis and the role of nutrients. Students equated breathing with respiration, assumed the heart functions to purify and form blood, and thought vitamins were a source of energy. Rural students from vernacular media believed the heart hoards emotions and feelings and plants release oxygen only to support living organisms. The study showed that misconceptions about respiration, vitamins, blood circulation and gaseous exchange persist across grade levels. Remedial materials in biology were developed, taking into account the nature of misconceptions and their sources. This material was tried in a sample of 101 rural and 115 urban students. Preliminary analysis of the data shows the materials are useful in helping to rectify some of the students' misconceptions.

KEYWORDS

Misconceptions, Biological Concepts, Remedial Materials

INTRODUCTION

From the time of Piaget, educationalists have been intensely involved in how students view concepts in science and mathematics. The works of Ausubel (1963, 1968) and Novak (1985) predate the popularization of conceptual change approaches by at least a decade. The importance of this work comes from its emphasis on examining "what a student already knows." Because the framework in which Ausubel worked depended largely on the logical operations of differentiation and integration, it fits particularly well into the research on biological sciences, where concepts and terminologies are structurally and functionally interrelated. From Piaget's (1929) work, assimilation has become

Mijung Kim and C. H. Diong (Eds.), Biology Education for Social and Sustainable Development, 259–270.

identified with constructivism and denotes the fitting of new experiences into existing mental schemes. Accommodation, a related term, describes the changing of mental schemes that are unable to explain one's new experiences (Geelan, 2000).

Over the last three decades, a significant body of research has focused on students' understandings of scientific phenomena (Duit, 2006). Students hold numerous misconceptions – interpretation of various phenomena, which differ, often radically from those accepted by the scientific community (Driver, 1981). Several investigations into students' understanding of biological concepts indicate that students of varying ages possess misconceptions about various biological concepts. Educators agree that the prevalence of misconceptions among students not only presents a serious obstacle to learning in biology but also interferes with further learning (Novak, 1970). To promote effective and meaningful learning, there is a need to identify the causes of such misconceptions and find ways to rectify them or prevent them from occurring. Education in schools today targets the notion of "Education for All, and Science for All": Science Education in schools in India is compulsory at the lower secondary level, but optional at the higher secondary level.

The Homi Bhabha Centre for Science Education (HBCSE), a constituent unit of the Tata Institute of Fundamental Research (TIFR) is engaged in improving science and mathematics education in the country. As part of its activities, the HBCSE conducts in-service training courses for teachers teaching science and mathematics. The author has been arranging a number of such training programmes for teachers from rural, urban and tribal areas, and is also involved in school visits programmes. Interactions with class IX students revealed that many scientific notions used by the students were frequently understood incorrectly. The understanding of these concepts was influenced by students' socio-cultural background. It was interesting to note that teachers also had misconceptions about biological concepts like, respiration, photosynthesis, form-function relationships of the heart, a balanced diet and vitamins. To find out students' and teachers' misconceptions, a systematic study was undertaken. Based on interaction and input received, the Concept Based Objective Tests (CBOT) was designed to find out students' understanding of the biological concepts mentioned above. Remedial teaching materials were developed to help students correct their misconceptions.

LITERATURE REVIEW

Identification of Misconceptions

It has been shown that if misconceptions are not detected and corrected, they can adversely affect students' subsequent learning. In order to identify and analyze misconceptions at an early stage, various forms of assessment should be used. Interviews are widely used to identify students' misconceptions or meaningful understanding of a particular concept. Fisher (1985) and Haslam and Treagust (1987) noted that multiple choice items can be marked objectively and efficiently, but may not be able to probe the learners' reasoning process and causes of conceptual problems. For this reason, the authors suggested the use of a two-tier misconception test to detect common misconceptions, as well as to help students reason. This type of assessment informs students that reasoning and thinking are important in understanding science concepts. Mann and Treagust (1998) suggested another diagnostic instrument with true or false type questions instead of multiple-choice items. Besides, Concept Evaluation Statements (Simpson and Marek, 1988; Westbrook and Marek, 1991), Proposition Generating Tasks (Amir and Tamir, 1994) and Writing Assays (Sanders, 1993) have also been used to assess students' understanding of biological science topics and concepts. Many researchers have combined these methods to study student misconceptions (Fielder et al, 1987).

Sources of Misconceptions

School textbooks, teachers cultural beliefs and practices are some of the principal sources of high school students' misconceptions of many science concepts (Deshmukh and Deshmukh, 2007). According to Perkins et al., (1988), replacing students' misconceptions with textbook theory amounts to affecting a theory change in students because the perspective offered by naïve theory is generally so different from the textbook theory that the information presented in class cannot be assimilated without major restructuring. Storey (1992) traced the sources of misconceptions by students to textbooks. Many concepts in biology are interrelated and they are links to understanding other concepts. An understanding of photosynthesis and organic and inorganic molecules will facilitate the understanding of food chains and food webs. The concept of conservation of energy is essential to the understanding of many feeding relationships in a food web, photosynthesis, and respiration. It is known that most of the concepts in biology are closely related to concepts in chemistry and physics. Many biological concepts such as genetics, evolution, metabolic processes, ecosystems, have their foundations in the physical sciences and students' understanding of biological processes breaks down because of their misconceptions in the physical sciences.

Misconceptions may originate from everyday experiences (Tekkaya, 2003). Bell (1985) noted that the terms 'energy' and 'food' are associated with human activities in such expressions as: to be 'energetic', needing 'to stay alive' and 'be healthy'. Many terms in biology are used in an alternative way in daily life; for this reason, some misconceptions may arise when words are used to mean one thing in everyday life and another in a scientific context, such as food, respiration, and energy. Gilbert et al., (1982), noted that the word -particle- is scientifically used to mean an atom, molecule or ion, but in daily use, particle refers to a small but visible piece of solid substance. On this note, when students combine a newly learned concept -all organisms require oxygen – with their previously held, more primitive concept – some microorganisms do not require oxygen -, they experience conceptual conflicts.

Studies have shown that teachers are sometimes a source of student misconceptions (Sanders 1993, Yip 1998) when concepts are wrongly or inaccurately presented. Sanders (1993) opined that inappropriate assessment strategies by biology teachers could also influence the development of misconceptions in students. Mintzes *et al.*), (2001) suggested several new assessment strategies, such as concept maps, V diagrams, clinical interviews, portfolios and conceptual diagnostic tests to encourage meaningful learning and conceptual understanding in the biological sciences. Students' misconceptions may be compounded by daily life experience, the use of everyday language in a scientific context, compartmentalization of concepts, teaching strategies and textbooks. By reviewing the possible source of misconceptions, it is suggested that conceptual development can be promoted by classroom instruction that avoids excessive factual details, establishes meaningful connection between new and existing concepts and takes into account students' prior knowledge.

Remediation of Misconceptions

To promote meaningful learning, attempts must be made to eliminate or prevent misconceptions. One such method involves the use of a conceptual change approach. According to Posner *et al*, (1982), a conceptual change approach proposes that if students are to change their ideas, they must become dissatisfied with their existing knowledge. Also, the new concepts they are to learn must be intelligible, plausible, and fruitful. Several research studies suggested that instructional strategies leading to conceptual change such as analogies, concept maps, conceptual change texts and refutational texts could be employed to rectify students' misconceptions. Confrey (1982) confirmed that misconceptions research has documented students' beliefs, indicating that they enter instruction with conceptual configurations that are culturally embedded, tied to the use of language or other concepts, have historical precursors and are embedded in a cycle of expectation, prediction, and confirmation or rejection.

Conceptual Change text (Remedial Materials)

Conceptual change texts are designed to make students aware of both their misconceptions and scientifically accepted concepts. Misconceptions are directly stated within the text to help students understand and apply the target scientific knowledge through the use of more plausible and intelligible explanations (Sungur *et al.*, 2001). Thus, conceptual change instructional techniques are designed to correct students' misconceptions and to teach concepts in a meaningful manner. Recall that misconceptions can arise when learning fails to induce conceptual change in students' minds (Erdmann, 2001). These strategies not only help teachers analyze the ideas of their students but also help students better understand biological concepts. Chi and Roscoe (2002) conceive conceptual change as a repair of misconceptions whereas diSessa (2006) reckons it is the reorganization of diverse kinds knowledge into complex systems in students' minds. To Vosniadou (2002), conceptual change is a process that enables students to synthesize models in their minds, beginning with their existing explanatory frameworks. According to Champagne *et al.,* (1985), the effects of prior knowledge requires a change from the view that learning is an absorption of transmitted knowledge, to the view that learning is conceptual change. Conceptual change is a process of transition from ordinary ways of perceiving, directing attention, conceptualizing, reasoning and justifying. With time, learners transform prior knowledge to accommodate new scientific ideas (Posner *et al.*, 1982).

AIMS OF THE STUDY AND RESEARCH METHODOLOGY

This study aims to investigate the students' misconceptions in secondary level biology with respect to life processes, such as respiration, circulation, reproduction, excretion, photosynthesis, nutrition, and to develop and test remedial materials for their effectiveness in correcting misconceptions.

The study was conducted in three phases. In the preparatory phase, a review and analysis of the current misconceptions in Biology from the perspectives of students' knowledge and conceptions, learning materials, and teachers and teaching practices, were undertaken. In the design phase, design remedial materials were done up using the findings from the preparatory phase. Subject experts validated the remedial materials. A Concept Based Objective Test (CBOT) was developed to study the effectiveness of the remedial materials. Pre- and post-test single group quasi-experimental design was used to study the effectiveness of the remedial material. In the evaluation phase, the evaluation of the effectiveness of the remedial materials was carried out.

216 students (77 girls, 139 boys), aged 14–16 years who followed the TATE board syllabus of class IX were selected using cluster sampling. The sample comprised 115 urban and 101 rural students from one urban English medium school and two rural vernacular schools. Interviews of students were conducted to understand the nature of the students' misconceptions.

The Concept Based Objective Tests (CBOT) on respiration and photosynthesis, and transport of material and excretion, were prepared to study the effectiveness of remedial materials on correcting misconceptions. Two remedial modules were prepared based on the CBOTs. For identification of the students' misconceptions, an open-ended test was administered in the first phase. Based on the students' responses, remedial materials were designed, developed, and field-tested to assess their effectiveness in correcting misconceptions. Remedial materials are basically conceptual change texts which address the learning difficulties of students and incorporate suitable learning and instructional strategies. The ADDIE model of Instructional Design was used to develop the remedial materials which focused on: (i) correcting wrong notions or ideas of students (ii) providing fine structure of each learning concept (iii) relating one concept to another, and (iv) the historical development of concepts or theories.

CBOTs were constructed based on students' responses. Most of the distracters were the students' responses obtained from an open-ended test. The CBOT on photosynthesis and respiration consisted of 26 items and CBOT on transport of materials and excretion consisted of 32 items. Content validity of these tests was ensured by a panel of experts in Biology and their reliability was ensured using the split-half method. Reliability of the tests on respiration and photosynthesis was 0.73 and 0.69 for transport of material and excretion. These tests were used to conduct the pre- and post-tests. Interviews with students were conducted to ascertain sources of students' misconceptions.

RESULT AND DISCUSSION

BOT-Respiration and Photosynthesis

Pre- and post-test scores differed between rural and urban schools (Table 1). In both urban and rural schools, students scored significantly higher in post-tests than in pre-tests.

Students equated breathing with respiration. They had poor conceptual understanding of "cellular respiration" and "breathing" and thus were not able to distinguish between the two concepts. Respiration was often misconceived as breathing – the taking in of oxygen through the nose and giving out of carbon dioxide. Other typical misconceptions of respiration include notions such as the following: "the taking in of oxygen and release of impure air is observed only in animals and humans", "dolphins respire through gills" and "plants release oxygen, simply because this was mentioned in the science textbook".

Respiration is taught from primary school as a characteristic of living things. Terms like 'respiratory system', 'respiratory organ', external respiration, and 'respiratory centre', in which 'respiratory' meant 'breathing', are commonly used in textbooks and by science teachers – the main sources of misconception. As Soyibo (1983) has demonstrated, these terms are misleading, ambiguous, confusing and capable of breeding students' misconceptions, as was borne out in this study. The use of the term "external respiration" in everyday language is also a source of students' misconception of respiration (Driver, 1989; Sanders, 1993).

On photosynthesis, the prevalent misconceptions were: "photosynthesis takes place during the day, whereas respiration takes place only at night", "plants do not respire during the day, so there is no respiration during the day", "plants release carbon dioxide at night, so we should not sleep under a tree". School textbooks were a main source of these misconceptions.

Table 1. Pre-test and post-test results of CBOT on the topic of respiration and photosynthesis

	1. CBOT-Respiration and Photosynthesis					
	Urban schools (n = 55)			*Rural schools (n = 42)*		
	Pre-test	*Post-test*	*Correlation coefficient, r value*	*Pre-test*	*Post-test*	*Correlation coefficient, r value*
Mean	9.85	11.45		8.17	9.60	
Standard Deviation	2.59	3.67	0.52	2.24	2.79	0.28
t-test		2.64			2.58	

Emphasis on the process of photosynthesis must have resulted in the misconception that cellular respiration occurs only at night in plants (Waheed and Lucas, 1992). The concept of photosynthesis, which is usually taught at upper and secondary school levels, is considered important, yet quite difficult to teach and to learn. Amir and Tamir (1990) reported a number of prevalent misconceptions about photosynthesis among students in Israel, such as (i) plants get organic materials ("food") from the soil (ii) water and minerals taken in from the soil are sources of plant "food" (iii) photosynthesis is the respiration of plants (iv) photosynthesis takes place during the day whereas respiration takes place only at night. Wandersee *et al.* (1994) also found these misconceptions among college students.

CBOT-Transport of Materials and Excretion

Post-test scores were higher for students from both rural and urban schools (Table 2). Students' naïve conceptions on the functions of the human heart were: "the heart converts impure blood into pure blood", "the heart pumps pure blood to different parts of the body", "our emotions are stored in the heart", and "the heart is an organ actively responsible for blood formation". Students' understanding of the structure and functions of the human heart was limited. Words in Marathi (vernacular language) for oxygenated and deoxygenated have added to the confusion, so has popular literature that portrays the heart as the origin of feelings. Use of colours, blue on the right side of the heart, red on the left, has also created a misconception that blood in the right side of the heart is blue.

Students' misconceptions of human physiology have been associated with the way teachers and textbooks present the information and the incorrect use of language in class (Barrass, 1984). Even teachers consider purification as a function of the heart (Deshmukh & Deshmukh, 2007). Since the heart functions as a physical pump and is not concerned with blood purification, filtration, or blood cell formation, usage of terms such as 'purification', 'pure blood', 'impure blood' 'oxygen rich', 'carbon dioxide rich', and 'emotions' by teachers and in science textbooks can create misconceptions. Buckley (2000) observed that when children explain blood circulation, their misconceptions were similar to those portrayed in school textbook illustrations.

Table 2. Pretest and posttest scores of rural and urban school students

2. CBOT-Transport of material (Item-32)						
	Urban Schools (n = 60)			Rural Schools (n = 59)		
	Pre-test	Post-test	Correlation coefficient, r value	Pre-test	Post-test	Correlation coefficient, r value
Mean	14.18	17.50		12.03	15.10	
Standard Deviation	3.46	5.09	0.70	3.59	2.77	0.42
t-test	4.17			5.19		

Misconceptions on the circulatory system and heart have been associated with the way teachers and textbooks present information and with incorrect use of language (Abimbola and Baba, 1996). Misunderstanding about the blood circulatory system can escalate when teachers themselves have misconceptions. Yip (1998) evaluated science teachers' knowledge on the circulatory system. Teachers were asked to underline incorrect statements about blood circulation and to provide justifications for their choices. Most teachers were unable to relate blood flow to blood pressure and blood vessel diameter (Dikmenli & Cardak, 2004). Although teacher education programs focus on teaching methodology, few provide deep understanding of science content.

SUMMARY OF FINDINGS

It is apparent students are not 'blank slates'; they are in school with their ideas and naive conceptions of science and the world around them. Students' naive ideas about science often conflict with scientists' conception of science. The language used by teachers and school science textbooks was a source of conflict and confusion to some students. Everyday use of terms, such as respiration, a weak heart, impure blood, and pure blood, impure air and so on in nonscientific contexts hinders students' understanding of scientific concepts. It was observed that concepts on photosynthesis, circulation, respiration and excretion were difficult to understand for many students who were in the concrete learning stage. Science teachers, particularly those in upper primary schools, were not aware of their own or their students' misconceptions. Students with particular misconceptions are also unaware that their conceptions of science are incorrect. When told their ideas were wrong, students often had a difficult time correcting their misconceptions, especially if they have held a misconception for a long time. Instructional and remedial learning curriculum materials with an emphasis on (i) correcting wrong notions or ideas (ii) providing fine structure of a concept and sub-concepts, and (iii) relating one concept or sub-concept to another were found to be effective in rectifying student misconceptions. The questioning technique, explanations, animations, teacher demonstrations, lab-based practical work, and student-centred teaching approaches were shown to be more constructive in helping students understand and form scientific concepts.

CONCLUSIONS AND IMPLICATIONS

This study shows misconceptions on respiration, photosynthesis, function of heart, transport system and excretion are prevalent among students in both rural and urban schools. Authors of science textbooks, teachers and students are unaware of misconceptions in school textbooks. Writers of science textbooks should expunge misconceptions in their books which students and teachers conventionally regard as infallible documents. Appropriate models of instruction should be explored to facilitate science learning and concept formation. As an example, the Biological Science Curriculum Study Model (Binghamton University, New York) 5E Model of instruction has been recommended as an instructional model. The 5 E's of the model are: Engage, Explore, Explain, Elaborate and Evaluation. The 5E cycle (i) focuses on major misconceptions (ii) begins with an 'engage' phase that requires active participation by students

(iii) includes additional phases that develop and expand the information and ideas (iv) engages students by requiring them to articulate and (v) concludes with an 'evaluation' phase that emphasizes student synthesis and/or application, plus self-assessment. A conventional teaching method of instruction is not sufficient in overcoming student misconceptions. Models of teaching that help students to overcome their misconceptions by diagnosing the misconceptions, creating dissatisfaction with the misconceptions, and providing opportunities to practice the goal conceptions are necessary.

Teacher preparation programs should take cognizance of student (and teacher) misconceptions to better prepare competent and effective science teachers who are able to teach science concepts correctly. Data banks of students misconceptions can be used to structure pedagogies to facilitate concept learning formation. Appropriate content upgrading combined with pedagogical content knowledge in preparatory and in-service training programs, as well as research-based instructional and learning curriculum materials have been recommended as a result of the findings of this study.

Research suggests teachers can act as clarifiers of student alternative ideas and misconceptions to guide students in correcting their naïve or alternative conceptions. Appropriate teaching strategies that use cognitive conflicts to enable learners to experience anomalies in an attempt to produce rationally-based conceptual change can be introduced into the subject curricula. Adequate observational theory, metaphors, models, and analogies should be used to make a new conception more intelligible and plausible. Students need an awareness of fundamental assumptions of scientific theory, a demand for consistency among their beliefs about the world, an awareness of the epistemological and historical foundations of modern science and some sense of the fruitfulness of new conceptions, to make science learning through conceptual formation a meaningful endeavour.

ACKNOWLEDGEMENTS

I am very grateful to my mentor, Dr. Veena M. Deshmukh, Honorary Professor, K. K. College of Education, Mumbai for her guidance, motivation, encouragement and support. I express my sincere and deepest gratitude to my centre, HBCSE, that gave me permission and financial support for travel and accommodation expenditure to attend this conference. I thank the many students, teachers and schools involved in this study for their wholehearted support.

REFERENCES

Abimbola, I. O. & Baba, S. (1996). Misconceptions & alternative conceptions in science textbook: The role of teachers as filters.*The American Biology Teacher, 58*, 14–19.

Amir, R. & Tamir, P. (1990). Detailed analysis of misconceptions as a basis for developing remedial instruction: the case of photosynthesis. *Paper presented at the AERA annual meeting, Boston MA, April 1990.* Retrieved September 22, 2010 from http://*citeseerx.ist.psu.edu/viewdoc/download; jsessionid...?*doi=10.1.1...

Amir, R & Tamir, P. (1994). In-depth analysis of misconceptions as basis for developing research based remedial instruction: The ease of photosynthesis. *The American Biology Teacher, 56*, 94–100.

Ausubel, D. P. (1963). *The psychology of meaningful verbal learning.* New York: Grune and Stratton.

Ausubel, D. P. (1968). *Educational psychology: A cognitive view.* New York: Holt, Rinehart and Winston.

Barras, R. (1984). Some misconceptions and misunderstandings perpetuated by teachers and textbook of biology, *Journal of Biology Education,* 18, 201–206.

Bell B. (1985). Students' ideas about plant nutrition: What are they? *Journal of Biological Education, 19,* 213–218.

Buckley, B. (2000). Interactive multimedia and model-based learning in biology. *International Journal Science Education, 22,* 895–935.

Champagne, A. B., Gunstone, R. E, & Klopfer, L. E. (1985). Instructional consequences of students' knowledge about physical phenomena. In L. West & A. L. Pines (Eds.), *Cognitive structure and conceptual change,* (pp. 61–90). New York: Academic Press.

Chi, M.T.H., & Roscoe, R.D. (2002). The processes and challenges of conceptual change. In M. Limon & L. Mason (Eds.), *Reconsidering conceptual change: Issues in theory and practice* (pp. 3–27). Amsterdam: Kluwer.

Deshmukh, N. D. (2009). A Study of Students' and Teachers' Misconceptions in Biology at the Secondary School Level. *Proceedings of the International Conference entitled "Intercultural Education:* Published by the Hellenic Migration Policy Institute, Greece. ISBN: 978-960-98897-0-4

Deshmukh, N. D & Deshmukh, V. M. (2007). A Study of Students' Misconceptions in Biology at the Secondary School Level. *Proceedings of epiSTEME-2: An International Conference to Review Research on Science, Technology and Mathematics Education* (pp. 137–141). Delhi, India: Macmillan India Ltd.

Dikmenli, M. & Cardak, O. (2004). A study on misconceptions in the 9th grade high school Biology textbook, *Eurasian Journal of Educational Research, 17,* 130–141.

diSessa, A. A. (2006). A history of conceptual change research: Threads and fault lines. In K. Sawyer (Ed.), *Cambridge handbook of the learning sciences.* Cambridge, UK: Cambridge University Press.

Driver, R. (1981). Pupils' alternative frameworks in science. *European Journal of Science Education,* 3(1), 93–101.

Driver, R. (1989). Students' conceptions and the learning of science. *International Journal of Science Education, 11,* 481–489.

Duit, R. (2006). *Bibliography STCSE – Teachers' and Students' Conceptions and Science Education.* Kiel, Germany: IPN – Leibniz Institute for Science Education (http://www.ipn.uni-kiel.de/aktuell/stcse/stcse.html).

Erdmann, M. M. (2001). Improving conceptual change concerning photosynthesis through text design. *Learning and Instruction, 11,* 241–257.

Fisher, K. M. (1985). A misconception in biology: Amino acids and translation. *Journal of Research in Science Teaching, 22*(1), 63–72.

Fielder, Y., Amir, R. & Tamir, P. (1987). High school students' difficulties in understanding osmosis. *International Journal of Science Education,* 9, 541–551.

Geelan, D. R. (2000). Sketching some postmodern alternatives: Beyond paradigms and research programs as referents for science education. *"Electronic Journal of Science Education," 5*(2), Retrieved September 24, 2010 from http://wolfweb.unr.edu/homepage/crowther/ejse/geelan.html

Gilbert, J. K., Osborne, R. J., & Fenshman, P. J. (1982). Children's science and its consequences for teaching". *Science Education, 66*(4), 623–633.

Haslam, R. & Treagust, D. F. (1987). Diagnosing secondary students' misconceptions of photosynthesis and respiration in plants using a two-tier multiple choice instrument. *Journal of Biological Education, 21*(3), 203–211.

Jere Confrey (1982). A Review of the Research on Student Conceptions in Mathematics, Science, and Programming. *Review of Research in Education, 16*(1990), 3–56.

Lloyd, C. L. (1990). The elaboration of concepts in three biology textbook: Facilitating student learning, *Journal of Research in Science Teaching, 27*(10), 1019–1032.

Maharashtra State Bureau of Text Book Production and Curriculum Research (MSBTBPCR), Pune, (2006). *Science and Technology Textbook for Class 9*.

Mann, M. & Treagust, D. R. (1998). A Pencil and paper instrument to diagnose students' conceptions of breathing, gas exchange and respiration. *Australian Science Teachers Journal, 44*(2), 55–60.

Mintzes, J.1., Wandersee, J. H. & Novak, J. D. (2001). Assessing understanding in biology". *Journal of Biological Education, 35*(3), 118–125.

Novak, J. D. (1970). *The improvement of biology teaching*. Cornell University Press.

Novak, J. D. (1985). Meta-learning and meta-knowledge strategies to help students learn how to learn. In L. West & A. Pines (Eds.), *Cognitive structure and conceptual change* (pp. 189–207). New York: Academic Press.

Perkins, D. N., & Simmons, R. (1988). Patterns of misunderstanding: An integrative model for science, math, and programming. *Review of Educational Research, 58*(3), 303–326.

Piaget, J. *The child's conception of the world*. New York: Harcourt Brace, 1929.

Posner, G. 1., Strike, K. A., Hewson, P. W., & Gertzog, W. A. (1982). Accommodation of a scientific conception: toward a theory of conceptual change. *Science Education, 66*(2), 211–227.

Sanders, M. (1993). Erroneous ideas about respiration: The teacher factor. *Journal of Research in Science Teaching, 30*(8), 919–934.

Simpson, W. D. & Marek, E. A. (1988). Understandings and misconceptions of biology concepts held by students attending small high schools and students attending large high schools. *Journal of Research in Science Teaching, 25*, 361–374.

Songer,C. J. & Mintzes, J. J. (1994). Understanding cellular respiration: An analysis of conceptual change in college biology. *Journal of Research in Science Teaching, 31*, 621–637.

Soyibo, K. (1983). Selected science misconceptions amongst some Nigerian school certificate students. In H. Helm & J. D. Novak (Eds.), *Proceedings of the international seminar: Misconceptions in science and mathematics* (pp. 425–427). Ithaca, NY: Cornell University.

Storey, R. D. (1992). Textbook errors and misconceptions in biology: Cell energetics, *The American Biology Teacher. 54*, 161–166.

Sungur, S., Tekkaya, C. & Geban, O. (2001). The Contribution of conceptual change texts Accompanied by concept mapping to students' understanding of the human circulatory system". *School Science and Mathematics* LO1 (2), 91–101

Tekkaya, Ceren, (2003). Remediating High School Students' Misconceptions Concerning Diffusion and Osmosis through Concept Mapping and Conceptual Change Text. *Research in Science & Technological Education, 21*(1), 2003

Vosniadou, S. (2002). On the nature of naive physics. In M. Limon & L. Mason (Eds.). *Reconsidering conceptual change: Issues in theory and practice* (pp. 61–67). Amsterdam: Kluwer.

Wandersee, J. H., Mintzes, J. J. & Novak, J. D. (1994). Research on alternative conceptions in science, In D.L. Gabel (Ed.), *Handbook of Research on Science Teaching and Learning*, (pp. 177–210). New York: Macmillan.

Waheed, T. & Lucas, A. M. (1992). Understanding interrelated topics: photosynthesis at age 14. *Journal of Biological Education, 26*(3), 193–200.

Westbrook, S. L. & Marek, E. A. (1991). Across-age study of student understanding of the concept of diffusion. *Journal of Research in Science Teaching, 28*(8), 649–660.

Yip, D. Y. (1998). Identification of misconceptions in novice biology teachers and remedial strategies for improving biology teaching. *International Journal of Science Education, 20*(4), 461–477.

Narendra D. Deshmukh
Homi Bhabha Centre for Science Education,
TIFR, Mumbai, India
nddeshmukh1965@gmail.com

BAOJUN YAO AND YUHONG HUANG

29. AN EXPLORATION OF BIOLOGICAL CONCEPT FORMATION IN THE CLASSROOM

ABSTRACT

This experiment explores biological concept formation in the classroom by means of the hypothesis testing model. The results suggest firstly, the character of biological concept formation begins at a higher level, grows slowly and then oscillates on a plateau, without the phenomena of mutative process, secondly the inquiry model of instruction is relatively more efficient in concept learning, and thirdly, there may be a threshold for concept learning.

KEYWORDS

Biological Concept, Concept Formation, Achievement, Biology

INTRODUCTION

Concept formation takes a long time to develop and is complex in daily life, so most psychologists use artificial materials to test the process of concept formation. Hull (1920) first used such materials, and Bouthilet (1948) and Bruner (1956) also researched concept formation using this kind of material.

Yang (1985,1986) undertook a series of experiments with the artificial material to research concept formation, and the results suggested that: (i) the Bouthilet's Hypothesis Testing Model is an ideal method of testing concept formation, (ii) when subjects use the method of analysis, the achievement is better than when they were merely reciting, (iii) the process of concept formation is a gradual-mutation process – first, it progresses step by step, then it comes to a sudden change; there is no phenomenon of a plateau.

Subsequently Mu (2002) researched the process of scientific concept formation using the Hypothesis Testing Model. The results showed that the process of scientific concept formation has three recognizable steps; firstly, it progressed gradually or oscillated, secondly, it came to a plateau, and thirdly, it arrived at a mutative process or a sudden change.

All these research studies used the Hypothesis Testing Model, in which subjects realize the character of a concept by discovery. However, in classroom conditions, students understand the character of a concept through learning. Brooks (1978), Klein (1987) and Schroth (1990, 2000) tested the effects on concept formation of the learning conditions produced by different instructional models. However, they

Mijung Kim and C. H. Diong (Eds.), Biology Education for Social and Sustainable Development, 271–276.

also used artificial materials during the tests. What about concept formation in relation to scientific concepts in the classroom? And what about differences in concept formation for different scientific concepts?

This experiment attempts to explore the process of concept formation in relation to different scientific concepts and different instructional models used in the classroom.

MATERIALS AND METHOD

In this experiment we randomly selected 60 Grade 1 students from one high school as our testees. In accordance with the corresponding concept character, we compiled the test, which includes 10 sections, each of which contains five questions. The questions in the test are all multiple-choice type. Each question has five options, which include one correct answer. The experiment examined the effect of two factors. Factor 1 comprises two different teaching methods – mass instruction and inquiring. Factor 2 comprises two different concept types – abstract concept and concrete concept. The 60 students studied these two concepts at the same time. Concept 1 was Osmosis, and Concept 2 Mitosis. For the learning of each concept, the 60 testees were divided into two groups, A and B, each group had 30 students. Group A received mass instruction and Group B, the inquiring mode of instruction. The lesson was taught by the same teacher according to requirements. The design of the experiment is shown in Table 1.

The experiment had three processes: (i) Separating the students into classes and teams according to their level of achievement in biology; the achievement levels were not significantly different among classes and teams. (ii) Carrying out concept teaching. The experiment used different teaching modes (mass instruction and inquiring) to carry out the teaching of the Osmosis and Mitosis concepts. (iii) Testing the efficiency of the students' concept formation. After the instruction, the results in terms of concept formation for the two concepts were measured separately.

Table 1. Experimental design of study

Instructional method	Osmosis	Mitosis
Mass instruction	$n_{1a} = 30$	$n_{2a} = 30$
Inquiring	$n_{1b} = 30$	$n_{2b} = 30$

p.s. 1 - Osmosis, 2 - Mitosis, a - Mass Instruction, b - Inquiring

During the test, the instructions were first read to the testees, and then the test, comprising five questions in each section, was put in order. The time allowed for each section was five minutes. After every section of the test, the testee was invited to describe the concept. If there was something wrong with the given answer, the examiner corrected it. At the same time, for the individual answers given, testees were asked to explain why they chose a particular option. Subsequently the right answers were fed back to the testee. The other sections of the test were then undertaken one after the other in the same manner. When the students described the concept correctly twice in a row, they were not required to describe the concept during the following test section; otherwise they were required to describe the concept during every test section until all 10 sections had been completed. If the students answered correctly in two test sections in a row, the test ended, otherwise the test continued until all 10 test sections were completed.

RESULTS

Table 2. Means and the standard deviations of test scores for each experimental group in the concept-forming process test for Osmosis and Mitosis

Groups		Osmosis			Mitosis	
	n	M	SD	n	M	SD
10	27	59.26	21.82	24	39.17	15.01
20	27	64.44	23.09	24	35.00	23.77
30	27	66.67	27.18	24	48.33	21.20
40	27	71.11	27.92	24	40.83	23.94
50	27	80.74	24.13	24	43.33	23.34
60	27	69.63	35.68	24	55.83	23.58
70	27	77.04	30.74	24	49.17	28.88
80	27	82.75	25.03	24	55.83	22.83
90	27	79.67	27.57	24	50.00	24.32
100	27	82.79	26.15	24	58.33	24.96

Table 3. Mean scores in the concept-forming process test for Osmosis under mass instruction and inquiring method of instruction

Groups		Mass Instruction			Inquiring			
	n	M	SD	n	M	SD	T	P
10	30	56.00	23.72	27	59.26	28.00	0.476	0.636
20	30	67.33	64.67	27	60.00	31.87	0.991	0.326
30	30	64.67	32.67	27	72.59	24.27	1.030	0.307
40	30	70.00	30.06	27	75.56	24.39	0.761	0.450
50	30	74.67	27.76	27	79.26	24.48	0.659	0.512
60	30	68.00	33.05	27	70.30	35.24	0.262	0.794
70	30	68.67	32.67	27	82.22	28.47	1.662	0.102
80	30	79.80	25.54	27	83.70	24.20	0.591	0.557
90	30	69.10	33.76	27	82.22	25.01	1.652	0.104
100	30	75.17	28.84	27	85.93	22.06	1.569	0.108

Table 4. Mean test scores in the concept-forming process test for Mitosis under mass instruction and inquiring method of instruction

Groups		Mass Instruction			Inquiring			
	n	M	SD	n	M	SD	T	P
10	21	40.00	15.49	26	33.08	18.71	1.360	0.181
20	21	34.29	24.61	26	30.77	19.78	0.543	0.590
30	21	47.62	22.34	26	34.62	23.02	1.951	0.057

40	21	37.14	21.25	26	32.31	23.02	0.734	0.467
50	21	47.62	21.34	26	30.00	19.80	2.924**	0.005
60	21	54.29	22.93	26	38.46	24.61	2.259**	0.029
70	21	50.48	30.08	26	39.29	19.98	1.534	0.132
80	21	56.19	24.18	26	44.62	22.13	1.710	0.094
90	21	47.62	24.06	26	39.23	19.89	1.306	0.198
100	21	57.14	25.52	26	44.62	20.64	1.862	0.069

DISCUSSION

By observing the results of concept formation for Osmosis and Mitosis, we found, firstly, that the means of the test score in the first group were 59.26 and 39.17. These marks were significantly higher than the score for the first group for an artificial concept, 20 (Yang, 1986). Secondly, the mean for the concept on Osmosis increased gradually up to the fifth group, but from the fifth to the tenth group, the mean did not rise significantly. The mean for the concept of Mitosis increased gradually up to the sixth group, but from the sixth to the tenth group the scores did not rise noticeably. One-way ANOVA yielded a statistically significant difference between the 10 groups: Osmosis (F=2.63, P = 0.008; Mitosis F = 2.691, P = 0.005).

The multiple comparisons of LSD showed that there was a significant difference in the mean for Osmosis between the first group and the fifth and later groups (except the sixth group). Furthermore, the fifth mean for Osmosis did not show a significant difference from the sixth and subsequent groups.

There were similar results for Mitosis. The difference was significant between the first group and the sixth but not significant between the six group and other groups after the sixth. Therefore the process of concept-forming occurred in two phases: the first phase was a period of gradual increase, and the second was a period of oscillation on a plateau. To sum up the above analysis, it can be said that the scientific concept-forming process in the classroom presents the character of a high jumping-off phase, a slow increase phase, and an oscillation on a plateau. Moreover, we want to know the effects of different kinds of teaching on the formation of different concepts.

The means for concept-forming for Osmosis and Mitosis with different teaching methods are presented in Tables 3 and 4. The t-test showed there were different effects with the different teaching methods for different types of concept-formation. For Osmosis, the two teaching methods had not yielded a significant difference in even one group; however, there were six groups which showed a significant difference between the two teaching methods for Mitosis. Thus we conclude that the effects of different kinds of instruction on concept formation in the classroom are varied. For some concepts, such as Mitosis, inquiring is more effective than mass instruction, while for other concepts, such as Osmosis, there is no significant difference between the two kinds of instruction.

A possible inference from these results is that there may be a threshold in concept formation, and that different concepts have different thresholds. The threshold for Osmosis is low, and both kinds of teaching method can enable students to reach this threshold, so we did not find a significant difference. For other concepts such as Mitosis, however, the threshold is higher, and only the inquiring method can enable students to reach that threshold, so the experiment yielded a significant difference between the two teaching models. This hypothesis needs to be further investigated in future studies.

EDUCATIONAL IMPLICATIONS

Our findings have implications for both science teachers and students. Firstly, for the formation of complex concepts in the classroom, there is no breakthrough in the later phase of concept formation, so the learning aims we can set are to reach the plateau. When students have reached the plateau, they need not spend more time learning the concept again because, according to the research, there is no significant further improvement in student achievement. Secondly, different concepts have different thresholds, so there are different effects with the different teaching methods for different types of concept formation.

REFERENCES

Bouthilet, L. (1948). The measurement of intuitive thinking.

Bruner, J. S. et al. (1956). A study of thinking. New York: John Wiley and Sons.

Yang, Z. L. (1985). An experiment on concept formation. *Psychological Science News*, (5), 31–35.

Yang, Z. L. (1986). An experimental research on concept formation process. *Acta Psychologica Sinica*, (4), 380–387.

Mu, X. Y. (2002). A comparative study of the scientific concept formation process of adults and middle school students. *Psychological Science*, *25*(5):569–640

Brooks, L. R. (1978). Nonanalytic concept formation and memory for instances. *Cognition and Categorization*, 169–211.

Klein, S B. (1978). Learning: Principles and applications. New York: McGraw-Hill.

Schroth, M.L. (1990). A comparison of concept formation strategies in pattern recognition tasks. *Journal of General Psychology*, *117*(3), 7–303.

Schroth, M.L. (2000). The effects of type and amount of pretraining on transfer in concept formation, *Journal of General Psychology*, *127*(3), 9–261.

Baojun Yao
School of Life Science, Jiangxi Normal University, Nanchang, P.R. China
755782564@qq.com

Yuhong Huang
Sanming College, Fujian, P.R. China

30. STUDENTS' KNOWLEDGE INTEGRATION AND DECISION MAKING: LEARNING FROM COLLABORATION DURING ENVIRONMENTAL FIELD STUDY

ABSTRACT

Environmental issues are complex and cannot be understood by one sole discipline or technique of science. The ability to collaborate in an interdisciplinary context does not arise all by itself, but may be developed through educational strategies. The purpose of the study was to provide students the opportunity to collaborate, to solve an environmental task, and determine how they share their knowledge and communication to solve the task. Sixteen secondary school grade two (age 14) and 16 Junior College grade one students (age 17) from public schools in Singapore participated. Participants collaborated in groups to collect data and analyze them to build an eco-village in Kahang, Malaysia. Communication, integration of knowledge with all members in the group and decision-making was necessary to solve the task. Discussions and fieldwork were video recorded and transcribed. Participants' reflection notes were also collected. Data from video recording and students' reflection were coded and thematized. Based on the findings, this study highlighted the importance of knowledge integration and decision-making and the development of responsibility, communication skills and leadership in science learning. The research study was mainly descriptive and qualitative in nature.

KEYWORDS

Collaboration, Knowledge Integration, Environmental Science, Field Study

INTRODUCTION

Science and technology has strived to understand and solve environmental changes and problems in local and global societies, however, its approach has been rather mechanistic and compartmentalized to address the complexity of the current environmental issues such as climate change or deforestation (Godemann *et al.*, 2008). Environmental issues cannot be understood by one sole discipline or technique of science. It requires an interdisciplinary approach and collaboration of various dimensions of sciences and society in order to

Mijung Kim and C. H. Diong (Eds.), Biology Education for Social and Sustainable Development, 277–284.

understand the complexity and uncertainty of and enhance the sustainability of our world. This highlights the need of collaborative participations among different disciplines of sciences, social sciences, and humanities to understand the issues and problems that we face in our time and place. The ways of knowledge integration would be the important aspect to facilitate environmental problems and sustainable issues.

With this realization, researchers stated the importance of interdisciplinary knowledge in research and education. Godemann *et al.* (2008) highlighted that the exchange of knowledge and the development of the common basis of understanding among group members would be necessary in knowledge integration. However, the ability to collaborate in an interdisciplinary context does not arise all by itself, but may be developed through strategic design and practice in education. This requires educational efforts to bring forth the skills of knowledge integration and interdisciplinary work in students' learning experiences.

The concern of interdisciplinary knowledge in educational contexts reflects on the idea of learning and knowledge building in social constructive approach. Knowledge building through collaboration has been regarded as a meaningful approach in problem solving for following reasons where students work collaboratively to understand problems, negotiate their own and others' ideas through deep discussion on problems, and take responsibility for collective answers to problems and further knowledge development. By engaging in group activity of problem solving, responsibility for their own and other's learning and knowledge can be shared and developed. Hence, students acquire interdisciplinary knowledge through the shared production of concepts and skills, which, as any higher order cognitive form of knowledge, initially exists in and through social interaction (Vygotsky, 1978).

As knowledge is actively developed through socially shared experiences and interaction, building interdisciplinary knowledge on environmental issues requires students' collaboration and communications to learn and problem solving skills. Thus, understanding how students interact in collaborative problem-solving situations is important. In addition, structuring the assignment problem and group dynamics needs to be taken into consideration. The purpose of this study was to provide students the opportunity for collaborative learning to solve environmental tasks and determine how students integrate their knowledge and communicate with one another to solve problems.

METHODOLOGY

Research Subjects

Sixteen Junior College (JC) grade one students aged 17 (11 boys) and 16 Secondary School (SS) grade two students aged 14 (1 boy) from public schools in Singapore participated. Both schools are classified in the middle socio-economic level. All participants were divided into groups. Each group consisted of 2–3 JC and 2–3 SS students.

Design of Field Trip

Participants were brought on a fieldtrip to Kahang Organic Rice Eco-farm (the farm hereafter) in Kahang, Malaysia. The farm is a certified organic rice farm 260 acre wide with rice-plots, several irrigation canals and a small lake for fish and prawn farming. It grows organic brown rice without chemical fertilizers or pesticides. The crops are harvested twice a year. However, due to economic reasons, a section of the farm was converted to conventional farming in 2008 which used chemical fertilizers and pesticides.

Data Collection

Participants were asked on how they can build an eco-village in Kahang area and the possibilities of using alternative energy resource such as solar and wind power. In addition, they needed to think of the consequences to the organic farm and crops, ways to deal with domestic and agricultural waste and water pollution. They were challenged with the impact of the eco-system with the development of the eco-village around the farm. Based on their findings, each group had to present their final report. A pre-field and an on-site field study were carried out by each group.

I. Pre-field Study

The duration of the pre-field study was four weeks. Participants were instructed to carry out a research using internet or the library as a New-Age farmer on the following crops: rice, mung bean, banana, papaya, durian, watermelon. Each group also selected one research tool among 6 areas; soil chemistry; weather station; brine shrimp as bio-indicator; soil physical properties; insect search and water chemical quality. Each group met once a week to discuss their findings from library or internet search and also learned how to use the lab equipments regarding their research topic (data loggers, GPS detector, chemicals, breeding brine shrimps, etc.) during this period.

II. On-site Field Study

The duration of the on-site field study was three night and four days and consists of two rounds of students' collaborative work. There was no internet access in this rural site where the field work was conducted. Participants were required to solve guiding research questions suggested by the researchers through using their pre-field study notes, relevant books, apparatus, equipment, and research tool. They need to select the location for sample collection and discuss how to complete data collection and analysis in three days. Appendix A shows the questions given to the six groups of participants to aid them in their data collection and analysis in round 1.

In round 2, participants were re-assigned new groups. The new group contained a mixture of participants from the 6 different research groups. Hence, each member in the previous group collaborated and shared their research findings with the new group. The group made their final proposal for building an eco-village based on the information.

DATA ANALYSIS

The group of soil chemical participants was randomly selected and observed for their collaborations throughout the field work, discussion meetings, and reflection writing during the round 1. All activities were video recorded and watched several times. Data was analyzed to investigate the distinctive dynamics of participants' interactions during their research and discussion, that is, collaboration between the six research groups as well as collaboration between JC and SS participants. For example, the number of times JC participants and SS participants together discussed things and what manner they discussed. Similarly, we chose a random group during the round 2. There were two students from the soil chemical group. Their work was observed and video recorded for data analysis. Data was analyzed to understand how participants integrated scientific data and findings from different research groups and made decisions through group discussion.

Participants resented the sites of their data collection and suggested areas for planting and building houses to more than two hundreds of audience including farm workers, JC students and school teachers from outdoor camp activities in that region. Throughout their decision-making and presentation, the participants explained and justified their ideas using primary scientific data collected from the farm, secondary data collected from their pre-field study research, and information collected from the farmers.

Throughout the study, participants recorded their reflection notes on their learning experiences of researching and collaborating with others during pre-field and on-site field study. The writing records and data from discussion, fieldwork, and presentation were cross-checked and thematized according to interactive collaborations among group members and knowledge integration.

RESULTS

Importance and Appreciation of Collaborative Knowledge Building

The study reported a significant level of collaboration among group members as each member had worked on a different task previously and played expertise on different knowledge. Participants shared their knowledge and findings and also learned from others to create their ideas of ecological living and farming to build an eco-village in Kahang. Participants highlighted the importance of their involvement in knowledge sharing and contribution to problem solving in the situation. For example, one SS participant stated how her team contributed to problem solving with in-depth research and being well-prepared for possible questions raised by other participants.

More than 90% of JC participants and four SS groups reflected on difficulties on data collection and inaccuracies in analysis. According to the participants, they reported high pressure on providing as accurate knowledge and answers as possible as the role of expertise during their pre-field and on-site field study. In addition, they emphasized all members' research was related to the question and had to integrate the knowledge in order for solutions to the task. For example, one SS participant reflected upon realization that their work was inter-related and how they valued the work with others. Another JC participant shared that they developed appreciation for their own role and others' in problem solving process. Participants reported they experienced the responsibilities of expert knowledge and interrelation among various dimensions of knowledge, and dependency among others.

Collaboration with Different Levels of Knowledge

The study reported on the challenge of working with group members with different levels of knowledge. According to JC participants, SS participants were unable to follow group discussion and time was spent for explanation. In a consistent vein, SS participants revealed they were unable to understand JC participants. However, participants found ways to alleviate the difference in levels of knowledge through communication. SS participants reported they continued to ask questions if they did not understand and JC participants explained to them.

The findings suggest an inter-dependent relationship. JC participants took the role of teaching or guiding SS participants as they were more knowledgeable in using lab equipments and analyzing data. For instance in the soil chemical group, JC participants took the role of leadership and explained how to measure the chemicals in the soil samples. SS participants were also challenged to think of factors why plant growth is increased when added phosphorus. In forming mentor-mentee relationships, they found their own way to cope with different levels of knowledge among themselves.

Challenges of Collaborative Decision-making and Communication

Participants reported the many different opinions they encountered during the process of collective decision making. They had to work out how they wanted to settle the tension and gaps among diverse opinions, location of sample collection and many others to reach their final conclusion. They realized that their final proposal on building an eco-village in Kahang needs to be based on evidence and knowledge. Furthermore, collaboration requires respecting others' opinions. One JC participant reflected that good ideas perceived by some may not appeal to others. Their proposal was difficult to conclude with many conflicting suggestions. Another highlighted everyone played a part in the decision-making as his group leader asked for everyone's opinions first before any making any decisions. Participants with the role of group leader reported higher responsibility during decision making process. One JC participant highlighted the need to consider everyone's thoughts and feelings but make the correct decision and not the popular one.

The findings also showed SS participants' difficulty in communicating the final decision as they were not as knowledgeable as the JC participants. Group discussion and communication were reported to be challenging when there were much difference in knowledge levels, personality, age and gender and individual roles (leader versus member). Participants realized the importance to develop communication and decision making skills in scientific research and development. Through these experiences, participants experienced various dynamic relationships among themselves and challenges of group decision making and collaboration. Many understood they needed to know what their responsibilities were and how they needed to participate in the group work over time.

Deepening the Level of Thinking

This study reported the effect of collaboration between two different grade groups. SS participants were observed to benefit from the collaboration during the task. The researchers observed the initial lack of participation of SS participants due to age and knowledge difference. Over time, the researchers observed that care and trust, guidance and scaffolding in the group were developed. SS participants learned how to work and established rapport among them. Based on their reflective writing, it was evident they appreciated the opportunities to collaborate with the seniors.

DISCUSSION AND CONCLUSION

This environmental field trip was designed to provide participants the experience of collaboration and knowledge integration and sharing. It was also planned for problem-solving and decision making. The study showed that there are some potential benefits and concerns in the dynamics of collaborative decision making and field work among different group members. Collaboration among different research groups developed participants' responsibility to do research and share knowledge as accurately as possible. They experienced the need to collaborate and depend on others' knowledge and support when they learnt from others. Participants were given opportunities to learn how to communicate with others who do not have the same knowledge. JC participants had to help SS participants make sense of the content they acquired in technical and procedural content and problem solving skills. This study suggests that group work on several different research topics to solve the key problem can generate an opportunity to develop students' communication skills. The positive notion of a mentor-mentee relationship may be explained in the realm of Confucius culture where juniors respect seniors and seniors take care of juniors as a virtue of good human beings (Phuong-Mai *et al.*, 2009) which supported the dynamic grouping strategies in this study. Further research is required to discuss the effects and concerns of collaboration and grouping strategies as this is a complex notion of human relationship.

Researchers of information exchange have found that meta-knowledge of expertise in the group has a positive influence on the exchange of unshared information (Godemann, 2008). If the group members know who has what knowledge in what areas, the quality of group discussion and decision-making is improved (Littlepage *et al.*, 1997), even if group members often do not build up a correct idea of the expertise of the others. Hence, the inter- and intra-collaboration among groups are positively increased and affect on knowledge integration. In this case, grouping design in this study suggested much potential to enhance students' abilities to communicate and make decision, thus increasing the interdisciplinary level of learning and knowledge building.

Collaborative learning may further bring forth the development of leadership. Grouping two different levels of participants developed participants' different meanings of relationships such as care, trust, guidance and scaffolding among the group members. Senior participants learnt to communicate and lead their juniors such as collecting all opinions for decision making, caring for their emotional feelings such that their collaboration would benefit all members.

In addition, the field trip opened a new dimension of learning science for all participants such as data analysis using scientific methods. Participants developed their understanding of the importance of evidence for conclusion. Despite these challenges of understanding in-depth knowledge and skills, most reflected that the learning experience was enjoyable and wanted to learn more in research such as types of equipments available, techniques for data collection and analysis.

REFERENCES

Godemann, J. (2008). Knowledge integration: a key challenge for transdisciplinary Cooperation. *Environmental Education Research, 14*(6), 625–641.

Hmelo-Silver, C., & Barrows, H. S. (2008). Facilitating collaborative knowledge building. *Cognition and instruction, 26*(1), 48–94.

Littlepage, G., Robinson, W., & Reddington, K. (1997). Effects of task experience and group experience on group performance, member ability, and recognition of expertise. *Organizational behaviour and human decision processes, 69*(2), 133–147.

Phuong-Mai, N., Terlouw, C., Pilot, A., & Elliott, J. (2009). Cooperative learning that features a culturally appropriate pedagogy. *British Educational Research Journal, 35*(6), 857–875.

Polk, M., & Knutsson, P.(2008). Participation, value rationality and mutual learning in transdisciplinary knowledge production for sustainable development. *Environmental education research, 14*(6), 643–653.

Vygotsky, L. S. (1978). *Mind in society: The development of higher psychological processes.* Cambridge, MA: Harvard University Press.

APPENDIX A

Table 1. Guiding questions for the participants to aid them in the data collection and analysis

Groups	Guiding research questions
Insects	What are the insects that may damage or help the crops? How are you going to catch the insects? How are you going to identify the insects?
Soil Chemistry	What are the nutrients suitable for planting these crops? What chemicals are you looking for in the soil? (e.g. Ca^{2+}, ...) How are you going to determine the chemicals in the soil?
Physical Properties of Soil	What are the types of soil suitable for planting these crops? What are the physical properties of the soil that you are measuring for the soil? (e.g. pH, particle size, water content, ...) How are you going to determine the physical properties of the soil?
Chemical Quality of Water	What do you mean by water pollution? In particular, what are the chemicals that constitute water pollution? What will you be doing to determine the chemicals in the water?
Bio-indicators	How are you going to carry out the Brine Shrimp test? How do you determine the state of health of the water?
Weather station	Research into alternative forms of energy (Solar, Wind). How much electricity can you generate from the sun and wind? (e.g. how much solar radiation/wind can produce how much electricity?) What are the weather conditions that are suitable for planting these crops?

Mijung Kim
National Institute of Education, Nanyang Technological University, Singapore 637616
Current address: Department of Curriculum and Instruction. University of Victoria, Victoria BC, Canada V8P5C2, mjkim@uvic.ca

Hoe Teck Tan
School of Science and Technology, Singapore 138572
tanhoeteck@hotmail.com

WOON KEAT FOO-LAM, MENG LENG POH AND YEN PING SOH

31. IMPORTANCE OF LECTURE FEEDBACK IN H2 BIOLOGY LECTURES IN A JUNIOR COLLEGE

ABSTRACT

Timely feedback is crucial in the effective teaching of GCE A Level Biology. In Singapore, junior colleges adopt the lecture-tutorial system in curriculum delivery. However, pedagogical effectiveness during lectures is hindered by many challenges that include large lecture size, diverse learning abilities of students and difficulty in monitoring students' learning. Hence, it is an uphill task to employ the best teaching practices that foster deep learning. We have administered post-lecture feedback for all Biology topics taught since 2007, and monitored the efficacy of this mode of student feedback on their understanding of biological concepts. Our findings, based on consolidated feedback from five student cohorts, have shown a positive correlation in the use of post-lecture feedback with students' ability to grasp concepts, and provided evidence that students improved in their capability to make connections between related themes in the subject. Students thus learn better and deeper when given timely and targeted feedback. The use of pre- and post-lecture tests, in which students from the "lecture feedback group" fared better compared to the control group, further substantiated our findings. There is a need to look into a less time-consuming and more efficient means of soliciting and collating feedback from large student numbers.

KEYWORDS

Curriculum Delivery, Lecture-Tutorial System, Diverse Learning Abilities, Deep Learning

INTRODUCTION

Junior colleges and pre-university centres in Singapore are designed for students who wish to pursue a university degree after two and three years respectively of pre-university education. Lessons are typically conducted in a lecture-tutorial system, with lectures as the main platform for mass transmission of information to a large number of students. Despite mixed criticisms of lecturing as a pedagogical method, junior colleges have yet to find practical alternative teaching methods for most GCE A Level teaching subjects. Critics point out that lecturing is essentially one-way communication that does not involve significant student participation, and therefore fails to promote active learning. Nonetheless, lectures remain an efficient

Mijung Kim and C. H. Diong (Eds.), Biology Education for Social and Sustainable Development, 285–296.

means by which large numbers of students can be informed on conceptual content of many examinable subjects.

Given the drawbacks of the lecture teaching mode, there are many challenges involved in teaching H2 Biology topics effectively. Some of these challenges stem from the issue of large lecture group size, while others are related more specifically to the nature of the Biology topics. A large lecture group size is associated with great variability in students' background knowledge, academic competence and future goals, which makes it difficult for the lecturer to address their diverse needs. Furthermore students arrive with preconceived views and misconceptions of the content knowledge. It is also difficult and costly to employ the best teaching practices that promote deep learning which involves personalised instruction, rich and timely feedback and interactive learning environments. Within the H2 Biology curriculum, concepts are introduced initially in their basic form and then applied in multiple contexts. Yet, students often compartmentalise what they learn, missing out opportunities to link their knowledge, interrelate various concepts and conceptualise their understanding (Brown *et al.*, 2006).

Consequently, timely feedback becomes important in effective lecturing. Previously, student feedback for lectures was carried out only at the end of a school term. So far, an efficient and systematic way of soliciting real-time classroom feedback is possible only in classrooms built with expensive infrastructure and equipment, and is usually limited to small classes. Otherwise, the 'quick show of hands' method has remained the only way to obtain immediate feedback from a class (Tay and Tan, 2008). There are many scenarios where student responses need to be analysed and consolidated. Conducting assessments during the lecture to assess students' understanding of the materials before proceeding to the next part of the topic is also necessary to gauge how much the students have learnt.

From research on how students learn, two well-supported principles have emerged that are particularly relevant to addressing these challenges. First, students' learning improves and their understanding deepens when they are given timely feedback (Butler and Winne, 1995; Corbett and Anderson, 2001). "Feedback" here refers to corrections, suggestions and explanations that are tailored to the individual's current performance and that encourage revision and enhancement in learning. Second, for students to benefit from the information they are learning, students need to practice making connections between related ideas (Eylon and Reif, 1984). Adapting instruction to students' needs is also consistent with the principle of student-centred teaching and hence should derive similar benefits (Slunt and Giancarlo, 2004).

Use of post-lecture feedback has been documented in several papers (Magnan, 1988; Chizmar and Ostrosky, 1998; Bartlett and Morrow, 2001), but such studies have not been conducted in the context of junior colleges in Singapore. In Hwa Chong Institution (College), lecture feedback has been administered for all Biology topics taught since 2007, and the efficacy of this mode of student feedback monitored with regards to its impact on students' understanding of biological concepts. The questions in the feedback form allow the lecturer to evaluate two basic issues. One, if the main concepts covered in a lecture are conveyed to students, and two, if there are any concepts which might have confused a significant proportion of the lecture group. This study therefore aims to investigate the effectiveness of lecture feedback in fostering better and deeper learning, and if its use can potentially translate to better student scores in assessments.

METHODOLOGY

We have been administering the post-lecture feedback form to JC1 and JC2 students since 2007.

Construction of the Post-lecture Feedback Questionnaire

The mode of lecture feedback involves a written questionnaire consisting of two main questions: (i) What are at least two important t points you have learnt from today's lecture? and (ii) What are at least two areas that you found most difficult to understand from today's lecture?

Administration of Lecture Feedback

Feedback forms were distributed to students before the commencement of each lecture. While the lecture was in progress, students could pen in their responses to the questions on the feedback form. In the last five minutes of the lecture, students were given time to complete the form before submission. This has been dutifully carried out for all H2 Biology topics. For this research paper, feedback for three lecture series, namely Organisation of the Eukaryotic Genome, Diversity and Evolution and Cell Signalling, were analysed. These topics were chosen because of their relatively higher level of difficulty and greater complexity of concepts involved.

Reviewing Lecture Feedback Results at the Next Lecture

At the start of the following lecture, the lecturer spent at least ten minutes reviewing contents covered in the previous lecture. This review was tailored to the specific learning needs of the lecture group, as ascertained based on students' feedback collected from the previous lecture. The lecturer clarified doubts pertaining to the previous lecture and recapped important concepts before teaching new content. Requests to re-explain certain concepts as well as queries on particular conceptual points were also addressed during the review.

Generation of Frequently-asked Questions (FAQs)

There was insufficient time for the lecturer to answer all questions posed by students during the first ten minutes of a lecture. Usually, the lecturer focused on questions pertinent to the major concepts in the topic. The quantity and diversity of questions raised by students have prompted us to generate a list of Frequently-Asked

Questions (FAQs), classified by topic, since 2008. This list was compiled by the lecturer at the end of each lecture or entire lecture series.

Study Design

We included the administration of a pen-and-paper survey (see Appendix Section 5.1) on the use of lecture feedback at the end of the lecture series for each of the three topics. An SMS survey (see Appendix Section 5.2) was also carried out. To provide a quantitative measure of the effectiveness of lecture feedback, pre- and post-lecture quizzes were conducted prior to the start and upon completion of the Organisation of the Eukaryotic Genome lecture series.

Pen-and-paper Survey

The pen-and-paper survey asked student in an open-ended format to relate the positives and negatives of lecture feedback. All 2010 JC1 H2 Biology students were surveyed for the topic Organisation of Eukaryotic Genome, and all 2010 JC2 H2 students for the topics Diversity and Evolution as well as Cell Signalling.

SMS Survey

The SMS survey used the standard five-level Likert scale for responses (see Appendix Section 5.2). Ten questions were given. A total of 610 JC1 and JC2 H2 Biology students responded to the survey. The purpose of the SMS survey allowed the authors to assess the strengths of the lecture feedback as a means of improving students' conceptual understanding, an avenue for asking questions and a gauge of student learning at timely junctures during the lecture series.

Pre- and Post-Lecture Quizzes

The 2010 JC1 Biology cohort of 22 Civics Tutorial (CT) groups (classes) was divided into two lecture groups, each group comprised 11 CT groups. Division of the cohort was done such that there was an equivalent representation of CT groups covering the range of academic capabilities from high to average to low in each lecture group. Academic competence of each CT group was evaluated based on the computed average class scores for a most recent common Lecture Test then. As a consequence of this means of division, the number of students in each lecture group was not directly comparable. One lecture group of 274 students was designated the "Lecture Feedback Group", for which lecture feedback was conducted as described, while the other group of 247 students formed the "Control Group" for which no lecture feedback whatsoever was carried out. The assignment of either lecture group as the "Lecture Feedback Group" or "Control Group" was entirely random, and also not made known to the students.

The three-part lecture series for the topic was conducted concurrently in two different venues. The same set of lecture notes was used as the main teaching material in the lecture series. Teaching resources including online animations, video clips, as well as summary diagrams and organisation charts used for mid-lecture overview and end-lecture review were standardised for both lecture groups. Both the pre- and post-lecture quizzes were multiple-choice quizzes, each consisting of five multiple-choice questions (MCQs) on the topic. The five MCQs in each quiz cover a gradated range in level of difficulty from easy to medium to difficult. The scope of each set of MCQs spanned the entire topic.

RESULTS AND DISCUSSION

Pen-and-paper Survey

Effectiveness of lecture feedback in teaching and learning was evaluated by three means: (i) a four-question open-ended pen-and-paper survey that solicited students' responses about the usefulness of lecture feedback, individual preferences on doing lecture feedback and suggestions for improvement (see Appendix), (ii) an SMS survey of ten questions (see Appendix), and (iii) pre- and post-lecture quizzes for a selected JC1 lecture series. (i) and (ii) were conducted on both 2010 JC1 and JC2 H2 Biology cohorts at the end of the first semester. Pooled student responses to question 1 in the pen-and-paper survey administered on the 2010 JC1 and JC2 H2 Biology cohorts for three different lecture series are shown in Table 1.

For all three lecture series, students most frequently related the effectiveness of lecture feedback in enhancing their understanding to the consolidation and reiteration of main points from the previous lecture, as well as the clarification of doubts, before moving on to new content in the subsequent lecture. This was observed in nearly 80% of students surveyed. Potential misconceptions can be identified from student inputs to question 2, which are specific to the particular lecture topic, and addressed during the review of feedback at the beginning of the next lecture.

Table 1. Student responses to positive aspects of lecture feedback

	Type of positive responses	Number of positive responses (n = 845)	% positive responses
1	• Increased ability to understand new concepts • Clarification of doubts and misconceptions • Recap of key concepts	669	79.2
2	• Provision of out-of-syllabus information • FAQs for independent learning • Increased depth in learning; • Exploration of new domains of knowledge	207	24.5

3	• Peer learning – gaining insights and learning through questions asked by peers	280	33.1
4	• Increased lecturer-student interaction • Allows less vocal students to raise questions • All-inclusive learning environment • Addresses issues overlooked by lecturers	171	20.2

A significant proportion of students cited they gained substantially from the ability to pose questions that were promptly addressed by the lecturer either at the start of the next lecture or in a list of frequently asked questions (FAQs) prepared by the lecturer and uploaded for students' reference. The most frequent response about the FAQs was how they facilitated a better grasp of key concepts with more detailed explanation of points of doubt. The students' positive perception of the FAQ lists mirrors the usefulness of the second question in the post-lecture feedback form requiring students to pen down what they were unsure of about the lecture content, and reaffirms its importance as a feedback device because it leads to very concrete and relevant statements of what students want to know more about (Mosteller, 1989). Other comments on the usefulness of the FAQs have been extremely positive with benefits such as: (i) FAQs provide supplementary, out-of-syllabus information and thought-provoking concepts, which promote deeper learning,
(ii) FAQs contain coloured diagrams and links to online animations that reinforce conceptual understanding; (iii) FAQs facilitate recap and hence aids independent learning, and (iv) classification of FAQs by subtopic makes it easier to interrelate different concepts within the topic.

Students appreciated the fact that they could learn from answers to queries raised by their peers and saw the topic or concept from a different perspective that enhanced their understanding. One other noteworthy benefit is the ability of students to draw links between different topics or different parts of a topic.

Based on the response in question 3, 77.8 % of both the JC1 and JC2 cohorts indicated that they liked the method of lecture feedback employed, citing the very same benefits of lecture feedback mentioned above as reasons. Students further revealed that they were in favour of the use of lecture feedback as a means of interacting with the lecturer, which is often very difficult to initiate in large lecture groups (Angelo and Cross, 1993; Chizmar and Ostrosky, 1998; Webster and Hooper, 1998; Harwood, 1996). Additionally, students preferred pen-and-paper feedback to online modes, the former commonly perceived as being more immediate, convenient and effective. The small number of students who were not supportive of the use of lecture feedback mostly lamented their inability to pen down at the end of the lecture what they find dubious as they needed more time to review the lecture content.

SMS Survey

Results of the lecture feedback SMS survey were similar between the JC1 and JC2 student cohorts, and are thus pooled (Table 2). The mean scores did not veer to the extremes of the rating scale (of 1–5) owing to the large sample size. Findings based on these SMS survey results were similar to those from the pen-and-paper survey.

Results of questions 1, 2 and 5 provided evidence that the lecture feedback served to strengthen students' grasp of concepts and enhance their comprehension of difficult lecture material through clarification of queries raised via the post-lecture feedback form. Students expressed their agreement for the effectiveness of the FAQ lists produced by the lecturer that addressed specific student responses about areas of doubt in the topic. Question 3 addresses the aspect of learning from peers, which students felt was facilitated by the lecturer's responses to questions posed by the lecture group. This is in agreement with the findings of Olmstead (1999). The aforementioned benefits of lecture feedback are affirmed in part by the responses of students to questions 6 and 10. Students generally did not agree that the use of lecture feedback was not beneficial and that the first ten to fifteen minutes of a lecture spent reviewing feedback collected from the previous lecture is not a valuable use of lecture time. Responses to question 9 revealed students' positive perception of the lecturer's use of lecture feedback as a demonstration of his respect for and interest in student opinion, as reported also by Angelo and Cross (1993), Chizmar and Ostrosky (1998), Webster and Hooper (1998), Harwood (1996) and Bartlett and Morrow (2001). Results of question 4 point to the students' consensus view that the process of completing the post-lecture feedback questionnaire enabled some degree of self-monitoring in their learning. Question 8 reflected students' general lack of favour for the post-lecture feedback to be administered online.

Table 2. Student responses to SMS survey on lecture feedback

Question	Sample Size	Minimum Score	Maximum Score	Mean Score	Standard Variation
Question 1	610	1	5	3.75	0.79
Question 2	610	1	5	4.17	0.74
Question 3	610	1	5	3.87	0.82
Question 4	610	1	5	3.40	0.84
Question 5	609	1	5	3.84	0.80
Question 6	610	1	5	2.36	0.87
Question 7	610	1	5	3.16	0.84
Question 8	610	1	5	2.61	1.23
Question 9	606	1	5	3.80	0.85
Question 10	593	1	5	2.48	0.99

Pre- and Post-lecture Quizzes

The pre-lecture quiz was administered at the beginning of the lecture series, while the post-lecture quiz was conducted after the entire lecture series has been completed. Both quizzes are each scored out of a total of 5 marks. Deviation in the raw score of the pre-lecture quiz from the post-lecture quiz is obtained for every student as an improvement (positive difference) or a deprovement (negative result). The mean deviation is then calculated for the "Lecture Feedback Group" and the "Control Group" respectively. The "Lecture Feedback Group" shows an average improvement of 0.726 marks, which is higher compared to the mean 0.670-mark improvement of the "Control Group". This is implicative of students' enhanced learning in the "Lecture Feedback Group" as a consequence of the use of lecture feedback, which is the only key variable in lecture delivery for both groups, thereby providing conclusive evidence of the effectiveness of this pedagogical practice.

CONCLUSIONS

Based on feedback consolidated from the pen-and-paper and SMS surveys, the use of lecture feedback has improved students' learning of the lecture topic in a large lecture environment, which is consistent with the findings of Chizmar and Ostrosky (1998).

One of the most important advantages of the lecture feedback is that the explanations are particularly tailored to the needs of the individuals and thus greatly encourage enhanced learning. Reviews involving reiteration of specific concepts and clarification of doubts through lecturer's responses to specific questions posed allow instruction to be adapted for the students. This is an approach similar to student-centred teaching in the classroom where students actively participate in discovery learning processes from an autonomous viewpoint.

Another advantage is that the lecturer is able to address any likely misconception that may arise from the questions raised, allowing students to learn from one another as well as see new ideas being raised. Students are thus able to draw better links between previous topics learnt and the current topic taught as a result of such active exchanges of ideas. Lecture feedback hence fosters not only better, but also deeper learning. At the same time, by directly addressing student interests, this means of lecture feedback serves as a tool for keeping the lecturer in touch with his students (Magnan, 1991), and given the overwhelming number of student responses generated, encourages students' active involvement in the learning process (Angelo and Cross, 1993). The latter is congruent with the principles of social constructivism, which emphasises the active involvement of the learner in the learning process vis-à-vis teacher-centred pedagogies with the learner playing only a passive, receptive role.

Lecture feedback conducted via a written questionnaire provides an avenue for students to pose questions, and in particular, anonymously, which was a welcome feature for most students. The questions were readily addressed in the following lecture and if not, in a list of FAQs compiled by the lecturer at the end of each lecture or lecture series. The aforementioned benefits of the use of lecture feedback that were cited by students are the same ones identified as reasons for why they like the method of lecture feedback employed. We are, based on our experience, convinced of the effectiveness of lecture feedback in enhancing student learning, given that it provides regular, relatively detailed feedback useful for ascertaining students' understanding of a particular topic – what they are learning and how they well they are learning – information that is otherwise scarce in a typical lecture setting (Magnan, 1988; Chizmar and Ostrosky, 1998).

However, there are drawbacks related to this form of lecture feedback, identified from students' responses to question 4 in the pen-and-paper survey, that if rectified, will significantly enhance the positive impact of lecture feedback on teaching and learning. Pertaining to the need for a more time-effective means of collecting feedback, which we will be exploring in the near future, students suggested the use of online platforms such as Wikispaces, asynchronous discussion forums or SMS for administration of lecture feedback. Another area of improvement is to resolve the tedious nature of looking through all the questions posed at the end of each lecture and answering them by the next lecture. One possible solution is to have all tutors assist in sieving out questions from feedback forms of their respective classes so that the lecturer can have more time to craft answers that address the key concepts in the topic. Finally, the format of the feedback form can be improvised to include a checklist for students to mark against sections they have difficulties understanding.

ACKNOWLEDGEMENTS

The authors wish to express their deep appreciation to Miss Brenda Seah for collating the responses to the pen-and-paper survey, and to Mr Kock Kian Hong for his help with statistical analysis. The authors also wish to thank their school, Hwa Chong Institution, Singapore and its Biology Unit (College Section) for their continued support.

REFERENCES

Angelo, T. A. & Cross, K. P. (1993) *Classroom Assessment Techniques*, 2nd Ed., Jossey-Bass Publishers, San Francisco A, 148–153.

Bartlett, M. G. & Morrow, K. A. (2001). "Method for assessing course knowledge in a large classroom environment: An improved version of the minute paper," *American Journal of Pharmaceutical Education, 65*, 264–267.

Brown, William E. et al. (2006). "Improving the Feedback Cycle to Improve Learning in Introductory Biology Using the Digital Dashboard," *Proceedings of World Conference on E-Learning in Corporate, Government, Healthcare, and Higher Education.*

Butler, D. L. & Winne, P. H. (1995). "Feedback and self-regulated learning: A theoretical synthesis," *Review of Educational Research, 65,* 245–281.

Chizmar, J. F. & Ostrosky, A. L. (1998). "The one-minute paper: some empirical findings," *Journal of Economic Education, 29*, 3–10.

Corbett, A. T. & Anderson, J. R. (2001). "Locus of feedback control in computer-based tutoring: Impact on learning rate, achievement and attitudes," *Proceedings of CHI 2002, Human Factors in Computing Systems,* ACM, 2001, 245–252.

Eylon, B. & Reif, F. (1984). "Effects of internal knowledge organization on task performance," *Cognition and Instruction, 1,* 5–44.

Harwood, W. S. (1996). "The one-minute paper," *ibid., 73,* 229–230.

Magnun, B. (1991). "Teaching idea: The one-minute paper," *Teaching Concerns,* University of Virginia.

Mosteller, F. (1989). "The "muddiest point in the lecture" as a feedback device," *On Teaching and Learning, 3.*

Olmsted, J. A. (1999). "The mid-lecture break: When less is more," *Journal of Chemical Education, 76,* 525–527.

Slunt, K. M. & Giancarlo, L. C. (2004). "Student-centered learning: A comparison of two different methods of instruction," *Journal of Chemical Education, 81,* 985–988.

Tay, A. & Tan, K. K. (2008). "Mobile real-time feedback/teaching system," Presentation at *International Conference on Teaching and Learning with Technology,* 5–6 August 2008, Suntec City, Singapore.

Webster, T. R. & Hooper, L. (1998). "Supplemental instruction for introductory chemistry courses," *ibid., 75,* 328–331.

APPENDIX

Pen-and-paper Survey Questions

1. How has the use of lecture in this lecture improved / enhanced your learning of the topic?
2. Name one specific point / idea / concept that you have learnt from the lecture feedback that you may not have realised from the actual lecture conducted.
3. Do you like this method of lecture feedback? Why or why not?
4. Give any additional comments / suggestions for improvement to this method of lecture feedback.

SMS Survey Rating Scale and Questions

1	2	3	4	5
Strongly Disagree	Somewhat Disagree	Neutral	Somewhat Agree	Strongly Agree

1. The lecture feedback improves understanding, clears doubts and reiterates concepts.
2. The lecture feedback provides an avenue for students to pose questions and the lecturers to address the relevant concepts.
3. The lecture feedback allows me to learn from my peers through the questions they posed.
4. The lecture feedback allows me to gauge my level of understanding and reflect on my learning progress.

5. The list of frequently asked questions (FAQs) generated addresses questions that the lecturer has no time to cover in lectures, and reading the FAQs allows me to reinforce my conceptual understanding.
6. The use of the lecture feedback is not beneficial to the large lecture group.
7. The lecture feedback helps me draw links between different subtopics / topics.
8. I would prefer if the responses from the lecture feedback were done by e-mail.
9. I feel the use of the lecture feedback demonstrates the lecturers' interest in my learning.
10. The lecture feedback detracts from valuable lecture time.

Woon Keat FOO-LAM
Hwa Chong Institution
661 Bukit Timah Road
Singapore 269734
foowk@hci.edu.sg,

Meng Leng POH
Hwa Chong Institution
pohml@hci.edu.sg

Yen Ping SOH
Hwa Chong Institution
sohyp@hci.edu.sg

DEVELOPING TEACHER EDUCATION AND BIOLOGY SCIENCE CURRICULUM

Developing biology teachers and science curriculum lies at the core of any commitment to ensuring the relevance and effectiveness of biology instruction and learning. The 11 papers in this theme explore how teacher's proficiency can be developed and how they can in turn impart to students a thirst for knowledge and inquiry-based learning. The need to reform curriculum in certain contexts is also examined in this theme through a number of case studies across Asia.

So what makes a science teacher excellent? Myrna Paez-Quinto seeks to answer this million dollar question. Her study selected recipients of the Teaching Excellence Award in Biology, Chemistry and Physics using purposive sampling. Results from a variety of data collection methods showed that there were five characteristics of an excellent science teacher and the common thread is that teacher's beliefs are most important in influencing their approach and teaching practice and hence, the quality of education. These findings are presented in *"What makes a Science Teacher Excellent: Beliefs"*.

Esther Daniel also highlights the power that biology teachers wield in sparking and sustaining strong student interest in the discipline. In *"Orchestrating Biology Instruction: Teaching Students to Yearn for Knowledge"*, she ponders if the focus on teaching of biology content has caused teachers to neglect their crucial role of helping students cultivate a sense of wonder at science. She summarizes the challenges to biology instruction in her paper, citing the example of how pre-service teachers already have negative ideas about science teaching even before they embark on their professional career. Daniel also argues that biology curriculum and instruction has to become more relevant, current and interdisciplinary, especially to engage this present generation of digital natives. She suggests different ways in which biology can be taught more effectively, for example, by tapping on cooperative teaching techniques, the use of technology, incorporating social issues and ethics in learning, and a focus on biology education for sustainable development.

A similar focus on developing teachers through professional development is examined in *"Empowering Biology Teachers through Development of Content and Pedagogical Content Knowledge"*. Hassan H Tairab sought to increase the pedagogical content knowledge of 22 biology teachers through a series of professional development training activities, like workshops and conferences. Quantitative and qualitative data collected suggest that teachers follow different pathways to acquire meaningful content representation. Also, the series of the professional development activities implemented at the beginning of the research

Mijung Kim and C. H. Diong (Eds.), Biology Education for Social and Sustainable Development, 297–300.

impacted their content as well as pedagogical content knowledge (PCK). Another important conclusion is that teachers' PCK can be meaningfully assessed and characterized through data directly from teachers based on their own practice and reflection. This has implications for teacher education programs which might be enhanced by incorporating components of PCK.

Other factors that could improve teaching outcomes are discussed in Koichi Morimoto's *"Enhancing Elementary Biology Education of Undergraduate Students in Japanese University Through Teachers' Teaching Proficiencies"*. This paper explores the outcomes of learning in elementary science education in a student-centered approach and found that participants were better able to explain the concepts taught, when the lecturer used a diversity of methods. Frequent interaction between the lecturer and students also ensured that prompt replies were given to queries. The study concludes that keeping students engaged actively is an effective way to improve their academic performance.

Another study looks at some of the effects of meaningful reception learning by using advance organizers (AO) that emphasize deductive thinking process. A series of classes were conducted on a topic to fifth graders, followed by the administration of a pre-test, post-test, retention test and affection test. A learning process termed the "cobweb condition" was created, by first presenting the various phenomena relating to new knowledge. Advance organizers were introduced, and students adapted AO to various events through adaptation and progressive learning. Shogo Kawakami, Koichiro Watanabe, Aya Matsumoto conclude that reception learning is more effective than discovering learning for teaching abstract content, especially to underachievers. Their findings are summarized in *"Development of Meaningful Reception Learning in Japan: A Case Study"*.

How innovative thinking can be fostered in students is explored in *"A Study of the Value of Education in the History of Bioscience to the Training of Students' Innovative Thinking"* by Ying-Chun Zhang and Yan-Ting Tang. By suggesting multiple examples of biosciences in history, they argue that the history of bioscience plays a significant role in developing students' innovative thinking, creativity, and scientific views.

Other papers in this theme focus on the reform and development of science curriculum in specific contexts. In *"Fostering Creativity and Sustainability Through the 2009 Science Curriculum in Korea"* Heui-Baik Kim and Sun-Kyung Lee review the contents and pedagogies of the Korean national curriculum revision in 2009. In reviewing the implications and recommendations for science curriculum revisions, they highlight the importance of re-defining the concept of scientific literacy for it to be meaningfully implemented. Another noteworthy observation is the need for more practical integrations of scientific concepts with other inquiry processes or real-life contexts within the science curriculum. Linked to this is the importance of adopting appropriate pedagogy so as to create authentic learning experiences that will help achieve competencies necessary for a sustainable society through science education.

A comparative study of science education in Japan and Ukraine is presented in *"A Comparison of Life Science and Environmental Education in Japan and*

Ukraine: A Need to Improve the Japanese Curriculum". Kseniya Fomichova and Futaba Kazama find that the yearly instructional time in teaching science to students in Japan is significantly lesser than in Ukraine. Compared to other developed nations, Japan is teaching the least science topics in grade 8 curriculum.

A need for reform is also called for in *"Educators' and University Students' Perceptions of Common-Resource Dilemmas – The Need for Adjusted Curriculum in Indonesia"*. Sebastian Koch, Jan Barkmann, Leti Sundawati, and Susanne Bögeholz summarize common-resource dilemmas and state that solutions cannot rely on the actions of individuals only. Specifically in the Indonesian context, stagnancy of the national educational system on management of natural resources has been a longstanding issue. Koch *et al.* looked at the pre-conceptions of Indonesian biology educators and students' perception on local resource conservation issues, specifically in the overexploitation of rattan. Qualitative results showed that their pre-conceptions of resource depletion of rattan were fraught with errors and inadequate. Hence the writers call for an adjusted curriculum that includes current local issues about sustainability concerns. In particular they stress the need for greater accountability to the local population and responsibility towards sustainable living.

Another way to promote responsibility towards sustainable living is discussed in Emilia Fägerstam's study, *"Teachers' View on Relationship between Outdoor Environmental Education and a Sense of Place"*. This study set in Sydney found that contact with nature is important in fostering an Australian identity in a multicultural society. It also found that outdoor environmental education deepens students' sense of place.

A multi-pronged approach towards developing students' sense of responsibility towards environmental sustainability is also necessary. Hong Kim Tan's paper *"Singapore Students' Learning Experiences on Sustainable Development: A Review of the Roles of Civil Society and External Organisations"* reviews some of the key considerations to establish and refine programmes on educating students towards sustainable development.

Taken together, the papers in this theme present diverse recommendations for improving outcomes for science education across different contexts, and span the entire spectrum of teacher training and development, presentation of scientific concepts and the reform of curriculum. Several writers also sound the call for more extensive and meaningful collaborative relationships amongst educators, students, local communities and other advocacy groups to ensure science education remains current and relevant to students' lives and real-life challenges on sustainability.

ESTHER DANIEL

32. ORCHESTRATING BIOLOGY INSTRUCTION: TEACHING STUDENTS TO YEARN FOR KNOWLEDGE

ABSTRACT

Biology teachers hold a lot of power in their hands. This power is to orchestrate the learning environment so creatively that students are stimulated to want to know more. It may be a simple spark as a story or an interesting fact, but it is enough to light the fire of curiosity. Much research points to the fact that the direct teaching of biology content overshadows the process of discovering the wonders of natural science. New research also indicates that changes need to be made within the biology curriculum to make it more relevant and current as well as interdisciplinary. Biology teaching and learning needs to break loose out of its rigid structure and become more fluid and non-linear to become more appealing to our present generation of digital natives.

KEYWORDS

Biotechnology, Digital Natives, Biological Knowledge, Society and Nature, Interdisciplinary Teaching

INTRODUCTION

A biology teacher is introducing the topic of biotechnology at the start of a biology lesson. She asks, "When do you think *Homo sapiens* stumbled upon the process of biotechnology?" One of her students (21st Century born) was quick to answer, "Dolly!" Everyone knows the student is referring to the famous Dolly the sheep that took the world by storm in 1996 as the first mammal to be cloned. Then the teacher shows an animated video about the Sumerians in 6000 BC in Mesopotamia carrying out fermentation of bread made from barley grains, crushed after which water is added (yeast spores carried by air finds its way into the mixture). The end of the video shows the Sumerians drinking the product with a long Sumerian straw. The teacher asks, "Would anyone like to try answering the question again?" After some moments of silence the teacher informs her students, "Although the ancient Sumerians did not realise it, they used anaerobic respiration of yeast to ferment barley grains into beer as far back as 6000 BC. This means that the Sumerians were the first biotechnologists!" After a moment's silence, a voice is heard,

Mijung Kim and C. H. Diong (Eds.), Biology Education for Social and Sustainable Development, 301–310.

"8000 years ago right?" This scenario above could perhaps overcome the misconception of what biotechnology is all about as well as make the students realize that the history associated with the growth of biological knowledge is awe-inspiring. With this single introduction the biology teacher can branch out to teach not only biotechnology and its applications but also the biological concepts of anaerobic and aerobic respiration. The teacher can even teach dispersion of spores of fungi. However, this kind of non-linear teaching and learning is not what always happens in a biology classroom. School biology remains very much structured today as it was in yesteryears.

The science of biology in schools today covers the traditional content of all knowledge associated with living things. The question that arises here is, "How is the biological knowledge of today"? Biology is constantly evolving. What started with basic classical departments of botany, zoology, ecology, microbiology and anthropology (Grimme, 2000) have now become almost 80 sub disciplines (and still expanding) including nanobiology, epigenetics, synthetic biology, genomics (Younès, 2000), bioinformatics, systems biology (EMBO, 2007) and such.

Other alternate ways of looking at biological knowledge which have been explored is related to the significant 'understanding of self and responsible behaviour, of maintaining health and wellbeing, and of environmental citizenship'. (Page & Reiss, 2010, p. 1). Looking at how fast current biological knowledge is advancing, biologists believe that the revolution of biological knowledge has just begun and no one knows what amazing biological discoveries the coming decades can usher in. The sequencing of the human genome was the pinnacle of biological discovery in the final minutes of the 20th Century. At the present time, the molecular secrets of the human genome are being unlocked one by one (Kerfeld, Levis & Perry, 2001). The study of science springing from basic elements was also discussed by Daniel and Rohaida (2001).This is exciting as humankind waits for more astonishing moments of biological breakthroughs (Hopkin, 2010). How are all these stimulating discoveries related to classroom biology? Walker (2006) believes that tremendous creative thought can be stimulated as students strive through experimental and problem solving as these processes of discovery are at the heart of the study of biology.

BIOLOGY EDUCATION RESEARCH

What does recent research say about biology teaching and learning? One of the consistent issues being uncovered repeatedly is that it difficult to study biology. Apparently biology subject matter learnt in the classroom is irrelevant to daily life. This situation has led to biology students tending to memorise facts that appear unrelated to the real world situation. Students' motivation to study biology also seems low (Tekkaya et al.,2001; Wieman, 2007; Setiawan, 2008 in Nugraini et. al.,2009). Research has also revealed that students may struggle with learning biology because of a lack of critical thinking skills (Ursu, 2010). Other research have indicated boring textbooks with excessive details (Tekkaya, et al., 2001) and chalk and talk methods (Daniel, 2010) have made biology learning to appear complicated and has turned off students towards Biology.

As late as the end of the last decade it has been found that much of biology in schools is still taught using strict cook book procedures, as stated by Hammond *et. al.*, (2010),

> *The influence of scientific discoveries on daily life has never been greater, yet the percentage of students pursuing careers in science and technology has dropped dramatically in the Western World. Student disenchantment begins even before high school, where students must typically memorize scientific facts and occasionally perform experiments following a strict protocol that teaches abstract concepts with little relevance to daily life. p. 1*

In Malaysia, it has been found that many a time students are taught about the natural world in the confines of the classroom and this could be a reason why the students do not seem to enjoy learning about living things (Daniel, 2005). Kamisah Osman *et al.*, (2006) found that among 1,690 science teachers (413 of whom were Biology teachers), 525 (31.1%) of the teachers (130 or 31.5% of whom were Biology teachers) indicated that there was a great need to improve on the management and delivery of science instruction. Furthermore, 654 (38.7%) of the teachers (163 or 39.5% of whom were Biology teachers) indicated that there was a great need to improve in generic pedagogical knowledge and skills. In addition, 668 (39.5%) of the teachers (173 or 41.9% of whom were Biology teachers) felt that there was a great need to improve in the planning of science instruction. Biology teachers' content knowledge has also been found to be low (Komathi, 2007) and did not manage to create positive dynamics in the biology classroom. Ho (2010) has reiterated the above situation and reported that teachers still prefer traditional teaching approaches, despite exposure to new approach; teachers are over dependent on commercial teaching materials as they claim they have no time to prepare materials on their own; and the teaching and learning process is examination-oriented

It was found that even the pre-service biology teachers displayed ideas, such as, "A biology teacher must teach students how to recall and remember facts", "Biology has too much content and needs to be memorized", and "Too much time to finish the syllabus, so give facts only" (Mazalan Kamis 2008; Daniel, 2010). These teachers have not even started their formal teaching career, and yet they have many negative ideas.

How can biology be taught more effectively? Cooperative teaching techniques have shown that this technique has the capability to enhance scientific thinking, attitudes, values, practical, social and language skills, as well as augment the learning environment (Lord, 2001). The delegates of the Biology Education Summit, 2008, had suggested that an up to date biology curriculum must prepare students to answer the critical questions in biology, give students the skills to think and work across disciplines, and emphasize the use of mathematics (Musante, 2008). The introduction of more quantification into the life sciences has also been touched on before (Wilmsen & Bisseling, 2005). Much research has also pointed to the use of technology to enhance the teaching and learning of biology (Huppert *et al.*, 2002; Soderberg & Price, 2003). Research has also pointed to adding clear social issues and ethics in the teaching and learning of biology. Real world problems help to link biological concepts together and students will be able to see the real biology rather than just a heap of irrelevant facts and concepts in thick textbooks to be memorised (Chamany *et al.*, 2008).

Another very important aspect is that of biology education for sustainable development. Daniel (1996) had already initiated the infusion of biology education for sustainable education. Effective life science education can help to create a community that is able to address global environmental issues and provide a framework for creating positive human behaviour towards the environment (van Eijck & Roth, 2007). However, this it is a slow process to convince teachers of science and in particular biology to infuse concepts of sustainable development into their lessons (WWF Malaysia, 2009).

Slowly but surely, biology education research has been accumulating as to how this life based subject can be taught in a more meaningful way, such that students understanding of its concepts may be enhanced (Morse, 2010). The consensus is that teaching out-dated facts is not the way. Rather, the teaching of biological discovery will be more significant for students. This is the challenge, to teach current biology using state of the art innovative teaching techniques.

CREATING A LEARNING ENVIRONMENT FOR TEACHING AND LEARNING BIOLOGY

Aristotle is recognized as the originator of the scientific study of life at around 334BC. He observed, dissected and studied at least 110 animals. Aristotle's zoological reports were unmatched for almost 2000 years. Since Aristotle tried to record the study of animals in a systematic and comprehensive way, biology has predominantly been a descriptive quest (Wong, 2007).

At the turn of the 19th Century and the beginning of the 20th Century, Dewey (1903) and his cooking laboratory pedagogy attempted to introduce interdisciplinary science through his progressive curriculum. Dewey's idea was to make the curriculum as experiential as possible. The laboratory pedagogy was based upon the belief that the classroom was a small society by itself and teachers should strive to create an environment which was analogous to a process of creating a civilization.

Thirty years ago, Yager (1983) created a list of what biology education should be and the actual state that it was in. Some of the items stated by Yager are given in Table 1. Some similar thoughts were also put forward by Hernandez (1981).

If an honest look is considered at the present state of our biology education we really have not moved on since the last Century (Sathasivam & Daniel, 2010; Foong & Daniel, 2010, Lee & Daniel, 2010). Sathasivam found that science teachers' and in particular biology teachers' methods of assessment were really to ascertain the retention of information rather than interpretation and application. Foong and Daniel as well as Lee and Daniel found that reasoning, argumentation and decision making skills rarely happened if at all in the biology classroom. One aspect that must be enhanced in biology learning environments and perhaps in turn will augment biology instruction overall is our understanding of students' learning styles. *Do not then train youths to learning by force and harshness, but direct them to it by what amuses their minds so that you may be better able to discover with accuracy the peculiar bent of the genius of each.* — Plato

Tanner and Allen (2004) made an interesting observation about learning styles. They stated that a learning style is a 'phenotypic characteristic' and is the 'emergent interaction' that happens between one's brain's neurophysiology and the experiences of the individual's environment. These learning styles are as flexible as the brain's plasticity and can change according to different learning environments.

Table 1. Comparison of critical elements in biology education

Desired State of Biology Education	Actual State of Biology Education
Decision making involving biological knowledge in biosocial contexts	Uncovering a correct answer to discipline bound problems
Curriculum is problem centred, flexible and culturally as well as biologically valid	Curriculum is textbook centred, inflexible; Only biological validity is considered
Individualised and personalised instruction recognizing student diversity	Group instruction geared for the average student and directed by the organization of the textbook
Testing and evaluation should test the use of biological knowledge to interpret personal and social problems and issues.	Replication of assigned information.
Philosophical position should influence all aspects of curriculum and teaching practices	Curriculum and teaching practices are largely atheoretical and routine.

Source: Yager (1983)

One way of narrowing the gap between learning styles and the complexities of biology instruction is the integration of technology in biology classrooms. There exists an incompatibility between the present teaching of school biology and teaching biology with technology (Table 2). Computer technology has brought the idea that learning can be customised to suit individual students and that the teacher is no longer the sole source of knowledge in the biology classroom. Hence 'doing' is the key word as opposed to acquisition through assimilation.

The students of today are digital natives. They speak an entirely new 'language'. How is the learning style of the digital native? The most prominent is that digital natives receive and process information rapidly. In addition, they process multiple forms of information media simultaneously. It is effortless for them to be sending SMSs, sending email, or even playing a video game and talking on the hand phone all at once. Such is the learning path of a digital native. The social aspect in their lives is all about being constantly digitally connected to a larger network of friends (Gibson *et al.*, 2010). In designing suitable learning experiences and learning environments, the teachers who are digital migrants must see that scientific knowledge has to be created and shared constantly through various forms of communication in the science classroom. For this reason the present science teacher training programmes must also enhance the technological, content and pedagogical experiences of the student teachers who will be involved in the creation of lessons for the future science classroom (Daniel, 2010).

Table 2. Incompatibility between school biology and technology

School Biology	Technology
Uniform learning	Customisation learning
Teacher as expert	Diverse learning sources
Standardisation assessment	Specialisation
Knowledge in the head	Reliance on outside sources
Coverage	The knowledge explosion
Learning by acquisition	Learning by doing

Note: Modified from Collins and Halverson (2009).

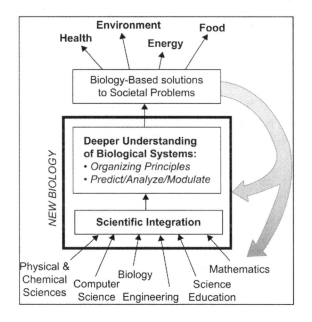

Figure 1. A New Biology for the 21st Century (Source: AIB, 2010).

NEW DIRECTIONS FOR BIOLOGY TEACHER EDUCATION: THE NEXT STEPS?

Society and nature are in a continuous state of transition. Therefore biological scientific inquiry has to be too. The 20th Century saw the advancement of all scientific knowledge in strides that we could never have imagined a hundred years ago. In particular, the progress of biological discoveries has culminated in a burst of excitement especially in the field of molecular genetics which has seeped into all areas of science. However, fragmentation of knowledge is what we have in schools (Vohra, 2000). This means that, "Biology Education must change to meet the potentials and demands of the new biology and to realize the promise of science to society in the future" (AIB, 2010, p.7). The American Institute of Biological Sciences has put out a unique for a 21st Century Biology (Figure 1). The brave new idea calls for an interdisciplinary outlook that integrates the various giant disciplines to address the four main problematic issues of health, energy, food and the environment that have become pressing issues of our times. A very similar outlook given by Page and Reiss (2010) has been stated earlier in this paper. In fact Borght (2000) had already hinted at this interdisciplinary approach almost a decade ago.

However, for interdisciplinary teaching to be successful, it will require new materials (such as textbooks), spaces (such as new design laboratories) and approaches.

The digital native students of today have ideas of acquiring knowledge far removed from yesteryears. These digital natives are calling out to teachers of biology to engage them, to challenge them, to help them to develop critical, analytical and communication skills as well as enrich them with research and experimentation skills. They are asking that we make biology lessons relevant in real life and give them ownership of the lessons. They wish to capture the passion and enthusiasm that is needed to keep biology alive and grand as it has been in the past. It is appropriate here to state the French pilot and writer Antoine de Saint-Exupery's words,

"If you want to build a ship, don't drum up people together to collect wood and don't assign them tasks and work, but rather teach them to long for the endless immensity of the sea."

HOW COULD A BIOLOGY CLASS BE IN THE NEAR FUTURE? PERHAPS, A SCENARIO AS FOLLOWS?

After completing the study of the human nervous system in a biology class, the students ask the teacher about how the brain is affected by music. The teacher suggests that they conduct a simple research and asks them to think about it. After a few days the students having searched for information on brains including those of other animals ask if they could conduct a simple research on the brains of birds as it would be difficult to perform any kind of experiment on human subjects in the school. The teacher agrees and tells them to plan the research and that they can conduct the research after school. The students plan and list out a few materials needed for their research. The teacher assists them in obtaining the materials to build a 'test cage'. After a week the students who have been consistently working after school have completed building the 'test cage' in which the birds would be able to step on a lever and obtain food pellets while various type of music is played. The rationale of the students is that different kinds of music may influence bird behaviour which reflects the workings of the brain. The students decide to use chicks. They place the 'test cage' in a part of the biology laboratory and every day after school the students expose the chicks to different kinds of music (jazz, rock, ballads, classical etc.) for different lengths of time. They observe the behaviour of the chicks and count the times the chicks step on the lever for food. The students also record temperature readings and the growth of the chicks (weight and length). After a week or two the students write up a report and present their findings to the school. They also try and interpret the findings for the human brain. In this scenario, not only will the students learn more about animal brains, but they will also learn important scientific research skills and thinking skills. Furthermore, the students will acquire knowledge in measurement and graphing skills as well as transference of knowledge and skills from one issue to another. After watching their friends there is a possibility that other students will be motivated to conduct other creative simple research experiments.

Is the scenario above imaginary? Far from it. The scene is an episode in a Malaysian school in 1980 when the Internet was as yet not discovered. The biology teachers of today and tomorrow can do so much more. Biology will soon move beyond the present and zoom into nano gene biology. Exactly where it will move to from there will remain a mystery for future biologists to discover. Perhaps, it is time for biology teachers to hold a baton and begin to orchestrate biology education to transform from the content centred approach to a more contemporary research centred interdisciplinary approach where the students will be made to yearn and want to know more and be able to discover for themselves.

REFERENCES

American Institute of Biological Sciences, (2010). *Emerging life science core concepts: Big ideas.* Available at: http://www.aibs.org/events/biology_education/emerginglifesciences.html

Borght, C. V. (2000). *New directions in Biology teacher education.* Available at: http://intl.concord .org/cbe/papers/vander_borght.html

Chamany, K., Allen, D. & Tanner, K. (2008). *Making biology learning relevant to students: Integrating people, history, and context into College Biology Teaching.* Available at: http://www.lifescied .org/cgi/content/full/7/3/267

Collins, A. & Halverson, R. (2009). *Rethinking education in the age of technology: The digital revolution and schools.* New York: Teachers College Press .

Daniel, E. G. S. (1996). Once upon a pond. *The Science Teacher, 63*(4), 20–22.

Daniel, E. G. S.& Rohaida Mohd Saat. (2001). Elemental education. *The Science Teacher, 68*(9), 9.

Daniel, E. G. S. (2005). Paddy fields, cyber cafes and science teachers: Urban and rural primary science teaching in Malaysia. *Electronic Journal of Literacy through Science, 4*(11).

European Molecular Biology Organisation -EMBO, (2007). *New biology for new curricula.* 6th EMBO International Workshop on Science Education 17–19 May 2007 | Heidelberg | Germany.

Foong, C.C. & Daniel, E.G.S. (2010). *Instructional Support for Argumentation in the Science Classroom.* . Paper presented at the Taylor's 5th Teaching and Learning Conference 2010: Learning Beyond Tomorrow: An Evolutionary Process, Taylor's University, Malaysia.

Gibson, T. L., Koontz, D. A. & Hende, M. V. D. (2010). *The digital generation: teaching to a population that speaks an entirely new language.* Available at: http://david.koontz.name/ digital/Presentation_files/THE_DIGITAL_GENERATION.pdf

Grimme, L.H. (2000). The Necessity to direct Trends into Biology Education and Training at the Tertiary Level. Available at: http://www.intl.concord.org/cbe/pdf/grimme.pdf

Hammond, C., Karlin, D. & Thimonier, J. (2010). Creative research science experiences for high school students. *PLoS Biology 8*(9), 1–3.

Hernandez, D. (1981). *Strategies and methods for teaching/learning biology for general education*. An occasional paper,UNESCO.

Hopkin, K. (2010). *New frontiers in Biology*. Available at: http://www.hhmi.org/biointeractive/ genomics/overview.html

Huppert, J., Lomask, S. M. & Lazarowitz, R. (2002). Computer simulations in the high school: students' cognitive stages, science process skills and academic achievement in microbiology. *International Journal of Science Education, 24*(8), 803–821.

Kerfeld, C. A., Levis, M. & Perry, L.J. (2001). Teaching and Exploring the Social Implications of Twenty-first Century Molecular Biology in a Laboratory-Based General Education Course

Lee, S.S. & Daniel, E.G.S. (2010). *Linking theory to Design of the 'Living Cell Kit'*. Paper presented at the Taylor's 5th Teaching and Learning Conference 2010: Learning Beyond Tomorrow: An Evolutionary Process, Taylor's University, Malaysia.

Lord, T. R. (2001). 101 Reasons for using cooperative learning in Biology teaching. *The American Biology Teacher, 63*(1), 30–38.

Morse, M.P. (2010). Preparing biologists for the 21st Century. *American Institute of Biological Sciences.*

Musante, S. (2008). Critical conversations: The 2008 Biology education summit. *BioScience, 58*(8), 685–689. Available at: http://www.bioone.org/doi/full/10.1641/B580804

Nugraini, S. H., Koo Ah Choo & Hew Soon Him, 2009). *The proposed conceptual framework of e-audio visual biology for teaching and learning in Indonesian senior high schools*. Available at: http:// www.recsam.edu.my/cosmed/cosmed09/AbstractsFullPapers2009/.../S20.pdf

Page, G. & Reiss, M. (2010). *Biology education research*. Available at: http://www.prints.ioe.ac.uk/ 5869/1/Page_Reiss_JBE_Editorial.pdf

Samudi Raju, K. (2007). *Content knowledge and classroom dynamics of biology teachers*. Unpublished Masters Thesis, University of Malaya: KL

Sathiasivam, R. & Daniel, E. G. S. (2010). *'Theories- of-action' of primary science teachers on assessment literacy*. In proceedings of the Taylor's 5th Teaching and Learning Conference 2010: Learning Beyond Tomorrow: An Evolutionary Process, Taylor's University, Malaysia.

Soderberg, P. & Price, F. (2003). An examination of problem-based teaching and learning in population genetics and evolution using EVOLVE, a computer simulation. *International Journal of Science Education, 25*(1), 35–55.

Tanner, K. & Allen, D. (2004). Approaches to biology teaching and learning: Learning styles and the problem of instructional selection—Engaging all students in science courses. *Cell Biology Education, 3,* 197–201.

Ursu, D. (2010). *Biology Concepts and Connections Require Critical Thinking*. Available at: http://www.suite101.com/content/biology-concepts-and-connections-require-critical-thinking-a248407

van Eijck, M. & Roth, W-M. (2007). Improving science education for sustainable development. *PLoS Biology 5*(12), 2763–2769.

Walker, J. (2006). *Ashes to ashes, dust to dust, and dirt to dirt: Creative Biology*. Available at: http://hti.math.uh.edu/curriculum/units/2000/02/00.02.06.pdf

Wilmsen, T. A. & Bisseling, T. (2005). Biology by numbers—Introducing quantitation into life science education. *PLoS Biology 3*(1), 25–26.

Wong, K. M. (2007). Teaching biology in the 21st Century. *Science Matters@Bekerkely, 4*(27). Available at: http://sciencematters.berkeley.edu/archives/volume4/issue27/story1.php

Yager, R.E. (1983). *The Crisis in biology education*. Available at: http://www.cdbeta.uu.nl/ tdb/fulltext/1983-yager.pdf

Younès, T. (2000). *Biological education: Challenges of the 21st Century*. Available at: http://intl.concord.org/cbe/cbe_paper_index.html

Esther Daniel
Department of Mathematics and Science Education
Faculty of Education Building
University of Malaya, 50603 Kuala Lumpur, MALAYSIA
esther@um.edu.my

KOICHI MORIMOTO

33. ENHANCING ELEMENTARY BIOLOGY EDUCATION OF UNDERGRADUATE STUDENTS IN JAPANESE UNIVERSITIES THROUGH TEACHERS' TEACHING PROFICIENCIES

ABSTRACT

Lectures are generally the main strategy used to teach elementary science students in universities and are teacher-centered. This paper investigates the outcomes of learning in elementary science education when students are engaged in their own learning improvement of their academic performance. Some 123 undergraduate freshmen participated in this study. The elementary science lessons conducted included 3rd to 6th grade science topics. At the end of all the science lessons, a test was used to measure the students' performance and how well they were able to explain the contents taught. The high test score of participants showed participants were kept engaged in the learning through a diversity of methods used by the lecturer. Instructional methods were aimed at sustaining interest in the learning and it was observed that students were actively involved in their own learning. In addition, frequent interactions between students and the lecturer further helped ensure the lecturer was able to check students' ideas to give prompt replies to their queries. The elementary science lessons conducted were student-focused and as a result, the students became active learners and were able to acquire the biological knowledge. It is concluded that engaging students in their learning is an effective way to improve their academic performance.

KEYWORDS

Elementary Science, Engaging, Teaching Proficiencies, Biology

INTRODUCTION

It is recently reported that universities in Japan have been tasked to increase the academic levels of graduate education (Morimoto, 2009). For secondary education, passing the TIMSS and PISA are the desired outcomes of students. For higher education level, it is the Assessment of Higher Education Learning Outcomes (AHELO). However, more can be done to increase the teaching proficiency of elementary school teachers as it ultimately translates into improved student performance in elementary science in universities.

Mijung Kim and C. H. Diong (Eds.), Biology Education for Social and Sustainable Development, 311–316.
© 2012 Sense Publishers. All rights reserved.

According to Irie *et al.*, 2008, approximately 40–60% of the newly employed elementary school teachers did not have confidence in teaching certain topics and concepts in Biology. Among the topics identified were, "the birth of animals", "the observation of animals and the plants" and "dissection". Lectures were generally the main strategy used to teach elementary science students in universities. Students did not always listen to the lecturer's explanation, some slept during the lectures, and others found it the delivery too teacher-centered. Students' results had not improved despite an increase in the number of periods for science lessons. An enhancement of teaching capabilities was expected to lead to an improvement in students' academic performances in universities. Many proposals were made in response to the data collected (Yamazaki, 2004; Kawakami, 2009; Hashimoto, 2010). For example, lessons should include experiments and observations. More importantly, teachers should first and foremost engage students in their own learning and follow up with an evaluation of students' understanding. Students who were engaged were motivated to acquire the biology knowledge and the ability to inquire (Lee & Ursel, 2001). Other strategies such as teaching students problem-solving skills, and peer discussions may be employed later in the lessons.

However, there is limited literature on improvements in the teaching of Biology in the universities. This paper investigates the effects of engaging students in their own learning and improvements in academic performance in elementary science education in University.

METHOD

A total of 123 undergraduate freshmen participated in the study. The elementary science lessons that were conducted included 3rd to 6th grade science topics (see Appendix A) and student presentations. At the end of all the science lessons, a test was used to measure how well the students performed and how well they were able to explain the content taught. Most of the lessons were carried out the following manner: the lecturer presented study materials to the participants in every lesson and used a variety of strategies to keep participants engaged and motivated throughout the lessons. Students were later invited to participate and explain their answers to questions posed by the lecturer. Examples of the questions include "What are the names of these plants?", "Explain the development of human body." Participants could opt to reply the questions with biological drawings or writings, after which, the lecturer would explain his answers.

RESULTS AND DISCUSSION

Figure 1(a) illustrates how students were engaged in the science lessons and their learning outputs in the form of biological drawings. For example, the lecturer involved student participants in learning about insect body morphology by identifying the various parts of an insect. During the learning exercise to identify the anatomical parts of an insect, the students were not able to identify the thorax. It was noted that the lecturer pointed out the errors to the participants before he taught the definition of thorax as a body segment containing three pairs of legs.

Students were able to eventually identify the part of an insect correctly. The test score was high; 80% of students drew the insect body correctly in the final test.

Similarly, this instructional process was repeated for another science topic. The lecturer told the class: "Draw two muscles on the humerus bone of the human body" and students were invited to draw and show their answers before the lecturer explained his. Most students could not draw the structure precisely. (In order to move a muscle, the muscle must be inserted to another bone over the joint by the tendon.) Students did not draw the tendon and the end of the muscle where it was inserted before the joint. A video of the chicken's wingtip was screened in class to show that the movement of the wing tip is only possible with the tendon. Figure 1(b) shows a student's drawings before and after watching the video. In another science lesson, 35% (n=35) of the students could not draw the liver at the precise location and 28% drew it at the wrong place. Students were curious and motivated to learn when lecturer showed a T-shirt printed with human digestive organs on it. They were engaged in the lesson thereafter. At the end of the lessons, 93% of students were able to identify the location of the organs correctly in the test.

Students' engagement in the science lessons was also illustrated through biological writings (Table 1). For example, the lecturer taught student-participants to fill in the K-W-L (Know-Want to know-Learned) chart for the topic on the development of the human body, where K, W and L refer to what they already knew of a subject matter, what they want to find out in the lesson and what they have learnt at the end of the lesson respectively. The lecturer engaged students through videos from the Japanese Broadcasting Company, NHK, and biological photographs from elementary science textbooks. It was observed that the KWL chart was an effective way to assess and encourage learning as students were taught to reflect on their own learning using the chart.

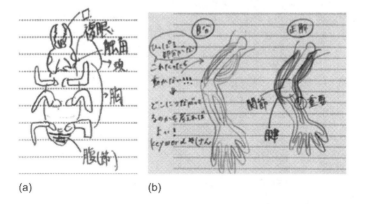

(a)   (b)

Figure 1. (a) A student's biological drawing of an insect to show its body parts, (b) A student's drawing of the wing and bone before and after watching an instructional video.

According to Bebbington (2005), advanced level students cannot recognize commonly found plants in their own country even though these were covered in the elementary and secondary school science curriculum. Student-participants in the study were also unable to identify them correctly. Results of the final test scores showed participants who scored at least 75% were able to identify the commonly found plants in Japan. For example, 75% of participants correctly identified *Vicia angustifolia* and 89%, *Oxalis corniculata*. However, there was no quantitative data surveyed before the study to compare how large the improvements in their scores were.

Table 1. *An example of a student's biological writing of what he knew (K) of human development before the science lesson, what he wanted (W) to find out from the lesson before writing down his answers, and what he had learnt (L) at the end of the lesson*

Know	Learned	Want to know
The umbilical cord.	The apoptosis.	The relationship between
The fetus has a tail and	The heart develops	cancer and the apoptosis.
webbed feet.	twisty.	The relationship between
The human development is	The ovoviviparity of a	evolution and tail of the fetus.
similar to sea urchin	fish.	
development.		

CONCLUSION

The high scores of student participants in the tests showed that participants were kept engaged during the instructional process through a variety of teaching methods that sustained their interests. Hence, the students were actively involved in their own learning. In addition, the frequent interaction between participants and the lecturer further helped ensure the lecturer was able to check students' ideas and understanding of science in order to give prompt replies. The elementary science lessons conducted were student-focused and as a result, the students became active learners and were able to acquire the biological knowledge. Thus, it is concluded that engaging students is an effective way to improve their academic performance. The next step would be to conduct a survey to determine the teaching proficiencies of lecturers and modify their teaching pedagogies so as to cater to the different learning needs of their students.

REFERENCE

Bebbington, A. (2005). The ability A-level of students to name plants, Journal of Biological Education, *39*(2), 62–67.

Linda E Lee, Samantha Ursel. 2001. Engaging Students in Their Own Learning. Education Canada, *40*(4), 12–13.

Kathy Ferrell (2007) May I go to the bathroom. *Science scope. 31*(1) 31–37

Koichi Morimoto, Hisako Tanahashi, Takeshi Nakai, Maki Shibuya and Hayato Akazawa. (2009). Nara University of Education Curriculum Framework, *Journal of Japan Association of Universitites of Educations, 27*, 207–216.

Kaoru I., R. Otake and Tatsushi K. (2008). Actual conditions of science instruction by newly employed elementary school teachers in regard to such matters as the utility of science, attitude toward inquiry, and confidence in science lessons. *Journal of research in science education, 48*(3). 13–24

Takahito Y. (2004). Practical problems of science teacher education. *Science education monthly, 53*(621), 4–6.

Tateo H. (2010) A training program for elementary school teachers who can find great pleasure in teaching science. *Science education monthly, 59*(697), 16–19.

Shogo K., (2009). Present situation and challenge for teacher training: here's a reason it doesn't and cannot change. *Science education monthly, 58*(678), 32–34.

APPENDIX A

3rd to 6th Grade Science topics taught in the study before the test were as follows:

I.   3rd grade science B: the insect body, the plant body, the sun and earth, 3rd grade science A: the electricity, the wind, the rubber, the magnet, the mass

II. 4th grade science B: the human body bone and muscle, the living things and season, the moon and stars, 4th grade science A: the battery, the metal and heat, the air and heat, the water its three states

III. Research programs presentation

IV. 5th grade science B: the plant germination, the animal birth, the river, the weather, 5th grade science A: the pendulum, the electromagnetic, the solution

V.   6th grade science B: the human body, the vascular bundle, the stratum, the moon and sun, 6th grade science A: the lever, the usage of electricity, the combustion, the acid and base

VI. Test

Koichi Morimoto
Nara University of Education
Takabatakecho Nara, Nara 6308528
Japan
morimoto@nara-edu.ac.jp

EMILIA FÄGERSTAM

34. TEACHERS' VIEWS ON THE RELATIONSHIP BETWEEN OUTDOOR ENVIRONMENTAL EDUCATION AND A SENSE OF PLACE

ABSTRACT

This paper addresses how Environmental Education Centre officers and high school science teachers in Sydney view the relationship between outdoor environmental education and students' attachment to a sense of place. This study also examines the EEC officers' and teachers' own associations of a sense of place. Semi-structured interviews with thirteen EEC officers and eight science high school teachers were conducted. Findings revealed that a sense of place can be viewed as familiarity with the local environment and as part of a broader social-ecological system. Outdoor environmental education was one factor in increasing students' sense of place. Encounters with nature were regarded as important in increasing the identity of being an Australian in a multicultural society with immigrant students around the world. In particular, it increases students' understanding of the social-ecological systems in which they are a part. This study suggests that outdoor environmental education improves students' sense of place and could further instil positive feelings for nature and develop accountability and responsibility towards sustainable living. The study is mainly descriptive and qualitative.

KEYWORDS

Environmental Education, Outdoor, Sustainability, Sense of Place, Responsibility

INTRODUCTION

Education for sustainable development is important in an era of globalisation when people move between different parts of the world and live in cities. To live more ecologically and be socially responsible might promote feelings of connectedness and attachment to nature and society (Gruenewald, 2003; Lugg, 2007), but place attachment or sense of place is seldom in focus in the literature concerning environmental or sustainability education. A place-attachment model which integrates developmental attachment theory and place theory is provided by Morgan (2010), whereby place attachment emerges from a child's explorative and pleasurable interactions with the environment. Outdoor education may thus, play a significant role in giving students the opportunity to encounter nature and thereby develop a relational ethical perspective important in education for sustainable development (Manteaw, 2101; Nicol, 2003; Sandell & Öhman, 20101).

In what way does schooling contribute to students' development of a sense of place for which they live? What does it mean to have a sense of place? These are not easy questions. This study, part of a PhD project in outdoor education involving both Sweden and Australia, aims at examining this and finding answers to how teachers view the relationship between outdoor environmental education and students' development of a sense of place.

A sense of place could be understood as "resulting from interconnected social, environmental and behavioural processes" (Shamai, 1991) and "a living ecological relationship between a person and a place " that includes, "physical, biological, social, cultural, and political factors with history and psychological state of the persons who share the location" (Kincheloe et al., 2006). According to Manteaw (2010), the essence of education for sustainable development is fundamentally about values, behaviours, attitudes, beliefs and life-styles, which without it becomes difficult to live and act in a sustainable way. Also, recent research in system ecology emphasizes the impossibility to divide ecological systems from social systems and the urgent need to find ways to develop and maintain social-ecological systems in a sustainable way (Berkes & Folke, 1998; Chapin *et al.*, 2009). Yet, the relation between outdoor education and environmental or sustainability education is fairly often discussed on a theoretical basis (e.g. Lugg, 2007; Nicol, 2003).

Education for sustainable development needs to consider the affective aspect of education as well as the cognitive outcomes. There are a few empirical studies examining effects from a student perspective (e.g. Bogner, 1998) but studies giving voice to teachers' views are rare. Teachers' understanding of how the development of a sense of place could be an aspect of outdoor environmental education has limited attention, even though the notion of a sense of place is receiving increased attention outside the field of geography and psychology.

OBJECTIVES

The purpose of this study is to examine high school science teachers' and environmental education centre (EEC) officers' views of the relevance of outdoor environmental education in relation to a sense of place in a multicultural context (Sydney, Australia). The research questions include: (1) What is the importance of a sense of place according to the participants? (2) How do the participants consider outdoor environmental education contributions to students' development of a sense of place? (3) What does a sense of place mean to these participants where outdoor education is important in their teachings?

METHOD

Twenty-one interviews with high school science teachers and EEC officers were conducted in the Greater Sydney region. The duration of each was typically around 60 minutes, with one lasting 120 minutes and another lasting 20 minutes. Interviews were semi-structured and audio recorded before being transcribed.

Design and Data Collection

Thirteen EEC officers (six men) were interviewed. Participants had different vocational backgrounds. For example, some are high school teachers in biology or environmental education while others have a degree in geography or biology. One officer was selected at each centre, except on one occasion when two officers from the same centre were interviewed. The interviews took place at the respective EECs. The majority of EECs participating in this study are run by the Department of Education and Training in New South Wales but three are run by non-government organisations. All were curriculum-orientated and programs ranged from Kindergarten to Year 12.

Eight high school teachers (four men) were interviewed at the schools where they worked. The schools include both government and non-government ones and are situated in different socio-economic areas in Sydney, with different closeness to natural environments. One was a girls' school but the others were co-educated schools. These experienced teachers taught science at all levels (Year 7 to 12). Most teachers visited EECs as fieldwork is mandatory in NSW curricula.

Data Analyses

Qualitative findings were based on an inductive thematic analysis which seeks to find themes and subthemes embedded in the data. The themes and subthemes are the product of a thorough reading and re-reading of the transcripts and field notes that make up the data (Bryman, 2008). The transcripts were read several times for the author to be familiar with the material, notes and codes written during the analyses. The codes were mainly descriptive but to some extent also interpretative (Miles & Huberman, 1994). Examples of codes were: local environment, part of the community, relation to nature, fear of nature, lack of knowledge, responsibility. Finally, the main themes built up from the three research questions were supplemented by several subthemes emerging during the analysis.

RESULTS

The results reported a sense of place was not easily defined but familiarity from two somewhat different aspects was discussed by a majority of the participants. The qualitative results were as below:

319

A Sense of Place - Familiarity with the Local Environment

Most of the participants discussed a sense of place from a student's perspective. From a geographical point of view, this was considered the most relevant method to develop the meaning of a sense of place in students. The importance of having students know their local environment was emphasized. The school and nearby nature were what they were familiar with or what they should become familiar with. This view can be broadened to include a larger geographical area as they grow older. Participants also emphasized it important that students developed a love of nearby nature by exploring and experiencing it in outdoor activities. There would be no further environmental responsibility without that love attachment.

A Sense of Place - Part of a Social-ecological System

Other participants viewed a sense of place to be more holistic: a community with both natural and cultural aspects (inter-related). It includes the physical place and the actions and participation as citizens in the community. Without real life experiences provided during outdoor education, there might be misconceptions about the relations between the natural and social world.

However, participants reported the belonging to both a cultural and a natural world was not unproblematic. One participant identified himself as belonging to a part of the land millions of years old but whose culture did not always behave responsibly to ecological needs and found this insight problematic. He drew parallels to the Aborigines' historical sense of place for the land and their way of living on the land. He concluded the current way of living does not lend itself to a more sustainable way of living. It would seem a sense of place is contradictory to this participant.

Why Outdoor Environmental Education is Considered Important

In this study, participants highlighted the love for nature and environment concern. They reported that learning to live in a community, connectedness to history and other cultures, living sustainably are other important factors. In particular, all participants agreed that students' first hand experiences and immersion in the situations were regarded as highly important. Hence, experience was considered the first step to understanding and cultivating an interest on a personal level. Many educators also emphasized the benefits associated with the outdoor environment for multicultural students. It is the possibility of touching, smelling and visualizing while explaining concepts that would be helpful. They believe that by using the natural and cultural environment outdoors, a personalised understanding of academic concepts, as well as a more holistic view of belonging to a natural world would occur.

One participant reported that she would adapt the outdoor education program to be more emotionally driven than knowledge driven to get their students to appreciate the natural environment.

How Does Outdoor Environmental Education Contribute to Students' Development of a Sense of Place?

(i) Participation in Community Life Creates a Sense of Belonging to a City and a Country Many EEC officers expressed a similar opinion that many students, especially those from Sydney's poorer western suburbs, were excluded from natural areas but also inner city areas. One urban EEC officer reported many students' excitement and surprise when they visited tourist spots such as The Rocks with Sydney Harbour Bridge. School trips and camps gave students the possibility to experience environments they may never experience otherwise. Out-of-school experiences were one way to broaden their students' world and change their ideas of what they always thought Sydney was. Participants also wanted the students to realize that visiting those places was something they could do themselves too.

From the teachers' point of view, experiences of less familiar parts of the city could be seen as encouraging the students to participate in and enjoy community life other than their usual practice. It leads them to begin thinking of what an environment is and to realize that the environment is also the place where they live every day. By incorporating local community into outdoor teaching, students develop a sense of where they live and go to school, how they fit in with their local community and how they and their parents interact with others. Students are building their own sense of place but need support from parents and teachers. The teacher is an important person in maintaining this. However, this scenario was reported to be uncommon. An urban EEC officer highlighted that many student immigrants lacked a sense of belonging to Australia and they did not always see the relevance of learning about Aboriginal and European history at the EEC. This participant encouraged the students to exchange their views of places where they feel at home to connect to Sydney and enhance their sense of belonging to the city.

(ii) Participation in Outdoors Creates a Sense of Belonging to a Natural World All participants agreed the natural outdoors brings feelings of affection such as joy and positivity that create a sense of place. Developing a sense of place by building a personal relation with nature was seen as one of the major benefits of outdoor education. By immersing students in nature, the teachers hoped to instill a love for nature. However, participants held a common view that students spend too much time indoors and are denied outdoor experiences because of their parents' anxiety, after school schedules and the lack of natural environments nearby.

(iii) Ecological Knowledge of the Place Needed To Develop a Sense of Place
The participants reported that ecological knowledge was considered important in developing a sense of place for students, without which it would be difficult to really understand the Australian nature. Many teachers stressed students' lack of knowledge of the unique flora and fauna in Australia and the fact that learning about animals is limited to television and other media. For instance, students think North American animals also live in the Australian bush. Giving students a one-on-one experience is an unusual experience even for students knowledgeable in Australian native species such as wallabies and koalas from books.

In particular, fear of nature and Australian animals were discussed by the EEC officers. They acknowledged the possible dangers from snake and spider bites but insisted that with knowledge and typical cautiousness during bushwalking, outdoor education was not something to be afraid of. In fact, it is a good opportunity to educate students on ecological content so that they get to enjoy the outdoor lessons safely. All agreed that students' fear for nature often decreased after a day in the bush and after experiencing that they could walk around safely.

What Does a Sense of Place Mean to the Participants where Outdoor Education is Important in their Teachings?

Some participants reported there are other desired outcomes of outdoor education. They wanted their students to develop the love for nature and a sense of responsibility and accountability towards the environment – it is education for sustainable development. For example, almost all participants highlighted that students need to learn to live without large gardens and pools that use huge volumes of water. Participants perceived that students need to know how to appreciate the environment and want to act responsibly; these attitudinal values can only come about after developing a love for nature and their sense of belonging towards it.

DISCUSSION

Qualitative findings from this study emphasized the importance of outdoor environmental education in many aspects. The experience with nature was not something to be taken for granted. In today's context, trips to nearby nature are not common and students are alien to nature and afraid of animals. Louv (2008) discusses in his book, "Last child in the woods", how children become more and more separated from first-hand experiences in nature in a mainly American context. He calls attention to what he called a nature-deficit disorder. Lack of free time, fear from parents and competition for time from multimedia are a few of the things he discusses as hindrances to developing relations with nature. This was also a common view held by participants regarding urban Sydney children. This knowledge and sense of belonging to the neighbourhood was considered important before learning complex global relations.

Participants concluded that students are in many ways denied experiences in natural and unfamiliar urban environments. This results in a lack of understanding of what it means to live in Australia both from an ecological and a cultural point of view. The uniqueness and vulnerability of the Australian flora and fauna, and the fragility of the ecosystems are not common knowledge to Australian students and this knowledge is considered important in the perspective of sustainable development. Ecological knowledge was also discussed as a part of a sense of belonging to a society and country from a multicultural point of view.

Sandell and Öhman (2010) discuss educational potentials of encounters with nature from a Swedish perspective. They suggested six potentials of encounters with nature as follows: experienced-based meaning of nature; a relational ethical perspective; the addition of a fourth perspective to sustainable development; human ecology in practice; sensing the quality of a simple life; and democracy, dynamic and dwelling. The findings from this study reveal that all but the fifth aspect was something considered important. Meaningful experiences and relations are discussed above and the fourth aspect of sustainable development is also somewhat relational, "a comprehensive existential perspective that originates from aesthetic and emotional relations with nature – the direct encounter with nature". Feeling of love, joy and wonder was something that the participants wanted to inculcate in students. A further sustainable stewardship was seen as a logical consequence. This would be difficult to interpret and evaluate but research about life experiences (Chawla, 2006; Chawla and Cushing, 2007) reveal that childhood experiences do have an impact on future attitudes and behaviour.

Outdoor environmental education was seen as important in helping students develop a sense of place or belonging. Sandell and Öhman (2010) discuss the linkage between a sense of place and sustainable development in their sixth perspective: democracy, identity and dwelling. Lugg (2007) also stresses the importance of outdoor learning when it comes to connectedness and relational and experiential ways to promote sustainable literate citizens in a context of higher education.

CONCLUSION

Many participants reported that their students appreciated outdoor lessons at EEC and around the schools. However, they revealed that outdoor education in the multicultural city of Sydney was not always easy. A major factor was students' fear of animals and the unfamiliar surroundings. A majority also discussed their lack of experience with nature. They suggested this lack of experience with nature led to students' fearfulness.

More importantly, a sense of place is a concept that is not easily defined. There were many different associations about its meaning. In this study, there were two different views; a sense of place as a particular local environment or a sense of place as a wider social-ecological system. This was the case from both the participants' view and that of the students. However, all participants agreed that outdoor environmental education helped students develop a sense of place.

First-hand experiences were considered very important. Students had the opportunity to know places outside the suburb where they lived, visit places such as the city, and that gave them an opportunity to feel more connected to the local region. By taking students out into nature, it was hoped that these experiences would lead to a sense of place and stewardship in the long term.

REFERENCES

Agarwal, P. (2005). *Operationalising 'sense of place' as a cognitive operator for semantics in place-based antologies.*

Berkes, F., & Folke, C. (Eds.) (1998). *Linking social and ecological systems: management practices and social mechanisms for building resilience.* Cambridge University Press: Cambridge.

Bryman, A. (2008). *Social research methods.* Oxford: Oxford University Press.

Chapin, S., Carpenter, S., Kofinas, G., Folke., Abel, N., Clark, W., Olsson, P., Stafford Smith, M., Walker, B., Young, O., Berkes, F., Biggs, R., Grove, M., Naylor, R., Pinkerton, E., Steffen, W., & Swanson, F. (2009). Ecosystem stewardship: sustainability strategies for a rapidly changing planet. *Trends in Ecology and Evolution, 25*(4), 241–249.

Chawla, L. (2006). Research methods to investigate significant life experiences: review and recommendations. *Environmental Education research, 12*(3–4), 359–374.

Chawla, L., & Flanders Cushing, D. (2007). Education for strategic environmental behaviour. *Environmental Education research, 13*(4), 437–452.

Gruenewald, D. (2003). The best of both worlds: A critical pedagogy of place. *Educational Researcher, 32*(4), 3–12.

Kincheloe, J., Mcinley, E., Lim, M., & Calabrese Barton, A. (2006). Forum: a conversation on sense of place' in science learning. *Cultural Studies of Science Education, 1*, 143–160.

Lugg, A. (2007). Developing sustainability-literate citizens through outdoor learning: Possibilities for outdoor education in higher education. *Journal of Adventure Education and Outdoor Learning, 7*(2), 97–112.

Louv, R. (2008). *Last child in the woods- saving our children from nature-deficit disorder.* Chapel Hill, North Carolina: Algonquin Books of Chapel Hill.

Manteaw, B. (2010). Education in global environmental politics: why the discourse of education for sustainable development needs attention. *International Journal of Environment and Sustainable Development, 9*(1/2/3), 74–89.

Miles, M., & Huberman, M. (1994). *Qualitative data analysis.* Thousand Oaks, California: SAGE Publications Inc.

Morgan, P. (2010). Towards a developmental theory of place attachment. *Journal of Environmental Psychology. 30*, 11–22.

Nicol, R. (2003). Outdoor education: research topic or universal value? Part three. *Journal of Adventure education and Outdoor Learning. 3*(1), 11–28.

Sandell, K., & Öhman, J. (2010). Educational potentials of encounters with nature: reflections from a Swedish outdoor perspective. *Environmental Education Research, 16*(1), 113–132.

Tranter, P., & Malone, K. (2008). Out of bounds. Insights from Australian children to support sustainable cities. *Encounter: Education for Meaning and Social Justice, 21*(4), 20–26.

Emilia Fägerstam
Department of Behavioural Sciences and Learning, Linkoping University
581 83 Linkoping, Sweden and Department of Education
Macquarie University, NSW 2109, Australia
emilia.fagerstam@liu.se

MYRNA PAEZ-QUINTO

35. WHAT MAKES A SCIENCE TEACHER
EXCELLENT: BELIEFS

ABSTRACT

This research is a preliminary model/theory building based on Pandit's process of building grounded theory from case studies and is qualitative in nature. The purpose of the study is to describe, analyze, and categorize what makes an excellent science teacher. Science teachers who were recipients of Teaching Excellence Award in Biology, Chemistry and Physics (in the Philippines) were selected using purposive sampling. Multiple methods of data collection were used, including, interviews, classroom observations and students' evaluation. The analysis showed that an excellent science teacher typically believes in: (i) using a variety of approaches to stimulate learning, (ii) promoting student-centered teaching, (iii) developing knowledge of the subject matter, (iv) undertaking lifelong learning and pursuing quality education, and (v) being a reflective practitioner and an active learner. It is concluded the beliefs of an excellent science teacher influence how they approach their teaching and the process of instruction, thereby positively affecting the quality of education.

KEYWORDS

Beliefs on Teaching, Excellent Science Teachers, Reflective Practitioners

INTRODUCTION

Science education is of great importance because of its links to technology and industry which are widely accepted as key components for national development (Batomalaque, 2009). In this connection, the low achievement levels of 13-year old Filipino students in mathematics and science in spite of various changes made by educators and the government is proving to be worrisome has repeatedly been noted (Ogena and Ibe, 1998). The poor performance at the Second International Science Study (SISS) and the Third International Mathematics and Science Study (TIMSS) surfaces a problem in the educational system.

The Republic Act 774 recognizes that the teacher is the key to effective teaching-learning process. Several studies have shown the effects of excellent classroom teaching performance of teacher on student achievements (Salandanan, 2001). Cruickshank and Haefel (2001) stressed that only effective teachers bring about high student achievement. What are the strategies to become effective?

Mijung Kim and C. H. Diong (Eds.), Biology Education for Social and Sustainable Development, 325–330.
© 2012 Sense Publishers. All rights reserved.

What influenced effective teaching in their classroom practices? It has been widely reported that teachers' beliefs greatly influence their classrooms practices. The relationship between teachers' beliefs and instructional practices has attracted increasing attention in science education in recent years. Cho (2008) conducted a study based on the assumptions that teachers are highly influenced by their beliefs. Beliefs determine how teachers approach their teachings and influence the instruction process (Hampton, 1994) and the way they interact with their students (Pohan and Aguilar, 2001). Thus, it is necessary to understand the beliefs and principles effective science teachers embrace (Richard 1996).

The purpose of this study is to investigate the beliefs of an excellent effective science teacher. Data collected were used to formulate a preliminary model/theory of the beliefs of excellent science teachers. The study adopted the process of grounded theory. The process involved five analytic phases of grounded theory building (not strictly sequential): research design, data collection, data ordering, data analysis, and literature comparison (Pandit 1996). Details of the nine phases are shown in Fig 1.

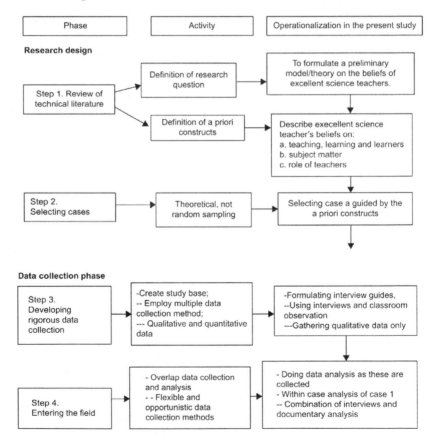

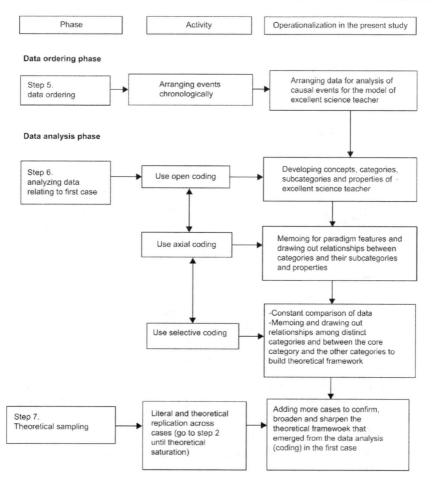

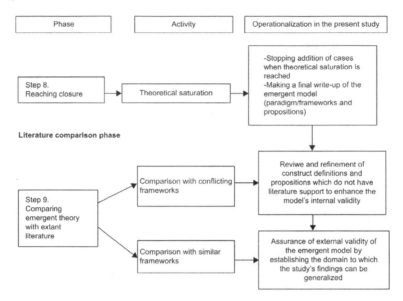

Figure 1. Paradigm of the process employed in this study based on Pandit's (1996) Grounded Theory Approach.

RESULTS AND DISCUSSION

The qualitative interpretation of the beliefs of excellent science teachers in these three areas are presented as follows: (i) teaching, learning and learners, (ii) subject matter, and (iii) role of the teacher.

Beliefs on Teaching, Learning and Learners

Excellent teachers believe in teaching and learning by: (i) using different approaches to promote and generate meaningful learning, (ii) facilitating learning, and (iii) employing student-centered teaching approaches. Excellent science teachers believe there are different approaches that generate learning which tap on the activation of their practical knowledge. They also believe there are different approaches that promote meaningful learning among the students such as authentic learning, knowledge application and knowledge development. Similarly, approaches to facilitate learning meant students are kept engaged in the learning process and a variety of pedagogies are necessary to conduct a learning activity. Teaching should be student-centered and this can be achieved through adaptive teaching with a focus on the development of students' capacity.

Beliefs on the Subject Matter

Excellent teachers believe in developing the knowledge of the subject matter. Hence, they believe in using different techniques to promote conceptual understanding and knowledge of the subject matter in learners. Promoting conceptual understanding involves the use of technology and adapting appropriate instructional materials.

Beliefs on Teacher's Role

Excellent teachers believe in promoting lifelong learning. They believe in pursuing quality education themselves and in providing quality education to their students. Excellent science teachers are reflective practitioner and active learners. Figure 2 illustrates the "Beliefs of Excellent Science Teachers".

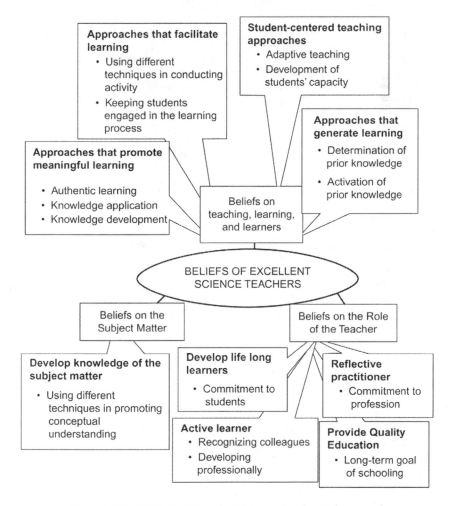

Figure 2. The "Beliefs of Excellent Science Teachers" framework.

CONCLUSION

Based on the findings, excellent science teachers believe in using different approaches to generate and promote meaningful learning, facilitating learning to promote student-centered teaching, developing knowledge of the subject matter, promoting lifelong learning and quality education, and are reflective practitioners and active learners. It is concluded the beliefs of an excellent science teacher influence how they approach their teaching and the process of instruction, thereby positively affecting the quality of education.

REFERENCES

Baiocco, S. A., & DeWaters, J. N., (1998). Successful College Teaching- Problem Solving Strategies of Distinguished Professors. A Viacom Company, USA

Balsicas, N., (2005). Teaching Practices of the National Science Teacher Awardees. Unpublished Dissertation. University of the Philippines, Quezon City. M

Blair, T. R. (1998). Emerging Patterns of Teaching. Merill Publishing Company, London.

Batomalaque, www.criced.tsukuba.ac.jp/pdf/09

Borgatti. S. (2005). Introduction to grounded theory. RetrievedDecember, 2007, from http://www .analytictech.com

Charmaz, K. (2003). Grounded theory: Objectivist and constructivist methods.

In N. Denzin & Y. Lincoln (Eds.), Strategies of qualitative inquiry (p.265). London: Sage

Corbin, J., & Strauss, A. (1990). Grounded theory research: Procedures, canons, and evaluative criteria. Qualitative Sociology, *13*, 3–21.

Cruickshank, R, Bainer, S. L. & K. Metcalf (1992). The Act of Teaching. Mcgraw- Hill College. Boston.

Easterby-Smith, M., Thorpe, R., & Lowe, A. (1991). Management research: An introduction. London: Sage.

Eisenhardt, K. M. (1989). Building theories from case study research. Academy of Management Review, *14*, 532–550

Glaser, B. & Strauss A. (1967) The discovery of grounded theory: strategies for qualitative research. Chicago: Aldine.

Pandit, N. R. (1996). The creation of a theory. A recent application of the grounded theory method. The Qualitative Report, 2(4). Retrieved September 11, 2007, from http://www.nova.edu.sss/QR/QR2-4/pandit.htmlSalandanan, G. (2000). Stauss, A., & Corbin, J. (1990). Basics of qualitative research: Grounded theory procedures and techniques. Newbury Park, CA:Sage

Wiles, J. & Bondi, J., (1989). Curriculum Development. McMillan Publishing Co. USA

Yin, R. (1989). Case study research: Design and Methods. London:Sage

Myrna Paez-Quinto
Department of Biological Sciences
Far Eastern University, Manila Philippines
myrnazaldy2003@yahoo.com

KSENIYA FOMICHOVA AND FUTABA KAZAMA

36. A COMPARISON OF LIFE SCIENCE AND ENVIRONMENTAL EDUCATION IN JAPAN AND UKRAINE: A NEED TO IMPROVE THE SCIENCE CURRICULUM OF TWO COUNTRIES

ABSTRACT

The study examines and compares the Science Education System, Life Science and Environmental Education System (LSEE) in Japan and Ukraine secondary schools (SS). It analyzes national standards for LSEE curriculum in these two countries and other selected states from grade 7 to 12 to determine which of Japan or Ukraine is closer to approaching the international standards of developed countries. In addition, the study aims to identify themes that might be proposed for introduction into Japan's and Ukraine's curriculum or as sources of social education. Japan and Ukraine were chosen for the comparison as Japanese science education has recently been criticized as superficial, but its social education recognized as developed. In Ukraine, it is the opposite. Results show all Japanese and Ukrainian students acquire basic knowledge in LSEE from the SS curriculum. However, the yearly instructional time in science in Japan is 2 to 4.5 times less than in Ukraine. Compared to England and the USA, it is 25% lower in grade 8 and 5.5% lower than the international average. Japan is the country with the least science topics in grade 8 curriculum, and has the lowest average percentage of students taught TIMSS science topics in Biology and Earth Science, as compared to developed countries. This is even lower than the international average. Thematic analysis of curriculum showed that Ukrainian students are prescribed to learn 68 topics in LSEE while Japanese students are prescribed to learn from 34 to 44 topics. However, in Japan, there is more life science and environmental TV programmes available to school students than in Ukraine. A major revision of science curriculum is in progress in Japan to increase topics and instructional time in science. Themes that are not included into Japanese and Ukrainian curriculum according to the study might be recommended to be taught in schools or used as resources for social education.

KEYWORDS

Biology Education, Environmental Education, Curriculum, Social Education, Lifelong Learning

Mijung Kim and C. H. Diong (Eds.), Biology Education for Social and Sustainable Development, 331–342.

INTRODUCTION

Introduced by the United Nations (UN), Science and Environmental education are the keyconcepts themes of the Decade of Education for Sustainable Development (DESD) (UN DESD 2009, UNESCO 2010). Although DESD was proclaimed in 2002, the question of integrating environmental science education into existing secondary school subjects or as a subject on its own has been discussed for a few decades (Hungerford & Peyton 1994). The current practice in schools is to teach it under the subject of Biology (Life Science). Education in Life Science is of special importance as governments and institutions have set up high goals to ensure standards of environmental protection (Carey 1998). However, Life Science and Environmental Education (LSEE) should not be restricted only to school matter. There should be another significant source of science knowledge for a pupil – social education for lifelong learning (Abell & Lederman 2007, UN DESD 2009). Thus, the study analyses LSEE system from two angles: national standards for school curriculum and knowledge that is available from a source of social education (television). The research covers grades 7–12 of Japanese and Ukrainian secondary school (SS), compulsory subjects and topics and aimed to determine whether Japan or Ukraine is closer to approaching the international standards of developed countries. In addition, the study aims to identify themes suitable for introduction into Japan's and Ukraine's curriculum or as sources of social education.

RESEARCH OBJECTIVES AND METHODS

Overall objective of the research was to analyze and compare the minimum range of topics in LSEE that every Japanese or Ukrainian student had to learn by standards set by the Ministry of Education, and the information students were able to obtain from a basic source of social education (television). The instructional time, the prescribed and taught topics and the teaching issues in LSEE, termed under the Biology curriculum in Ukrainian SS and General Science, A, B in Japan SS, were studied. A database of compulsory LSEE topics was created and analysed. Data was compared with education statistics of developed countries such as England, Italy and the USA, and also with the international average. LSEE programmes available in Japan and Ukraine for students, their themes and the percentage of time devoted to the total broadcasting time were noted.

RESULTS AND DISCUSSION

Differences in the Science Education System and LSEE in Japanese and Ukrainian SS

Table 1 presents similar and different characteristics of science education in Japanese and Ukrainian SS. Both education systems are similar with governments standardizing and centralizing science curricula. In both countries SS is classified into Lower SS (no streaming) and Upper SS (streaming and specialization of subjects); all science textbooks are approved by the government and a degree from a teacher education program or certification exam complete with a teaching mentoring or induction program is required to be a SS teacher. However, several significant differences are reported in Table 1. For example, Ukraine shows a 12-year education system that is free-of-charge for its students and all subject curricula is compulsory, as compared to a 9-year system and optional subject curriculum in Japan. Japan's school education system does not separate Science into subjects in Lower Secondary, as opposed to Ukraine where learning of Biology starts from grade 7. Japanese LSEE curriculum does not include a detailed classification of living things. Ukrainian national standards for LSEE subjects include such classification, but they are more outdated and have less emphasis on experiments.

Compulsory LSEE national curriculum for Japanese and Ukrainian secondary school were combined in a database and analyzed. The total number of themes was 74. Table 2 shows an example of thematic analysis for LSEE curriculum taught in grades 7 and 8. For example, both countries include themes such as the structure and life cycle of plants, plant cells and plants' relation to the environment in their LSEE curriculum. However, themes such as internal structure of stems and roots, organs and tissues of plants and their functions and algae are not included in Japan's LSEE curriculum, in contrast to the Ukraine curriculum.

It was determined that by national standards for lower and upper SS that Japanese students have to learn 34science topics if they choose "General Science A" in upper SS and 39 topics— if "B". Five more topics are prescribed for study in elementary school. Therefore, the total number of topics (including those that are a part of grades 5 and 6 curriculum) is 39 (if students choose "A") or 44, if "B". From the 74 science topics Ukrainian students have to learn 68. Of the 6 topics not in the prescribed Ukrainian curriculum, 5 dealt with present environmental problems and issues, such as: "Global Warming", "Impact of the Introduced Species", "Causes and Consequences of Greenhouse Effect", "Sustainable Society, its Importance and Awareness"; "Destruction of Tropical Rain Forests".

International Data of Life and Earth Science Curricula in Grade 8

Table 3 presents quantity of life and environmental science topics in the Intended Curriculum (grade 8) in Japan and Ukraine in comparison with selected developed countries, using data from the International Association for the Evaluation of Educational Achievement: Trends in International Mathematics and Science Study at the Fourth and Eighth Grades (TIMSS) (2007). It states the number of topics prescribed for studying in life science and environmental education in Japan and Ukraine is fewer than in other developed countries such as England, Italy and the USA. Ukraine has a higher percentage of students who were taught TIMSS topics in Biology and Earth Science than Japan.

Table 4 shows the intended and taught TIMSS topics in Japan, Ukraine and selected developed countries. TIMSS topics such as common infectious diseases, preventive medicinal methods are some topics not included in students' learning in Japan but are taught in Ukraine. Furthermore, results show Earth science environmental topics such as environmental concerns, supply and demand of freshwater concerns are also not taught in Japan while students learnt these in

Ukraine. Table 1 in Appendix 1 shows an example of an identical theme in both LSEE curricula in Japan and Ukraine SS in Grade 7. Instructional time (hours) and content taught are however different. Table 2 in Appendix1 shows the competency and confidence of teachers teaching TIMSS topics in LSEE in Japan and Ukraine and other countries.

Analysis of Life Science and Environmental Television Programmes as a Source of Social Education in Japan and Ukraine

Results showed that from October to November 2008, 146 hours of life science and environmental television programmes featured four main themes: Eco-life (including ecotourism), Animals, Life and Environmental Science, Safety of Food and Drinking Water, Health were broadcast by 6 of Japanese television channels (3 national and 3 private). Eco-life was shown only in Japan while only 81 hours of the other three themes were shown in Ukraine. In addition, 37 hours of airtime in Ukraine concerns the last theme. The airtime for programmes devoted to the other three themes was 1.8 to 3.2 times fewer than Japan. Japan's television channels devote approximately 8% of their total broadcasting time to life science and environmental programmes, four times more than in Ukraine. On the other hand, in Ukraine, there are more programmes on the theme "Safety of Food and Drinking Water, and Health" at 2.08%, compared to 1.26% in Japan.

Table 1. Comparison of the science education system and the LSEE system in Japan and Ukraine SS[1,2,3,4]

	Science Education System Differences	
Characteristic	*Japan*	*Ukraine*
1. Yearly system	6-3-3 years	3(4)-5-2 years is being changed into 6-3-3 years (2002)
2. Free of charge and required years	Free of charge – 9; required – 9	Free of charge – 12; required – 9
3. School types	Public and private	Public
	General and "Super Science High Schools" starting from the 10th year	General and specialized schools starting from the 1st, 4th, 7th year
	Cram schools	Free courses provided after lessons by school teachers (lower and upper SS); courses for charge provided by universities (upper SS)
4. Subjects for choice	Yes (starting from the 10th year)	No (all subjects are compulsory), Upper SS: several streams
5. Subjects of lower SS	Course "General Science"	"Physics", "Biology", "Chemistry", "Geography"
6. Subjects of upper SS	"Science A or B" + 1 compulsory (from 4: "Physics", "Chemistry", "Biology", "Earth Science", I) + 1 not compulsory (from 4, II)	Subjects of lower SS + "Astronomy", "Ecology", "Computer Science"

7. Current school reforms	Curricular reform (2002) – more emphasis on science education	According to the global standards (from 10 to 12 years, started 2002)
8. Curriculum for students with different levels of ability	One curriculum for all students with no grouping	Different curricula for different groups of students according to the ability level
9. Current requirements to be a secondary school science teacher	No requirement to have a degree in a certain subject	A degree in the subject the teacher is teaching; e.g. – a biologist cannot teach "Chemistry", etc.
10. Teaching approach	b) observing natural phenomena and describing what is seen	
	A lot of emphasis	Some emphasis
	c) providing explanations about what is being studied	
	A lot of emphasis	Some emphasis
	d) designing and planning experiments or investigations	
	A lot of emphasis	Very little emphasis
11. Instructional time in SS per year, h.	Until 2009:105 (7); 105 (8); 80 (9); 2010: 105 (7); 140(8);105(9);70(10);105(11); 105(12)	210 (7); 210 (8); 245 (9); 209–489 (10); 226–437 (11); 245–437 (12)

LSEE System Differences (Grades 7 – 12)		
12. Curriculum	Japan	Ukraine
*Separate subject "Biology" in lower SS**	No	Yes
Separate subject "Biology" in upper SS	Yes	Yes
*Separate subject "Ecology" in lower and (or) upper SS**	No	Yes
Possibility of choosing the field as a main course in upper SS	Yes	Yes
*Possibility of not studying the field in upper SS**	Yes	No

335

Outdoor school environmental activities provided by the curriculum	Yes		Yes
Appropriate introduction of themes covering recent environmental problems or achievements of science and technology into educational programs	Yes		No
Detailed classification of living things and studying its ranks separately*	No		Yes

*denotes differences between Japan and Ukraine in LSEE; references: 1 – Ishikida (2005), 2 – Martin *at el*. (2008a), 3 – MEXT (2010), 4 – Ministry of Education and Science of Ukraine (2009)

Table 2. An example of thematic analysis of LSEE curriculum in Japanese and Ukrainian SS[5,6,7]

Country	Japan		Ukraine	
	Students intended to be taught topic	*Grade at which the topic is intended to be taught*	*Students intended to be taught topic*	*Grade at which the topic is intended to be taught*
Biology topics taught Structure and life cycle of plants	In curriculum	7	In curriculum	7
Cells of plants	In curriculum	7, 8	In curriculum	7
Organs, tissues of plants, their functions*	Not included	Not applicable	In curriculum	7
Symbiotic relationships between certain plants	In curriculum	7	In curriculum	7

Internal structure of sterns and roots*	Not included	Not applicable	In curriculum	7
Plants' relations to the environment, seasonal changes in growth	In curriculum	7	In curriculum	7
Reproduction and development of plants, mechanism, types	In curriculum	7, 9	In curriculum	7
Structure, functions and variety of flowers, sterns and roots	In curriculum	7	In curriculum	7
Spore plants, their structure,	In curriculum	7	In curriculum	7
life cycle, environment	Not included	Not applicable	In curriculum	7
Algae: classification, structure, life cycle, variety, value in nature and human life; adaptations to environment*				

*denotes differences between Japan and Ukraine in thematic analysis of the LSEE curriculum references: 5 – MEXT (2009a); 6 – MEXT (2009b); 7 – Ministry of Education and Science of Ukraine (2010)

Table 3. Summary of TIMSS topics in the Intended Curriculum (Grade 8) in Japan, Ukraine and selected developed countries[8]

Country		Japan	Ukraine	England	Italy	USA	International average
Number of Science Topics in the Intended Curriculum	*Biology (Highest: 14)*	8	9	13	14	14	11
	Earth Science Environmental (Highest: 4)	1	4	2	4	3	
Average Students Taught TIMSS Topics (%)	*Biology*	32	69	85	89	84	66
	Earth Science	44	95	67	71	81	57

reference: 8 – Martin *at el.* (2008b)

Table 4. Intended and taught TIMSS (mostly taught during or before the year of assessment topics (Grade 8) (Background data on intended curriculum provided by national research coordinator[9])

Country Biology topics taught	Japan Students intended to be taught topic	Grade at which the topic is intended to be taught	Percent-age of students taught the topic (%)	Ukraine Students intended to be taught topic	Grade at which the topic is intended to be taught	Percent-age of students taught the topic (%)	International Average Students intended to be taught topic	Grade at which the topic is intended to be taught	Percent-age of students taught the topic (%)
Trends in human population and its effect on the environment	Not included	-	4	Not included	9, 11	40	-	-	48
Life cycles of organisms, including humans, plants, birds, insects	In curriculum	3, 12	36	In curriculum	6–7,9,11	87	-	-	68
Impact of natural hazards on humans, wild life and the environment	In curriculum	6,9–12	8	In curriculum	6,7,9–12	39	-	-	51
Common infectious diseases*	Not included	-	5	In curriculum	6–7,9,11	99	-	-	60
Preventive medicine methods*	Not included	-	3	In curriculum	7–10	100	-	-	57
Cell structure and functions	Not included	9–12	15	Not included	10	95	-	-	83
Earth Science Topics (environmental) – Environmental Concerns*	Not included	9–12	13	In curriculum	1–8	99	-	-	63

| Earth resources | In curriculum | 6,9–12 | 5 | In curricul-um | 6–8 | 93 | - | - | 57 |
| Supply and demand of fresh water resources* | Not included | - | 8 | In curricul-um | 7 | 93 | - | - | 47 |

*denotes differences between Japan and Ukraine in thematic analysis of the LSEE curriculum reference: 9 – Martin *et al.*, (2008b)

CONCLUSIONS

The study shows all students in Japan and Ukraine acquired basic knowledge in LSEE from SS curriculum and outdoor activities. They are able to choose LSEE as a main subject or stream in grades 10–12. In Japanese upper SS, the subject 'General Science A' or 'B' is compulsory with 11 themes to read. Ukrainian students have to study Biology in both lower and upper SS. The yearly instructional time in teaching science in Japan is 2 to 4.5 times lesser than in Ukraine. Compared to England and the USA, it is 25% lower in grade 8 and 5.5% lower than the international average. Japan is the country teaching the least science topics in grade 8 curriculum and has the lowest average percentage of students taught TIMSS science topics in Biology and Earth science, as compared to Ukraine, England, the USA and Italy. This is even lower than the international average. Japanese SS teachers reported they were less confident teaching TIMSS topics in LSEE than their colleagues from Ukraine and other countries

Japanese and Ukrainian secondary school life and environmental science curricula were divided on 74 topics. The analysis included only topics compulsory for studying. Ukrainian students are prescribed to learn 68 topics in LSEE while Japanese students are prescribed to learn only between 34 to 44 topics, depending on whether they choose 'General Science A' or B. School teachers report that in most schools, only "A" is taught. In addition, a Biology topic taught to Ukrainian students is more complex, includes more instructional time and scientific terminology than the same topic taught to Japanese students. However, in Japan, there is more life science and environmental TV programmes available to school students than in Ukraine, with the exception of those pertaining to the theme "Safety of Food and Drinking Water, and Health".

The current Ukrainian LSEE is closer to international educational standards with regards to biological or life science topics prescribed in SS curriculum. However, it has less emphasis on experiments and is more outdated (themes on current environmental concerns and issues are not included in the curriculum). A major revision of science curricula is in progress in Japan to increase topics and instructional time in science. Themes not included in the Japanese and Ukrainian curriculum according to this study might be recommended for teaching in schools or as resources for social education, such as media programmes. Insufficient knowledge and skills in LSEE will affect a country's economy and social issues in environmental awareness and management, as well as in research and development

(R&D), especially in terms of the ability of the country's specialists to compete successfully with those in other countries.

REFERENCES

Abell, K. & Lederman, N. G. (2007). Handbook of research on science learning. Mahwah (NJ): Lawrence Erlbaum Associates, Inc., Publishers. USA;

Carey, J. (1998). We are now starting the century of biology. http://www.businessweek.com/1998/35/b3593020.htm;

Hungerford, H. R. & Peyton, R. B. (1994). Procedures for developing an environmental education curriculum (revised): a discussion guide for UNESCO training seminars on environmental education. http://unesdoc.unesco.org/images/0013001304/130454eo.pdf

Ishikida, M. Y. (2005). Japanese education in the 21st century, 6, 72–109. Linkoln (NE): iUniverse, USA;

Martin, M. O., Olson, J. F., Berger, D. R., Milne, D., & Stanco, G. M. (Eds.). (2008a). TIMSS 2007 encyclopedia: a guide to mathematics and science education around the world (Volumes 1, 2). TIMSS & PIRLS International Study Center, Lynch School of Education, Boston College., USA;

Martin, M. O., Mullis, I. V. S., Foy, P. collaboration with Olson, J. F., Erberber, E., Preuschof f, C.,Galia, J. (2008b). TIMSS 2007 international science report: findings from IEA's trends in international mathematics and science study at the four and eighth grades, 207–280. TIMSS & PIRLS International Study Center, Lynch School of Education, Boston College, USA;

Ministry of Education, Culture, Sports, Science & Technology of Japan (MEXT). (2010). Elementary and secondary education. Retrieved June 8, 2010, from http://www.mext.go.jp/english/shotou/index.htm;

Ministry of Education and Science of Ukraine. (2009). Zagalni vidomosti pro zagalnu serednyu osvitu v Ukraini [General information about common secondary school education in Ukraine]. Retrieved July 9, 2010, from http://www.mon.gov.ua (in Ukrainian);

Ministry of Education, Culture, Sports, Science & Technology of Japan (MEXT). (2009a). Koutou gakkou gakushuu shidou youryou kaisetsu, rika-hen risuu-hen [Explanation of Governmental guidelines for high school teaching, science volume and mathematics volume]. http://www.mext.go.jp/component/a_menu/education/micro_detail/__icsFiles/afieldfile/2010/01/29/1282000_6.pdf (in Japanese);

Ministry of Education, Culture, Sports, Science & Technology of Japan (MEXT). (2009b). Chuugakkou gakushuu shidou youryou kaisetsu, rika-hen [Explanation of Governmental guidelines for junior high school teaching, science volume]. http://www.mext.go.jp/component/a_menu/education/micro_detail/__icsFiles/afieldfile/2011/01/05/1234912_006.pdf; (in Japanese);

Ministry of Education and Science of Ukraine. (2010). Navchalni programy dlja zagalnoosvitnih navchalnyh zakladiv 5–12 klasy 12-richnoi shkoly: biologiya, geographiya [Course of study for grades 5–12 of 12 years secondary school: biology, geography]. Retrieved May 7, 2010, from http://www.mon.gov.ua/main.php?query =education/average/ new_pr (in Ukrainian);

The United Nations Decade of Education for Sustainable Development (UN DESD). (2009). About ESD (Education for Sustainable Development). http://www.desd.org/About%20ESD.htm;

UNESCO. (2010). Education for Sustainable Development. http://www.unesco.org/en/science-and-technology/sustainable-development/

APPENDIX 1

Table 1. An example of an identical theme in both LSEE curricula in Japan and Ukraine SS in Grade 7.[10,11]

Identical Theme (Japanese and Ukrainian Secondary School, Grade 7)	
Japan	*Ukraine*
Theme	
2. Reproduction and development of plants. Plants breeding by and without seeds	2. Reproduction and development of plants
Instructional Time, h.	
not prescribed, approximately 4; total for the subject per year (grade 7) – 24	10; total for the subject per year (grade 7) – 60 + 10 reserved
Contents	
Group of seed plants. Group of non-seed plants and their characteristics. Spore plants: ferns and mosses. Their structure, life cycle, value in nature and human life. Environment of spore plants	Agamogenesis, its kinds. Vegetative reproduction. Plants regeneration. Sexual breeding. Structure and variety of flowers. An inflorescence. Pollination, fertilization. A seed, a fruit, their structure. The influence of environmental conditions on the germination of a seed. Growth and development of plants. Seasonal changes in the life of plants
Demonstration of	
seed and non-seed plants	experiments showing the conditions of seeds' germination; living objects, herbarium samples
Laboratory and Practical Works	
observing spore plants (ferns and mosses) and finding distinctions between seed and non-seed plants	1) "Structure and variety of flowers"; 2) "Structure and variety of fruits"; 3) "Vegetative reproduction of plants"

reference: 10 – MEXT (2009b), 11- Ministry of Education and Science of Ukraine (2010)

Table 2. Summary of Students Whose Teachers Feel "Very Well" Prepared to Teach the TIMSS Science Topics (Grade 8) [12]

Country	Percentage of students whose teachers report feeling very well prepared to teach the TIMSS science topics, %					
	Biology and Earth Science (Environmental) Topics					
	Major Organs and Organ Systems in Humans and Other Organisms	*Cells and Their Functions, including Respiration and Photosynthesis as Cellular*	*Role of Variation and Adaptation in Survival/ Extinction of Species in a*	*Interaction with Living Organisms and the Physical Environment in the*	*Trends in Human Population and its Effects on the*	*Impact of Natural Hazards on Humans, Wildlife and the*

		Processes	Changing Environment	Ecosystem	Enviro-nment	Environ-ment
Japan	40	46	18	33	13	16
Ukraine	97	92	87	91	94	86
International Average	75	76	60	70	57	62

reference: 12 - Martin *et al.* (2008b)

Kseniya Fomichova and Futaba Kazama
Department of Eco-social System Engineering,
University of Yamanashi, 4-3-11, Takeda, Kofu,
Yamanashi, 400-8511, Japan.
white_kirin@ymail.com

YING-CHUN ZHANG AND YAN-TING TANG

37. A STUDY OF THE VALUE OF EDUCATION IN THE HISTORY OF BIOSCIENCE TO THE TRAINING OF STUDENTS' INNOVATIVE THINKING SKILLS

ABSTRACT

In view of the fact that the traditional classroom teaching does not give due attention to students' innovative thinking and ignores the scientific idea and the construction of scientific concepts, this study aims to discuss the intrinsic value of education in the history of bioscience in the high school biology curriculum. The study is of the view that the history of bioscience reflects the essential purpose of science education as well as conforming to the law of students' thinking development. It also has a great value in the training of students' ability to think innovatively, in providing the innovation development paradigm as well as demonstrating the process of innovative thinking, and in reflecting the nature of the innovative thinking.

KEYWORDS

Science Education, Bioscience, Scientific Thinking, Innovative Thinking

In this era of the knowledge economy, the worldwide competition in comprehensive national strength, after all, is the competition in talents especially the innovative talents. Who can train, attract and make the better use of the talents, especially the innovative talents, who will come to grasp the first resource of mastering the strategic initiatives and achieving the development goals in the fierce international competition. Establishing the innovative country is a natural choice for revitalizing the Chinese nation with the training of innovative talents as its core. Whether a country has enough science reserves or the innovation, its education is the foundation and the key lies in innovative education. Compared with the general education, the innovative education model emphasizes the formation of students' innovative ingenious and innovative spirit, especially the cultivation of creative thinking.

The training of innovative thinkers does not mean that once you have mastered a set of unique ways of thinking, you have the ability to think innovatively. The production of innovative thinking benefits from a long-term comprehensive blend of a variety of scientific thinking, such as critical thinking, intuitive thinking, and abstract thinking. The training of thinking abilities is subtle and long-term, and the outcomes are often not obvious in a short time. With an innovative plan in mind,

Mijung Kim and C. H. Diong (Eds.), Biology Education for Social and Sustainable Development, 343–352.

teachers should purposefully carry out the goals of cultivating innovative talents and innovative thinking when teaching his classes.

However, the current teaching practices seem to ignore or neglect pedagogical models that prepare or train students for innovative thinking. Consequently, science learning has become more of a process of acquiring knowledge than a process of learning by discovering science. Yang Zhen-ning once expressed his opinion about education in China as follows, "Chinese students are knowledgeable and are good at exams but not good at imagination and creation". How then can we train students in our classes to think innovatively? How can we guide and inspire our students to make flexible use of a variety of scientific thinking skills and processes? This is a problem demanding prompt solutions. The authors believe that the implicit educational content in the history of biological science is of great value to demonstrate how to fully develop students' innovative thinking.

THE EDUCATION IN THE HISTORY OF BIOSCIENCE REFLECTS THE ESSENTIAL PURPOSE OF SCIENTIFIC EDUCATION

In February, 2006 the State Council issued the "National Scientific Quality Action Plan (2006–2010–2020)" emphasizing the training of scientific quality of minors and regarded the project on scientific quality in minors as the first of four key projects. This was a major decision of strategic significance and profound historic significance, made by a central leader at a new stage of the development of China's socialist construction. The goal of educational sciences is not simply to impart knowledge, but with scientific knowledge as a carrier to establish a new ideology and culture, including new ways of thinking and values.

However, the traditional classroom teaching often pays attention to the accumulation of static, mature and not doubtful knowledge, neglects the exploration of scientific ideas and the construction of scientific concepts without paying due attention to the training of students' scientific thinking. John Dewey once moaned in the "Methods in Scientific Teaching" that "Too much emphasis on the content is the same with placing the carriage before the horse. In high school, scientific education should focus on drawing the horse to the right direction instead of filling the coach". The physicist Max von Laue once said: "It's the development of the thinking ability that counts instead of acquiring knowledge. Education is nothing more than a scientific thinking ability which is still in your mind to help you solve the new problems when all the other learned things have been forgotten". Obviously, the training of scientific thinking should and have been the basic aim of science education.

The Biology course is a major science curriculum in China's high school education. The biology classroom teaching not only imparts knowledge but also develop students' scientific thinking. By imparting to the students the scientific work and scientific processes that are involved in scientific discovery by other scientists, students can begin to appreciate how science come about through discovery and develop the scientific thinking process at the same time. The history of bioscience is all about the history of discovering science, the thinking process associated with discovering the truth by scientists, and the diversity and creativity of scientific methods. Students can get a strong sense of intellectual engagement of the scientific thinking processes with the teaching the history of bioscience. The history of bioscience lessons can provide a paradigm for students to use scientific thinking skills flexibly to help them develop innovative thinking skills.

EDUCATION IN THE HISTORY OF BIOSCIENCE CONFORMS TO THE LAW OF STUDENTS' THINKING DEVELOPMENT

Thinking is the indirect, general reflection of the objective realities in the human brain, with concept forming processes, judging and reasoning, and basic methods of making comparisons, generalizations, abstractions, analysis and synthesis, induction and deduction happening. Aristotle thought that in specific recollections, thinking can be equated to a series of concepts that reflects a connection among a series of continuing concepts. Scientific thinking is the indirect, general and active reflection of a conscious human brain to the intrinsic attributes and internal laws of the things in nature (including the objects, processes, phenomena, facts, etc) as well as the links and mutual relationship among things in the nature. Scientific thinking is based on the scientific theory and the scientizing of epistemological subject's thinking.

The authors believe that scientific thinking is an activity that lies in both the domains of scientific inquiry and the scientific cognition. The characteristics of this thinking is the rational thinking established on facts and logic, discarding the dross and selecting the essential as well as sifting out the true from the false of the abundant materials provided by sensibility so as to form the concept. The main tasks are to discover the intrinsic law, search the common characteristics, and infer and solve problems. Scientific thinking is characterized by rationality, logic, systems, and innovation, with the core of innovation in thinking, i.e. innovative thinking is the source of the generation of human intelligence. Innovative thinking is a thinking activity that, in the process of exploring the unknown, allows a person to fully exert the active function of knowledge, breaks the fixed logical channel, and explores the internal mechanisms of the movement of things with a flexible and original way, as well as from a multidimensional perspective. According to UNESCO statistics, in a list of 16 most important educational objectives listed by more than 500 educators in more than 50 developing countries, "the development of students' innovative thinking ranks the second position". The report shows the importance of training students to think innovatively.

The training for innovative thinking is a training of the mental faculty to for thinking development as well as to follow the law of ability training. The high school period is the crucial period of a student's life during which time students enter puberty and their cognitive structures are no longer as simple as children; instead their cognitive structures are able to reason and judge realities, events, and experiences and their emotional attitudes have acquired a certain level of development.

According to Jean Piaget's theory of genetic epistemology, the essence of cognition development is the construction and reconstruction of schema. Piaget stresses that the formation of knowledge is the result of continuous interactions between an individual and the outside world. The gradual development of human cognition, in fact, is that the schema gradually develops from a low level to a higher level, from a simple stage to a complex stage. In this process, the schema is influenced and promoted by the three factors, assimilation, accommodation, and balance. It can be understood this way: when an organism meets a stimulus, it always assimilates the stimulus according to the original schema, and if it succeeds, it gets the temporary balance, but if not, the individual accommodates by adjusting or reconstructing himself to achieve a new schema until he achieves a new balance.

High school students are in this period of the development of the abstract logical thinking, hence teachers should not only consider promoting the original schema of students but also not to exceed the development stages, which require the concern about students' current level, the appropriate choice of learning materials, the attention to the development process of the scientific concepts and principles, and the concern about the choice of teaching methods, as well as the novelty of the presentation of teaching contents, especially, with the large amounts of materials provided. This will enable students to adjust their cognitive structures and improve their capability of thinking actively to allow exploration. The history of bioscience, from an objective view, provides a wealth of materials for the development of students' thinking processes. Like a knowledgeable man in deep thought who is telling a continuous story, the history of bioscience vividly demonstrates how the scientific thinking can be leaned and developed in our students to help mold student's thinking processes, temperaments, intrinsic motivation to enable them to cultivate the habit of thinking innovatively.

FULLY UNDERSTAND THE VALUE OF EDUCATION IN THE HISTORY OF BIOSCIENCE TO TRAIN STUDNETS FOR INNOVATIVE THINKING

The history of bioscience is a source of stimulating the innovative thinking. The innovative thinking originated from a passion for doing science. Innovation needs passion which comes from a love and a strong interest in the study of a problem and the desire to solve the problem. In classroom teaching, teachers should try their best to use appropriately selected materials which can arouse students' interest so as to raise students' desire for scientific inquiry and research. The history of bioscience has many vivid examples about how scientists' carry out scientific research and interesting stories of their work and challenges which can improve students' interests in the learning of biology. On students' curiosity and the need to arouse students' interest during lessons, teachers should use students' prior knowledge and experiences to explore and plan fun learning activities to motivate their learning enthusiasm. For example, in the lecture on "metabolism and enzyme", before the introduction of "the concept of enzyme", the events leading to the discovering "enzyme" are introduced: the contributions of Lazzaro Spallanzani, Loius Pasteur, Eduard Buchner, James Sumner and other scientists are mentioned to show that enzyme is a kind of protein, and then the discovery by the American scientists Thomas Cech and Sidney Altman is introduced to explain the limitation of "enzyme is a kind of protein", and that "certain RNA of a small number of organisms also has catalytic action." Students are attracted by the ingenious experimental designs of the scientists, and at the same time, they are eager to learn what enzyme is all about. The use of the history of bioscience approach increases students' interest in the study "the essence of enzyme". Another example, in the lecture on "photosynthesis" where students often lose patience with the complex photosynthetic reactions and the lack of explanations, making them disinterested in exploring the topic further. Students' understanding of photosynthesis can be improved by introducing the historical cases on the discovery of photosynthesis: Jan Baptist van Helmont's willow experiment, Joseph Priestley's "green – candle – mouse" experiment, Sachs' "semi-shade leaves – iodine vapor" experiment, Stanley Enjierman's "*Spirogyra* – aerobic bacteria," Samuel Rubin and Carmen isotope experiment. These historical examples make students enjoy the wonderful scientific stories, and at the same time enable students to accurately understand the various "details" of the reactions, and the formulae of process of photosynthesis so that they can have a profound impression on photosynthesis.

The history of bioscience illustrates generations of scientific thought and the process of innovative thinking. Innovative thinking stems from the inspiration that emerges through the stimulation of passion, which is the qualitative leap through a long period of time of preparation and accumulation of thinking on a subject. It is the intuitive the thoughts that emerged spontaneously rather than thoughts or afterthoughts that emerged gradually through logical inference. Although the inspiration comes and goes without a trace, it still has some laws and patterns to follow. Inspiration is the state in which a thought is reached spontaneously after painstaking elaboration and refining. Once inspired, it works, and then comes the sudden enlightenment. As for Buluna, the generation process of intuitive thought is usually achieved by creating situations and providing them with rich materials, rather than a dependence on verbal information, especially not on knowledgeable written scripts of teachers.

Since High School students have already accumulated certain knowledge, teachers should broaden the horizon of the students by providing appropriate and more challenging learning materials to further broaden their scope of mind and to enlighten the learning process. The history of bioscience displays the generation process of innovative sparks when the passion of scientists is ignited and stimulated. The works of scientists and their passion for scientific inquiry are useful teaching materials that can be drawn from the history of bioscience to inspire, and motivate students into inquiry and innovative thinking. Charles Darwin travelled for five years aboard the vessel, the H.M.S. Beagle in 1831. During this long journey, Darwin observed many of nature's experiments, found many fossils, observed innumerable plants and animals, and made detailed notes and drawings of what he had observed. In 1836, after returning home from the journey, Darwin came to a conclusion that fauna and flora are not unchangeable. And then when he read the *Population Theory* of Malthus he had an inspiring thought that "the fitness survives". After much research, he finished his masterpiece *The Origin of Species*. The work of Darwin portrays practical scientific spirit, the power of scientific observation, and creative thinking that are all relevant and important for the training of students' scientific thinking processes.

The discovery of the process of vaccination is another example of the generation process of scientists' inspiration that is stimulated by inquisitive observation and opportunity. In the 18th century, when smallpox erupted in Europe, the country doctor Edward Jenner in 1796 found that milkmaids who caught the cowpox virus will not have smallpox. His observation inspired to do research and conduct experiments that led to the development of the process of vaccination against smallpox. These examples demonstrate that every discovery in the history of bioscience are about scientists making sharp and detailed observations, thinking creatively, and constructing knowledge with research and inspiration. The training of students for innovative thinking is possible if teachers understand the generation process of scientific thinking and creative thoughts in the history of bioscience so that they can be effective in developing the skills of innovative thinking in their students. Teachers should give space for the development of imaginative thinking in their students and provide solid basic knowledge for the generation of their unique inspirations.

The history of bioscience provides a paradigm for the development of innovative thinking. Innovative thinking is a complex process which requires one to think what others don't think, recognize what others do not discover, and the thinking is not be bound by the traditional mode of thinking but to take on new and a daring uncharted course to make breakthroughs. The history of bioscience is itself a history of discoveries, inventions, creations, and knowledge advancements in the biological field. It reveals the process of the scientists' exploration on the phenomenon of life and demonstrates the evolution of the biological thought and biologists' innovative thinking. Actually, without innovation, the history of bioscience cannot exist. The materials on innovative thinking by biologists are the best medicine for curing the conventional thinking and one dimensional thought processes of students. The history of bioscience includes a wealth of original materials.

Examples on innovative thinking from the history of bioscience can inspire students' minds, supplement the biology lessons with interesting references for the training of innovative thinking skills and promote the development of students' mental faculty for thinking innovatively. For example, in the lecture on "the basic laws of heredity", students' ability to think innovatively can be cultivated by introducing how Gregor Mendel discovered the laws of heredity with his pea experiments. Historical accounts of how Mendel planted peas, corn and many other plants in a small garden of his monastery to do hybridization experiments can excite students. When Mendel did his experiments with peas, he decisively abandoned the previous view of blending inheritance on the basis of scientific observation and statistical analysis. Besides, by means of the precise reasoning and bold imagination, he proposed a proper explanation for the phenomenon of separation, leading him to discover the law on the separation of genes for traits. Mendelian laws of inheritance were considered a heresy in the religious circle even after Mendel's death. When Mendel proposed his biological laws of heredity, biologists at the time did not recognize gametogenesis and changes in chromosome structure during fertilization. On the basis of experimental phenomenon, Mendel proposed that genetic factors exist in pairs in somatic cells and appear in the gametes. This hypothesis was marvelous and was beyond his age. Mendel's experiments provide excellent teaching materials which can be used to encourage students to advance different their opinions and to dare to put forward new and novel ideas about the genetics of hereditary. It is because of the innovative thinking and great contributions of past outstanding scientists that people have a more profound understanding of nature and the environment. The science process pursued by scientists in their quest to explore and discover the unknown provides an effective paradigm for students' development of thinking skills and understanding of science process skills. The process skills pertains to the ability to observe and think, make bold assumptions, do experiments, and draw conclusions. In the classroom teaching,, as long as teachers guide students and facilitate the learning process appropriately, students can make gradual improvements in their thinking abilities.

The history of bioscience reflects the intrinsic feature of innovative thinking. The innovative thinking must take doubt and negation as the premise, and no doubt, and criticisms on the traditional mode of thinking. The reflections and criticisms are the essential characteristics of innovative thinking. The history of bioscience reveals that scientists often question boldly about everything they observe or do in their experiments, as well as having the spirit of challenging assumptions to traditional thinking and sometimes authority. Through the study of the history of bioscience, students can learn that knowledge in the biological science accumulates and advances over time in the process of self-correction. Students can reach a conclusion by the logical inference of observations and facts. So they can realize that any conclusion is tentative and can be overthrown by the new discovery and facts. The process of science is beneficial for students to consciously be aware of how scientific knowledge advances so that they can admire rationality and the need for independent, logical thinking as they develop critical thinking skills. In the lecture on "the essence and function of enzymes", students' critical thinking can be cultivated by introducing the discovery of enzymes and experiments with enzymes. From the 1930s to 1980s, scientists defined enzyme as "the protein with biological catalysis which originates from the living cells". It took the American scientist James B. Sumner nine years to prove, by a series of experiments, that urease is a kind of protein, and he was later awarded the Nobel Prize in Chemistry. It is noteworthy that old textbooks define enzyme as "a special protein with biological catalysis which originates from the living cells". However, in the 1980s, American scientists Thomas Cech and Sidney Altman found that certain RNA of a small number of organisms also has biological catalytic function. Obviously, this discovery broke the verdict that protein is the origin of biology so that "protein" is replaced by "organism" in the new textbook. Thus it can be seen that the understanding of the nature of enzyme is gradually formed and advanced by several generations of scientists who have undertaken several centuries of painstaking investigations and constant questioning and revision of their research work. Another example, in the lecture on "the hormone regulation of animals", an account on work of Ernest Henry Starling, the first person to study hormones, can be introduced at the start of the lecture to train students in the scientific process of asking bold questions. In 1888, Ivan Pavlov found that the pneumogastric nerve can control the secretion of the pancreas. The young Starling was interested in Pavlov's test but he thought that Pavlov's test lacked scientific proofs. Therefore, he audaciously renovated the experimental approach and arrived at the following conclusion: the increase in the secretion of pancreatic juice is not the result of neuroregulation. Starling announced the result of his experiment and proposed his theory and never gave up the pursuit of science but continued with his research to demonstrate the regulatory function of "secretin" with sufficient proofs. Starling's daring spirit to doubt the work of others, criticize, and question scientific work to pursue the truth, and at the same time thinking and experimenting boldly and innovatively are attributes shared by all scientists. These admirable scientific qualities will intensely touch and motivate students to develop scientific and thinking skills.

It has been pointed out in the "General High School Biology Curricula Standard" that the history of bioscience should be emphasized in school science curriculum. Most teachers fail to make a profound analysis and explanation of the bioscience. They also tend to explain some ideas like scientists' ideology and the historical significance of the discoveries of past scientists inadequately. As a result, students were able to receive the knowledge of the history of science, but not thoroughly understand the scientific thoughts and the scientific processes that went into the development and advancement of science. "As long as the natural science is being considered," said Friedrich Engels, "the form of its development is hypothetic." Education in the History of Bioscience should focus on the ideation, the creativity, and the scientific thinking skills and processes as we teach and train students in science. This is not only the essence of science education but also the necessary prerequisites for empowering students in our country the scientific thinking skills and processes and the ability to think and do science innovatively.

REFERENCES

Shu-wen Li. (2006). Creative Thinking Methodology. Beijing: Communication University of China Press, 5–355.

National Scientific Quality Action Plan (2006–2010–2020). People's Daily, 2006–03–21.

J. Dewey. Method in science teaching. General Science Quarterly, 1916, (1) 39.

Yi-you Wang. the Teaching of Human Spirit In the professional courses. University Teaching in China, *1999*(2), 21–27.

Ai-lun Liu. Psychology of Thinking. Shanghai : Shanghai Education Publishing House, 2002. 36.

Guo-qaun Ma. Social Science Dictionary. Beijing : China International Radio Press, 1989. 85.

Wei-ping Hu The development of young scientific thinking ability and training. Contemporary Education Forum, 2008, (3), 5.

Shan-kan He. Introduction to Creative Thinking. Shanghai : Donghua University Press, 2006. 22.

AI-qi Dong. History of science education in high school biology Model. ［Master thesis］. Shandong Normal University, 2006, 10.

The People's Republic of China Ministry of Education. General High School Biology Curricula Standard (Experiment). Beijing: People's Education Press, 2003. 36.

Zi-qiang Yu. On the biology curriculum. Beijing : Education and Science press, 2006. 264–265.

A STUDY OF THE VALUE OF EDUCATION IN THE HISTORY

Ying-Chun Zhang
College of Life Sciences, Shaanxi Normal University
South Chang'an Road,Xi'an, 710062,China
yingchunzcn@yahoo.com.cn

Yan-Ting Tang
College of Life Sciences, Shaanxi Normal University
mabean@126.com

HEUI-BAIK KIM AND SUN-KYUNG LEE

38. FOSTERING CREATIVITY AND SUSTAINABILITY THROUGH THE 2009 SCIENCE CURRICULUM IN KOREA

ABSTRACT

Fostering scientific literacy in citizens is one of the main goals in science education, which includes higher-thinking abilities such as critical thinking skills and creativity, and it contributes to active participation in a knowledge-based, open society. Recently, education for sustainable development (ESD) has been considered as a critical strategy for solving unsustainable issues in the world such as climate change and biodiversity, which stresses complexity and harmony among the social, economic and environmental perspectives on those issues. ESD is also emphasized to build competencies in critical thinking, reflective thinking, future thinking, system thinking and problem solving based on sustainable literacy for achieving a sustainable future. The Korean national curriculum revision conducted in 2009 highlighted the converging competencies of creativity and integrity as key competencies. The 2009 revision of the science curriculum tried to move it from the compartmentalized branches of science and to re-organize the curriculum as a converging science under the themes of 'the Universe and Life' and 'Science and Culture.' It was recommended to apply inquiry-based activities and science-technology-society (S-T-S)-related science classes using various pedagogies, including project-based learning, problem-based learning, inquiry-based learning as well as observation, experiment, investigation and discussion to cultivate creative problem-solving and rational decision-making abilities for the future. This paper will review the contents and pedagogies of the 2009 science curriculum to explore the contribution of converging science education to a sustainable society. In addition, possible methods for integrating sustainable literacy into scientific literacy will be explored to re-orient science education based on reviews of syllabus details.

KEYWORDS

Creativity, Sustainability, ESD, Science Curriculum, Converging Science, Pedagogy

Mijung Kim and C. H. Diong (Eds.), Biology Education for Social and Sustainable Development, 353–365.

SCIENTIFIC LITERACY

In discussing the school science curriculum, scientific literacy makes a frequent appearance as an aim of science education. Scientific literacy can be defined as "what the general public ought to know about science" (Durant, 1993, p. 129) or commonly implies "appreciation of the nature, aims, and general limitations of science coupled with some understanding of the more important scientific ideas" (Jenkins, 1994, p. 5345), which is another expression of general understanding of science. Since the term was first introduced by Paul Hurd at the end of 1950 (Hurd, 1958), 'scientific literacy' has had different meanings according to the perspectives or purposes of people who use it. There is still no agreed definition or meaning of scientific literacy in implications for school curriculum, but most science educators understand the term through the characteristics of a scientifically literate person illustrated by the U.S. National Science Education Standards as one who:

– can ask, find or determine answers to questions derived from curiosity about everyday experiences
– has the ability to describe, explain, and predict natural phenomena– is able to pose and evaluate arguments based on evidence and to apply conclusions from such arguments appropriately
– be able to evaluate the quality of scientific information on the basis of its source and the methods used to generate it
– has the capacity to pose and evaluate arguments based on evidence and to apply conclusions from such arguments appropriately.

(National Research Council, 1996, p. 22)

Scientific literacy as a curriculum aim of science education was introduced with the slogan 'Science for All' in the 1980s and the summary report of 'Science for Every Citizen: Educating Canadians for Tomorrow's World' in Canada summarized well the goals for school science (Science Research Council of Canada, 1984):

– to develop citizens to participate fully in political and social choices facing a technological society
– to train those with a special interest in science and technology education for further study
– to provide an appropriate preparation for modern fields of work
– to stimulate the intellectual and moral growth of students

Implementing 'Science Education for All' in the school curriculum requires considerations of science content and pedagogy that can be conveyed for students in learning contexts. In the U.S., a list of scientific knowledge of each discipline for students' learning was proposed based on recommendations by 100 scientists who participated in Project 2061 (AAAS, 1990). The National Curriculum Council in the U.K. used a similar method with science educators selecting scientific knowledge that should be taught to students (Fensham, 2000). Interestingly, those efforts caused the expansion of the scope of scientific content to earth and space science, science and technology, nature of science etc. beyond physics, chemistry and life science. In detail, the U.S. National Academy of Science (1996) presented 8 content areas, including science as inquiry, physics, life science, earth, space science, science and technology, science in personal and social perspectives, history and nature of science, integrated concept of science, and the U.K. National Curriculum Council proposed 17 contents strands (National Curriculum Council, 1989).

This wider range of content knowledge requires the reduction of content through viable links and integration between knowledge in order to be implemented in the school curriculum, and information coherence, in reality, has been stressed in the curriculum design for science education in recent decades. In this context, the reconstruction of a content scheme in science education was proposed in the belief that teaching physics, chemistry, life science and earth science as separate courses is inefficient and not helpful for constructing meaning for students in science. In other words, a particular scope with a series of sequences should be taught to students through coordination, where the scope means the coherence of the curriculum content and the scientific ideas that should be taught in school science over the years. One of the approaches for providing coherence is 'concepts in real-world contexts' of the Dutch *PLON* physics project and of Salters' Chemistry in England. The other is 'the curriculum as story' approach used for the science materials of the Curriculum Corporation in Australia for the compulsory years of schooling, and the chemistry materials for Salters' A Level Chemistry in England (Fensham, 2000).

In the perspective focusing on 'scientific understanding of public issues,' it is important to consider scientific literacy as the application of science and technology in the real world and social participation based on scientific knowledge. The competency to produce rational decision making in social issues of science and technology is presented as an important aim for science education in this perspective. The social issues in science and technology are complex, and so a scientist or a group of scientists cannot easily solve them. Rational decision making requires judgments regarding the validity of evidence and the reliability of sources, because different claims are provided based on different perspectives. Science education for this area focuses on the logic and rationale of scientific argumentation as well as scientific inquiry and the interrelationship of individual and social values (Fensham, 2000). According to the notion that average students cannot learn all the important scientific concepts in a wide range (Kuhn, 1993), scientific argumentation was strongly suggested as a basic competency for all students to learn in the 1990s. This was also stressed in OECD/PISA science projects as high-level scientific thinking for drawing conclusions based on the scientific inquiry process or scientific knowledge, which was highlighted in the following competencies: recognizing scientifically investigable questions; identifying evidence/data needed in a scientific investigation; drawing or evaluating conclusions; and communicating valid conclusions (OECD/PISA, 1999).

SCIENCE EDUCATION FOR A SUSTAINABLE SOCIETY

Recently, emerging issues threatening the Earth's sustainability such as climate change and the loss of biodiversity have highlighted the importance of education for sustainable development as a strategy for facing and solving these unsustainable issues (UNESCO, 2009a; UNESCO, 2009b). Education for sustainable development (ESD) may be referred to as education for sustainability

(EfS) depending on the context and emphasis, and various efforts have been conducted in various sectors in the world since the United Nations (UN) designated the decade as the decade of ESD for 2005–2014 (Lee et al., 2005; UNESCO, 2005). Dealing with those unsustainable issues, however, is difficult due to the complexity that they were based on. Fostering competencies including critical thinking, future thinking, system thinking and participation in problem-solving processes needed for facing those issues and contributing to a sustainable society, which are closely related to scientific literacy in science education as Rauch (2010) indicated, is stressed. Exploring the link for application to science education may be what science education can contribute for a sustainable world. Indeed, the OECD Programme for International Student Assessment (PISA) (2009) defined 'literacy' as the 'capacity of students to use what they have learned and to analyze and reason as they pose, solve and interpret problems in a variety of situations,' which is the same emphasis on scientific literacy in science education.

SCIENTIFIC LITERACY REFLECTED IN KOREA'S SCIENCE CURRICULUM

Curriculum Objectives and Scientific Literacy

In Korea, the science curriculum was revised in 2007 and 2009, and the revisions have been applied in schools with minor revisions of the 7th science curriculum promulgated in 1998. Providing objectives with understanding scientific concepts, the acquisition of inquiry skills, cultivating an interest in science and scientific attitude, understanding the relationship of science, technology and society, the 7th science curriculum emphasizes enhancing scientific literacy among students through the national basic common curriculum (Ministry of Education, 1997). These objectives seem to correspond closely to the theme of scientific literacy proposed by Chiappetta and Koballa (2006), which includes 'science as a way of thinking, science as an inquiry, science as a knowledge system, science and technology, and interrelationships with society.' While there is no explicit mention of a way of thinking in science in the curriculum, the objectives may have been set up properly. However, an article analyzing middle school science textbooks pointed out a great lack of content related to ways of thinking and the relationship between S-T-S in them, while there is too much emphasis on the knowledge system and science as inquiry (Kim et al., 2006), which raises the issue of reaching the aim of cultivating scientific literacy in school practices. The excessive emphasis on the scientific knowledge system is not a problem unique to Korea, which was reported by other science educators (Chiappetta, Sethna, & Fillman, 1991; Lumpe & Beck, 1996).

Scope, Strand and Coordination of the 7th Science Curriculum

The 7th science curriculum sets up 'the national basic common curriculum' for all Koreans, in which the core knowledge and inquiry skills students from grade 3 to grade 10 need to learn, and are linked with each other (Table 1).

Table 1. Framework for designing the 7th curriculum in 1997

Grade / Field	3rd	4th	5th	6th	7th	8th	9th	10th
[Knowledge]								
Energy	- Activity with magnets - Making sound - Making shadow pictures - Measuring temperature	- Maintaining level - Stretching springs - Heat transfer - Turning on the light bulb	- Speed of object - Mirrors and lens - Making electric circuits - Energy	- Weight and pressure (in the water) - Handy tools - Electromagnets	- Light - Force - Waves	- Various motion - Electricity	- Work and energy - Action of current	- Energy
Materials	- Investigating materials around us - Dissolving the powered substance in water - Separating solid mixture	- Investigating properties of various liquids - Separating mixtures - Temperature and volume changes of objects by heat - Water showing phase changes	- Making solutions - Making crystals - Investigating properties of solution - Changes of solution	- Properties of gases - Various gases - Observing burning candles	- Three phases of matters - Molecular motion - Phase change and energy	- Nature of materials - Separation of mixtures	- Motion of materials - Regularities in material changes	- Materials
Life	- Life cycle of fruit fly - Raising living things in aquarium - Investigating various leaves - Observing the stems of plants	- Growing beans - Roots of plants - Features of various animals - Male and female of animals	- Flowers and fruits - What leaves of plants do - Observing small animals - Environment and living things	- Features of our body - Living things around us - Pleasant environment	- Organization of living things - Digestion and circulation - Respiration and excretion	- Structure and function of plants - Stimulus and response	- Reproduction and development - Genetics and evolution	- Life
Earth	- Various stones and soil - Soil in transport - Round earth, round moon - Sunny day, cloudy day	- Searching for constellation - River and sea - Investigating the earth's strata - Investigating fossils	- Weather changes - Journey of the water - Volcano and rocks - Family of the Sun	- Seasonal changes - Weather forecast - Earth shaking	- Structure of the Earth - Earth's crust materials - Composition and movement of sea water	- Earth and stars - Earth's history and tectonic movements	- Water cycle and weather changes - Movement of solar system	- Earth
[Inquiry]								
Inquiry Process SP[1]	✔ ✔ ✔			✔ ✔ ✔		✔ ✔ ✔		
Inquiry Process IP[2]	✔ ✔			✔ ✔		✔ ✔ ✔		
Inquiry activities[3]	✔ ✔ ✔			✔ ✔ ✔		✔ ✔ ✔		

[1] SP means simple process skills such as observation, classification, measurement, expectation, and inference
[2] IP means integrated process skills such as problem recognition, hypothesis formation, control of variables, data transformation, data analysis, drawing conclusions, and generalization.
[3] Inquiry activities include teaching and learning activities such as discussion, experiment, investigation, field trip, and project.

Features of the Revised Science Curriculum in 2007 & 2009

2007 Science Curriculum

The 2007 science curriculum, the partially revised version of the 7th curriculum in 2007, reflects the spirit of the 7th science curriculum, but is more focused on scientific literacy and creativity in science. This revised curriculum explicitly discusses fostering scientific literacy through science education in the goal statement of the curriculum:

"to understand basic concepts in science through investigation with interest in and curiosity regarding natural phenomena and objects, and to foster scientific literacy needed to solve problems in everyday life creatively and scientifically based on a scientific way of thinking and creative problem-solving skills." (MEST, 2007)

The 'Open Inquiry' newly included in the 2007 science curriculum aimed to increase students' interest in science and creativity, and students can select and investigate topics and themes that they are interested in (Ministry of Education, 2007). The themes for 'Open Inquiry' provided as examples in the curriculum are closely related to everyday life, which include transportation, natural disasters, sports and science for 7th-grade students, universe, optical equipment and plastics for 8th graders; sea, science in my house and drug abuse for 9th-grade students; and the future of science, profession and career, electromagnetic waves for 10th-grade students. All the themes and topics provided in the curriculum can be tasks for inquiry into the culture competencies of a scientifically literate person 'who can solve problems encountered in everyday life contexts.'

Table 2. Content structure of 'Life' in the 2007 science curriculum

Grade	Life	Grade	Life
3rd	Life cycle of animals Animal's world	7th	Organization and diversity of living organisms Plant nutrition
4th	Life cycle of plants World of plants	8th	Digestion and circulation Respiration and excretion
5th	Plant structure and functions World of micro-organisms Human body	9th	Stimulus and response Reproduction and development
6th	Ecosystems and environments	10th	Inheritance and evolution Life science and the future of the human species

2009 Science Curriculum

Still maintaining the spirit of the 7th curriculum as another revision with minor revisions, the 2009 curriculum emphasizes 'creativity and personality' as competencies for people in the future society. In the 2009 science curriculum, the integrated content and coherence approach among a wide range of knowledge is strengthened and aims at facilitating students' applications of scientific knowledge based on understanding content rather than memorizing fragmented knowledge.

INTEGRATED APPROACH IN THE 2009 SCIENCE CURRICULUM

Integrated Science

Integrated science for high school students takes two different approaches under the theme of 'The Universe and Life' and 'Science and Culture.' 'The Universe and Life' uses a storyline-centered approach to answer the big questions, "Where are we in the universe?" and "How did it come to be?" The former "Where are we in the universe?" consists of content elements, including "universe – galaxy – solar system - Earth – human – cell – compound – atoms – the fundamental particles," while the latter includes those of "the Big Bang – fundamental particles – atoms – stellar evolution – solar system – the chemical evolution – biological evolution" (Table 3). This storyline focuses on the process and history from the birth of the universe to the birth of the Earth, and to the emergence and flourishing of life forms on Earth with an integrated approach.

'Science and Culture,' using an approach focused on context and cultural emphasis, intends to cultivate the characteristics of a scientifically literate person in "understanding science and technological issues encountered in everyday life and, therefore, presenting rational opinions on them." To this end, this curriculum emphasizes the relevance between science and society or culture through highlighting the development and use of science and technology in various contexts (Table 4).

Biological Science I, II

Biological Science I, another selective subject in the 2009 science curriculum, indicates characteristics of this subject to cultivate basic biological literacy for democratic citizens in a modern knowledge-based society through an integrated understanding of life science. The objectives of this subject are to understand the basic concepts in integrated ways, to cultivate scientific inquiry skills, to foster a scientific attitude for problem solving in life science-related contexts and to recognize the interrelationship of S-T-S. In other words, Biological Science I aims for students to become aware of the usefulness of biological science through understanding biological concepts in everyday life contexts, to investigate scientifically biological-science-related information or phenomena, and to communicate clearly their own opinions on information or phenomena with other people in a creative way. Biological Sciences I consists of four domains, understanding biological science, cells and continuity of life, homeostasis and health, humans in nature, which include contents of "cells and cell division, inheritance, biological activity and energy, homeostasis and physiological control, defense mechanism, composition and function of ecosystems, and biodiversity and environment" (Table 5).

Table 3. Contents of 'Science (Part I)' in the 2009 curriculum

Domain			Content
The Universe and Life	Origin of the universe	Origin of the universe	Expansion of the universe, Hubble's law, line spectrum, age of the universe
		Big Bang and fundamental particle	Fundamental particle, protons, neutrons, formation of atomic nucleus
		Formation of atoms	Hydrogen and helium atoms, cosmic microwave background radiation
		Stars and galaxy	Beginning of a new star and its evolution, synthesis of heavy elements, galaxy structure, interstellar chemical compounds, covalent bond, reaction rate
	Solar system and the Earth	Formation of the solar system	Formation process of the solar system, solar energy, terrestrial planets, Jovian planets
		Dynamics of the solar system	Kepler's law, Newton's law of motion, planetary motion, motion of the earth and the moon, the Earth's revolution and rotation
		Atmosphere of planets	Escape velocity, difference of planetary atmosphere, structure and feature of molecules
		Earth	Earth's evolution, Earth system, distribution of terrestrial elements, terrestrial magnetism
		Beginning of life	Early Earth, chemical reaction and chemical evolution, carbon compounds, basic elements of life, DNA, proteins, structure of the cell membrane
	Evolution of life	Evolution of life	Beginning of primitive life, photosynthesis and oxygen in the atmosphere, fossils, geographical age, prokaryotic cells, eukaryotic cells, diversity of life
		Continuity of life	Genes and chromosomes, genetic code, cell division, gene replication, assortment of genes, gene transfer through reproduction

Table 4. Contents of 'Science (Part II)' in the 2009 curriculum

Domain			Content
Science and culture	Information and communications, new material	Generation of information and data processing	Generation of information, sensor, digital information processing
	Information and communications, new material	Storing and utilizing information	Storage medium, display, application of information processing
		Semiconductor and new material	Feature of semiconductors, semiconductor devices, polymer
	Science and technology for human health	Mineral resources	Type of minerals, generative process of minerals, exploration, practical use
		Food resources	Breeding, fertilizer, food safety, ecosystems and biodiversity
		Scientific health care	Nutrition, metabolism, disease and immunity, sterilizing water, detergent, natural and synthetic medicine, physical examination
		Frontier science for the treatment of disease	Advanced diagnostic medical images, cancer development, diagnosis and treatment of cancer
	Energy and environment	Energy and culture	Energy type, energy conservation, energy conversion, law of energy conservation, energy efficiency, fossil fuel
		Carbon cycle and climate change	Earth's energy balance, green house effect and climate change, carbon cycle, reduction of carbon dioxide during photosynthesis
		Energy problems and the future	Formation and depletion of energy resources, new and renewable energy, nuclear energy, sustainable development and energy

Table 5. Contents of 'Biological Science I' in the 2009 curriculum

Domain		Content
Understanding biological science		Characteristics of life (including systematic phases of organizations in living organisms)
Cells and continuity of life	Cells and cell division	Cell cycle and cell division, genes, chromosomes
	Inheritance	Mendel's law, human genetic traits, expression of genetic traits (chromosome aberration and gene abnormality)
	Biological activity and energy	Biological activity of cells, systemic integration of digestion, circulation, respiration, excretion
Homeostasis and health	Homeostasis and physiological control	Functions of the nervous system, signal transduction and transmission, stimulus and response process, muscle contraction, control of body temperature, control of blood glucose levels, control of osmotic pressure
	Defense mechanism	pathogens, antigen, antibody, immunity

Humans in the natural environment	Composition and function of ecosystem	Interaction between living organisms and environment, population and community, biogeochemical cycle and energy flow
	Biodiversity and environment	Conservation of biodiversity, practical use of biotic resources, relevance to the environment, sustainable development

In particular, the biodiversity and environment domain emphasizes the need for ecosystem conservation in conjunction with the importance of biodiversity and the environment. In addition, measures for sustainable development are explored due to their relationship with ecosystem conservation.

Table 6. Contents of 'Biological Science II' in the 2009 curriculum

Domain		Content
Cells and metabolism	Characteristics of cells	Nucleus, comparison between prokaryotic cells and eukaryotic cells, cytoplasm, cell membrane, diffusion, osmosis, active transport, structure and function of enzyme
	Cells and energy	Energy conversion through the cellular membrane, fermentation, ATP, structure and function of mitochondria, glycolysis, TCA cycle, electron transport systems, structure and function of chloroplast, light reaction, dark reaction
Genes and biotechnology	Gene and its expression	Properties of genetic information, DNA replication, expression of genetic traits, control of gene expression
	Biotechnology	Biotechnology and its practical use
Evolution of life	Origin of life and biodiversity	Origin of life, classification system of living organisms
	Principle of evolution	Variation, natural selection, genetic equilibrium, speciation

Biological Science II is a selective subject for cultivating competencies to creatively and scientifically solve problems related to life phenomena, based on an understanding of biological concepts and diverse inquiry skills. Thus, systematic understanding of biological concepts, cultivation of scientific inquiry skills and fostering of scientific attitudes, and recognition of the interrelationship of S-T-S were set as objectives.

Biological Sciences II is divided into three domains: cells and metabolism, gene and biotechnology and biological evolution (Table 6). Cells and metabolism include 'characteristics of cell and cells and energy' to help students to understand biological activities physically and chemically related to cells as the basic unit of life. The genes and biotechnology domain consists of 'genes and its expression, and biotechnology' intends to provide an understanding of the features and functions of genes at the molecular level. Evolution of life includes 'the origin of life and biodiversity, and principle of evolution' to support understanding the origin of life on Earth and the changes in life caused by changes of genes.

Biological Science II covers comprehensive biological phenomena from the molecular level to a broad variety of life to provide a comprehensive awareness and understanding of life and to forecast a positive future for science and human beings.

IMPLICATIONS AND RECOMMENDATIONS FOR FUTURE CURRICULUM

This paper briefly summarized Korea's science curriculum in relation to scientific literacy in the context of education for sustainable development. Implications and recommendations for science curriculum revisions are provided as follows.

First, scientific literacy as a curriculum aim is necessary to refocus on the context of education for sustainable development. Scientific literacy in science education has been emphasized in much of the literature since the 1980s, and most curriculum revisions have indicated it as a big slogan, but it has limitations in realization in schools due to the slippery and ambiguous identity of scientific literacy. However, to implement meaningful science education, the meaning of scientific literacy must be re-examined for science education to contribute to a sustainable society in the context of education for sustainable development.

Second, given the complexity of issues in the real world, more practical integrations of scientific concepts with other concepts, with inquiry process or with real-life contexts need to be done in constructing the science curriculum. Indeed, issues related to the development of science or science itself are not limited to an inward relationship inside science, but are involved in an outward relationship with society and technology (Dillon, 2009); thus, integrated science learning has the potential to provide scientific solutions for social and economic problems. In this sense, scientific concepts were converged with scientific concepts of different areas or with social and cultural contexts to formulate 'The Universe and Life' and 'Science and Culture' in the 2009 science curriculum revision, which was meaningful for more relevant science education in the future.

Third, appropriate pedagogy is required for achieving competencies required for a sustainable society through science education. Inquiry-based learning, problem solving learning, place-based learning, and project-based learning associated in science can provide chances for students to be connected to the real world through real actions and experiences, which are often considered as pedagogy for education for sustainable development. Through these authentic learning experiences, students can not only understand the complexity of issues from scientific, social and economic perspectives and the interrelationship of science-technology-economy-society but also build the competencies needed for achieving a sustainable future. In the 2009 science curriculum in Korea, students can understand scientific inquiry methods and processes through diverse pedagogy, including observations, experiments, investigations and discussions, etc., which contributes to fostering scientific thinking skills for creative problem solving and rational decision making in society (MEST, 2009). While the emphasis on diverse pedagogy in the science curriculum does not always lead to actual implementation in schools, a positive result was reported in Canada, which implemented a curriculum differently by introducing approaches for students to participate in problem solving and decision making in the existing science curriculum without a curriculum revision (CMEC, 1997).

Fourth, support is essential for the intended curriculum to be implemented in school settings. A study that evaluated the curriculum implementation of General Natural Science in the Netherlands reported difficulties in changing traditional science lessons in schools (De Vos and Reiding, 1999). Science education is the culture (Osborne and Dillon, 2008), and diverse support is necessary for a new culture to be implemented in schools. In particular, support for teachers who have initiatives for this culture, including building the capacity to implement new curriculum through teacher training, developing useful instructional materials and providing online consulting, etc., is essential.

Lastly, an overall program evaluation of the curriculum implementation is needed, which was not conducted appropriately after the curriculum revision. An investigation into the status of implementing the curriculum may be conducted during the curriculum revision process, but it is difficult to reflect the real performance. In the U.K., the evaluation of Twenty First Century Science included knowledge and understanding, attitudes toward science and the degree of changes in classroom science (2007). In most cases, the former two elements are included in the evaluation, but the last element is easily overlooked or neglected. To identify the changes that have occurred in classrooms or further impacts on sustainable society through curriculum implementation, a comprehensive evaluation of curriculum implementation needs to be conducted. The evaluation results should be reflected in the next curriculum revision.

REFERENCES

AAAS (1990). *Science for All Americans*. Washington, DC: American Association for Advancement of Science.

Aldridge, B. G. (Ed.) (1996). *Scope, sequence, and coordination: A framework for high school science education*. Arlington, VA: National Science Teachers Association.

Chiappetta, E. L., & Koballa, T. R. (2006). *Science instruction in the middle and secondary schools-Developing fundamental knowledge and skills for teaching* (6th ed.). Columbus, OH: Pearson/Merrill Prentice Hall.

Chiappetta, E. L., Sethna, G. H., & Fillman, D. A. (1991). A quantitative analysis of high school chemistry textbooks for scientific literacy themes and expository learning aids. *Journal of Research in Science Teaching, 28*, 939–951.

Durant, J. R. (1993). What is scientific literacy? In Durant, J. R. & Gregory, J. (Eds.), *Science and culture in Europe* (pp. 129–137). London, UK: Science Museum.

Council of Ministers of Education, Canada (CMEC) (1997). *Common framework of science learning outcomes K to 12: Pan-Canadian protocol for collaboration on school curriculum for use by curriculum developers*. Toronto, ON, Canada: CMEC.

De Vos, W., & Reiding, J.(1999). Public understanding of science as a separate subject in secondary schools in the Netherlands. *International Journal of Science Education, 21*, 711–719.

Dillon, J. (2009). On scientific literacy and curriculum reform. *International Journal of Environmental & Science Education, 4*(3), 201–213.

Fensham, P. (2000). Providing suitable content in the 'science for all' curriculum. In Millar, R., Leach, J. & Osborne, J. (Eds.). *Improving science education*. Buckingham, UK : Open University Press.

Hurd, P. D. (1958). Science literacy: Its meaning for American schools. *Educational Leadership, 16*, 13–16, 52.

Kim, H., Choi, S., Hwang, Y., Lee, J., Kim, S., & Lee, M. (2006). An analysis of middle school science textbooks based on scientific literacy. *Journal of Korean Association for Research in Science Education, 26*(4), 601–609.

Lee, S., Lee., J., Lee, Y., Lee, S., Min, K., & Shim, S. (2005). Development of the National Strategy for UN Decade for ESD in Korea. Presidential Commission for Sustainable Development, Korea.

Lumpe, A. T., & Beck, J. (1996). A profile of high school biology textbooks using scientific literacy recommendations. *The American Biology Teacher, 58*, 147–153.

Minitry of Education, Science & Technology, Korea (2009). *2009 Science curriculum*. Seoul, Korea: Ministry of Education, Science & Technology, Korea.

National Curriculum Council (1989). *Science: Non-statutory Guidance*. London: National Curriculum Council.

National Research Council (1996). *National Science Education Standards*. Washington, DC: National Academy Press.

Osborne, J. & Dillon, J. (2008). Science education in Europe; Critical reflections. London: The Nuffield Foundation.

Rauch, F. (2010). *Education for Sustainable Development and Science Education. Proceedings of 20th Symposium on Chemistry and Science Education*. University of Bremen, Bremen, Germany. p. 6.

Twenty First Century Science (2008). Retrieved 7 December 2008 from http://www.21stcentury science.org.

UNESCO (2005). DESD International Implementation Scheme. UNESCO.

UNESCO (2009a). Climate change and education for sustainable development. UNESCO Policy Dialogue Series 3. UNESCO.

UNESCO (2009b). Bonn declaration. UNESCO World Conference on Education for Sustainable Development. UNESCO.

Heui-Baik Kim
Seoul National University,
Gwanak-gu, Seoul 151–742, Korea
hbkim56@snu.ac.kr

Sun-Kyung Lee
Cheongju National University of Education
Cheongju, Chungbuk 361–712, Korea
sklee@cje.ac.kr

SHOGO KAWAKAMI, KOICHIRO WATANABE
AND AYA MATSUMOTO

39. DEVELOPMENT OF MEANINGFUL RECEPTION LEARNING IN JAPAN: A CASE STUDY

ABSTRACT

Meaningful reception learning is a learning theory using advance organizers (AO) that emphasizes the deductive thinking process. AO is introduced prior to learning and it is a general and abstract concept that organizes the learning that follows. Our study group has clarified that charts and models can be used as AO. The effects of meaningful reception learning are: (i) more students understand science, (ii) advanced learning can be introduced smoothly, and (iii) students find science classes interesting because they understand. We report here that meaningful reception learning was applied to fifth graders on the topic, the structure of flowers, to verify the effects and problems of meaningful reception learning. The key factor in introducing AO lies in creating an environment in which learners are given opportunities to ask questions. Meaningful reception learning cannot be replaced with discovery learning. Meaningful reception learning, as well as discovery learning, is included in problem-solving learning. Problem-solving learning can be enhanced by introducing meaningful reception learning. Meaningful reception learning is appropriate for learning abstract concepts. In that context, meaningful reception learning works well with many classes in junior high schools whereas discovery learning plays a pivotal role in elementary schools.

KEYWORDS

Meaningful Reception Learning, Advance Organizer, Problem-Solving Learning, Discovery Learning, Structure Of Flowers

INTRODUCTION

The current goals of science learning, as explained in the Manual of the Course of Study for Science(1) are "to be in close contact with nature, to carry out observations and experiments with expectations to cultivate problem-solving ability as well as love for nature, so that students can understand the natural things and phenomena, and cultivate scientific perspectives." Emphasis is placed on conducting observations and experiments "with expectations". Hidaka (2007) observed that students are sometimes confused when they are asked to have expectations and self-responsibility for their own learning. Pointing out

Mijung Kim and C. H. Diong (Eds.), Biology Education for Social and Sustainable Development, 367–374.

the difficulty of having expectations within the framework of the current science learning methods, Hikada raised these questions: "How could children discover specific problems and have expectations without a framework to comprehend nature? Isn't it necessary to stand on the side of students and encourage them to realize problems based on the reality?". Kawakami (2007) argued that "attitude to study for the sake of discovery distances students from understanding the objective of experiments explicitly, thus experiments become meaningless operation". Under the current learning model, it is difficult for students to find scientific principles or generalizations through observations and experiments with "expectations".

Studies on meaningful reception learning for science lessons in Japan was launched by Kawakami and Sugiura (1985), and continued in later years with studies by Kawakami and Tajika (1987), Tajika and Kawakami (1988), and Kawakami and Tajika (1990). This series of studies led to the conclusion that the introduction of AO to science learning contributes not only to the embedding of basic knowledge but also to obtaining applied skills to handle new learning problems. Furthermore, the outcome showed that using AO is effective, especially for the learning of underachievers.

Our research led us to form the "Meaningful Reception Learning Study Group", based on the assertion that "recent disinterest in science results from not teaching advanced knowledge in science classes". A new study on teaching science at a higher level than that required was carried out in cooperation with school teachers. Ten units of science lessons to which meaningful reception learning can be applied were presented by Kawakami, Terada, Kato, Tsuboi, Yagi, Fujita, Yamada, Isogai, Oda and Kobayashi at the 50th Meeting of the Society of Japan Science Teaching held at Yokohama National University. The book "Science classes to re-empower teaching" was published subsequently (Kawakami 2003).

In our 2007 study, meaningful reception learning using advance organizers schematized by Ausubel (1968) was applied as a teaching method so that children could carry out experiments and observations with "expectations" for better discoveries. A series of classes applying meaningful reception learning was planned by means of AO and put into practice for the unit, "Structure of Flower", for fifth graders in order to examine the effects and the problems of meaningful reception learning. According to Ausubel and Robinson (1969), advance organizers (AO) are defined as information "introduced in advance of learning itself, and are presented at a higher level of abstraction, generality, and inclusiveness". The provision of AO activates learners' existing knowledge and links it firmly to related new inputs.

RESEARCH METHOD

A series of classes were given for the unit "Structure of Flower" class of fifth graders in a municipal elementary school in Nagoya. The flow of the lessons is shown in Table 1. A pre-test, post-test, retention test and affection test were administered. Before the start of the classes, a questionnaire survey was carried out to assess how much the students were interested in plants. Students had to respond to the question, "From now we are going to study about plants. We have already learned about plants. Are you interested in plants?" on a four-point scale (1-very much, 2-somewhat, 3-not so much, 4-not at all).

Table 1. Lesson flow and advance organizers

Period	Content of learning
1.2	Let's find out the structure of flower
	Advance organizer A:
	Showing the chart below, "A flower consists of a pistil, stamens, petals and calyxes, set in order from the center. Therefore, you can start investigating any flower from the center."

3	Let's find out the structure of male/female flowers
4	Let's find out how fruits are formed
	Advance organizer B:
	"When pollen from stamens attaches to the pistil (pollination), the base of the pistil becomes a fruit with seeds inside it."
5	Let's find out the structure and function of pollen①
6	Let's find out the structure and function of pollen②
7	Let's find out how fruits are formed
	Advance organizer C:
	"Flowers are evolved from leaves. The trace can be found in fruits transformed from pistils."

The pre-test was carried out to clarify how prepared the students were in understanding the lesson topic in terms of the previously learned content, new knowledge that they were about to learn and how much background information they had. It had 28 questions on the structure of the flower. The purpose of the post-test was to evaluate whether the classes were effective in the students' learning and whether they understood the progressive content that had been integrated into the unit. The retention test, using the same questions as the post-test, took place when a certain period of time had passed after the classes, to examine how far their academic capability has been retained. In the affection test, a column on "Today's impression" was added to the worksheet. It contained the questions, "Did you enjoy today's class? " (*1-enjoyed very much, 2-somewhat, 3-not so much, 4-not at all), and "Did you understand today's class?" (1-well understood, *2-somewhat understood, 3-did not understand well, 4-not at all understood). A space was provided for students to describe their impressions. The follow-up questionnaire had this question, "We have been studying about flowers.

Do you want to know more about flowers?" (1-very much, 2-somewhat, 3-not so much, 4-not at all).

RESULTS

In each test, the participants were grouped into high score and low score groups according to their academic grades in the first trimester, as assessed by their teachers. Table 2 shows the average test scores (maximum = 100 marks) of all students, high score group, and low score group for the pre-test, post-test and retention test.

Table 2. (a) Average score of each test, (b) Fun of science class

	All students	High score group	Low score group
Pre- test	68.3	79.1	59.1
Post- test	89.3	95.2	82.3
Retention test	89.0	95.4	77.0

(a)

Answer \ Period	1.2	3	4	5	6	7
1	55.6	36.1	55.6	83.3	72.2	80.6
2	44.4	61.1	44.4	16.7	25.0	19.4
3	0	2.8	0	0	2.8	0
4	0	0	0	0	0	0

(b)

In the results of the preliminary survey questionnaire, 5.6% of the students answered that they were "very much" interested, 11.1% were "somewhat" interested, 50.0% "not so much" and 33.3% "not at all" interested in the subject. In the follow-up questionnaire, 44.4% of the students answered they wanted to know "very much" more about the subject, 52.8% chose "somewhat", 2.8% "not so much", with no student answering "not at all". Table 3 presents the results of the affection test; the figures show the number of students for each option expressed as a percentage the total student number of the class.

Table 3 shows the result on the student's level of understanding for the science concepts. The figures in the table are the percentage of students who selected the answer to the total student number in the class.

Table 3. Level of understanding

Answer \ Class	1.2	3	4	5	6	7
1	72.2	55.6	58.4	77.8	72.2	69.4
2	27.8	38.9	41.7	19.4	27.8	27.8
3	0	2.8	0	2.8	0	2.8
4	0	2.8	0	0	0	0

DISCUSSION

In the high score group, the average score increased 16.1 points between the pre- and post-tests, which confirmed the learning effect of this teaching method. An average score increase of 0.2 point was seen between the post- and the retention tests, which means the students were able to retain the knowledge. In the low score group, a 23.2-point rise between the pre-test and post-test shows the effectiveness of learning in the classes. A 5.3-point decrease between the post-test and the retention test suggests the students had forgotten what they had learned one month after instruction.

Figure 1 shows the changes in test scores of each student in the pre-test, post-test and retention test. Here the students were classified into three categories according to the test score; a group that "understood well" scored at least 80%; a group that "mostly understood" scored between 60%, but less than 80% and a group that "understood little" scored less than 60%. Changes in the number of students in each group are indicated by arrows.

There was a significant increase in the level of understanding between pre-test and post-test, indicating the effectiveness of reception leaning in the classes. Students who answered they "understood well" in the pre-test continued to choose the answer that they "understood well" in the post- and retention tests. From this, we can conclude that the instruction was effective for students who "understood well" before learning this unit. 92.3% of students who said that they "did not understand well", opted for either "understood well" or "mostly understood" as answers. It is considered that the instruction was effective for students who "did not understand well". 85.2% of the students who "understood well" in the post-test answered they "understood well" in the retention test, which suggests these students retained what they had learned very well. Of those who "mostly understood" in the post-test, 62.5% chose they "understood well", and 25.0% answered that they "mostly understood" in the retention test. It is believed that most of the students who "mostly understood" in the post-test successfully retained the learning content. However, there were some students whose answers shifted from "mostly understood" to "did not understand well", or from "understood well" to "mostly understood" between the post-test and retention test. Therefore it cannot be said that the instruction was effective for everyone.

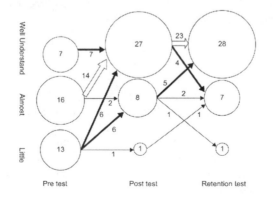

Figure. 1 Changes in the number of students according to the scores of pre-/post-and retention tests.

In the preliminary questionnaire, 16.7% of students answered they were "very much" or "somewhat" interested in plants, while 97.2% of students wanted to know "very much" or "somewhat". This result shows students' interest in the structure of flower was improved substantially by the instruction in the classes.

Throughout the study, when the question, "Did you enjoy the lesson on the structure of the flower?" was asked, no student answered they did not enjoy the classes. Those who answered they enjoyed "very much" or "moderately" typically described their impressions as follows: "I did not understand lilies, but then I understood and now I got it.", "I felt something sticky at the base of pistil.", "I learn there are not only stamens and pistils but also male and female flowers", "I cannot wait to see the result of the experiment", "The stamens of a flower in bloom and those of a bud were different", "It was like an egg of something", "Morning glory is white and fluffy. I found lilies have many spots", "Some pollens are thorny, some are round", "When I see pollen myself, they look the same size, but their actual size is different when you see them with a microscope", "Fruits are formed by piled leaves", but "How is a structure of a fruit such as strawberries?".

In order for students to learn science the fun way, they have to conduct observations and experiments directly by themselves. The reason why no students in the test responded that the classes were not interesting is indication the students were not bored with the lesson and were hence learning the scientific concepts. Because observations and experiments were included in every lesson, the students were given sufficient time to do their hands-on practical work during the class. When asked about how deeply they understood the lessons, most students answered they "understood well" or "mostly understood", showing that most of the students discovered the learning goal planned for the lesson and were able to understand it. Compared with the morning glory, the structure of flowers such as the lily and the dayflower are not easy for students to understand. However the more complicated the structure is, the more the students enjoyed in the experimental inquiry and observations. This shows the capacity of children's motivation to clarify scientific ideas and for discovery, as they are surprised and inspired by the existence of flowers whose structures are different from what they knew.

SUMMARY

Advance organizers were used to plan a series of biology lessons to evaluate reception learning in a three-step model. In step 1 (Awareness of problems involved), various phenomena relating to new knowledge were presented or recalled, allowing learners to wonder why things happen the way they are. This learning process is termed "creating a cobweb condition". Students were presented AO in step 2 (Introduction of advance organizers). In step 3 (Adaptation/ generalization, progressive learning), students adapt AO to various concrete events by means of experiments and observations, and confirming the content of AO. When adaptation and generalization include advanced content, the content takes on a progressive character by itself, therefore progressive learning can be easily integrated.

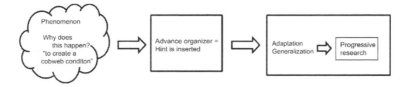

Figure. 2 Steps to carry out classes by meaningful reception learning approach.

Reception learning cannot be replaced with discovery learning. Reception learning as well as discovery learning is included in problem-solving learning. Problem-solving learning can be enhanced by introducing reception learning. These methods should be chosen carefully according to the development stage and lesson content of the subject grade. To illustrate this, the approach that should be used in the teaching of photosynthesis is discussed.) In discovery learning, students are taught: "The mechanism is called photosynthesis", only after confirming the existence of carbohydrate by means of the iodine reaction. On the other hand, in reception learning, students are taught, "Plants produce carbohydrates by photosynthesis. Let's verify it by experiments". In another instance, when teaching biological substances to students, molecular/atomic theory is introduced after various experiments in the former learning method, while such experiments are carried out after explaining molecular/atomic theory in the latter. The steps are reversed.

Our study concluded that reception learning is more effective than discovery learning for teaching abstract content, especially to underachievers. Our views are that discovery learning is suitable for science classes in elementary school. Science in junior high school includes a number of notional content, therefore reception learning dominates in many situations. Teachers are required to determine which learning style is appropriate after evaluating their students' level of understanding.

It is not our intent to deny discovery learning or inquiry learning. We believe that for the improvement and advancement of science education, it is essential to employ heuristic, inductive problem-solving learning and receptive, and deductive problem-solving learning flexibly, while at the same time reviewing whether a learning method is suitable or how students respond to it. We encourage teachers to adopt receptive learning in the science education process without depending too much on heuristic problem-solving learning so that "problem-solving learning using both heuristic and receptive learning" can be achieved. In so doing, it will contribute to further enhancement of effective science teaching.

REFERENCES

Ministry of Education, Culture, Sports, Science and Technology. (2007). Manual of the Course of Study for science at elementary school, *Japan.* 92–104.

Hidaka, T. (2007). Science classes without hesitation to teach; a trial of "knowledge transmission – instantiation" learning. pp. 2–10, Gyosei Publ., Japan.

Kawakami, S. (2007). Enhancement and progress in discussion of science study. *Science Education Monthly, 56*(4), 4–7.

Ausubel, D.P. & F. G. Robinson. (1969). School leaning. New York: Holt, Rinehart & Winson.

Mayer, R.E.(1983). Can you repeat that?: Qualitative and quantitative effects of reception and advance organizers on learning from science prose. *J. of Educational Psychology, 75*, 40–49.

Kawakami, S. & Y. Sugiura. (1985). The effect of the advance organizer concerning the understanding of the structure of the flowers in third grade elementary education (in Japanese with English summary). *J. of Research in Science Education, 25*(3), 15–25.

Kawakami, S. & H. Tajika. (1987). Effects of the advance organizer on teaching biological science in the junior high school (in Japanese with English summary). *Bull. of Jap. Curriculum Research and Development, 12*(2), 25–30.

Tajika, H. & S. Kawakami. (1988). Effects of the advance organizer on teaching biological science in an elementary school (in Japanese with English summary), *J. of Research in Science Education 29*(1), 29–37.

Kawakami, S. & H. Tajika. (1990). Effects of the advance organizer on science lessons (in Japanese). Bull. of Curriculum Research Center, *Aichi University of Education, 4*, 197–202.

Kawakami, S. (2003). Science classes to re-empower teaching (in Japanese), Toyokan Publ., Japan

Kawakami, S., K. Watanabe & A. Matsumoto. (2009) . A study of meaningful reception learning" (in Japanese). *J. of Center for Research, Training and Guidance in Educational Practice, 12*, 183–190.

Kawakami, S. & K. Watanabe. (2010). Development of meaningful reception learning in Japan (in Japanese). *J. of Research in Science Education, 50*(3), 1–14.

Shogo Kawakami
Gamagori Museum of Earth, Life and the Sea
kawakami@nrc.gamagori.aichi.jp

Koichiro Watanabe
Kanare Elementary School, Nagoya ,

Aya Matsumoto
Meiho Lower Secondary School, Nagoya, Japan

HONG KIM TAN

40. SINGAPORE STUDENTS' LEARNING EXPERIENCES ON SUSTAINABLE DEVELOPMENT: A REVIEW OF THE ROLES OF CIVIL SOCIETY AND EXTERNAL ORGANISATIONS

ABSTRACT

This paper examines the roles played by civil society and external organizations in complementing Singapore schools to develop a sense of responsibility towards environmental sustainability. A review of the key considerations to establish and refine programs for educating students on sustainable development is reported. Successful implementation of the programs can ensure students' initial encounters with environmental issues will serve as sources of inspiration or challenges to themselves for a passionate commitment on environmental sustainability.

KEYWORDS

Singapore Schools, Co-curricular Programs, External Organizations, Sustainable Development

INTRODUCTION

Education is a cumulative and ongoing process that occurs from experience in a range of settings in formal curriculum and informal settings (Rennie, 2007). Increasingly, informal learning takes place in a variety of contexts and through a wide variety of media. Factors outside schools have a strong positive influence on students' educational outcomes (Schibeci 1989, Falk *et al.*, 1986). With the involvement of more stakeholders from external organisations and communities, learning outside formal institutions is certainly of growing importance and this review aims to contribute further to our understanding of its complementary roles and explore factors that must be considered when we attempt to put together a holistic learning experience in our students. One important factor to consider is the sense of responsibility towards ensuring environmental sustainability.

ROLE OF EDUCATION ON ENVIRONMENT ISSUES IN SINGAPORE SCHOOLS

Singapore schools play a key role in laying the foundation for maintaining a population which will have the knowledge and willingness to care for and act

Mijung Kim and C. H. Diong (Eds.), Biology Education for Social and Sustainable Development, 375–384.
© *2012 Sense Publishers. All rights reserved.*

responsibly to protect our environment. Key competency domains in Singapore's education system include critical and inventive thinking, information and communication skills, civic literacy, cross cultural skills and global awareness. In view of the importance of global awareness and civic literacy skills on nurturing our young for the future, aspects pertaining to the need for ensuring environmental sustainability are incorporated into the schools' formal curriculum in all levels (via the Humanities and Science syllabuses). The coverage of these curricula is regularly revised and structured introduction of related topics is carried out in appropriate subjects. Opportunities are provided for students to create and apply their knowledge to solve real-world problems within the largely academic treatment of the content. Students are also taught in field trips, community involvement projects and their student clubs where such co-curricular programs and projects develop the whole child.

Role of Academic Curriculum on Environmental Issues

Starting from the Primary Level (primary one to six), concepts of biodiversity and life-cycles are introduced. Through the subject Social Studies, environmental issues such as air and water pollution are discussed with the aim of developing a sense of responsibility to the environment. The Civics and Moral Education Syllabus covers aspects such as the respect for life and nature and being a responsible decision-maker, a caring member of the global community living in harmony with our environment. Hence, students learn the importance of showing respect and responsibility towards environmental preservation and conservation through these subjects (CPDD, 2010a).

Continuing to the Secondary Level, concepts such as the interdependence of living things and ecosystem are introduced to Years 7 and 8 (Lower Secondary) science students. This prepares them for the study of human activities that leads to the maintenance or destruction of the diversity of species in Years 9 and 10 (Upper Secondary) Biology subject. In Geography, students examine the possible strategies and challenges involved in managing environmental issues. At the lower secondary level, students learn to evaluate Singapore's approaches to environmental protection. At upper secondary, they learn about the issues involved in the sustainable development of tropical rainforests. In addition, they learn to analyze sustainable development as applied to contexts such as tourism and industrial development. Through the subject Social Studies at secondary level, the discussion extends to studying the environmental impact of globalization, for example on deforestation and the haze problem in Southeast Asia. Hence, students are exposed to a broad spectrum of environmental issues including wildlife conservation and become aware of the need to maintain a balance between economic development and environmental conservation. The syllabuses also equip them with skills to make informed decisions on how they can contribute towards achieving this balance through the study of these science and humanities subjects (CPDD, 2010b).

At the Pre-University Level, importance of genetic variation in natural populations, significance of genetic engineering in improving the quality and yield of crop plants and animals, as well as the ethical and social considerations of genetically modified (GM) organisms are covered. Possible impact of GM organisms on wildlife is also emphasized. In Geography, students go to the root of environmental issues by comparing resource use in developed and less developed countries and discussing changes in society that affect people's appraisal and use of resources. These resources could include animal and plant by-products. Therefore, students are equipped with the skills, knowledge and attitudes to work towards achieving a balance between economic development and conservation of the natural environment through this curriculum (CPDD, 2010c).

Role of the Co-curricular Programmes on Environment Issues

The Singapore Green Plan 2012, highlights our commitment towards ensuring Singapore's environmental sustainability. It was formulated with inputs from the People, Private and Public (3P) sectors to cultivate an environmentally conscious population, promote resource conservation and clean technology and increase our effort in protecting the local and global environment (Singapore Green Plan, 2010).

In line with this plan, the Ministry of Education (MOE) collaborates with and facilitates schools' collaborations with external agencies to organize activities that will capture students' interest. These collaborations include short-term programs to enthuse the general student population and intensive longer term programs that have a greater impact on selected students. External organizations such as the Agency for Science, Technology and Research (A*STAR), Singapore Science Centre, Sungei Buloh Wetland Reserve and Institutes of Higher Learning have been organizing outreach programs to cultivate and maintain students' interest in environmental issues. The outreach program by Jurong Bird Park, for example, involves training student volunteers to serve as wildlife conservation ambassadors and also providing training for preschool teachers on how to conduct exciting and enriching field trips to this park (Jurong Bird Park Outreach Program, 2010).

Various programs and resources are available to support schools in achieving environment-related learning outcomes. One of the resources is the Wireless Learning Trail at the Sungei Buloh Wetland Reserve. The trail was designed by the Geography Unit at MOE in partnership with the National Parks Board, the Infocomm Development Authority of Singapore (IDA) and iCELL Network Pte Ltd. to support schools in exploring environmental issues and wildlife conservation issues through field-based learning. The trail equipped students with portable devices (Ultra Mobile PC) to receive text, images, video and audio files related to the sights and sounds of this wetland reserve from bar codes located along the Mangrove Boardwalk. The barcodes also provide access to activity sheets that guide student learning about the unique flora and fauna of the mangrove ecosystem (Wireless Learning Trail, 2010). The activities, which comprise a series of station activities, are specially designed to cater to the different learning styles and abilities of the pupils and to engage them in active learning beyond the classroom and textbooks. An experiential and inquiry approach is the focus of this trail whereby pupils get to see, touch and explore the wonders of nature around them. When learning is made more fun and meaningful, students' interests are stimulated. These measures will serve to enhance engagement of students towards establishing balanced human-nature relationships between these students and the world around them.

A key aspect of any environmental education program is environment conservation. Tan *et al.* (2009) described a case study of the Nature Learning Camp which is currently the longest running environmental awareness and learning program for students in Singapore. Originating from a local reforestation-stewardship project, hundreds of students learnt environmental science and conservation values under the guidance of a biologist from the National Institute of Education, school teachers, volunteers and officers from government bodies such as the National Parks Board and Public Utilities Board. The teachers who had participated in this program gained a level of expertise close to that of practicing scientists and eventually assumed responsibility of the organization of the Nature Learning Camp as well as other environment education programs. The early beginnings of the Wallace Environmental Learning Laboratory (WELL), part of the Wallace Education Centre in Dairy Farm Nature Park, can be traced to this reforestation-stewardship project. This learning laboratory, established by Raffles Girls' School and the National Parks Board, sponsored by GlaxoSmithKline and supported by the Economic Development Board (EDB), is the first outdoor environmental learning laboratory in Singapore. It is developed with the objective of promoting environmental education through fieldwork and is a one-stop learning centre for scientific research, national education, community service, teacher training and international exchange (WELL, 2010).

Another program which many local schools participated in is the International Coastal Cleanup, Singapore (ICCS). This annual event, conducted in 70–100 countries, is coordinated by the US-based agency, The Ocean Conservancy, a non-profit organization. In Singapore, the event is coordinated by volunteers of the Raffles Museum of Biodiversity Research of the National University of Singapore (NUS). The extent and scope of the ICCS has grown over the years, from just carrying out beach cleanups to enhanced education programs about the marine environment. Students learn about issues concerning marine debris, about the importance of environmental conservation for protecting wildlife and the need do their part in protecting aquatic environments (International Coastal Cleanup, 2010).

The Roots & Shoots (Singapore) program is supported by the Jane Goodall Institute (Singapore) (JGIS). It is an affiliate of the Jane Goodall Institute headquartered in the United States and was established in 2007. The Roots & Shoots program focuses on educating youths on the importance of individuals taking informed and compassionate action to improve the environment for all living things. JGIS leads outreach programs to schools, mentoring programs to train the educators and students to connect the Roots & Shoots groups of Singapore with each other and with groups from around the world in working to make a difference for animals, people, and the environment (Cool Projects, 2010). The Singapore American School organized a recycling project which involved the participation of over 1000 students; NUS organized a campus recycling education campaign aimed at increasing recycling rates from a campus rate of 12% to the national rate of 56%; members also serve as coastline ambassadors to increase awareness of the need to protect our precious coral reefs and marine wildlife.

Some schools have customized the lower secondary curriculum to include an environment education component. For example, Marsiling Secondary School was accorded Centre of Excellence for Environmental Education since 2007 and its program is closely aligned to the school's vision of nurturing world-ready citizens. This program aims to develop in their students an environmentally conscious mindset. Portions of the Geography and Science syllabuses are integrated into two environment education modules (Niche School Program, 2010). In these modules, students use the problem-based learning approach to study the environmental challenges facing Singapore and the world. The impact of pollution on wildlife was one of the challenges examined. At Commonwealth Secondary School, an inter-disciplinary team of teachers has designed an Environmental Education curriculum for their students, using the Teaching for Understanding framework. Apart from school-wide Green Events, there is a structured and differentiated program for each level, with various hands-on activities to enable students to engage with environmental issues. Activities organized includes environmental seminars, learning journeys to the Sungei Buloh Wetland Reserve, clean-up of Sungei Pandan and Pandan Reservoir as well as assigning students to community outreach programs as green ambassadors (Environmental Education, 2010).

The Raffles Institution's Community Education programme is structured to provide exposure to community involvement and service learning. Going beyond the simplicity of charity, students are given opportunities to act and think critically about how they can make a difference in the lives of others (Raffles Ecological Literacy Programme, 2010). They are presented with the chance, not only to serve and interact, but also to plan innovative community outreach programmes. This develops in them an in-depth understanding of developmental, governance, sociological, economic and ecological issues. One of the programmes, the Raffles Ecological Literacy Programme, enables students to understand and care for our Earth and for the people that inhabit it. They are empowered to take responsibility and act for social justice and environmental advocacy through local and international projects, field trips, seminars and discussions.

Strengthening and Leveling Up the Capacity of Teachers

Teaching approaches and activities must be able to enthuse and inject in students a keenness to explore and discover. The key to inspiring students is the teacher. Teachers need to be equipped with a wide repertoire of teaching skills that will enable them to stimulate their students' interest. When conducting out-of-classroom programs, activities tend to be less structured, learner centered, open access and require more intrinsic motivation. Teachers would encounter occasions of uncertainty as they fear of being unable to answer questions based on unfamiliar territory. To address these concerns, Lim and Ng (2011) reported that NUS and National Institute of Education (NIE) in Nanyang Technological University (NTU) offer Biology programs with biodiversity and environmental conservation courses. At NIE (NTU), undergraduates who read Biology as an academic subject take compulsory Biology courses such as Biodiversity in Natural Ecosystems, Animal Diversity and Evolution and Ecology. They also made trips to places such as Bukit Timah Nature Reserve, Sungei Buloh Wetlands Reserve, Pulau Ubin and WELL for diversity outdoor classes. These courses provide pre-service teachers with solid fundamental knowledge in biodiversity and conservation so that they can be champions and ambassadors of biodiversity conservation in the Singapore school system.

FACTORS TO CONSIDER WHEN ESTABLISHING AND REFINING LEARNING EXPERIENCES

Most educators accept the premise that first-hand experiences are essential to the educational process and an excellent method for introducing and reinforcing certain concepts is out-of-classroom experience. However, Openshaw and Whittle (1993) indicated that there are areas of hindrances faced by students who have not adequately acquired the necessary background knowledge and skills before carrying out field studies. For example, students lack interpretation skills. The use of pre-visit preparatory material would help to structure visits for them (Tunnicliffe, 2004) and overcome potential difficulties and enhanced their ability to adjust to the study site (Cotton and Cotton, 2009). Gunckel (1999) found that students, after interacting with the natural environment, often continue with their classroom studies without connecting their field experience to a larger conceptual picture. An ecological exploration curriculum developed to help students build a conceptual framework before participating in field experiences would better integrate their field discoveries into their own understandings.

Studies on field trip learning by Falk (1983) indicated that students in the age range 10–12 are ready for day-long trips to novel settings but younger students may not be as receptive. He suggested planning for more than one trip for that location. The first visit should emphasize activities that will familiarize students with the setting while succeeding visits can focus more on conceptual learning. It was reported students showed improved attitudes towards wanting to learn more about the subject matter and an interest in returning to the field trip site during revisits to field trip sites (Knapp, 2000).

Well-designed worksheets serve to focus students' attention on what they are supposed to look at and explore. For example, some worksheets require students to carefully examine an organism and sketch a particular aspect of the organism. On the other hand, some are only factual lists that hardly require students to look at specimens in the habitat (Tunnicliffe, 2004). Thus, design and close supervision on the use of worksheets is another important factor to consider depending on what the intended outcomes are. Building up students' question-posing capabilities through the use of real-world problems and analyze case study has been found to improve their problem-solving ability (Dori and Herscovitz, 1999). This strategy is thus useful to increase students' awareness of the need and feasibility of seeking practical solutions to a given problem.

Stake and Mares (2005) reported that it was important schools and supporting organizations recognize the role of social support from other stakeholders such as the family and alumnus members. Rennie (2007) emphasized that effective helpers encourage students to actively explore and reflect, rather than simply directing them to the 'right' answer. Development of effective environmental policies in schools also needs to be considered in order to promote environmental knowledge in the school population as schools with strong orientation towards the environment are more capable of helping students with their understanding of environmental concepts (Barraza and Cuarón, 2004). For example, Nkosi (2002) carried out community education programs on diversity conservation resulted in community involvement by related communities and government organizations, and hence a higher level of emphasis on environment issues.

DISCUSSION

Kwan and Stimpson (2003) examined context variables that helped shape the environmental curriculum in Singapore schools. They observed there was commitment to environmental education in schools and, at times, a passionate commitment among a significant minority of teachers and curriculum developers. Teachers and school administrators have been increasingly supportive of initiatives to equip students with skills to make informed decisions on how they can contribute towards environmental conservation.

Interdisciplinary approaches are necessary to enable academic and co-curricular programs to develop a sense of responsibility towards ensuring environmental sustainability. There is a need for both teachers and students to explore the contributions that each traditional discipline has to offer towards the building of environmental literacy. There must be ongoing efforts to level up the capacity and quality of teachers in the areas of content as well as pedagogies through in-service workshops and attachment programs as well as stepped up efforts to expose teachers to current developments in environmental education through workshops, conferences, local and overseas study trips as well as attachment to local research institutes and overseas institutions. Lock (2010) surveyed published studies on Biology fieldwork and identified time, cost, health and safety issues, curriculum, assessment as well as teacher enthusiasm and expertise as key factors that impact on teachers who are actively engaged in fieldwork. When establishing and refining programs for educating students on sustainable development, due consideration should also be given to providing students with the relevant background knowledge and skills before embarking on field studies.

It is also important to enlist the support of parents, school administrators and community organizations. The complementary roles that parents, schools and out-of-school establishments play must be harnessed through careful integration of learning experiences so that each activity extends what can be learned in classrooms. These considerations will result in the organization of more enjoyable, successful and sustained environmental education programs. Areas for future research should include studies on processes that lead to the development of more favorable attitudes towards environmental protection as well as instruments for measuring changes in environmentally relevant behavior. Improved attitudes and motivation, leading to environmentally friendly behavior would certainly contribute towards our ongoing efforts towards ensuring environmental sustainability.

As indicated by the programs described above, much effort has been made to cultivate an awareness and understanding of the environment, encourage experiential learning and promote active involvement in the protection and maintenance of the environment amongst the local student population. Overall, these experiences with external organizations contribute towards cultivating care and respect for the environment in students by exposing them to a broad spectrum of environmental issues so that their views can take on global perspectives and inculcate a sense of interconnectedness beyond the confines of our national borders.

REFERENCES

Barraza, L., & Cuarón, A. D. (2004). How values in education affect children's environmental knowledge. *Journal of Biological Education, 39*(1), 18–23.

Bebbington, A. (2004). Learning at residential field centres. In Braund, M., & Reiss, M. (Eds.), *Learning science outside the classroom.* (pp. 55–73). London: RoutledgeFalmer.

Braund, M. (2004). Using freshwater habitats. In Braund, M., & Reiss, M. (Eds.), *Learning science outside the classroom.* (pp. 35–53). London: RoutledgeFalmer.

Braund, M., & Reiss, M. (2004). The nature of learning science outside the classroom. In Braund, M., & Reiss, M. (Eds.), *Learning science outside the classroom.* (pp. 1–12). London: RoutledgeFalmer.

Cool Projects. (2010). Retrieved July 1, 2010, from the Roots & Shoots website: http://www .janegoodall.org.sg/Jane_Goodall/_Roots_and_Shoots.html

Cotton, D.R.E., & Cotton, P.A. (2009). Field biology experiences of undergraduate students: the impact of novelty space. *Journal of Biological Education, 43*(4), 169–174.

CPDD (2010a). (Curriculum Planning and Development Division) *Primary Level syllabuses.* Singapore: Ministry of Education. Retrieved July 1, 2010, from the Singapore Examinations and Assessment Board website: http://www.seab.gov.sg/psle/2010subjectInfo.html

CPDD (2010b). *GCE 'O' Level syllabuses.* Singapore: Ministry of Education. Retrieved July 1, 2010, from the Singapore Examinations and Assessment Board website: http://www.seab.gov.sg/oLevel/ schoolCandidates/2011_GCE_O.html

CPDD (2010c). *GCE 'A' Level syllabuses.* Singapore: Ministry of Education. Retrieved July 1, 2010, from the Singapore Examinations and Assessment Board website: http://www.seab.gov.sg/aLevel/ syllabus/schoolCandidates/2011_GCE_A.html

Cutter, E. G. (1993). Fieldwork: An essential component of biological training. *Journal of Biological Education, 27*(1), 3–4.

Dori, Y. J., & Herscovitz, O. (1999). Question-posing capability as an alternative evaluation method: Analysis of an environmental case study. *Journal of Research in Science Teaching, 36*(4), 411–430.

Environmental Education. (2010). Retrieved July 1, 2010, from Commonwealth Secondary School website: http://www.commonwealthsec.moe.edu.sg/sites/SchoolPortal/publicportal/school_res.aspx

Falk, J. H. (1983). Field trips: A look at environmental effects on learning. *Journal of Biological Education, 17*(2), 137–142.

Falk, J. H., Koran, J. J., & Dierking, L. D. (1986). The things of science: Assessing the learning potential of science museums. *Science Education, 70*(5), 503–508.

Gunckel, K. L. (1999). Ecosystem Explorations. *Science and Children, 37*(1), 18–23.

Hart, P. (2007). Environmental education. In S. K. Abell & N. G. Lederman (Eds.), *Handbook of Research on Science Education*. (pp. 689–726). New Jersey: Lawrence Erlbaum Associates Publishers.

International Coastal Cleanup, Singapore. (2010). Retrieved July 1, 2010, from http://coastalcleanup.nus.edu.sg/aboutcleanup.html

Jane Goodall Institute, Singapore (JGIS). (2010). Retrieved July 1, 2010, from http://www.janegoodall.org.sg/Jane_Goodall/Welcome.html

Jurong Bird Park Outreach Programme. (2010). Retrieved July 1, 2010, from Jurong Bird Park website: http://www.birdpark.com.sg/l2_t1.aspx?l2=16&l1=6&langid=1

Knapp, D. (2000). Memorable experiences of a science field trip. *School Science and Mathematics, 100*(2), 65–72.

Kobierska, H., Tarabula-Fiertak, M., & Grodzińska-Jurczak, M. (2007). Attitudes to environmental education in Poland. *Journal of Biological Education, 42*(1), 12–18.

Kwan, W.B.F., & Stimpson, P. (2003). Environmental education in Singapore: Curriculum for the environment or in the national interest? *International Research in Geographical and Environmental Education, 12*(2), 123–138.

Leemimg, F. C., Dwyer, W. O., Porter, B. E., & Cobern, M. K. (1993). Outcome research in environmental education: A critical review. *The Journal of Environmental Education, 24*(4), 8–21.

Lim, S. S. L. & P. K. L. Ng. (2011). Formal biodiversity education. In Ng, P. K. L., R.T. Corlett & H.T.W Tan (Eds.), *Singapore Biodiversity: An encyclopaedia of the natural environment and sustainable development*. (pp. 176–181). Singapore: Tien Wah Press (Pte.) Ltd.

Lisowski, M., & Disinger, J. F. (1991). The effect of field-based instruction on student understandings of ecological concepts. *The Journal of Environmental Education, 23*(1), 19–23.

Lock, R. (2010). Biology fieldwork in schools and colleges in the UK: an analysis of empirical research from 1963 to 2009. *Journal of Biological Education, 44*(2), 58–64.

Lopushinsky, T., & Besaw, L. (1986). Field experiences for non-science students. *Journal of College Science Teaching, XVI*(1), 21–24.

MacKenzie, A. W., & White, R. T. (1982). Fieldwork in geography and long-term memory structures. *American Educational Research Journal, 19*(4), 623–632.

Manzanal, R. F., Barreiro, L. M. R., & Jimerez, M. C. (1999). Relationship between ecology fieldwork and student attitudes toward environmental protection. *Journal of Research in Science Teaching, 36*(4), 431–453.

Multidisciplinary Learning Trail. (2010). Retrieved July 1, 2010, from Corporation Primary School website: http://www.corporationpri.moe.edu.sg/cos/o.x?c=/wbn/pagetree&func=view&rid=52055

Niche School Programme. (2010). Retrieved July 1, 2010, from Marsiling Secondary School website: http://www.mslportal.edu.sg/marsiling/main/homepage/dsa.html

Night Safari Educational Programmes. (2010). Retrieved July 1, 2010, from the Wildlife Reserves Group website: http://www.nightsafari.com.sg/l2_t1.aspx?l1=6&l2=36&langid=1

Nkosi, B.S. (2002). Community education for biological diversity conservation in the Shiselweni Region of Swaziland. *Journal of Biological Education, 36*(3), 113–115.

Nurturing Our Young For The Future: *Competencies for the 21st Century*. (2010). Retrieved July 1, 2010, from the Ministry of Education website: http://www.moe.gov.sg/

Openshaw, P. H., & Whittle, S. J. (1993). Ecological field teaching: How can it be made more effective? *Journal of Biological Education, 27*(1), 58–66.

Orion, N. (1993). A model for the development and implementation of field trips as an integral part of the Science curriculum. *School Science and Mathematics, 93*(6), 325–331.

Raffles Ecological Literacy Programme. (2010). Retrieved July 1, 2010, from Raffles Institution website: http://www.ri.edu.sg/main/rafflesprog/studentdev

Reiss, M., & Braund. M. (2004). Managing learning outside the classroom. In Braund, M., & Reiss, M. (Eds.), *Learning science outside the classroom*. (pp. 225–234). London: RoutledgeFalmer.

Rennie, L. J. (2007). Learning Science outside school. In S. K. Abell & N. G. Lederman (Eds.), *Handbook of Research on Science Education*. (pp. 125–167). New Jersey: Lawrence Erlbaum Associates Publishers.

Rickinson, M., Dillon, J., Teamey, K., Morris, M., Choi, M.Y., Sanders, D., & Benefield, P. (2004). A review of research on outdoor learning. London: Field Studies Council.

Rowe, S., & Humphries, S. (2004). The outdoor classroom. In Braund, M., & Reiss, M. (Eds.), *Learning science outside the classroom*. (pp. 19–33). London: RoutledgeFalmer.

Schibeci, R. A. (1989). Home, school and peer group influences on student attitudes and achievement in Science. *Science Education, 73*(1), 13–24.

Singapore Green Plan 2012. (2010). Retrieved July 1, 2010, from http://app.mewr.gov.sg/web/Contents/Contents.aspx?ContId=1342

Stake, J. E., & Mares, K. R. (2005). Evaluating the impact of science-enrichment programs on adolescents' science motivation and confidence: The Splashdown Effect. *Journal of Research in Science Teaching, 42*(4), 359–375.

Tan, K. C. D., Lee, Y.-J., & Tan, A.-L. (2009). Environmental education in Singapore: Learning to manage urban landscapes and futures. In N. Taylor, R.K. Coll, M. Littledike, & C. Eames (Eds.), *Environmental education in context: An international perspective of the development of environmental education* (pp. 243–251). Rotterdam, The Netherlands: Sense Publishers.

Tunnicliffe, S. D. (2004). Learning at zoos and farms. In Braund, M., & Reiss, M. (Eds.), *Learning science outside the classroom*. (pp. 95–112). London: RoutledgeFalmer.

Uitto, A., Juuti, K., Lavonen, J., & Meisalo, V. (2006). Students' interest in biology and their out-of-school experiences. *Journal of Biological Education, 40*(3), 124–129.

Wallace Environmental Learning Laboratory. (2010). Retrieved July 1, 2010, from http://www.well.sg/

Wellington, J. (1990). Formal and informal learning in science: The role of the interactive science centres. *Physics Education, 25*(5), 247–252.

Wireless Learning Trail. (2010). Retrieved July 5, 2010, from Sungel Buloh Wetland Reserve website: http://www.sbwr.org.sg/events/wirelesslearningtrail/

Hong Kim Tan
Natural Sciences and Science Education,
National Institute of Education
Nanyang Technological University, Singapore
hongkim.tan@nie.edu.sg

SEBASTIAN KOCH, JAN BARKMANN, LETI SUNDAWATI
AND SUSANNE BÖGEHOLZ

41. UNIVERSITY STUDENTS' PERCEPTIONS OF COMMON-RESOURCE DILEMMAS – THE NEED FOR ADJUSTED CURRICULUM IN INDONESIA

ABSTRACT

Many of Indonesia's forest resources are degraded by over-utilisation due to *de facto* resources that are common property in the open-access areas. Consequences include social, economic, ecological, cultural as well as worldwide repercussions on resource degradation. The purpose of this study is to examine the pre-concepts of Indonesian biology student teachers and agronomy students on local resource conservation issues – overexploited common-resource dilemmas in Central Sulawesi, especially of the non-timber forest product, rattan. Nineteen future teachers and agricultural advisors at Tadulako University were interviewed. Qualitative results showed that students' pre-conceptions of resource depletion of rattan use were widely erroneous. Socio-economic impacts of over-exploitation on rural livelihoods were also not emphasised. The students do not recognise the need to balance short-term individual exploitation benefits with long-term community interests in resource conservation. Education is a long-term solution to solve this common-resource situation (in open-access situations) in order to ensure sustainable long-term resource utilisation. We conclude that socio-economic and institutional aspects of rural forest use need to be stressed in adjusted curricula development.

KEYWORDS

Education, Natural Resource, Common Resource, Sustainable, Indonesia

INTRODUCTION

Indonesia has the world's third largest tropical rainforests (FAO, 2006) but is responsible for two-thirds of forest loss in South and Southeast Asia (Achard *et al.*, 2002). Its deforestation rate at 2.0% per annum is also one of the highest worldwide. Over-exploitation of forest products, expansion and intensification of agriculture by smallholders, expansion of industrial agriculture, commercial lumbering and international oil and gas operations contribute to the high rate of deforestation (Butler & Laurence, 2008). The importance of the non-industrial,

Mijung Kim and C. H. Diong (Eds.), Biology Education for Social and Sustainable Development, 385–392.

individual appropriation of forest land and forest products suggest that the solution to biodiversity loss points to a substantial local factor.

Common-resource dilemmas are characterised by the use of an accessible natural resource (limited) by competing users (Musgrave & Musgrave, 1984). Short-term incentives exist that prompt the single users to seek the advantages of exploitative resource use. Hardin (1968) highlighted that such competition often leads to an over-exploitation of the resource that could principally be avoided. Environmental psychologists explain the apparent irrationality of resource over-exploitation with three so-called *traps;* the social trap, the temporal (or time delay) trap, and the spatial trap. The *social trap* (Platt, 1973) focuses on the unequally distributed costs and benefits of resource appropriation. The benefits of resource appropriation accrue to the individual while the costs are borne by the whole community. The *time delay trap* (Messick & McClelland, 1983) refers to the fact that some of the consequences of today's action – such a sudden breakdown of a resource stock following excessive resource extraction – may manifest themselves in the future only. Finally, the *spatial trap* (Vlek & Keren, 1992) describes situations in which the consequences of actions at a certain place affect other people or groups elsewhere. For example, the rattan over-exploitation dilemma (cf. Siebert, 2004) in the open-access Lore Lindu region, Central Sulawesi has negative consequences for the community; the social trap where the individual users benefit solely from the selling of rattan; the time trap as these exploitation leads to rattan loss; the spatial trap where other groups of individuals are affected by the decreasing rattan resources.

Solutions to such common-resource dilemmas cannot rely on the actions of individual users alone. Institutional changes should include governmental regulations (e.g. hunting bans, assignment of property rights), binding voluntary commitments (*Community Conservation Agreements)*, effective recourse to generally accepted traditions of resource use, or the introduction of economic incentives (Ostrom, 1990; Ostrom *et al.*, 2002). However, these changes require a strong government backing to enforce these regulations and commitments.

Indonesia is a member of the Convention on Biological Diversity (CBD) (UNCED, 1992). Article 13 of the CBD requests that all signatory countries to distribute information and raise public awareness about the importance of biological diversity (UNESCO, 2005). Many reports (e.g. Gordon, 1954; Edney & Harper; 1978; Ernst, 2008) suggest strong institutions, an educational system and personal capacity to propose potential solutions to the loss of biodiversity. However, there are indications the respective competences are lacking.

In particular, little is known about the knowledge of environmental issues in Indonesia, especially its future educational multipliers (Sudarmadi *et al.*, 2001). Multipliers of an *education for sustainable development* (ESD) need integrated knowledge and competences on the economic, ecological, social and institutional factors that shape the complexity of the utilisation and degradation of natural resources (Kassas, 2002). Hence, students graduating from universities are likely to become educational multipliers or key decision makers (Wong, 2001) and thus, likely to have a decisive impact upon the development of natural resources in the future (Wallis & Laurenson, 2004).

Stagnancy of the Indonesian educational system (including tertiary education) on uses of natural resources has already been noted a decade ago (Rudebjer & Del Castillo, 1999). Higher education needs to educate learners of the need to use natural resources in a sustainable manner (General Directorate of Higher Education, 2003). It is not surprising that single concepts of ESD are included only occasionally in the curriculum (Supriatna, 2007). Currently, Environmental Education is not an independent subject at primary and secondary education; it is integrated into existing subjects (Nomura, 2009). At the university level, natural resource management is provided in undergraduate courses only in some programmes. For example, University of Indonesia (UI) and Institut Pertanian Bogor (IPB), include environmental education components only in the graduate courses. In addition, teacher colleges only attempt to include environmental components in their training (Nomura, 2009).

The purpose of this study is to examine the pre-concepts of Indonesian biology student teachers and agronomy students on local resource conservation issues – overexploited common-resource dilemmas in Central Sulawesi, especially of the non-timbre forest product rattan. The non-empirical research questions are: (i) How do students perceive the common-resource dilemma situation concerning intensive rattan extraction in the Lore Lindu region? (ii) Which of the courses of action do the students envision to solve the dilemma? and (iii) What kinds of knowledge should future environmental educators and decision-makers in relevant fields of natural resource management possess, concerning common-resource dilemmas?

DATA COLLECTION AND METHODS

Nineteen problem-centred in-depth interviews (Witzel & Reiter, 2010) were conducted with agronomy and biology student teachers from Universitas Tadulako, Palu, Central Sulawesi. The interview guide was based on extensive consultations with local and international experts on resource use issues in Central Sulawesi, and included short interventional materials on several aspects of rattan utilisation. It operationalised values, risks and coping appraisal constructs from Protection Motivation Theory (Rogers & Prentice-Dunn, 1997). Responses were analysed following qualitative content analysis (Mayring 2000), and coded with MaxQDA. To verify the inter-subjectivity of coding, check-coding was conducted by a second researcher.

RESULTS

Qualitative results of the interview reported all participants recognised government action was rarely a sufficient means to solve the common-resource dilemma. However, most participants reported government actions were still one of the key factors to solve the dilemma.

Findings of this study also indicated that participants did not have prior knowledge of the ecological and socio-economic problems of rattan extraction. Most cited exclusively ecological, and often largely irrelevant problems of rattan extraction. While the majority of the participants referred to a loss of the resource, only a few mentioned the consequences for future generations. Socio-economic impacts on living conditions of the local population were also not emphasised. Participants did not recognise the need to balance short-term individual exploitation profits with long-term community interests in the resource conservation.

When asked what the courses of action to improve the implementation of ESD in the university curricula should be, participants only highlighted the need to integrate 'practical learning' (e.g. field practicals). There was no mention of any need to identify how the local population was dependent on the resource use, nor was there any suggestion on ways to help the people to be less dependent on the common resource.

A Model to Examine 'Knowledge'

Based on De Jong & Ferguson-Hessler (1996), a knowledge model (Figure 1) concerning common-resource dilemmas was used to understand the factors contributing to open-access situations. The model involves three types of knowledge (situational, conceptual and procedural) in the knowledge domains; (i) ecological knowledge, (ii) socio-economic knowledge, and (iii) institutional knowledge. Situational knowledge covers information that has to be screened from a certain problem description. Conceptual knowledge comprises additional knowledge beyond information scrapped from the problem description. The additional knowledge has to be integrated with the problem situation in order to classify the specific type of problem – this helps in recognising an open-access resource use problem. Based on the problem description, procedural knowledge accomplishes the transition from one problem state to another state, e.g. a state that allows for the identification of potential solutions.

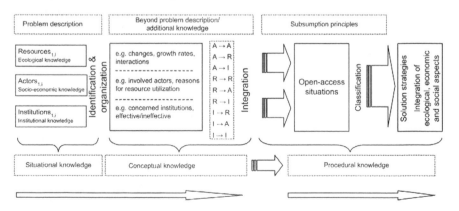

Figure 1. Knowledge model concerning common-resource dilemmas.

DISCUSSION

This study shows that a comprehensive understanding of ecological, economic, social, and institutional interrelationship exists. The future educators and advisors lack the needed competencies themselves. The qualitative results suggest that a more applied cross-disciplinary curriculum development that highlights ecology-society linkages (Menzel & Bögeholz, 2009) and natural resource depletion is necessary. For example, environmental education curriculum needs to evolve towards more interdisciplinary ESD (Fien & Tilbury, 2002). In addition, fostering of knowledge in each of the knowledge domains (i) ecological knowledge, (ii) socio-economic knowledge, and (iii) institutional knowledge is of major importance, to deal with common-resource dilemmas adequately.

In conclusion, the findings reveal a knowledge gap on the consequences of common-resource dilemmas. Consequences of this knowledge gap include social, economic, ecological, cultural as well as worldwide repercussions on resource degradation. Education is a long-term solution to solve this common-resource situation (in open-access situations) in order to ensure a more sustainable long-term resource utilisation. All students need to eventually acquire the knowledge of these consequences on forest resource utilisation and perhaps, come up with sustainable solutions.

Therefore, the education curriculum should be tailored to include current local issues reporting on sustainability concerns. In addition, it would be best to allow students to interact with affected stakeholders and policy makers for authentic case studies (Clark, 2001). In this way, learners are educated on local and socially relevant knowledge and would hopefully be able to explore adequate measures to balance human needs and conservation efforts. It is a concern that traditional teaching methods are still predominant in much of Southeast Asia (Lim, 2010; Wahyudi & Treagust, 2004). Therefore, once the adjusted curriculum is in place in the Indonesian education system, the next step is an adjustment of educators' teaching methodology.

REFERENCES

Achard, F., Eva, H., Stibig, H.-J., Mayaux, P., Gallego, J., Richards, T. & J.-P. Malingreau (2002): Determination of Deforestation Rates of the World's Humid Tropical Forests. *Science, 297*, 999–1002.

Butler, R. & W. Laurence (2008): New strategies for conserving tropical forests. *Trends in Ecology & Evolution, 23*(9), 469–472.

Clark, T. (2001): Developing Policy-Oriented Curricula for Conservation Biology: Professional and Leadership Education in the Public Interest. *Conservation Biology, 15*(1), 31–39.

De Jong, T. & M. Ferguson-Hessler (1996): Types and Qualities of Knowledge. *Educational Psychologist 31*(2), 105–113.

Direktorat Jenderal Pendidikan Tinggi [General Directorate of Higher Education] (2003): *Basic Framework for Higher Education (KPPTJP IV). 2003–2010. Draft.*

Edney, J. & C. Harper (1978): The Commons Dilemma-a Review of Contributions from Psychology. *Environmental Management, 2*(6), 491–507.

Ernst, A. (2008): Ökologisch-soziale Dilemmata. *In*: Lantermann, E.-D. & V. Linneweber (Eds.), *Enzyklopädie der Psychologie. Serie IX Umweltpsychologie* (Vol. 1). Göttingen. Hogrefe. pp. 569–605.

FAO (2006): Global Forest Resources Assessment 2005 – Progress towards sustainable forest management. Rome.

Fien, J. & Tilbury, D. (2002): The Global Challenge of Sustainability in: Tilbury, D. Stevenon, R., Fien, J. & D. Schreuder (2002): *Education and Sustainability: Responding to the Global Challenge*. Gland. IUCN. pp. 1–12.

Gordon, H. S. (1954): The Economic Theory of a Common-Property Resource: The Fishery. *The Journal of Political Economy, 62*(2),124–142.

Hardin, G. (1968): The Tragedy of the Commons. *Science, 162*, 1243–1248.

Kassas, M. (2002): Environmental Education: Biodiversity. *The Environmentalist, 22*(4), 345–351.

Kementerian Lingkungan Hidup [Ministry of the Environment]: (2004): *Kebijakan Pendidikan Lingkungan Hidup*. Jakarta, Indonesia.

Lim, W. (2010): Asian Education must change to promote innovative thinking. *Nature, 465*, 157.

Mayring, P. (2000): Qualitative Content Analysis [28 paragraphs]. *Forum Qualitative Sozialforschung / Forum: Qualitative Social Research [Online Journal]*, 1*(2)*.

Menzel, S. & S. Bögeholz (2009): The Loss of Biodiversity as a Challenge for Sustainable Development: How Do Pupils in Chile and Germany Perceive Resource Dilemmas? *Research in Science Education, 39*(4) 429–447.

Messick, D. & C. McClelland (1983): Social Traps and temporal Traps. *Personality and Social Psychology Bulletin, 9*(1), 105–110.

Musgrave, R. & P. Musgrave (1984): *Public Finance in Theory and Practice*. 4th Edition, New York. McGraw-Hill.

Nolting, H.-P. & P. Paulus (2004): *Pädagogische Psychologie*. Grundriss der Psychologie, Band 20. Stuttgart. Kohlhammer Verlag.

Nomura, K. (2009): A perspective on education for sustainable development: Historical development of environmental education in Indonesia. *International Journal of Educational Development, 29*(6), 621–627.

Ostrom, E. (1990): *Governing the Commons – The Evolution of Institutions for Collective Action*. Cambridge. Cambridge University Press.

Ostrom, E., Dietz, T., Dolsak, N., Stern, P. C., Stonich, S. & E. Weber (Eds.) (2002): *The Drama of the Commons*. Washington, D.C. National Academy Press.

Platt, J. (1973): Social Traps. *American Psychologist, 28*(8), 641–651.

Rogers, R. & S. Prentice-Dunn (1997): Protection Motivation Theory. In: Gochman, D. (Ed.): *Handbook of Health Behavior Research I: Personal and Social Determinants*. New York. Plenum Press. pp. 113–132.

Rudebjer, P. & R. Del Castillo, (1999): *How Agroforestry is taught in Southeast Asia. A Status and Needs Assessment in Indonesia, Lao PDR, the Philippines, Thailand and Vietnam*. Bogor, Indonesia: Southeast Asian Network for Forestry Education (SEANAFE).

Siebert, S. (2004): Demographic Effects of Collecting Rattan Cane and Their Implications for Sustainable Harvesting. *Conservation Biology, 18*(2), 424–431.

Sudarmadi, S., Suzuki, S., Kawada, T., Netti, H., Soemantri, S. & A. Tri Tugaswati (2001): A Survey of Perception, Knowledge, Awareness, and attitude in Regard to Environmental Problems in a Sample of two Different Social Groups in Jakarta, Indonesia. *Environment, Development and Sustainability, 3*(2), 169–183.

Supriatna, A. (2007): Issues of Sustainable Development (ESD) in Teacher Education Curriculum in Indonesia: Progress and Challenges. Conference Paper, ESD-NET Training Workshop. Bangkok. UNESCO.

Tilbury, D. (1995): Environmental Education for Sustainability: defining the new focus of environmental education in the 1990s. *Environmental Education Research, 1*(2), 195–212.

UNCED. (1992): *Convention on Biological Diversity (CBD)*. Rio de Janeiro. United Nations Conference on Environment and Development.

UNESCO. (2005): *United Nations Decade of Education for Sustainable Development 2005–2014*. Draft International Implementation Scheme.

Vlek, C. & G. Keren (1992): Behavioral decision theory and environmental risk assessment: Assessment and resolution of four 'survival' dilemmas. *Acta Psychologica, 80*, 249–278.

Wahyudi & D. Treagust (2004): An Investigation of Science Teaching Practices in Indonesian Rural Secondary Schools. *Research in Science Education 34*(4), 455–474.

Wallis, A. & L. Laurenson (2004): Environment, Resource Sustainability and Sustainable Behaviour: Exploring Perceptions of Students in South West Victoria. *Asian Journal of Biology Education, 2,* 39–49.

Witzel, A. & H. Reiter (2010): *The Problem-Centred Interview*. London. Sage Publications.

Wong, K. (2001): Taiwan's environment, resource sustainability and green consumerism: Perceptions of university students. *Sustainable Development, 9*(4), 222–233.

Sebastian Koch, Susanne Bögeholz
Faculty of Biology, Albrecht-von-Haller-Institute for Plant Sciences, Didactics of Biology,Georg-August-Universität Göttingen (Germany). Sebastian Koch, corresponding author; Waldweg 26, 37073 Göttingen, Germany; skoch@gwdg.de

Jan Barkmann
Department of Agricultural Economics and Rural Development, Environmental and Resource Economics, Georg-August-Universität Göttingen (Germany)

Leti Sundawati
Faculty of Forestry, Department of Forest Management, Social Forestry Unit, Institut Pertanian Bogor (IPB) (Indonesia)

HASSAN H. TAIRAB

42. EMPOWERING BIOLOGY TEACHERS THROUGH DEVELOPMENT OF CONTENT AND PEDAGOGICAL CONTENT KNOWLEDGE

ABSTRACT

This research was concerned with building capacity of biology teachers through development of their content and pedagogical content knowledge (PCK). The objectives of the study were to (i) ascertain the knowledge base of biology teachers through exploring their current pedagogical content knowledge and identifying components that make up their PCK, (ii) explore the effectiveness of a professional development training program on developing the PCK of the participating biology teachers, and (iii) develop a mechanism by which biology teachers' content and PCK is assessed and documented. The sample comprised 22 biology teachers of different professional backgrounds and teaching experience. Participating biology teachers were engaged in a series of professional development activities to impact their PCK and subjected to various classroom observations as well as collaborative and reflective activities to document their practice. Quantitative and qualitative data collected from these activities were categorized and analyzed. The findings suggest teachers exhibited varied levels of content representation, varied level of PCK, and varied components that make up their PCK, indicating that teachers follow different pathways towards acquiring meaningful content representation. Furthermore, the series of the professional development activities implemented at the beginning of the research impacted their content as well as their PCK. The findings may also suggest that teachers' PCK can systematically be assessed and documented using the approach adopted in this research. Implications and future research orientations are suggested.

KEYWORDS

Teacher Knowledge, Teacher Professional Development; PCK

INTRODUCTION

Much of the recent debate on teacher education reform focuses on issues related to what sort of knowledge teachers might have in order to become effective practitioners and how this knowledge might inform classroom practice. This debate

Mijung Kim and C. H. Diong (Eds.), Biology Education for Social and Sustainable Development, 393–402.

has led to realization that empowering teachers is an essential component of any systemic reform efforts. Increasing teachers' knowledge in the disciplines and their pedagogical expertise will lead to transformation of classrooms so that students have the opportunity to learn science in meaningful and challenging ways. It is essential therefore to maintain teachers' professional growth through effective professional development programs.

Shulman (1986) categorized the domain of teacher knowledge into seven categories. Among the categories are content and pedagogical content knowledge. Shulman defined his notion of pedagogical content knowledge (PCK) as the capacity to transform the content knowledge the teacher possesses into forms that are pedagogically powerful, adaptive and takes into account the diverse abilities and background of students (Shulman, 1986). From this perspective, pedagogical content knowledge represents an attempt to determine what the teachers know about their subject matter and how they translate that knowledge into classroom practice. Shulman (1986) further identified pedagogical content knowledge (PCK) as "the most useful forms of content representation, the most powerful analogies, illustrations, examples, and demonstrations in a word, the ways of representing and formulating the subject that makes it comprehensible for others". That area of knowledge includes "an understanding of what makes the learning of specific topics easy or difficult: the conceptions and preconceptions that students of different ages and backgrounds bring with them to the learning of those most frequently taught topics and lessons". To make learning meaningful and useful; teachers must know the content sufficiently and flexibly so that they can teach it within wider contexts.

Recent studies have reconceptualized Shulman's notion of pedagogical content knowledge in the light of findings from more recent research. For example, on the basis of a review of literature, Putnam and Borko (1997), Loughran et al. (2008) and Lee and Luft (2008) discussed pedagogical content knowledge in terms of wider conceptions of teaching related to understanding of content, instructional strategies and representations, students' understandings, and knowledge of curriculum and curricular materials. Loughran et al, and Mulhall (2001) viewed pedagogical content knowledge as being "the knowledge that a teacher uses to provide teaching situations that help learners to make sense of particular science content." In a recent study and in an attempt to understand and portray science teachers' PCK with content representation (CoRe) and professional and pedagogical experience repertoire (PaP-eRs) approaches, Loughran et al (2004) considered five aspects of PCK: (i) approaches to the framing of ideas and effective sequencing, (ii) knowledge of students, (iii) insightful ways of testing for understanding, and (iv) knowledge of difficulties and limitations connected with teaching, (v) knowledge of alternative conceptions. Including these components, Loughran et al. (2004) developed the CoRe matrix of eight questions which include those five components of the PCK to codify teachers' PCK related to a specific content.

Other researchers such as Sherin (2002), Sherin et al (2000) discussed teacher pedagogical content knowledge from the perspective of a "knowledge system analysis" paradigm where the focus was on describing the knowledge categories that characterize effective teaching. Sherin (2002) compared this line of research with a cognitive modeling paradigm that focuses on short term classroom activities and describes aspects of teacher knowledge that can account for particular teaching behaviors. The content of teacher knowledge according to Sherin (2002) focuses on what the knowledge is about or what it is used for, whereas the form of teacher knowledge focuses on how the teacher knowledge is organized, linked, and represented in the teacher's mind.

The studies of Sherin *et al.,* (2000), Loughran et al. (2008), Sherin (2002), and Loughran *et al.* (2001) clearly suggest that possession of PCK will greatly impact teachers' classroom actions. This suggestion was supported by the various findings of research on teaching that showed the importance of PCK in teachers' planning and action when dealing with subject matter (Van Driel *et al.*, 1998), teachers' learning of new instructional strategies (Supovitz and Turner, 2000; Huffman *et al.*, 2003), and student learning (Loughran *et al.*, 2008).

While the concept of pedagogical content knowledge is debated in the literature, there is general agreement that the development of PCK is embedded in classroom practice, implying that teachers vary in their PCK according to practice. Teachers, who promote student learning, are likely to have well-developed PCK in that specific content they teach, which is characterized by specific observable behaviors such as showing comprehension and understanding, using various representational models and variety of teaching acts, and continuous checking for understanding and misunderstanding during teaching.

From the perspective of teachers having sound and articulated PCK, there is a growing attention been paid to the value of professional development training program in order to help teacher develop coherent and consistent PCK. On the other hand, there is a growing belief that professional development should be targeted and directly related to teachers' practice. This belief also focuses on the notion that professional development should be site-based and should be integrated into the regular practices of teachers so that it helps teachers help their students attain higher levels of content understanding and improved performance.

Various models for teachers' professional development programs (PD) have been suggested worldwide. Different programs emphasize content knowledge, pedagogical content knowledge, building communities of practitioners, and building on teachers' beliefs (Bell and Gilbert, 1996; Marx *et al.,* 1998; NRC, 1996; Supovitz and Turner, 2000). The essence of most of these models is that teachers collaborate in order to construct meaning, enact new practices in the classroom, reflect on their practice and, eventually, adapt materials and practices. The paradigm shift from working in isolation to working in a collaborative group is favorably received by teachers (Birman, 2002). From this perspective, a question may be raised: Is it possible to enhance science teachers' topic specific PCK in those content areas where their PCK is under-developed using specifically designed professional development training program? The Empowering Biology Teachers' Project is specifically designed to achieve this.

Research Rationale and Objectives

In the United Arab Emirates, frequent comments and observations received from the educational field and concerned individuals suggest that many biology teachers may have limited content knowledge which in turn may influence the development of their PCK. Content knowledge of biology is obviously fundamental to being able to help students learn. To communicate an accurate understanding of scientific knowledge to students, biology teachers need to understand the subject matter from multiple perspectives than that actually presented to the students. To teach as advocated by most science education reforms, teachers must hold deep and highly structured content knowledge that can be accessed flexibly and efficiently for the purposes of instruction. It appears that building capacity of biology teachers through development of content and pedagogical content knowledge is timely and urgently needed to empower them in ways that are advocated by science education reforms.

This study was therefore concerned with biology teachers' development of content and pedagogical content knowledge. It attempts to ascertain the knowledge base of biology teachers of specific topics at the elementary and the preparatory school levels. The objectives of this study were to (i) ascertain the knowledge base of biology teachers through exploring their current pedagogical content knowledge and identifying components that make up their pedagogical content knowledge (ii) explore the effectiveness of a professional development training program on developing the PCK of biology teachers, and (iii) develop a mechanism by which teachers' content and pedagogical content knowledge is assessed and documented. To achieve these objectives, the following key questions were asked: (i) How can biology teachers' PCK of selected biology content be typified and represented?, (ii) Do components of PCK differ from teacher to teacher?, and (iii) Can professional development training program accelerate the development of teachers' PCK?

METHODOLOGY

Participants

The sample consisted of 22 biology teachers selected from 12 schools of one educational zone in UAE. Ten of the participating biology teachers were female. Average age of the participants was 32 years, with 14 of them, expatriate teachers. Teaching experience of the participants ranged from 2 to 14 years. Of the 22 participants 15 were teaching the elementary levels, the remaining 7 were teaching at the preparatory level. The inclusion of individual participant was based on personal consent and his/her willingness to participate and to professionally develop further.

Data Collection

The study employed a multiple method approach by using a variety of data sources and data analysis methods to assess the complex and the multifaceted aspects of teachers' PCK and the related constructs, such as teacher beliefs and reflection over the period of research. The multiple methods used included: (i) assessment of participant's understanding of selected biological concepts and beliefs about biology teaching and learning, (ii) classroom observations, (iii) analysis of teachers' responses to hypothetical situations that described students' answers to questions about specific scientific concepts, and (iv) analysis of teachers' reflection reports and philosophies about teaching and learning at the beginning and at the end of the three month period.

Participants' understandings of selected biological concepts were assessed through specifically developed items to assess the development of scientific contents that may eventually lead to the development of the PCK. Three incidents describing content knowledge were developed and distributed to the participants at the beginning of the PD program and they were asked to provide best answers to these incidents.

Teaching beliefs were captured using an open-ended interview at the beginning and end of the study based on The Teachers' Beliefs Interview (TBI) (Luft *et al*, 2003). TBI depicts five major response areas: traditional, instructive, transitional, responsive, and reform-based. Traditional and instructive responses represent teacher-centered beliefs while responsive and reform-based responses represent student-centered beliefs. Transitional responses on the other hand reflect views that include students at the affective disposition level only.

The purpose the TBI was to help examine and typify the teachers' knowledge of learning outcomes, representations used, type of tasks, concepts relating to the planned concepts. Moreover, three classes were observed for each of the participating teachers and further interviews were conducted after the observations to clarify issues that emerged from the observations. Each observation consisted of a written summary of the lesson observed, the interactions between the teacher and students, and teacher behaviors that facilitated or impeded the achievement of lesson learning outcome(s).

The Professional Development Program

The teachers underwent a series of professional development training activities with the focus on content and content representation to enhance their PCK. Altogether there were three 2-hours workshops on the importance of teaching and learning of biology meaningfully, including the role of the teacher in content representation. The workshops were designed to help teachers learn science concepts at the same time to refine their teaching and learning abilities. Workshops were conducted separately for male and female teachers. Each workshop consisted of three phases, (i) an introductory phase, where the researcher explained the concept and the task and tried to engage participants and spur their interest and prior knowledge in the workshop, (ii) activity phase consisting of engaging teachers in hands-on activity, and sharing with the group about their experience with the activity, and (iii) a period for reflection and discussion to build knowledge from their activities by talking and/or writing, before the researcher summed up the workshop activities. In addition to these, specifically organized conferences were held individually and in groups with teachers after interviews and classroom observations to ascertain incidences or to clarify observed situations. This exercise provided evidence on the development of PCK of participating teachers. During engagement with hands-on activities, participants were encouraged to document their vision on how to teach specific topics and thereby developing narratives about how teachers explicate different teaching strategies and how they are enacted (Loughran *et al.*, 2004). In this way the teachers' PCK development, and its relations with general pedagogical knowledge and content knowledge, will be identified and documented. Data collected from these teaching narratives were qualitatively analyzed for evidence of the development of teachers' content and pedagogical content knowledge.

Validity and Credibility

The research incorporated various techniques in order to ensure standards of validity for its outcomes. First, triangulation was achieved by employing multiple sources for collecting data, including interviews with participants, classroom observations of teaching, and reflective summaries of reports written by participants. Not only would triangulation provide the means for observing data that might have been overlooked by relying on only one source of data collection, but it also allow seeing the same data from various perspectives and, hence, enhance validity and reliability.

RESEARCH FINDINGS

To answer the question about how we can typify and characterize the participants' PCK, analysis of classroom observations and reflection reports were summarized to typify the participants' PCK that pertains to 6 categories of observable behaviors namely comprehension, transformation, instruction, evaluation, reflection, and new comprehension. The frequency of these observable behaviors was coded along a continuum ranging from 1 to indicate low level of occurrence to 3 to indicate high level of occurrence (Table 1) There was a tendency in previous studies to find that that PCK was embedded in classroom practice, implying that teachers varied in their PCK according to practice. As shown in Table 1, teachers, exhibited varying degree of observable behaviors that characterized the development of their PCK before and after the completion of the PD workshops.

Table 1. Frequency of observable PCK behaviors

No.	Observable behaviors of PCK	Pre PD activities			Post PD activities		
		1*	2	3	1	2	3
1	Comprehension		√				√
2	Transformation		√			√	
3	Instruction			√	√		
4	Evaluation	√				√	
5	Reflection	√					√
6	New comprehension		√				√

*1 = low level, 2 medium level, 3 high level of occurrence

As shown in Table 1, it may be interpreted that teachers tend to do more teaching and less reflection and evaluation though teaching situations might require the teacher to engage in more reflection and evaluation activities. Ability to engage in these categories at a medium or a high level would most likely typify a development of coherent and articulated knowledge (Loughran *et al.*, 2004). Table 2 presents results in relation to characterization of participants' beliefs about biology teaching and learning.

Table 2. Frequency of categories of responses to the TBI (see text for details)

	Traditional	Instructive	Transitional	Responsive	Reformed based
Pre PD	7	8	3	3	1
Post PD	3	3	5	6	5

The incoming beliefs of participants can be described as having traditional instructive position as 15 of 22 teachers showed this. Four had high proportions of student – centered responses (responsive and reform-based) and remained very student centered at the end of the research. Three participants, on the other hand, had transitional beliefs and regressed to more teacher-centered views by the end of the study. However, after the completion of the professional development workshops and the eventually classroom observations and reflective reports, the number of participants who ascribed to responsive and reformed based beliefs increased to 11 from the initial four. With the shift towards a more student-centered teaching, it seems that teachers employed different mechanisms towards achieving this. Traditional and instructive oriented teachers were reduced to 6 from the initial 15, indicating that the PD activities may have impacted them positively to move towards responsive and reform based continuum.

To answer the question related to pathways teachers adopt when progressing towards developing coherent PCK, analysis of participants' interview transcripts, their responses to the hypothetical situations, and reflection reports resulted in seven components of PCK that were mostly common to all participants with varying degree of emphasis. The seven components were the typical PCK components identified by Shulman (1986) such as, knowledge of content, knowledge of goals, knowledge of students, knowledge of curriculum organization, knowledge of teaching strategies, knowledge of assessment, and knowledge of resources. Although these seven components are thought to be knowledge areas of teaching and characterized the teaching of all participants, the result of this study clearly shows that they were varyingly emphasized by participants.

Most teachers emphasized "knowledge of content" for example, as the primary knowledge area for biology teaching. For most of the participants, being a biology teacher, content knowledge would be an integral and important aspect of being an effective teacher. The teachers described their knowledge to be broader, but different from that of the knowledge of scientists. This category also includes teachers' knowledge of the nature of science, the scientific process, and of the relationship among the various science areas.

Participants often commented on how they linked their lessons to the goal of their biology classes. They frequently exhibited tendencies reflecting that they wanted their students to use biological knowledge in their real lives and to understand better how this knowledge was linked to their daily lives. While the seven components were common to all participants, the pathways of developing these components seem different, with experienced teachers tending to emphasize knowledge of students as a key issue in their teaching more than the less experienced teachers. Experienced teachers spoke strongly about their students and how their students preferred to learn, their difficulties and misconceptions and their interests, thereby providing structured details of their knowledge more than the inexperienced teachers. Participants' pathways towards developing PCK were also detected in their beliefs about assessment. All participants articulated and displayed at length how they adopted a variety of assessment methods and procedures for ascertaining students' understanding of concepts. Participants indicated that this knowledge of assessment allowed them to adjust their lessons to suit the needs of the students.

To explore the effectiveness of the professional development training program on the development of the PCK of biology teachers, the results showed that the PD activities were found to have high level of sensitivities to revealing and helping participants acquire sound and coherent knowledge and understanding of biology and hence strengthening their PCK perspectives. The series of the professional development activities implemented at the beginning of the research have impacted participants' content as well as pedagogical content knowledge. These findings may also suggest that teachers' PCK can systematically be assessed and documented using the approach adopted in this research by helping teachers to realize their own strengths and weaknesses through analysis and reflection on their own practice.

CONCLUDING REMARKS

The findings of this study revealed that there were seven components related to the development of the PCK which were shared by the participating biology teachers. This study showed that these seven components are interrelated within the context of teaching biology and play a role as a class of knowledge that is central to biology teachers' work. Therefore, on the basis of the findings of this study, teachers' PCK can easily be typified and characterized in ways that can be isolated and studied into more detailed ways. The findings of this study were in congruence with similar studies such as those of Loughran *et al.*, (2001, 2004), and Luft, (2001).

Most importantly is that teachers' PCK can be meaningfully assessed and characterized via collecting data directly from teachers through their own practice and reflection. This attempt to characterize PCK from the teachers' perspectives is expected to encourage both researchers and science teacher educators to find new ways to apply teachers' insights into educational policies and facilitate the growth of the PCK of science teachers. This will bring to the forefront the ongoing discussion about the importance of interweaving content and pedagogy into teacher education preparation programs to an extent that allows prospective teachers to develop the much needed PCK components. One aspect that might be suggested is that teacher education programs may be enhanced by incorporating the seven components of PCK as an integral part of their training programs.

REFERENCES

Bell, B., & Gilbert, J. (1996). *Teacher Development: A Model from Science Education*. London: Falmer Press.

Desimone, L., Porter, A., Garet, M., Yoon, K.; & Birman, B. (2002). Effects of Professional Development on Teachers' Instruction: Results from a Three-year Longitudinal Study. Educational Evaluation and Policy Analysis, *24*(2), 81–112.

Huffman, D., Thomas, K., & Lawrenz, F. (2003). *School Science and Mathematics, 103*(8), 378–387.

Loughran, J., Milroy, P., Berry, A., Gunstone, R., & Mulhall, P. (2001). Documenting science teachers' pedagogical content knowledge through PaP-eRs. Research in Science Education, *31*, 289–307.

Loughran, J., Mulhall, P. & Berry, A. (2008). Exploring pedagogical content knowledge in science teacher education. *International Journal of Science Education, 30*(10), 1310–1319.

Loughran, J., Mulhall, P. & Berry, A. (2004). In search of pedagogical content knowledge in science: Developing ways of articulating and documenting professional practice. *Journal of Research in Science Teaching, 41*(4), 370–391.

Luft, J. (2001). Changing inquiry practices and beliefs: the impact of an inquiry-based professional development program on beginning and experienced secondary science teachers. *International Journal of Science Education, 23*(5), 517–534.

Luft, J., Roehrig, G., & Patterson, N. (2003). Contrasting landscapes: A comparison of the impact of different induction programs on beginning secondary science teachers' practices, beliefs, and experiences. *Journal of Research in Science Teaching, 40*, 77–97.

Marx, W., Freeman, J., Krajcik, J., & Blumenfeld, P. (1998). Professional development of science teachers. In B.J. Fraser & K.G. Tobin (Eds.) *International Handbook of Science Education* (pp. 317–331). Dordrecht: Kluwer Academic Publishers.

NRC (1996). *National Science Education Standards*. Washington, DC: National Academy Press.

Putnam, R., & Borko, H. (1997). Teacher learning: Implications of new views of cognition. In B. J. Biddle & T. L. Good & I. F. Goodson (Eds.), International handbook of teachers and teaching (pp. 1223–1296). Dordrecht: Kluwer Academic Publishers.

Sherin, M. (2002). When teaching becomes learning. Cognition and Instruction, *20*(2), pp. 119–150.

Sherin, M., Sherin, B., & Madanes, R. (2000). Exploring diverse accounts of teacher knowledge. Journal of Mathematical Behavior, *18*(3) 357–375.

Shulman, L. (1986). Those who understand: Knowledge growth in teaching. *Educational Researcher,* *15*(2), 4–14.
Supovitz, J., & Turner, H. (2000). The effects of professional development on science teaching practices and classroom culture. *Journal of Research in Science Teaching, 37*, 963–980.
Van Driel, J., Verloop, N., & De Vos, W. (1998). Developing science teachers' pedagogical content knowledge. *Journal of Research in Science Teaching, 35*(6), 673–695.

Hassan H. Tairab
Department of Curriculum & Instruction, Faculty of Education,
United Arab Emirates University, United Arab Emirates
tairab@uaeu.ac.ae

INDEX

CPSIA information can be obtained at www.ICGtesting.com
Printed in the USA
BVOW012307131212

308133BV00005B/114/P